Processing for Android

Create Mobile, Sensor-aware, and XR
Applications Using Processing

Second Edition

Andrés Colubri

Apress®

Processing for Android: Create Mobile, Sensor-aware, and XR Applications Using Processing, Second Edition

Andrés Colubri
University of Massachusetts, Worcester, MA, USA

ISBN-13 (pbk): 978-1-4842-9584-7   ISBN-13 (electronic): 978-1-4842-9585-4
https://doi.org/10.1007/978-1-4842-9585-4

Managing Director, Apress Media LLC: Welmoed Spahr
Acquisitions Editor: Spandana Chatterjee
Development Editor: Spandana Chatterjee
Coordinating Editor: Mark Powers

Cover image designed by eStudioCalamar

Distributed to the book trade worldwide by Apress Media, LLC, 1 New York Plaza, New York, NY 10004, U.S.A. Phone 1-800-SPRINGER, fax (201) 348-4505, e-mail orders-ny@springer-sbm.com, or visit www.springeronline.com. Apress Media, LLC is a California LLC and the sole member (owner) is Springer Science + Business Media Finance Inc (SSBM Finance Inc). SSBM Finance Inc is a **Delaware** corporation.

For information on translations, please e-mail booktranslations@springernature.com; for reprint, paperback, or audio rights, please e-mail bookpermissions@springernature.com.

Apress titles may be purchased in bulk for academic, corporate, or promotional use. eBook versions and licenses are also available for most titles. For more information, reference our Print and eBook Bulk Sales web page at http://www.apress.com/bulk-sales.

Any source code or other supplementary material referenced by the author in this book is available to readers on GitHub (https://github.com/Apress). For more detailed information, please visit https://www.apress.com/gp/services/source-code.

Paper in this product is recyclable

To L. J. for accompanying during the writing of this book.
To my family and friends for always supporting me.
And to the Processing community for putting these tools to great use.

Table of Contents

About the Author

Andrés Colubri is a senior member of the Processing project and the main developer of the OpenGL renderer, the video library, and Processing for Android. He originally studied Physics and Mathematics in Argentina and later did an MFA in the Design Media Arts Department at UCLA. He uses Processing as a tool to bridge his interests in computer graphics, data visualization, and biomedical research. He is currently an assistant professor at the University of Massachusetts Chan Medical School (https://co-labo.org).

About the Technical Reviewer

 **Massimo Nardone** has more than 25 years of experience in security, web and mobile development, cloud, and IT architecture. His true IT passions are security and Android. He has been programming and teaching others how to program with Android, Perl, PHP, Java, VB, Python, C/C++, and MySQL for more than 20 years. He holds a Master of Science degree in computing science from the University of Salerno, Italy.

He has worked as a CISO, CSO, security executive, IoT executive, project manager, software engineer, research engineer, chief security architect, PCI/SCADA auditor, and senior lead IT security/cloud/SCADA architect for many years. His technical skills include security, Android, cloud, Java, MySQL, Drupal, COBOL, Perl, web and mobile development, MongoDB, D3, Joomla, Couchbase, C/C++, WebGL, Python, Pro Rails, Django CMS, Jekyll, Scratch, and more.

He was a visiting lecturer and supervisor for exercises at the Networking Laboratory of the Helsinki University of Technology (Aalto University). He also holds four international patents (in the PKI, SIP, SAML, and Proxy areas). He is currently working for Cognizant as head of cybersecurity and CISO to help clients in areas of information and cybersecurity, including strategy, planning, processes, policies, procedures, governance, awareness, and so forth. In June 2017, he became a permanent member of the ISACA Finland Board.

Massimo has reviewed more than 45 IT books for different publishing companies and is the coauthor of *Pro Spring Security: Securing Spring Framework 5 and Boot 2-based Java Applications* (Apress, 2019), *Beginning EJB in Java EE 8* (Apress, 2018), *Pro JPA 2 in Java EE 8* (Apress, 2018), and *Pro Android Games* (Apress, 2015).

Acknowledgments

First, I want to give recognition to Ben Fry and Casey Reas, who initiated the Processing project over two decades ago and have worked steadfastly since then to promote software literacy within the visual arts and visual literacy within technology. Also, very special thanks to Sam Pottinger for his hard work in Processing 4 and his help to make the Android mode compatible with it.

I would like to express my gratitude to all the Google Summer of Code students who contributed to the project in very important ways in the years since the first edition: Syam Sundar Kirubakaran (GSoC 2018), Deeraj Esvar (GSoC 2019), Aditya Rana (GSoC 2020), Rupesh Kumar (GSoC 2022), and Gaurav Puniya (GSoC 2023).

I extend my appreciation to Chris Coleman and Kate Hollenbach for their invitation to do a residence at the Clinic for Open Source Arts at the University of Denver in March 2023 to finalize the development of the Android mode for Processing 4.

Finally, I thank the Apress editors, Spandana Chatterjee, Nirmal Selvaraj, and Mark Powers, for helping steer this second edition through the finish line.

Introduction

Welcome to the second edition of *Processing for Android*! In this book, we will explore the exciting world of creative coding and mobile app development using the Processing programming language specifically tailored for the Android platform. Whether you are an experienced programmer, an artist looking to expand your creative horizons, or a beginner interested in exploring the intersection of technology and art, this book is for you.

Processing, initiated by Ben Fry and Casey Reas in 2001, has revolutionized the way artists, designers, and developers approach creative coding. Its intuitive syntax and powerful capabilities make it an ideal tool for creating applications with interactive graphics, sound, animations, and more. With the rise of smartphones and smartwatches, mobile apps became a widely available medium for exploring new ideas with code, making Processing for Android a very useful tool to learn, prototype, and produce app projects.

Written by Andrés Colubri, an experienced software developer, computational scientist, and media artist who has been an active contributor to the Processing project for more than ten years, this book is a comprehensive guide that will take you on a journey from the fundamentals of Processing coding to building complex Android applications. No matter if you are new to Processing or have previous experience with the language, this book will equip you with the knowledge and skills necessary to develop engaging and innovative apps.

The book is designed with a hands-on approach to learning. Through a series of step-by-step tutorials and practical examples, you will learn how to set up your Processing development environment, navigate the Processing for Android interface, and harness the power of the Android platform to craft app-based experiences. From creating interactive animations to working with sensors, cameras, GLSL shaders, and virtual and augmented reality, you will gain a deep understanding of the capabilities that are offered by Processing for Android.

In addition to technical instruction, this book explores the artistic and creative possibilities that you can unlock with Processing for Android. You will be inspired by the diverse range of examples and full projects showcased throughout the book, demonstrating how Processing can be used to create visually sophisticated and conceptually rich mobile apps. Whether you are interested in generative art, data visualization, or immersive experiences in VR or AR, the combination of Processing and Android provides an exciting playground for your creativity.

This second edition is a major update of the book, with all code examples and figures from the first edition carefully revised to reflect the latest changes in the Processing software and the Android platform. Furthermore, several of the full projects at the end of each section were significantly rewritten to make them more concise and easier to follow while still highlighting the key techniques of their corresponding section. An entire new section comprising three chapters devoted to VR and AR was added, as well as a chapter where shader programming in Processing is described in depth and illustrated with many code examples from basic to advanced.

As you progress through the chapters, you will not only acquire the technical skills to create Android apps with Processing but also gain a deeper understanding of programming concepts and computational thinking. This book encourages you to experiment, explore, and push the boundaries of what is possible with Processing for Android.

So if you are ready to embark on an exciting journey into the world of creative coding and mobile app development, *Processing for Android* is your gateway. Let's dive in and unlock the potential of this powerful combination of art, technology, and Android!

Happy coding and creating!

PART I

■ ■ ■

First Steps with Processing for Android

CHAPTER 1

■ ■ ■

Getting Started with the Android Mode

In this chapter, we will introduce the Processing software and its Android mode, the community behind these projects, and how we can start using Processing to create apps for Android devices.

What Is the Processing Project?

The Processing project is a community initiative with the goals of sharing knowledge, fostering education, and promoting diversity in computer programming. The Processing software is a central part of this initiative, guided by the Processing Foundation (`https://processingfoundation.org/`), whose main mission is to "promote software literacy within the visual arts and visual literacy within technology-related fields – and to make these fields accessible to diverse communities." This community grew off the original Processing software, a programming language and environment created in 2001 by Casey Reas and Ben Fry at the MIT Media Lab as a teaching and production tool in computational arts and design. The Processing software has been continuously developed since then and is available for download at `https://processing.org/`, with its source code released under free software licenses. From now on, we will simply refer to Processing when talking about the Processing software.

Processing consists of two complementary parts: the Processing programming language and the Processing development environment. Together, they form a "software sketchbook" that allows users to quickly implement, or "sketch," their ideas with code while also providing them with enough room to iteratively refine these ideas into fully developed projects. Processing has been used to create many beautiful and inspiring works in generative art, data visualization, and interactive installations, just to mention a few areas. There are several online resources listing some of these works, including CreativeApplications.Net (`www.creativeapplications.net/category/processing/`), OpenProcessing (`https://openprocessing.org/`), and "For Your Processing" on Tumblr (`https://fyprocessing.tumblr.com/`).

The Processing Language

The Processing language is a set of functions, classes, and constants we can use to program screen drawing, data input/output, and user interaction, originally implemented in Java and now available in Python, JavaScript, and other programming languages. The core team of people behind Processing (`https://processing.org/people/`) has carefully constructed this language, technically called "Application Programming Interface" or API, to simplify the development of graphical and interactive applications by means of a simple and consistent naming convention, unambiguous behavior, and a well-defined scope.

© Andrés Colubri 2023
A. Colubri, *Processing for Android*, https://doi.org/10.1007/978-1-4842-9585-4_1

The Java implementation of the Processing language has been part of Processing dating back to 2001 and encompasses around 200 functions. A defining feature of this language is that it offers us the possibility of creating interactive graphics with very little code. It also includes several simplifications with respect to the Java language, with the purpose of making it easier to teach to people who are not familiar with computer code. The following program illustrates these features of the Processing language:

```
color bg = 150;

void setup() {
  size(200, 200);
}

void draw() {
  background(bg);
  ellipse(mouseX, mouseY, 100, 100);
}
```

The output of this program is a window of 200 by 200 pixels, with a white circle that follows the movement of the mouse on a gray background. The functions setup() and draw() are present in most Processing programs, and they drive its "drawing loop." All the initialization of the program should take place in setup(), which is called just once when the program starts up. The draw() function, containing all the drawing instructions, is then called continuously several times per second (by default, 60 times) so that we can animate the graphical output of our program. Another term specific to Processing is the word "sketch," which refers to a Processing program by highlighting the concept of code sketching we mentioned earlier.

The Processing Development Environment

The Processing Development Environment (PDE) is the software that provides users with a minimalistic code editor to write, run, and refine Processing sketches (Figure 1-1). The PDE also incorporates an uncluttered user interface to handle all the sketches created with it and to add libraries and other external components that extend the core functionality of the PDE, such as p5.js, Python, or Android modes.

The ease of use and simplicity of the PDE and the Processing language are the key elements to realize the concept of a "code sketchbook." A stumbling block for many people wanting to start working with code is the complexity of a modern development environment like Eclipse or IntelliJ, in terms of a lengthy installation and an overwhelming user interface. In contrast, the PDE addresses these issues by providing an easy install process and a clean interface, while the simple structure of a Processing sketch enables users to obtain visual feedback rapidly. Processing's aim is to enable an iterative development process analogous to sketching with pen and paper, where we can start with a simple idea and then refine by continuous code sketching.

■ **Note** The Processing language can be used outside of the PDE, for example, in advanced Integrated Development Environments or IDEs, such as Eclipse or IntelliJ. All of Processing's drawing, data, and interaction API can be used when writing a program with these IDEs; but many of the simplifications that the Processing language has with respect to Java will be lost.

Those of us who are familiar with Java have probably noticed that the code shown in Listing 1-1 is not a valid Java program. For example, there is no explicit definition of a main class encapsulating all the code, nor the additional instructions required in Java to initialize the graphical display and the user input. This sketch needs to be run inside the PDE, which applies a "pre-processing" step to the Processing code to convert it into a complete Java program. However, this step occurs behind the scenes, and we do not need to worry about it at all. Only when using an advanced IDE like those noted previously, we need to make sure to incorporate the Processing API into a syntactically correct Java program.

We can download the latest version of Processing from the main website (`https://processing.org/download`). As we pointed out in the previous paragraph, installation is very easy, only requiring unpacking the zip (on Windows and macOS) or tgz (on Linux) package that contains the PDE and all other core files. We should be able to then run the PDE without any additional steps, from whichever location inside the home or applications folder.

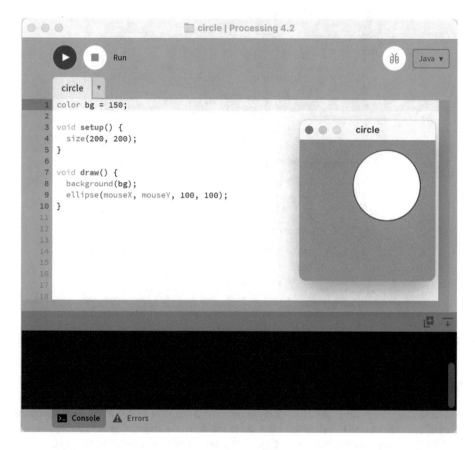

Figure 1-1. *The Processing Development Environment showing a running sketch in the Java mode*

The PDE saves our sketches inside a "sketchbook" folder. Each sketch is stored in a subfolder inside the sketchbook, which in turn contains one or more source code files with the pde extension. By default, Processing creates the sketchbook inside the documents folder located in the user's account (e.g., /Users/andres/Documents/Processing on macOS), but we can change this location by selecting the desired sketchbook folder in the Preferences window, available under the "Processing ➤ Settings" menu on macOS and "File ➤ Settings" on Windows and Linux (Figure 1-2). Notice the sketchbook location at the top.

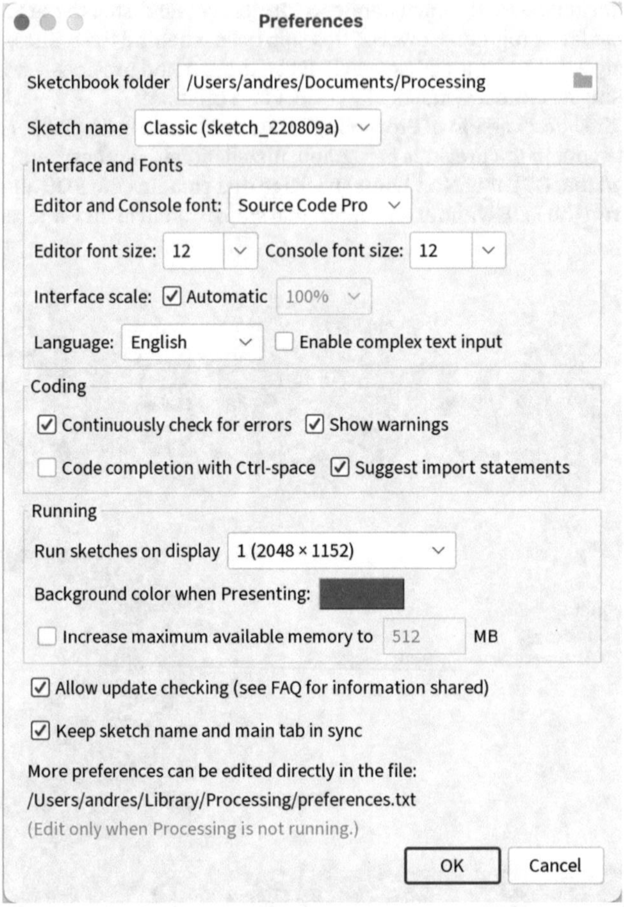

Figure 1-2. *The Preferences window on macOS*

Extending Processing

As we mentioned at the beginning, the Processing project is not only the PDE and the language but also, and very importantly, the community built around the use of the software and the "goal to empower people of all interests and backgrounds to learn how to program and make creative work with code, especially those who might not otherwise have access to these tools and resources," as stated in the home page of the Processing Foundation. Thanks to Processing's open nature and modular architecture, many people have contributed with improvements and extensions to the "core" software over the years. These contributions fall within one of the following four categories:

- Libraries: Modules (comprising one or more Java code files built into a jar package and additional documentation and example files) that make it possible to access new functionality in the sketches, for example, OpenCV library for computer vision applications on PC or Mac computers, or TensorFlow Lite for running machine learning tasks on Android.

- Programming modes: Alternative code editors and related PDE customizations that allow using an entirely different language within the PDE, for example, the Android mode itself! We will see in the next sections of this chapter how to install the Android mode on top of the default PDE.

- Tools: Applications that can only run from Processing and provide specific functionality to help while writing code, debugging, and testing the sketch, for example, the color picker (discussed in Chapter 2).

- Examples: Packages of contributed code sketches that can be used as learning material or reference, for example, the sketches from the *Learning Processing* book by Daniel Shiffman (`http://learningprocessing.com/`).

The possibility of extending Processing through contributed libraries, modes, tools, and examples has enabled the growth of Processing into application domains that were not part of the original software, such as mobile apps, computer vision, and physical computing, while keeping the core functionality simple and accessible for new programmers.

The Contribution Manager

By default, Processing includes one default mode, Java, where we can write and run sketches on Windows, Mac, and Linux computers using the Java implementation of the Processing language. Processing also bundles several "core" libraries, some of which are OpenGL (for drawing hardware-accelerated 2D and 3D scenes), PDF (to export graphics as PDF files), and data (which allows handling data files in formats such as CSV and JSON).

We can use the Contribution Manager (CM) to install additional contributions, which makes the entire process very seamless. A screenshot of the CM is shown in Figure 1-3. The CM has five tabs, the first four for each type of contribution – libraries, modes, tools, and examples – and the fifth tab for updates. All the contributions that are registered by their authors in a central repository are accessible through the CM and can also be updated through the CM when new versions become available.

■ **Note**   Contributions that are not available through the CM can be installed manually. You need to download the package containing the library, mode, tool, or examples, typically in zip format, and extract it into the sketchbook folder. There are separate subfolders for libraries, modes, tools, and examples. See `https://processing.org/reference/libraries/` for more info.

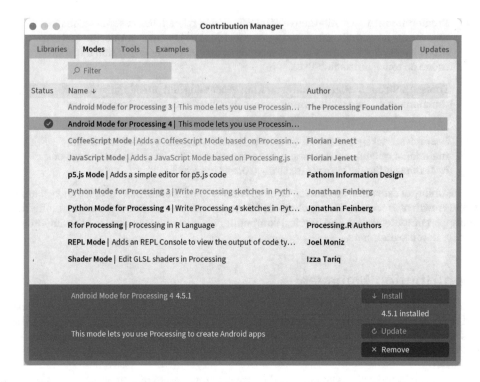

Figure 1-3. *The Contribution Manager in Processing showing the Modes tab*

Processing for Android

Processing for Android, just like the Processing software itself, is also several things. Primarily, it is a community effort that started in 2009 with the purpose of supporting the development of Android apps using Processing and translating some of the concepts of the project to the context of mobile apps: iterative sketching, simplicity, and accessibility.

If we look more closely into the technical details, Processing for Android is made of two parts: the processing-android library and the custom PDE programming mode itself. The library is the package that contains all the functions of the Processing API but re-implemented for the Android platform. The Android mode provides a customized version of the PDE that allows us to write Processing code and run it on an Android device or in the emulator. The Android mode includes the processing-android library, which we need for our Processing code to run without errors. However, we don't need to worry about these distinctions at this point, since Processing will let us install and use the Android mode and will make sure that all the required libraries are placed in the right places. But knowing about the difference between the android library and the mode would be important for those readers who may be planning to use Processing for Android in more advanced applications.

■ **Note**   The processing-android library can be imported from an IDE like Android Studio, allowing using all the Processing functionality in a regular Android app. This advanced use is covered in Appendix A.

Installing the Android Mode

Once we have installed Processing in our computer, we should be able to open the PDE by running the Processing application and then to install the most recent release of the Android mode through the CM. The mode also requires the Android Software Development Kit (SDK) to work. The Android SDK is the set of libraries, tools, documentation, and other supporting files provided by Google to develop and debug Android apps. So let's follow these next steps to install the Android mode and, if needed, the SDK:

1. Open the CM by clicking the "Manage Modes…" option that appears in the drop-down menu in the upper-right corner of the PDE (Figure 1-4).

2. Select the entry for the Android mode in the Modes tab and click the "Install" button.

3. After installation is complete, close the CM and switch into the Android mode using the same drop-down menu from Figure 1-4.

When switching into the Android mode for the first time, it will ask us to locate or download the Android SDK (Figure 1-5). Because the SDK is very large (up to several GBs), it could be a good idea to use the one that is already installed to save disk space. However, if that SDK is also used by another development tool, such as Android Studio, it may get updated or changed outside Processing, which may lead to incompatibilities with the Android mode. If that's the case, then it may be better to allow Processing to download and install its own copy of the Android SDK, which will not interfere with the SDK in use by other development tools. If no valid Android SDK is detected, Processing will ask to manually locate an SDK, or automatically download it (Figure 1-5).

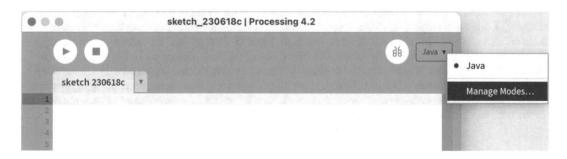

Figure 1-4. Opening the Contribution Manager to add a new mode

---

■ **Note** Version 4.5+ of the Android mode requires Android version 13, corresponding to API level 33 (https://source.android.com/docs/setup/about/build-numbers). The mode's automatic SDK download will retrieve this version from the Google servers.

Figure 1-5. *Pop-up dialog in the Android mode allowing us to search for an existing SDK in our computer manually or download a new copy of the SDK from Google's servers*

Finally, pre-releases of the Android mode, as well as older versions that are no longer are available through the CM, are all deposited in the GitHub releases page (https://github.com/processing/processing-android/releases). So, if we are interested in trying these versions out, we could install them manually by downloading the corresponding zip file and extracting it into the modes folder in the Processing's sketchbook.

Interface of the Android Mode

The editor in the Android mode is very similar to that of the Java mode. The toolbar contains the play and stop buttons to launch a sketch (on a connected device) and to stop its execution (on the device or in the emulator). Code autocompletion and integrated debugger in the editor are available as well. The main menu contains several Android-specific options as well (Figure 1-6). The "File" menu has options to export the current sketch as a package ready to upload to the Google Play Store, or as a project that can be opened with Android Studio. The "Sketch" menu contains separate options to run the sketch on a device or in the emulator, as well as a separate "Android" menu containing several options, among them the type of output to target with the sketch – regular app, wallpaper, watch face, VR, or AR app – and the list of Android devices currently connected to the computer. We will cover all these options in the next chapters!

Figure 1-6. *Android-specific options in the interface of the Android mode*

Running a Sketch on a Device

Once we have written some sketch code with the PDE, we can then run it on an Android phone, tablet, or watch. The first thing we need to do is to make sure that "USB Debugging" is turned on on our device. The process to do this varies by device and which version of the Android OS we have installed on it. In most of the cases, this setting is in the Developer Options, under system Setting. On Android 4.2 and higher, the Developer Options are hidden by default, but we can enable them by following these instructions:

1. Open the Settings app.

2. Scroll to the bottom and select About phone.

3. Scroll to the bottom and tap Build number seven times.

4. Return to the previous screen to find Developer Options near the bottom.

After turning USB Debugging on (which we need to do only once), we need to connect the device to the computer through the USB port. Processing will then try to recognize it and add it to the list of available devices in the "Android" menu.

■ **Note**   Version 4.5+ of the Android mode only supports devices that are running Android 4.2 (API level 17) or newer.

Let's use the code in Listing 1-1 as our first Processing for Android sketch. It is okay if we do not understand every line of code in it, as we will go over the Processing API in detail in the next chapters. It simply draws a black square in the half of the screen that receives a touch press.

Listing 1-1. Our first Processing for Android sketch

```
void setup() {
  fill(0);
}

void draw() {
  background(204);
  if (mousePressed) {
    if (mouseX < width/2) rect(0, 0, width/2, height);
    else rect(width/2, 0, width/2, height);
  }
}
```

It is possible to have several devices connected simultaneously to the computer, but only one can be selected in the Devices menu as the "active" device, which will be where our sketch will be installed and run. Figure 1-7 shows our first sketch already loaded in the PDE and the selected device to run it on.

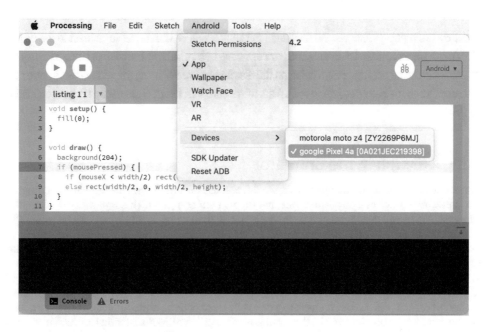

Figure 1-7. *Selecting the device to run the sketch on*

After we have picked the active device, we can hit the run button or select "Run on Device" under the "Sketch" menu. Then, we should see some messages scrolling down in the PDE's console, while Processing compiles the sketch, packages it as an Android app, and installs it on the device. One important detail is that the computer needs to be connected to the Internet the first time we run a sketch. The reason is that Processing uses a tool called Gradle to build the app from the sketch's source code, but Gradle is not part of the initial Android mode installation. The Android mode will automatically download the Gradle tool the first time it tries to run a sketch. It can be offline when running sketches after the first time. If everything goes well, the sketch should launch and show up on the screen of the device, as shown in Figure 1-8.

Figure 1-8. *Running a sketch on a connected phone*

■ **Note**   If we are running Windows, we may need to install a special USB driver to connect to the device (`https://developer.android.com/studio/run/oem-usb.html`). In the case of Linux, we may need to install some additional packages depending on the distribution we are using (`https://developer.android.com/studio/run/device.html`). Also, make sure that the USB connection is not configured as "Charge Only."

Running a Sketch in the Emulator

If we do not have a device to run our sketch on, we can still use the emulator. The emulator is a program that creates a "software replica" of a physical device that runs on our computer. This replica is called an Android Virtual Device (AVD), and even though it is generally slower than a real device, it can also be useful to test our sketch on hardware we don't currently have.

The first time we run a sketch in the emulator, Processing will download the "system image" containing all the information needed to emulate the AVD in our computer (Figure 1-9). However, it will initially ask us if we want to use the "ARM" or the "x86" images. The reason for this is that Android devices use ARM CPUs (central processing units), while our desktop or laptop computers often have x86 CPUs (ARM and x86 denote different "architectures" that CPUs can have to process the instructions from our code). When emulating an AVD with an ARM image on an x86 CPU, the emulator will convert ARM instructions into x86 instructions one by one, which could be slow. But if we use the x86 image on an x86 CPU, our computer will be able to simulate the AVD's CPU directly and therefore much faster. One drawback of using x86 images is that we must install an additional software on Mac or Windows called HAXM. Processing already downloaded HAXM together with the Android SDK, so it will install it for us in case we decide to use x86 images. However, with the ARM-based Mac computers (M1, M2, etc.), we do not have this issue since their CPUs have the same ARM architecture as the emulated devices.

We should also keep in mind that HAXM is only compatible with Intel processors, so the emulator won't work with x86 images if our computer has an AMD CPU. Linux has its own AVD acceleration system and does not require HAXM, so we can use x86 images on a Linux computer with an AMD CPU. We would need to perform some extra configuration steps though, which are described here: `https://developer.android.com/studio/run/emulator-acceleration.html#vm-linux`.

Figure 1-9. *System image download dialog in the Android mode*

After finishing the download, which can take several minutes depending on our Internet connection (the system images for the emulator are over 1GB in size), Processing will boot up the emulator and then will launch the sketch in it. Once our Listing 1-1 is running in the emulator, it should look like the one shown in Figure 1-10.

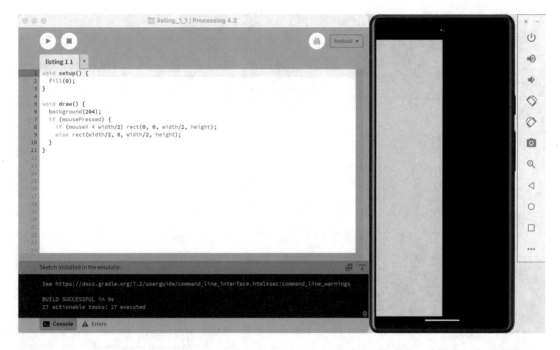

Figure 1-10. *Running our sketch in the emulator*

Summary

In this first chapter, we have learned what the Processing project and software are and how we can use Processing to create apps, thanks to its Android mode. As we saw, some of the main features of the Processing software are its minimal interface and the simple structure of a program, called a "sketch." These features allow us to start writing, testing, and refining our own sketches, either on a device or in the emulator, very quickly.

CHAPTER 2

The Processing Language

If you are not familiar with the Processing language, read this chapter for an introduction to how to create 2D shapes, use geometry transformations and color, and handle touchscreen input in Processing. The chapter ends with a step-by-step example of a drawing sketch, which we will use in Chapter 3 to learn how to export and upload an app created with Processing to the Play Store.

A Programming Sketchbook for Artists and Designers

As we learned in the first chapter, the Processing language, together with the Processing Development Environment (PDE), makes it easier for users who are new to programming to start creating interactive graphics. The language has been designed to be minimal and simple for learning and yet expressive enough to create many kinds of code-based projects, including generative art, data visualization, sound art, film, and performance. It includes around 200 functions across different categories: drawing, interaction, typography, etc., as well as several classes that help with the handling of form, color, and data.

    The creators of Processing were also inspired by the concept of sketching: when we have an idea and use a paper sketchbook to draw it down, we often create many iterations or variations of the original idea as we refine it or make changes. Processing supports a similar way of working with computer code by making it easy for us to obtain visual feedback from the code so we can quickly iterate and refine a programming idea. This is why you will see Processing described as a "coding sketchbook" in many places. The next section describes the basic structure in Processing that allows us to sketch with code by getting animated graphics to the computer screen.

The Structure of a Processing Sketch

Most of the time, we want our Processing sketches to run nonstop to animate graphics on the screen and keep track of user input. This means that instead of running our code just one time, Processing will continue running it repeatedly so that we can animate the visual output by programming how it changes from one frame to the next and how it's affected by any interaction of the user with the computer (desktop, laptop, phone, etc.). Because of that, we call these "interactive sketches" in contrast with "static sketches" that run just one time (we can create these with Processing too, but for now, we will focus on interactive sketches).

■ **Note**   All the code examples in this chapter can be run in the Java or the Android mode, since they don't rely on any features of the Processing language specific to either mode. This chapter also assumes some basic knowledge of programming, including conditions (if/else), loops (for/while), use of variables, and organizing our code with functions, so we will not go over those concepts.

© Andrés Colubri 2023
A. Colubri, *Processing for Android*, https://doi.org/10.1007/978-1-4842-9585-4_2

The structure of an interactive sketch in Processing is uncomplicated: it requires two functions, one called setup() and the other, draw(). The setup() function will contain the code that we need to run only one time at the beginning to set things up, and the draw() function will contain the code that generates the visual output of our sketch and Processing will run every time it has to draw or "render" a new frame on the screen of the computer, typically 60 times per second. Let's use these functions to create our first animated sketch in Processing!

A simple animation could be moving a vertical line from left to right across the screen. We do just that in Listing 2-1, where we have both setup() and draw(). In the setup() function, we run a few initial tasks: first, we set the size of the output window or "canvas" where Processing will draw to. In this case, we are initializing the canvas with fullScreen(), which makes it as large as the entire screen of the computer (or phone). Then we set the parameters of our line with strokeWeight(2), which sets the line weight (or thickness) to 2 pixels, and stroke(255), which sets the line color to white (we will go over the use of numbers to set color values later in this chapter). Finally, we set the value of the variable x, declared at the top of the code, to zero. This variable holds the horizontal position of the line, and setting to zero means placing it on the left side of the screen (also later in the chapter we will discuss about screen coordinates in more detail). In the draw() function, we start by setting the color of the entire canvas to a tone of gray with background(50) and then draw the line with line(x, 0, x, height). The line() function takes four parameters: the first two (x, 0) correspond to the first point of the line, and the last two (x, height), to the second point, so by calling this function, we get Processing to draw a line from (x, 0) to (x, height). The word "height" is a "constant" in Processing that always represents the height of the canvas and therefore cannot be used as a variable name by us (the Processing language includes several more constants like this; we will learn about some of them later in this and following chapters). Because the two points have the same x coordinate, we will get a vertical line running between the top (0) and the bottom (height) of the screen. The last two lines of code in the draw() function control the animation: by doing x = x + 1, we are increasing the value of the horizontal position of our vertical line by one unit; this means that the line will move to the right one pixel per frame. If we keep adding 1 to x enough times, its value will eventually be larger than the width of our canvas, and the line will no longer be visible. In that case, we put the line back at the left edge of the canvas by checking if x is larger than the width and resetting to zero with if (width < x) x = 0. The output of this sketch running on a phone is shown in Figure 2-1.

Listing 2-1. A sketch that draws a vertical line moving horizontally across the screen

```
int x;

void setup() {
  fullScreen();
  strokeWeight(2);
  stroke(255);
  x = 0;
}
void draw() {
  background(50);
  line(x, 0, x, height);
  x = x + 1;
  if (width < x) x = 0;
}
```

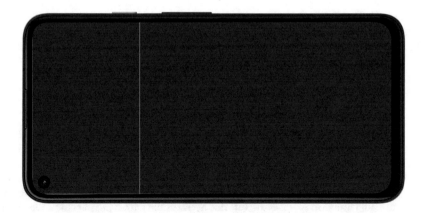

Figure 2-1. *Output of the animated line sketch, running on a Pixel 4a phone*

This continuous sequence of calls to the draw() function that Processing does automatically in any interactive sketch is called the "animation loop." Processing calls the draw() function during the animation loop at a default frame rate of 60 frames per second; however, we can change this default using the function frameRate(). For instance, if we add frameRate(1) in setup(), then the animation loop will draw 1 frame per second.

Sometimes, we may need to stop the animation loop at some point. We can use the noLoop() function for doing this and then the loop() function to resume the animation afterward. Processing also has a boolean (logical) constant named looping, which is true or false depending on whether the sketch is running the animation loop. We can build on top of our previous sketch to pause/resume the line movement if the user clicks the mouse (on a desktop/laptop) or taps the touchscreen (on a phone), as shown in Listing 2-2. This code introduces another new function from the Processing language called mousePressed(), where we can put code that should be run only when the user presses the mouse (or taps the touchscreen). We will see a few more interaction-handling examples in this chapter and then will deep-dive into touchscreen interaction more specific for mobile development in Chapter 5.

Listing 2-2. Pausing/resuming the animation loop

```
int x = 0;

void setup() {
  fullScreen();
  strokeWeight(2);
  stroke(255);
}

void draw() {
  background(50);
  line(x, 0, x, height);
  x = x + 1;
  if (width < x) x = 0;

}
```

```
void mousePressed() {
  if (looping) {
    noLoop();
  } else {
    loop();
  }
}
```

We can also write static sketches without setup/draw, which are useful if we only want to create a fixed composition that does not need to be animated. Processing runs the code in these sketches only one time. Listing 2-3 contains a simple static sketch that draws the white circle in Figure 2-2. Here, we use the function ellipse() to draw a circle centered at coordinates (400, 400) and width and height equal to 300 pixels (by setting different width and height values, we would get an ellipse of any proportions we like.) We use the fill() function to paint the interior of the circle with a purple color. We also use the size() function, which allows us to set the width and height of the output canvas. We apply this function instead of fullScreen() if we only want to use an area of the device's screen for drawing and interaction. Processing will paint the pixels outside of the drawing area with a light gray color, as seen in Figure 2-2, and we will not be able to change this color. Tapping on this area will not result in any interaction events with the sketch.

Listing 2-3. Static sketch without setup() and draw() functions

```
size(1000, 1000);
background(255);
fill(150, 100, 250);
ellipse(500, 500, 400, 400);
```

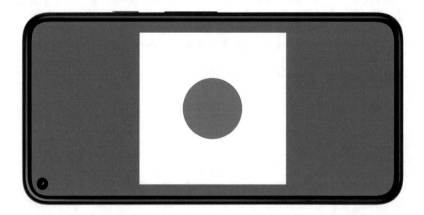

Figure 2-2. *Output of the static sketch in Listing 2-3*

Drawing with Code

We just saw in the examples from the previous section how the Processing language allows us to "draw with code." Even though these examples were very simple, they already point to some general concepts for code-based drawing in Processing. First, we need to specify the coordinates of the elements we want to draw on the screen. Second, there are functions, such as line() and ellipse(), that allow us to draw various shapes by setting numerical values that define their form, size, and position. Third, we can set the visual "style" of these shapes (e.g., stroke and fill color) by using functions like fill(), stroke(), and strokeWeight(). In the next sections, we will delve into these techniques in more depth to learn how to draw different kinds of shapes.

Coordinates

One of the most important concepts in code-based drawing is knowing how to locate points on the computer screen using numeric coordinates. Processing draws the graphical output of our code into a rectangular grid of pixels, numbered from 0 to width-1 along the horizontal direction (the x axis) and 0 to height-1 along the vertical direction (the y axis), illustrated in Figure 2-3. As we saw before, we can set the precise width and height of this grid by using the size() function with our desired values as arguments. If we use the fullScreen() function instead, then the width and height of the grid will be automatically set to the width and height of the entire screen of our device.

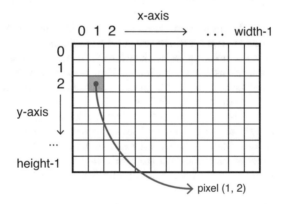

Figure 2-3. *Diagram of the screen's pixels*

The X coordinates run from left to right, while the Y coordinates run from top to bottom. So the pixel (0, 0) represents the upper left corner of the screen, and the pixel (width-1, height-1) represents the lower right corner. The arguments of most of the 2D drawing functions in Processing refer to the pixel coordinates of the screen. Processing also offers two internal constants, conveniently called width and height, that hold the values we set in the size() function or determined automatically when using fullScreen(). The following "toy" sample code, where we set a very small output size so we can see each single pixel, would produce the output in Figure 2-4 (although the actual output of running this code on a computer would be so small that we would likely not be able to differentiate its parts):

```
size(12, 8);
stroke(200, 0, 0);
fill(100, 200, 100);
rect(2, 1, width - 1, height - 2);
```

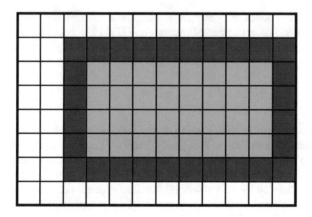

Figure 2-4. *Pixels covered by a stroked rectangle in Processing*

We should set the size of the shapes we draw with Processing according to the constraints of the screen size. In general, it is recommended to use the width and height constants when referring to the size of the screen instead of entering predetermined values, because the width and height of our output will likely change between devices, especially if we use the fullScreen() function. Even when we set the width and height in the size() function, if we later change the arguments of size(), we would then need to go through the code updating any references to the original width and height values. This won't be necessary if we use the width and height constants. The code in Listing 2-4 provides a demonstration of this technique. With this code, we generate a rectangular checkboard of 4×4 by drawing rectangles that have size equal to a quarter of the width and height of the output canvas. The result is shown in Figure 2-5, as it would appear on a Pixel 4a phone. If we change the values in size(1000, 1000) to something else, the result would still be a grid of 4×4 rectangles, because those rectangles will be resized automatically according to the value of width and height.

Listing 2-4. Using screen coordinates

```
size(1000, 1000);
noStroke();
fill(255);
background(0);
rect(0, 0, width/4, height/4);
rect(width/2, 0, width/4, width/4);
rect(width/4, height/4, width/4, height/4);
rect(3*width/4, height/4, width/4, height/4);
rect(0, height/2, width/4, height/4);
rect(width/2, height/2, width/4, width/4);
rect(width/4, 3*height/4, width/4, height/4);
rect(3*width/4, 3*height/4, width/4, height/4);
```

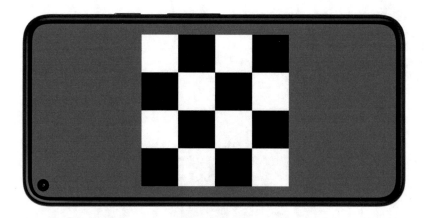

Figure 2-5. Using screen coordinates to draw a grid of rectangles

Form

All the shapes we draw in Processing have a form in two or three dimensions. One way to think of a shape is as a perimeter or boundary that separates the inside of the shape from the outside. We already saw that Processing includes functions to draw common shapes such as rectangles or ellipses by providing the coordinates of their center and size. Processing will automatically construct the perimeter of these shapes for us. But to construct the perimeter of an arbitrary shape in Processing, we need to explicitly provide the coordinates of the vertices alongside the perimeter. We can do this by listing the vertices between the beginShape() and endShape() functions as shown in Listing 2-5, whose output is presented in Figure 2-6.

Listing 2-5. Using beginShape() and endShape()

```
size(600, 300);

strokeWeight(2);

// Draw a rectangle in the bottom of the screen
beginShape();
vertex(5, 250);
vertex(590, 250);
vertex(590, 290);
vertex(5, 290);
endShape(CLOSE);

// Draw a star-like shape in right side
beginShape();
vertex(330, 25);
vertex(390, 90);
vertex(510, 10);
vertex(460, 120);
vertex(510, 270);
vertex(410, 180);
vertex(310, 270);
vertex(360, 150);
endShape(CLOSE);
```

```
// Draw a small triangle right above the star shape
beginShape();
vertex(350, 30);
vertex(410, 30);
vertex(390, 75);
endShape();

ellipse(70, 80, 70, 70);
```

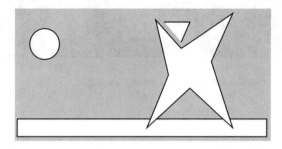

Figure 2-6. *Composition created by drawing several shapes*

We can learn a few important lessons from this example. First, shapes are drawn on top of each other according to the order they appear in the code; this is why the rectangle in the bottom, which is the first shape to be drawn, is partially obstructed by the star-like shape, which is drawn afterwards. Second, shapes can be open or closed. When a shape is open, the stroke line that goes around its perimeter will not connect the last and the first vertices, as we can see in the triangle shape. But if we add the argument CLOSE in the endShape() function, which is the case for the two first shapes, the stroke line will wrap around and result in an uninterrupted boundary delineating the shape. Third, we can combine common (also called "primitive") shapes drawn with functions like ellipse() or rect() with arbitrary shapes drawn with beginShape/endShape.

By applying some basic trigonometry, we can draw shapes that are regular polygons. The vertices alongside the perimeter of a regular polygon have coordinates x = r * cos(a) and y = r * sin(a), where r is the radius of the circumference, sin() and cos() are the sine and cosine functions, and a is an angle between 0 and 360 degrees (for a great intro/refresher about trigonometry, check Chapter 3 from Daniel Shiffman's book *The Nature of Code*, available online at https://natureofcode.com/book/chapter-3-oscillation/). For example, in Listing 2-6, we draw three regular polygons: a square, a hexagon, and an octagon.

Listing 2-6. *Drawing regular polygons*

```
size(900, 300);

fill(200, 100, 100);
beginShape();
for (float angle = 0; angle <= TWO_PI; angle += TWO_PI/4) {
  float x = 150 + 100 * cos(angle);
  float y = 150 + 100 * sin(angle);
  vertex(x, y);
}
endShape(CLOSE);
```

```
fill(100, 200, 100);
beginShape();
for (float angle = 0; angle <= TWO_PI; angle += TWO_PI/6) {
  float x = 450 + 100 * cos(angle);
  float y = 150 + 100 * sin(angle);
  vertex(x, y);
}
endShape(CLOSE);

fill(100, 100, 200);
beginShape();
for (float angle = 0; angle <= TWO_PI; angle += TWO_PI/8) {
  float x = 750 + 100 * cos(angle);
  float y = 150 + 100 * sin(angle);
  vertex(x, y);
}
endShape(CLOSE);
```

Here, we use a for loop to iterate over the angle that gives us the polygon vertices alongside its perimeter. In Processing, because it's built on top of the Java language, we can use all the control structures from Java (if/else, for, etc.) that we need for code-based drawing. So in this loop, we increase the angle variable by a fraction of 2π (which is 360 degrees expressed in radians and represented in Processing by the TWO_PI constant) until we go around the entire perimeter of the polygon, calculating its vertices with the cos/sin formula at each value of the angle. We can see the output of this code in Figure 2-7.

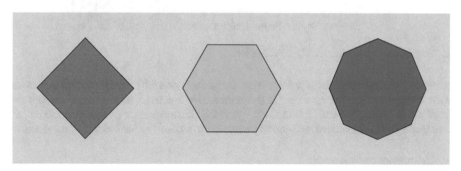

Figure 2-7. *Output of the polygon code example*

Color

Color is a fundamental element of visual design, and Processing provides many functions to let us set the color of the interior of our shapes (the fill color) and their edges (the stroke color), in addition to the background color of the entire output canvas.

By default, we can set colors using RGB (red, green, and blue) values between 0 and 255, as illustrated in the code of Listing 2-7 and its output in Figure 2-8. As we saw at the beginning of this chapter, if we pass a single value to the background(), fill(), or stroke() function, we will get a gray color (with the extremes of black and white when the value is 0 and 255, respectively). This is equivalent to passing the same number (e.g., (0, 0, 0)) as the three RGB values.

Listing 2-7. Setting fill and stroke colors using RGB values

```
size(600, 300);
strokeWeight(5);
fill(214, 87, 58);
stroke(53, 124, 115);
rect(10, 10, 180, 280);
stroke(115, 48, 128);
fill(252, 215, 51);
rect(210, 10, 180, 280);
stroke(224, 155, 73);
fill(17, 76, 131);
rect(410, 10, 180, 280);
```

Figure 2-8. *Output of setting stroke and fill RGB colors*

We can also set an optional fourth parameter in the stroke() and fill() functions. This parameter represents the transparency or "alpha value" of the color and allows us to draw semitransparent shapes, as it is demonstrated in Listing 2-8, with its output in Figure 2-9. If we are using a single number to paint with a gray hue, Processing will understand the second parameter in stroke() or fill() as the alpha value.

Listing 2-8. Using color transparency

```
size(600, 600);

background(255);

fill(0, 0, 255);
ellipse(525, 300, 150, 150);

fill(0, 255, 0, 120);
ellipse(450, 300, 270, 270);

fill(255, 0, 0, 50);
ellipse(300, 300, 500, 500);

fill(255, 0);
ellipse(300, 300, 600, 600);
```

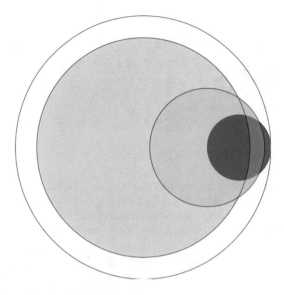

Figure 2-9. *Output of setting alpha values in fill()*

As we have seen so far, we can draw shapes of different kinds (points, lines, polygons) and set not only their fill and stroke color but other style attributes or parameters as well. We used the stroke weight before, but there are many more attributes we will learn about later. We can think of these attributes as "style parameters" that once they are set, they affect everything drawn afterward. For example, each circle in Listing 2-9 has a different fill color, but if we comment out the second fill() call, then the first and second circles will be red, since the fill color set at the beginning affects the first two ellipse calls. Figure 2-10 shows the outputs of this sketch in these two situations, with the left half beginning the output with the second fill() enabled and the right half showing the output of the second fill() commented out.

Listing 2-9. Setting the fill color attribute

```
size(460, 200);
strokeWeight(5);
fill(200, 0, 0);
stroke(255);
ellipse(100, 100, 190, 190);
fill(255, 0, 200); // Comment this line out to make second circle red
stroke(0);
ellipse(250, 100, 100, 100);
fill(0, 200, 200);
ellipse(380, 100, 150, 150);
```

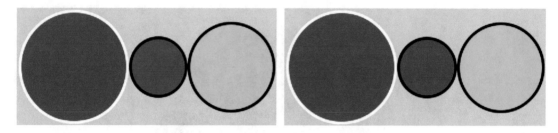

Figure 2-10. *Effect of the calling order of the fill() function*

Even though we can create almost any imaginable color using the RGB values, it can be hard to find the right combination of numbers for the color we need. Processing includes a handy Color Selector tool to help us pick a color interactively, which we can then copy into our sketches as RGB values. The Color Selector is available, alongside any other installed tool, under the "Tools" menu in the PDE (Figure 2-11).

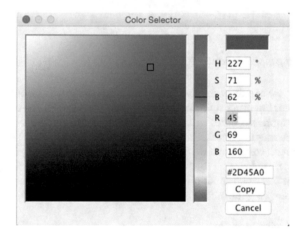

Figure 2-11. *Color Selector tool*

■ **Note** We can also specify colors in hexadecimal (hex) format, often used in web development, that is, fill(#FF0000) or stroke(#FFFFFF). The Code Selector tool provides the selected color in hex format as well.

Applying Geometric Transformations

So far, we have learned how to draw shapes and paint them with fill and stroke colors. In addition to all of this, Processing allows us to move our shapes around and change their size by applying translations, rotations, and scaling transformations (Figure 2-12).

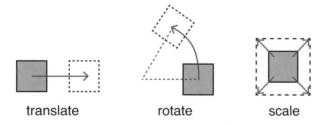

Figure 2-12. *The three types of geometric transformations*

Listings 2-10, 2-11, and 2-12 show applications of the translate(), rotate(), and scale() functions that we can use to apply translations, rotations, and scaling to any of the shapes we draw in our code. In all of them, we put the background() function in setup(); in this way, the canvas is cleared only once at the beginning, and so we can see the traces of the shapes as they move across the screen in each frame. The outputs of these examples are in Figure 2-13.

Listing 2-10. Translation example

```
float x = 0;

void setup() {
  size(400, 400);
  background(150);
}

void draw() {
  translate(x, 0);
  rect(0, 0, 300, 300);
  x += 2;
  if (width < x) x = -300;
}
```

Listing 2-11. Rotation example

```
float angle = 0;

void setup() {
  size(400, 400);
  background(150);
}

void draw() {
  rotate(angle);
  rect(0, 0, 300, 300);
  angle += 0.01 * PI;
}
```

Listing 2-12. Scaling example

```
f float s = 0;

void setup() {
  size(400, 400);
  background(150);
}

void draw() {
  scale(s);
  rect(0, 0, 10, 10);
  s += 1;
  if (100 < s) s = 0;
}
```

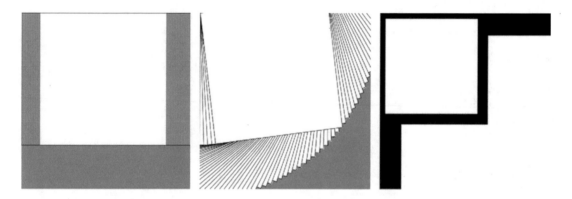

Figure 2-13. *Outputs of the translation (left), rotation (center), and scale (right) examples*

The result of applying a single translation, rotation, or scaling transformation is easy to understand; however, we may find harder to predict the effect of many transformations one after another. A way that could be helpful to think about geometric transformations is that they change the entire coordinate system in the Processing canvas. For instance, if we apply a translation of 20 units along the x axis and 30 units along the y axis and then apply a rotation, the shapes will rotate around point (20, 30) instead of (0, 0), which is the default center for 2D rotations. But if the rotation is applied before the translation, then the X and Y axes will be rotated, and the translation will be applied along the rotated axes. As a result of this, if we draw a shape at the end of a sequence of translate(), rotate(), and scale() calls, its final position will be different if we modify the order of the transformations. Figure 2-14 illustrates this situation with a rectangle drawn after translate() and rotate() calls in different orders. Even though this concept can be difficult to fully grasp at the beginning, it will become clearer with practice.

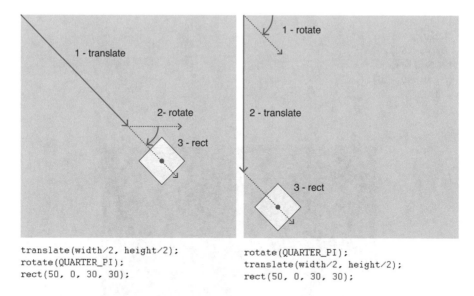

```
translate(width/2, height/2);        rotate(QUARTER_PI);
rotate(QUARTER_PI);                   translate(width/2, height/2);
rect(50, 0, 30, 30);                  rect(50, 0, 30, 30);
```

Figure 2-14. *The order of geometric transformations affects the result*

We can save the current transformation "state" with the pushMatrix() function and restore it with the corresponding popMatrix() function. We must always use these two functions in pairs, which allow us to create complex relative movements by setting transformations only to specific subsets of the shapes. For example, Listing 2-13 generates an animation of an ellipse and square rotating around a larger square placed at the center of the screen, with the smaller square also rotating around its own center. Figure 2-15 shows a snapshot of this animation.

Listing 2-13. Using pushMatrix() and popMatrix()

```
float angle;

void setup() {
  size(400, 400);
}

void draw() {
  background(170);
  translate(width/2, height/2);
  rotate(angle);
  rect(0, 0, 70, 70);
  pushMatrix();
    line(0, 0, 130, 0);
    translate(130, 0);
    rotate(2 * angle);
    rect(0, 0, 30, 30);
    pushMatrix();
      rotate(angle);
      line(0, 0, 50, 0);
      ellipse(50, 0, 15, 15);
    popMatrix();
```

```
  popMatrix();
  rotate(angle);
  line(0, 0, 0, 180);
  translate(0, 180);
  ellipse(0, 0, 30, 30);
  angle += 0.01;
}
```

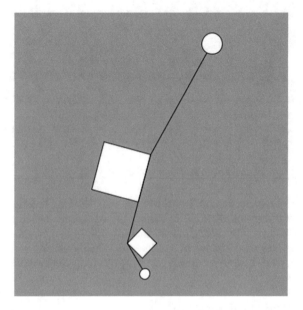

Figure 2-15. *Using pushMatrix() and popMatrix() to keep transformations separate*

■ **Note**   For readability of the code, we can consider indenting the code inside push and popMatrix(); many people use this style to know where a set of transformations start and end. But this is completely optional.

Responding to User Input

There are many ways to capture user input into our sketch. Keyboard and mouse (touchscreen in the case of mobile phones) are the most common. Processing provides several built-in variables and functions to respond to user input. For example, the variables mouseX and mouseY give us the position of the mouse pointer or touchscreen tap. In the Android mode, these variables represent the position of the first touch point on the screen (Processing also supports multitouch interaction, which is covered in Chapter 5). Both mouseX and mouseY are complemented with mousePressed, which indicates whether the mouse/touchscreen is being pressed. Using these variables, we can create a drawing sketch with very little code, like the one in Listing 2-14, where we simply draw a semitransparent ellipse at the (mouseX, mouseY) position. Its output on a phone would look like the one shown in Figure 2-16.

Listing 2-14. A free-hand drawing sketch using circles

```
void setup() {
  fullScreen();
  noStroke();
  fill(255, 100);
}

void draw() {
  if (mousePressed) {
    ellipse(mouseX, mouseY, 50, 50);
  }
}
```

Figure 2-16. *Drawing with ellipses*

While mouseX/Y stores the current position of the mouse/touch, Processing also provides the variables pmouseX and pmouseY, which store the previous position. By connecting the pmouseX/Y coordinates with the current ones in mouseX/Y, we can draw continuous lines that follow the movement of the mouse or touch pointer. Listing 2-15 illustrates this technique, with its output in Figure 2-17.

Listing 2-15. Using current and previous mouse positions

```
void setup() {
fullScreen();
strokeWeight(5);
stroke(255, 100);
}

void draw() {
  if (mousePressed) {
    line(pmouseX, pmouseY, mouseX, mouseY);
  }
}
```

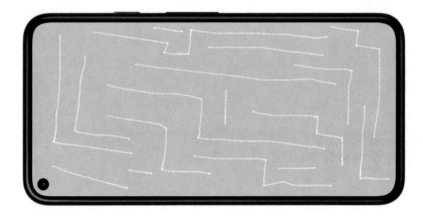

Figure 2-17. *Output of the drawing sketch where current and previous mouse positions are connected to create continuous lines*

We have one last example of a drawing sketch in Listing 2-16. Here, we also add a circle at the current mouse/touch pointer positions. This results in a line that resembles a chain made of connected links (Figure 2-18). The possibilities are virtually endless; it's only up to our imagination to come up with cool ways in which we can convert user input into interactive graphics using code!

Listing 2-16. Another free-hand drawing sketch

```
void setup() {
  fullScreen();
  strokeWeight(2);
  stroke(0);
  fill(255);
}

void draw() {
  if (mousePressed) {
    line(pmouseX, pmouseY, mouseX, mouseY);
    ellipse(mouseX, mouseY, 20, 20);
  }
}
```

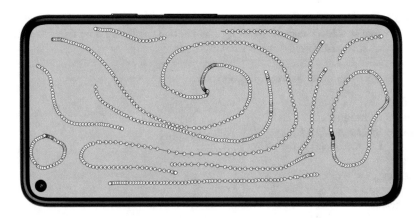

Figure 2-18. *Combining continuous lines with ellipses in drawing sketch*

Coding a "Vine Drawing" App

Our goal in this final section is to code a drawing app that incorporates code-generated shapes into hand-drawn lines. One possibility is to augment the scaffold provided by the lines with shapes that resemble growing vegetation, such as vines and leaves. Instead of trying to arrive to a fully organic look, which may be hard to do using only the functions we learned so far, we could limit our drawing to regular shapes that still suggest vegetation through color and randomness. Some sketching with pen and paper (Figure 2-19) may also help us to explore some visual ideas.

Figure 2-19. *Sketches for the vine drawing app*

We could draw leaves as clusters of regular polygons with begin/endShape, sprouting from random positions alongside the hand-drawn lines representing the main branches in the vine. Here, the random() function in Processing will be very useful to add some randomness to our shapes, so the resulting leaves do not look too regular. This function returns a floating-point (i.e., with decimal digits) random number between a minimum and a maximum value. For example, calling random(10, 20) would give us a random number between 10 and 20, such as 16.8. Every time we run random(), we will get a different result.

Let's draw a bunch with a random number of leaves. Also, the polygon representing each leaf could have a random number of sides. The code in Listing 2-17 contains code that does these two things, and Figure 2-20 shows the several different outputs from this code.

Listing 2-17. Drawing randomized leaves with polygons

```
size(600, 600);
translate(width/2, height/2);
int numLeaves = int(random(4, 8));
for (int i = 0; i < numLeaves; i++) {
  pushMatrix();
    float leafAngle = random(0, TWO_PI);
    float leafLength = random(100, 250);
    rotate(leafAngle);
    line(0, 0, leafLength, 0);
    translate(leafLength, 0);
    pushStyle();
      noStroke();
      fill(255, 190);
      float r = random(50, 100);
      beginShape();
      int numSides = int(random(4, 8));
      for (float angle = 0; angle <= TWO_PI; angle += TWO_PI/numSides) {
        float x = r * cos(angle);
        float y = r * sin(angle);
        vertex(x, y);
      }
      endShape();
    popStyle();
  popMatrix();
}
```

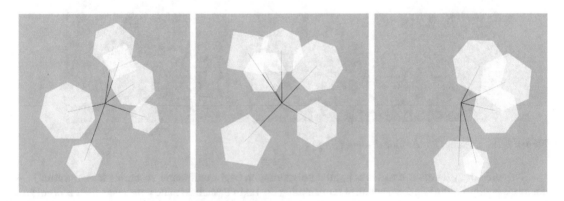

Figure 2-20. *Different outputs of the leaf drawing sketch*

This code gives us a reasonable range of variability in the output, but without being completely random. There are a couple of new things to note in this code. First, some of the random numbers need to be integer, for example, the number of leaves. So in that case, we can use the int() function in Processing to convert the floating-point result from random() into a whole number. Second, we are using another pair of functions called pushStyle() and popStyle(). Like what push/popMatrix does with transformations, push/popStyle keeps changes in style (e.g., fill and line color) separate so the changes do not affect any shapes drawn outside the push/pop block.

We already explored a few options for hand-drawn lines in the previous section. Listing 2-16 produced an interesting output by combining continuous lines with circles. If we set the lines and leaves to have bark (brownish) and green colors while also introducing some random variability, we may be able to get a complete vine drawing sketch. To do so, we could just take the code in Listing 2-17 and copy it inside a user-defined function that gets called every time we need a bunch of leaves alongside the hand-drawn lines.

One final question is when to draw the leaves. In order to keep our sketch simple, we could make this step automatic, for example, by using the random() function, but applying randomness all the time is not always a good idea because the output would feel too random. It's important that we take purposeful decisions in our code and do not leave everything to chance! We could try to use the user input so that if the mouse or touch pointer is moving quickly (e.g., the vine is growing fast), then new leaves are added to the drawing. An easy way to do this is calculating the distance between the current and previous mouse positions using the dist() function in Processing just like so: `dist(pmouseX, pmouseY, mouseX, mouseY)`. Listing 2-18 puts all this together, and Figure 2-21 shows a sample drawing made with the sketch.

Listing 2-18. Full vine drawing sketch

```
void setup() {
  fullScreen();
  strokeWeight(2);
  stroke(121, 81, 49, 150);
  fill(255);
  background(255);
}

void draw() {
  if (mousePressed) {
    line(pmouseX, pmouseY, mouseX, mouseY);
    ellipse(mouseX, mouseY, 13, 13);
    if (30 < dist(pmouseX, pmouseY, mouseX, mouseY)) {
      drawLeaves();
    }
  }
}

void drawLeaves() {
  int numLeaves = int(random(2, 5));
  for (int i = 0; i < numLeaves; i++) {
    float leafAngle = random(0, TWO_PI);
    float leafLength = random(20, 100);
    pushMatrix();
      translate(mouseX, mouseY);
      rotate(leafAngle);
      line(0, 0, leafLength, 0);
      translate(leafLength, 0);
      pushStyle();
        noStroke();
        fill(random(170, 180), random(200, 230), random(80, 90), 190);
        float r = random(20, 50);
```

```
      beginShape();
      int numSides = int(random(4, 8));
      for (float angle = 0; angle <= TWO_PI; angle += TWO_PI/numSides) {
        float x = r * cos(angle);
        float y = r * sin(angle);
        vertex(x, y);
      }
      endShape();
    popStyle();
  popMatrix();
  }
}
```

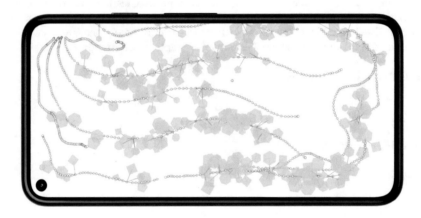

Figure 2-21. *Output of the vine drawing sketch*

Summary

We have now a basic knowledge of the Processing language that covers how to draw shapes, set colors, apply transformations, and handle user interaction through the mouse or touchscreen. Even though we learned only a small fraction of all the functionality available in Processing, what we saw in this chapter should give us enough tools to start exploring code-based drawing and to make our own interactive sketches and run them as Android apps.

CHAPTER 3

From Sketch to Play Store

In this chapter, we will go through all the steps involved in the creation of a Processing for Android project, from sketching and debugging to exporting the project as a signed app ready for upload to the Google Play Store. We will use the vine drawing sketch from the previous chapter as the project to upload to the store.

Sketching and Debugging

In the first two chapters, we talked about "code sketching," where immediate visual output and quick iteration are key techniques to develop projects with Processing. Another important technique that we did not mention yet is the identification and resolution of errors or "bugs" in the code, a process called debugging.

Debugging can take us as much time as writing the code itself. What makes debugging challenging is that some bugs are the result of faulty logic or incorrect calculations, and because there are no typos or any other syntactical errors in the code, Processing can still run the sketch. Unfortunately, there is no foolproof technique to eliminate all bugs in a program, but Processing provides some utilities to help us with debugging.

Getting Information from the Console

The simplest way to debug a program is printing the values of variables and messages along various points of the execution flow of the program. Processing's API includes text-printing functions, print() and println(), which output to the console area in the PDE. The only difference between these two functions is that println() adds a new line break at the end while print() does not. Listing 3-1 shows a sketch using println() to indicate the occurrence of an event (a mouse press in this case) and the value of built-in variable.

Listing 3-1. Using println() in a sketch to show information on the console

```
void setup() {
  fullScreen();
}

void draw() {
  println("frame #", frameCount);
}

void mousePressed() {
  println("Press event");
}
```

© Andrés Colubri 2023
A. Colubri, *Processing for Android*, https://doi.org/10.1007/978-1-4842-9585-4_3

Processing's console shows anything that is printed with these functions, but also warning or error messages indicating a problem in the execution of the sketch (Figure 3-1).

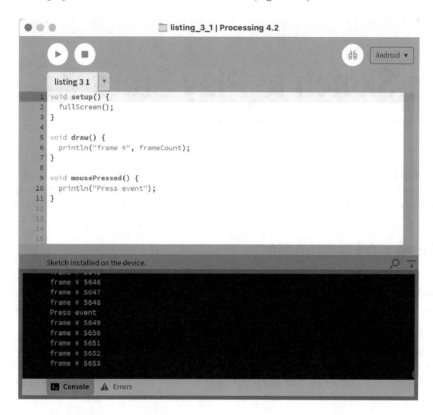

Figure 3-1. *Console area in the PDE, outlined with red*

The main problem of printing messages to the console for debugging is that it requires adding these additional function calls for each variable we want to keep track of. Once we are done with debugging, we need to remove or comment out all these calls, which can become inconvenient for large sketches.

■ **Note**   Comments in Processing work the same way as in Java: we can comment out a single line of code using two consecutive forward slashes, "//", and an entire block of text with "/*" at the beginning of the block and "*/" at the end. We can also use the Comment/Uncomment option under the "Edit" menu in the PDE.

Getting more information with logcat

We can obtain a lot of useful information from the Processing console, but sometimes, this may not be enough to find out what is wrong with our sketch. The Android SDK includes several command-line tools that can help us with debugging. The most important SDK tool is adb (Android Debug Bridge), which makes possible the communication between the computer we are using for development and the device or emulator. In fact, Processing uses adb under the hood to query what devices are available and to install the sketch on the device or emulator when running it from the PDE.

We can also use adb manually, for example, to get more detailed debug messages. To do this, we need to open a terminal console, and once in it, we would need to change to the directory where the Android SDK is installed. In case the SDK was automatically installed by Processing, it should be located inside the sketchbook folder, the modes/AndroidMode subfolder. Within that folder, the SDK tools are found in sdk/platform-tools. Once there, we can run the adb tool with the logcat option, which prints out the log with all the messages. For instance, the following is the sequence of commands we would need on Mac to run logcat:

```
$ cd ~/Documents/Processing/android/sdk/platform-tools
$ ./adb logcat
```

By default, logcat prints all messages generated by the Android device or emulator, not only from the sketch we are debugging but also from all processes that are currently running, so we might get too many messages. The print messages from Processing can be displayed if using logcat with the –I option. Logcat has additional options to only show error messages (-E) or warnings (-W). The full list of options is available on the Google's developer site (https://developer.android.com/tools/logcat).

Using the Integrated Debugger

The Android mode offers an "integrated debugger" tool that makes it easy to keep track of the internal state of a running sketch. We turn the debugger on by pressing the button with the butterfly icon on the left of the menu bar, next to the mode selector, or selecting the "Enable Debugger" in the Debug menu. Once enabled, we can access many additional options in the PDE to use when the sketch is running. For example, we can add "checkpoints" to any line in the code of our sketch. A checkpoint signals where the execution of the sketch should stop to allow us to inspect the value of all the variables in the sketch, both user defined and built-in.

We can create a new checkpoint by double-clicking on the line number in the left margin of the code editor. A diamond sign will indicate that the line has flagged with a checkpoint. When we run a sketch containing one or more checkpoints, Processing will stop execution when it reaches each checkpoint, at which moment we can inspect the value of the variables using the variable inspector window (Figure 3-2). We resume execution by pressing the continue button on the toolbar. We can also step line by line by pressing the Step button and see how each variable changes its value after each line.

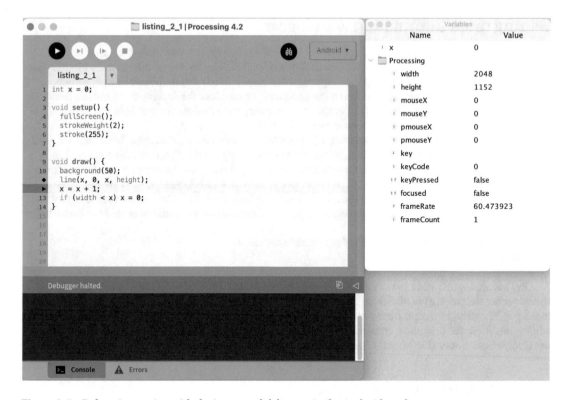

Figure 3-2. *Debugging session with the integrated debugger in the Android mode*

All this functionality in the integrated debugger could help us identify bugs in the code without the need of adding print instructions, although fixing a tricky bug is always challenging and can take a long time even with the debugger. At the end, it comes down to carefully understanding the logic of the code in the sketch and its possible consequences and edge cases, based on information we get from the debugger or print instructions. In this way, we can narrow down the portion of the code where the bug is likely to be.

Reporting Processing Bugs

Sometimes, an unexpected or erroneous behavior in a Processing sketch may be due not to a bug in our code, but in Processing itself! If you have strong suspicion that you have found a Processing bug, you can report it in the GitHub page of the project. If it is a bug affecting the Android mode, please open a new issue in the processing-android repository at `https://github.com/processing/processing-android/issues` and include as much information as possible to reproduce the bug and to help the developers replicate the bug and eventually fix it.

Preparing a Sketch for Release

After debugging a sketch in the PDE, we may want to bundle it for public release through Google Play Store. When working from the PDE, Processing creates a debug app bundle that can only be installed on our own device or emulator for testing purposes. Creating an app suitable for general distribution from our sketch requires some additional steps and considerations to make sure it can be uploaded to the Play Store.

Adjusting for Device's DPI

A first step to prepare our sketch for public release is to check that it can be run on most of the Android devices in use. When writing and debugging our sketch, it is often the case that we work with one or only a few different devices, so it may be hard to anticipate issues on devices we do not have access to. A common situation is that the graphics might look either too big or too small when running our Processing sketches on different devices. The reason for this is that both resolution (number of pixels) and physical screen size can vary quite a lot across phones, tablets, and watches, and so graphic elements designed with one resolution in mind and viewed on a screen of a particular size will likely look wrong on another. Since Android is designed to support various combinations of screen sizes and resolutions, we need a way in Processing to adapt the visual design of our sketch so it looks as intended across different devices.

The ratio of the resolution to the screen size gives what is called the DPI (dots per inch, which, in the context of computer screens, is equivalent to pixels per inch or PPI). The DPI is the basic magnitude to compare across devices. It is important to keep in mind that higher DPI does not necessarily mean a higher resolution, since two different devices with the same resolution may have different screen sizes. For example, the Galaxy Nexus (4.65" diagonal) has a 720×1280 pixels resolution, while the Nexus 7 (7" diagonal) has an 800×1280 pixels resolution. The DPIs of these devices are 316 and 216, even though their resolutions are very similar.

Android classifies devices in density buckets according to the following six generalized densities (a specific device will fall in one of these categories depending on which one is closest to its actual DPI):

- ldpi (low): ~120dpi

- mdpi (medium): ~160dpi

- hdpi (high): ~240dpi

- xhdpi (extra-high): ~320dpi

- xxhdpi (extra-extra-high): ~480dpi

- xxxhdpi (extra-extra-extra-high): ~640dpi

The generalized density levels are important in Processing to generate the app icons, as we will see later in this chapter, but not so much when writing our code. To make sure that the visual elements in our sketch scale properly across different devices, there is another built-in constant from Android that Processing makes available through its API. This is the "display density," a number that represents how much bigger (or smaller) is the pixel in our device when compared with a reference 160 DPI screen (e.g., a 320×480, 3.5" screen). Thus, on a 160 DPI screen, this density value will be 1; on a 120 DPI screen, it would be .75; etc.

■ **Note** Google's API Guide on Multiple Screen Support gives detailed information about the density independence on Android: `https://developer.android.com/guide/practices/screens_support.html`.

The display density is available in Processing as the constant named `displayDensity`, which we can use from anywhere in our code. The simplest way of adjusting the output to the device's DPI is to multiply the size of all the graphical elements in the sketch by `displayDensity`, which is the approach in Listing 3-2. As we can see in Figure 3-3, the size of the circles drawn by the sketch is the same across devices with different DPIs. Also, this example uses the `map()` function to convert the index variables i and j, which go from 0 to maxi and maxj, to the coordinate values x and y, which should be in the range (0, width) and (0, height), respectively.

Listing 3-2. Using displayDensity to adjust our sketch to different screen sizes and resolutions

```
void setup() {
  fullScreen();
  noStroke();
}

void draw() {
  background(0);
  float r = 50 * displayDensity;
  int maxi = int(width/r);
  int maxj = int(height/r);
  for (int i = 0; i <= maxi; i++) {
    float x = map(i, 0, maxi, 0, width);
    for (int j = 0; j <= maxj; j++) {
      float y = map(j, 0, maxj, 0, height);
      ellipse(x, y, r, r);
    }
  }
}
```

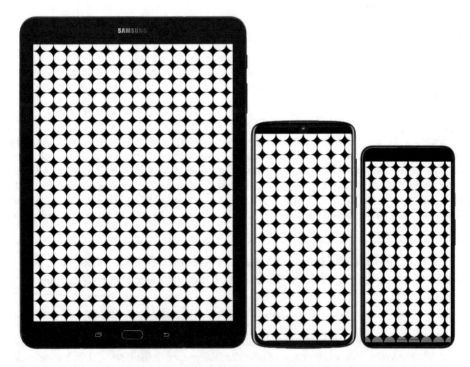

Figure 3-3. *From left to right, output of our sketch on a Samsung Galaxy Tab S3 (9.7″, 20480×1536 px, 264 dpi), a Moto Z4 (6.4″, 2340×1080 px, 403 dpi), and a Pixel 4a (5.81″, 2340×1080 px, 433 dpi)*

We can return now to our vine drawing sketch from the previous chapter and add `displayDensity` in the parts of the code where we need to scale the graphics. More specifically, any variable or value that represents the size of shapes and the position of vertices on the screen, or is related to handling mouse or touch pointer, should be multiplied by `displayDensity`. Listing 3-3 shows these changes applied to the original drawing sketch.

Listing 3-3. Adding displayDensity to the vine drawing sketch from Chapter 2

```
void setup() {
  fullScreen();
  strokeWeight(2 * displayDensity);
  stroke(121, 81, 49, 150);
  fill(255);
  background(255);
}

void draw() {
  if (mousePressed) {
    line(pmouseX, pmouseY, mouseX, mouseY);
    ellipse(mouseX, mouseY, 13 * displayDensity, 13 * displayDensity);
    if (30 * displayDensity < dist(pmouseX, pmouseY, mouseX, mouseY)) {
      drawLeaves();
    }
  }
}

void drawLeaves() {
  int numLeaves = int(random(2, 5));
  for (int i = 0; i < numLeaves; i++) {
    float leafAngle = random(0, TWO_PI);
    float leafLength = random(20, 100) * displayDensity;
    pushMatrix();
      translate(mouseX, mouseY);
      rotate(leafAngle);
      line(0, 0, leafLength, 0);
      translate(leafLength, 0);
      pushStyle();
        noStroke();
        fill(random(170, 180), random(200, 230), random(80, 90), 190);
        float r = random(20, 50) * displayDensity;
        beginShape();
        int numSides = int(random(4, 8));
        for (float angle = 0; angle <= TWO_PI; angle += TWO_PI/numSides) {
          float x = r * cos(angle);
          float y = r * sin(angle);
          vertex(x, y);
        }
        endShape();
      popStyle();
    popMatrix();
  }
}
```

Using the Emulator

We briefly discussed the emulator in the first chapter. Even when we have our own device, the emulator could be useful, because it allows us to test hardware configurations that we do not have access to. Processing creates a default Android Virtual Device (AVD) to run in the emulator, using the Pixel 6 settings (1080×2400 px, 411 dpi). We can create other AVDs with different properties to test our sketches on, using the command-line tool avdmanager, included in the Android SDK. We need to keep in mind that the emulator will likely run slower than an actual device, especially if creating high-resolution AVDs or with other high-end capabilities.

Since avdmanager is a command-line tool, we first need to open a terminal console and change to the tools directory where avdmanager and the emulator launcher are located inside the SDK folder. The sequence of steps to create a new AVD using the device definition for a Pixel C tablet, and then launching this AVD with the emulator, is as follows:

```
$ cd ~/Documents/Processing/android/sdk
$  cmdline-tools/latest/bin/avdmanager create avd -n processing-tablet -k "system-images;android-33;google_apis;x86_64" -d "pixel_c" --skin "pixel_c" -p ~/Documents/Processing/android/avd/processing-tablet
$ emulator/emulator -avd processing-tablet -gpu auto -port 5566
```

In the line running the avdmanager command, we provided four arguments:

- -n processing-tablet: The name of the AVD, which could be any name we wish to use.

- -k "system-images;android-33;google_apis;x86_64": The SDK package to use for the AVD; to find out which SDK packages are available in our SDK, we need to look at the system-images subfolder inside the SDK folder.

- -d "pixel_c": A device definition containing the hardware parameters of the device we want to emulate. We can list all the available device definitions by running the command "./avdmanager list devices".

- --skin "pixel_c": The name of the skin containing the images that the emulator will use to draw the frame of the device. This is optional; if a skin name is not provided, then the emulator window will not have a frame. The skin files need to be included in the SDK; when the Android mode downloads the default SDK, it also retrieves some skins from Google's servers and places them inside the skins subfolder inside the SDK folder.

- -p ~/Documents/Processing/android/avd/processing-tablet: The folder where we will store this AVD; in this case, we are using "android/avd/processing-tablet" inside the sketchbook folder, since this is the default location the mode uses for the default AVDs.

After we created a new AVD with the avdmanager, we can manually edit the configuration file that contains all the parameters of the AVD, which, in the case of this example, will be stored in "~/Documents/Processing/android/avd/ processing-tablet/config.ini". We can change the skin name and the path by modifying the values of the parameters skin.name and skin.path, respectively. If we remove the skin path altogether, we can set the AVD to any arbitrary resolution by entering a value of the form "wxh" as the skin. name, as shown in Figure 3-4.

```
● ● ●                          ○ config.ini — Edited⌄
hw.sensors.humidity = yes
hw.sensors.light = yes
hw.sensors.magnetic_field = yes
hw.sensors.magnetic_field_uncalibrated = yes
hw.sensors.orientation = yes
hw.sensors.pressure = yes
hw.sensors.proximity = yes
hw.sensors.rgbclight = no
hw.sensors.temperature = yes
hw.sensors.wrist_tilt = no
hw.trackBall = no
hw.useext4 = yes
image.sysdir.1 = system-images/android-33/google_apis/x86_64/
kernel.newDeviceNaming = autodetect
kernel.supportsYaffs2 = autodetect
runtime.network.latency = none
runtime.network.speed = full
sdcard.size = 512 MB
showDeviceFrame = yes
skin.name = 600x800
tag.display = Google APIs
tag.id = google_apis
test.delayAdbTillBootComplete = 0
test.monitorAdb = 0
test.quitAfterBootTimeOut = -1
vm.heapSize = 228M
```

Figure 3-4. *Adding a skin resolution to the AVD's config.ini file*

In general, the default device definitions together with a matching skin should be enough to have a working AVD to test our sketches on. The emulator command to launch the AVD includes the following arguments:

- -avd processing-tablet: The name of the AVD we want to launch.

- -gpu auto: Enables the emulator to use hardware acceleration on the computer to render the AVD's screen faster if it is available. Otherwise, it will use a slower software renderer.

- -port 5566: Sets the TCP port number to connect the console and adb with the emulator.

To use our new AVD in place of Processing's default, we should launch it manually as we did in this example, and then Processing will install our sketches in this AVD instead of the default AVD. However, we need to make sure to use the right port parameter, because Processing will only be able to communicate with phone emulators running on port 5566 and watch emulators on port 5576.

■ **Note** Google's Android developer site includes pages on avdmanager (`https://developer.android.com/tools/avdmanager`) and running the emulator from the command line (`https://developer.android.com/studio/run/emulator-commandline.html`) where we can find more information about these tools.

Setting Icons and Bundle Name

Android apps require icons of various sizes to be displayed at different pixel densities in the app launcher menu. Processing uses a set of default, generic icons when running a sketch from the PDE, but these icons should not be used for a public release.

To add our own icons to the project, we need to create the following files: icon-36, icon-48, icon-72, icon-96, icon-144, and icon-192 in .PNG format, for the ldpi (36×36), mdpi (48×48), hdpi (72×27), xhdpi (96×96), xxhdpi (144×144), and xxxhdpi (192×192) resolutions. Once we have these files, we must place them in the sketch's folder before exporting the signed bundle.

For the vine drawing app from the previous chapter, we will use the set of icons shown in Figure 3-5.

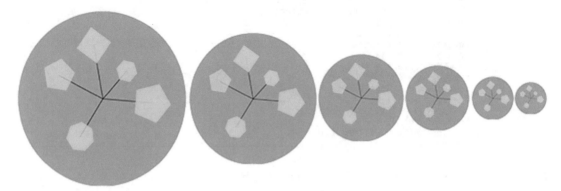

Figure 3-5. *Set of icons for the vine drawing app*

Google has published a set of guidelines and resources for icon creation, according to their material UI style, available at `https://m2.material.io/design/platform-guidance/android-icons.html`.

Setting Package Name and Version

Apps in the Google App Store are uniquely identified by a package name, which is a string of text that looks something like "com.example.helloworld". This package name follows the Java package naming convention, where the app name ("helloworld") is last, preceded by the website of the company or person developing the app in reverse order ("com.example").

Processing constructs this package name automatically by prepending a base name to the sketch name. The default base name is "processing.test", and we can change it by editing the manifest.xml file that Processing generates in the sketch folder after we run it for the first time from the PDE (either on a device or in the emulator). We can also set the version code and version name. For example, in the following manifest file generated by Processing, the base package name is "com.example", the version code is 10, and the version name is 0.5.4:

```
<?xml version="1.0" encoding="UTF-8"?>
<manifest xmlns:android="http://schemas.android.com/apk/res/android"
        android:versionCode="10" android:versionName="0.5.4"
        package="com.example">
    <application android:icon="@drawable/icon"
                android:label="Vines Draw">
        <activity android:name=".MainActivity"
                android:theme=
```

```
                    "@style/Theme.AppCompat.Light.NoActionBar.FullScreen">
            <intent-filter>
                <action android:name="android.intent.action.MAIN"/>
                <category android:name="android.intent.category.LAUNCHER"/>
            </intent-filter>
        </activity>
    </application>
</manifest>
```

If we save our sketch as "HelloWorld", then the full package name will be "com.package.helloworld" (Processing will set all the letters in the name to lowercase). Note that the package name of our app must be unique since there cannot be two apps on the Google Play Store with the same package name. Also, we should set the application name using the android:label attribute in the application tag. Android will use this label as the visible title of the app in the launcher and other parts of the UI.

Exporting As Signed Bundle

The Android mode simplifies the publishing of our sketch by signing and aligning the app so we can upload it to the Google Play Developer Console without any extra additional steps. All we need to do is to select the "Export Signed Bundle" option under the "File" menu (Figure 3-6).

Figure 3-6. *The "Export Signed Bundle" option in the PDE's "File" menu*

After selecting this option, Processing will ask us to create a new keystore to store the upload key to sign the app bundle. The keystore requires a password and additional information about the keystore issuer (name, organization, city, state, country), although those are optional. The keystore manager window that allows us to enter all this information is displayed in Figure 3-7.

Figure 3-7. *Entering the information needed to create a keystore in Processing*

Remember this password for the upload key, as you will have to use it every time you export a new signed bundle. If you lose access to the upload key, or it gets compromised, you can still create a new one and then contact Google support to reset the key. This is explained in this article from Play Console Help: `https://support.google.com/googleplay/android-developer/answer/9842756`.

The signed and aligned bundle will be saved in the build subfolder inside the sketch's folder, under the name [Sketch name in lowercase]_release.aab. Once we have this file, we can follow the instructions from Google to complete the app publishing process: `https://play.google.com/console/about/guides/releasewithconfidence/`.

If we follow all these steps with our vine drawing sketch, we should be able to generate a signed and aligned bundle ready to upload to the Play Store. We can also install it manually on our device using the adb tool from the command line:

```
$ cd ~/Documents/Processing/android/sdk/platform-tools
$ ./adb install ~/Documents/Processing/vines_draw/buildBundle/vides_draw_release.aab
```

If we install the final drawing app bundle either manually or through the Play Store, we should see it in the app launcher with the icon we created for it (Figure 3-8).

Figure 3-8. *The vine drawing app installed on our device*

Summary

This final chapter in the first part of the book covered several additional important topics, ranging from debugging our code using Processing's console, the integrated debugger, or the logcat option in adb; scaling the output of our sketches according to the device's DPI; and finally exporting our sketch as signed bundle to upload to the Play Store. With these tools, we are ready to share our creations with all the Android users around the world!

PART II

Drawing and Interaction

■ ■ ■

CHAPTER 4

Drawing Graphics and Text

In this chapter, we will take a closer look at the Processing API for drawing graphics and text, with several code examples illustrating the different functions in the API. We will also learn how to use the P2D renderer and the PShape class for better 2D performance.

Drawing Shapes

Chapter 2 gave us an overview of some basic elements of the drawing API in Processing. We saw how we can draw predefined shapes using functions like ellipse() or rect(), while we can also draw arbitrary shapes vertex by vertex with the beginShape(), vertex(), and endShape() functions. We will now learn more about the shape drawing API to create different types of shapes, including shapes with curved edges.

More Types of Shapes

We saw in Chapter 2 that if we provide the (x, y) coordinates of a list of vertices between beginShape() and endShape(), then Processing will connect those vertices one after another to draw a polygon shape on the screen. While we can draw pretty much any polygon with as many faces as we want, sometimes, we need to create a predetermined type of shape, say, triangles or quadrilaterals. We can specify a type argument in beginShape(), and by doing so, the vertices will be connected differently to construct our desired shape. All the valid shape types are POINTS, LINES, TRIANGLES, TRIANGLE_STRIP, TRIANGLE_FAN, QUADS, QUAD_STRIP, and POLYGON, shown in Figure 4-1.

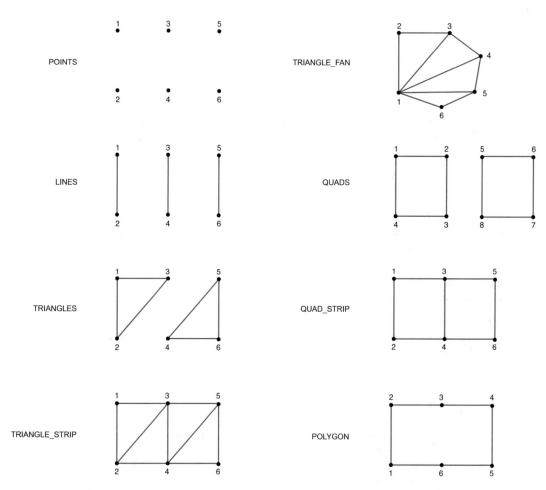

Figure 4-1. *All the shape types in Processing*

The number and order of the vertices are very important when we are drawing a shape with beginShape/endShape. Figure 4-1 illustrates how Processing uses each vertex in the shape, depending on the type. If we provide the vertices in a different order, for example, by switching vertices 2 and 3 in a shape of type QUADS, then the resulting shape will look distorted. Also, each type (except for points and polygon) requires a specific number of vertices to construct an individual shape, for instance, 3xN to draw N triangles, 4xN to draw N quads, etc. Although this may sound complicated at first, after some practice to familiarize with these rules, we would be able to create complex shapes of different types. Listing 4-1 gives an example of how the same vertices can lead to very different visual results when applying the various shape types, some of them quite interesting as we can see in Figure 4-2.

Listing 4-1. Drawing different shapes of different types using beginShape() and endShape()

```
int[] types = {POINTS, LINES, TRIANGLES,
               TRIANGLE_STRIP, TRIANGLE_FAN,
               QUADS, QUAD_STRIP, POLYGON};
int selected = 0;
```

```
void setup() {
  size(300, 300);
  strokeWeight(2);
}

void draw() {
  background(150);
  beginShape(types[selected]);
  for (int i = 0; i <= 10; i++) {
    float a = map(i, 0, 10, 0, TWO_PI);
    float x0 = width/2  + 100 * cos(a);
    float y0 = height/2 + 100 * sin(a);
    float x1 = width/2  + 130 * cos(a);
    float y1 = height/2 + 130 * sin(a);
    vertex(x0, y0);
    vertex(x1, y1);
  }
  endShape();
}

void mousePressed() {
  selected = (selected + 1) % types.length;
  println("Drawing shape", selected);
}
```

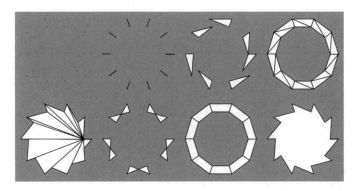

Figure 4-2. *Outputs for different shape types*

The code in Listing 4-1 also introduces a new function from the Processing API, called map(). This function does not draw anything on the screen, but rather it transforms or "maps" numbers from one range onto another, which is a very useful calculation. In this example, we use it for mapping the index variable i, which takes values between 0 and 10, into the variable a, which ranges from 0 to TWO_PI. This is because we want to get the angle around the circle that would correspond to each vertex so we can calculate their correct (x, y) coordinates using the trigonometric functions sine and cosine. We could have implemented the math of this mapping ourselves, but having the map() function doing it for us is very convenient, and we will use it many times throughout the book.

■ **Note** The POLYGON type is the default argument of beginShape(), so if we don't provide any explicit type, we will be creating a polygonal shape. Also, polygons can be open or closed, and this can be controlled with endShape(mode), with mode being either OPEN or CLOSE.

Curve Shapes

The vertex() function we have been using so far allows us to add vertices to a shape that Processing then builds up according to the type parameter we set in beginShape(type). Even though the examples we have seen so far resulted in polygonal shapes, we can use the same functions to create more organic-looking shapes with curved edges. It's just a matter of adding more vertices to get as close to a curve as we want! Let's look at Listing 4-2, where we use QUAD_STRIP as the shape type, and increase the number of angle subdivisions between 0 and TWO_PI. Doing this would result in shapes that are closer to a true circle, as we can see in Figure 4-3.

Listing 4-2. Creating a circular shape with quads by increasing vertex count

```
int numPoints = 100;
float outerRad = 250;
float innerRad = 220;

void setup() {
  size(600, 600);
  noStroke();
}

void draw() {
  translate(width/2, height/2);
  background(150);
  beginShape(QUAD_STRIP);
  for (int i = 0; i <= numPoints; i++) {
    float a = map(i, 0, numPoints, 0, TWO_PI);
    float x0 = outerRad * cos(a);
    float y0 = outerRad * sin(a);
    float x1 = innerRad * cos(a);
    float y1 = innerRad * sin(a);
    vertex(x0, y0);
    vertex(x1, y1);
  }
  endShape();
}
```

Figure 4-3. *Output of Listing 4-2, with vertCount equal to 5, 15, and 100 (from left to right)*

If we know how to calculate the positions of the vertices and draw enough of them, we could use beginShape/vertex/endShape as we have done so far to create virtually any kind of shape, whether polygonal or curved. To emphasize this, let's continue to iterate over the previous example, by adding an animation to the inner and outer radius of the ring. In Listing 4-3, we introduce a new variable that increases its value in each frame, a technique we used before in Chapter 2, and take advantage again of the periodic nature of the sine and cosine to set the values of the innerRadius and outerRadius variables. We should end up with the animation of an irregular ring that continuously expands and contracts. Figure 4-4 shows three frames from this animation.

Listing 4-3. Creating an animated shape with sine and cosine

```
int vertCount = 100;
float outerRad = 250;
float innerRad = 220;
float shift;

void setup() {
  size(600, 600);
  noStroke();
}

void draw() {
  translate(width/2, height/2);
  background(150);
  beginShape(QUAD_STRIP);
  for (int i = 0; i <= vertCount; i++) {
    float a = map(i, 0, vertCount, 0, TWO_PI);
    outerRad = 250 + 10 * cos(shift + 2 * a);
    innerRad = 220 + 5 * sin(shift + 4 * a);
    float x0 = outerRad * cos(a);
    float y0 = outerRad * sin(a);
    float x1 = innerRad * cos(a);
    float y1 = innerRad * sin(a);
    vertex(x0, y0);
    vertex(x1, y1);
  }
  endShape();
  shift += 0.1;
}
```

We use both the shift variable (which increases by 0.1 in each frame) and the angle around the circle to add a variable amount to the radius variables; this amount depends both on time (because of the shift variable) and the position around the circle (because of the angle) and changes periodically between a maximum and a minimum because of the use of sin() and cos(). If you are not familiar with the use of the trigonometric functions to create these kinds of animations, don't worry, practice makes perfect! Also, there are plenty of resources online to learn more about these techniques, including the Processing forum (`https://discourse.processing.org/`).

Figure 4-4. *Output of the animated shape example in Listing 4-3*

Using Bézier Curves

We just learned that by calculating vertex positions with the correct math formula and enough number of vertices, we could draw arbitrary shapes in Processing, including curved ones. A widely used type of mathematical curve, called the Bézier curve (after French engineer Pierre Bézier, who popularized their application for computer-aided car design in the 1960s), is very convenient to create complex curved shapes because it has "control points" that make it more intuitive to define their outlines. We could implement the formulas for the Bézier curves in the code ourselves if we wanted, but fortunately Processing offers functions that do that for us and can be quickly integrated into beginShape/endShape.

A Bézier curve passes through two vertices, and the tangent directions at those vertices are determined by two corresponding control points, as shown in Figure 4-5. We can set any of those vertices interactively, for example, using the mouse coordinates, which is demonstrated in Listing 4-4. A screen capture of its output is included in Figure 4-6.

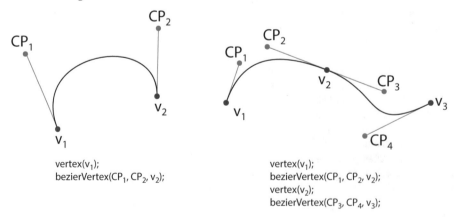

Figure 4-5. *A single Bézier curve passing through vertices v_1 and v_2 and with control points CP_1 and CP_2 (left) and two consecutive Bézier curves that join smoothly at vertex v_2 (right)*

Listing 4-4. Setting control point of a Bézier curve using the mouse coordinates

```
void setup() {
  size(500, 500);
}

void draw() {
  background(170);

  fill(250);
  stroke(50);
  strokeWeight(2);
  beginShape();
  vertex(50, 50);
  bezierVertex(50, 50, mouseX, mouseY, 450, 450);
  endShape(CLOSE);

  strokeWeight(2);
  stroke(50);
  line(450, 450, mouseX, mouseY);
  noStroke();
  fill(250, 100, 100);
  ellipse(mouseX, mouseY, 15, 15);
}
```

Figure 4-6. *Setting coordinates of Bézier control point with mouse*

We can have multiple Bézier curves in a single shape; in Listing 4-5, we took the code from the previous example and placed several vertex/bezierVertex calls, each one with a different pair of vertices and control points, which are set initially using the random function. As before, we can create an animation by having an angular variable that keeps increasing in each frame. In this way, we have movement both from the interaction (which moves the control point of all the curves) and the animation that rotates the shapes around the center of the screen. This example is also interesting because by moving the mouse, the shape appears to rotate in three dimensions, even though the rotation is entirely contained in the screen plane. Figure 4-7 shows one output frame from this sketch.

Listing 4-5. Rotating vertices of Bézier curves and simultaneously modifying their control points

```
float[] angle;
float[] radius;
float shift;
int num = 20;

void setup() {
  size(500, 500);
  angle = new float[num];
  radius = new float[num];
  for (int i = 0; i < num; i++) {
    angle[i] = random(0, TWO_PI);
    radius[i] = random(100, width/2);
  }
}

void draw() {
  background(255);

  float centerX = width/2;
  float centerY = height/2;

  fill(183, 7, 7, 50);
  stroke(183, 7, 7);
  strokeWeight(1);
  beginShape();
  for (int i = 0; i < num; i++) {
    vertex(centerX, centerY);
    float x = centerX + radius[i] * cos(angle[i] + shift);
    float y = centerY + radius[i] * sin(angle[i] + shift);
    bezierVertex(centerX, centerY, mouseX, mouseY, x, y);
  }
  endShape(CLOSE);

  shift += 0.01;
}
```

In this code, we use the arrays angle and radius to store the random values we get in setup() to later use in draw(). If we call random() in draw() instead, the coordinates of the curves will change randomly from one frame to the next, and as a result, the shape will jump around without retaining a coherent form.

Figure 4-7. *Output of Listing 4-5*

To finalize this section on Bézier curves, let's take on the challenge of drawing a continuous line with the mouse using Bézier curves. We can see in Figure 4-5 how to join smoothly two consecutive Bézier curves; they must share their last and first vertex, and the corresponding control points must lie on the same line that passes through the shared vertex. Our goal is to implement a very simple interaction mechanism for the user to enter the vertices and control points. One idea is to do it in two steps: in the first step, the user enters a new vertex at the end of the curve; in the next step, they enter the control point associated to that vertex.

To make our code more readable, we will use the PVector class in Processing, which allows us to store 2D and 3D positions and carry out basic vector algebra. A PVector object holds three values, x, y, z, and several methods to compute things like vector addition, subtraction, and length. The Processing online documentation includes a very clear tutorial on how to use the PVector class (`https://processing.org/tutorials/pvector/`).

Another new class that becomes handy in our Processing sketches is the ArrayList class (`https://docs.oracle.com/javase/8/docs/api/java/util/ArrayList.html`). This class is part of the Java core libraries comprising many programming utilities that we can use from Processing. ArrayList is very convenient in this example because it allows us to create a re-sizable array, in contrast with the built-in array type, which has a predefined fixed length. Because we are going to be drawing a continuous line using user input from the mouse, we do not know how many vertices will need to store in advance.

The finalized code of this example is in Listing 4-6, and we will spend some time looking at a couple of key details in this code.

Listing 4-6. Bézier curve drawing sketch

```
ArrayList<PVector> vertices;
ArrayList<PVector> cpoints;
Boolean addNewVertex;
PVector lastVertex;
PVector lastCPoint;

void setup() {
  size(500, 500);
```

```
    strokeWeight(2);
    vertices = new ArrayList();
    cpoints = new ArrayList();
    addNewVertex = true;
}

void draw() {
  background(255);

  noFill();
  stroke(0);
  beginShape();
  for (int i = 1; i < vertices.size(); i++) {
    PVector v0 = vertices.get(i - 1);
    PVector cp0 = cpoints.get(i - 1).copy();
    PVector v = vertices.get(i);
    PVector cp = cpoints.get(i);
    cp0.sub(v0);
    cp0.rotate(PI);
    cp0.add(v0);
    vertex(v0.x, v0.y);
    bezierVertex(cp0.x, cp0.y, cp.x, cp.y, v.x, v.y);
  }
  endShape();

  stroke(170);
  if (0 < vertices.size()) {
    line(lastVertex.x, lastVertex.y, mouseX, mouseY);
  }
  noStroke();
  if (addNewVertex) {
    fill(255, 0, 0);
  } else {
    fill(0, 0, 255);
  }
  ellipse(mouseX, mouseY, 10, 10);
}

void mouseReleased() {
  if (addNewVertex) {
    lastVertex = new PVector(mouseX, mouseY);
    lastCPoint = lastVertex.copy();
    vertices.add(lastVertex);
    cpoints.add(lastCPoint);
    if (1 < vertices.size()) {
      addNewVertex = false;
    }
  } else {
    addNewVertex = true;
  }
}
```

```
void mouseMoved() {
  if (!addNewVertex) {
    lastCPoint.x = mouseX;
    lastCPoint.y = mouseY;
  }
}
```

The input is handled with the functions mouseReleased() and mouseMoved(), which get called automatically whenever the user releases a button mouse (or ends tapping the touchscreen) and moves the mouse (or touch pointer). The boolean variable addNewVertex serves a very important role: it tells the sketch whether it should use the mouse coordinates to either create a new vertex or update the last control point. If addNewVertex is true when releasing the mouse, it means that the mouse coordinates should be used to create a new PVector object that stores the last position along the curve (lastVertex) but also is copied to create another PVector that represents the last control point. However, the control point has to be updated while the user moves the mouse pointer until the next mouse click, which is what happens in mouseMoved(). This may be hard to follow with words, but running the code should help us understand the logic.

The other key part of the code is the for loop between beginShape() and endShape(). This loop iterates over the contents of the vertices and cpoints ArrayLists, which store the vertices and control points collected so far, to draw the Bézier curves one after another. As we mentioned before, the control points of consecutive curves must lie on the same line passing through the shared vertex but pointing in opposite directions (see Figure 4-5); this is achieved in the code by taking a copy of the previous control point, cp0, and "mirroring" around the previous vertex, v0. We do this by subtracting v0 from cp0 (cp0.sub(v0)), rotating the resulting vector by 180 degrees (cp0.rotate(PI)), and adding v0 to the result. This new cp0 vector is the control point we need to smoothly join the curves. As the user draws with the sketch, it highlights whether it's placing a new vertex or a control point by drawing a red or blue circle at the mouse pointer's position. A sample drawing made with this sketch is available in Figure 4-8.

Figure 4-8. *Output of the Bézier curve drawing sketch*

Shape Attributes

Processing allows us to set several attributes that determine the final appearance of shapes. We have been using the fill and stroke colors attributes, but there are several more. For example, we can set not only the color of a stroke line but also its weight (how thick it is), endings caps, and joins connecting consecutive line segments, as demonstrated in Listing 4-7.

Listing 4-7. Setting stroke attributes

```
size(800, 480);
float x = width/2;
float y = height/2;
stroke(0, 150);
strokeWeight(10);
strokeJoin(ROUND);
strokeCap(ROUND);
beginShape(LINES);
for (int i = 0; i < 100; i++) {
  float px = x;
  float py = y;
  float nx = x + (random(0, 1) > 0.5? -1: +1) * 50;
  float ny = y + (random(0, 1) > 0.5? -1: +1) * 50;
  if (0 <= nx && nx < width && 0 <= ny && ny < height) {
    vertex(px, py);
    vertex(nx, ny);
    x = nx;
    y = ny;
  }
}
endShape();
```

Try this sketch with different values for the stroke joins (MITER, BEVEL, ROUND), caps (SQUARE, PROJECT, ROUND), and weight, and compare with the output shown in Figure 4-9.

Figure 4-9. *Output of sketch demonstrating stroke attributes*

Shape Styles

The current "style" in a Processing sketch is the collection of all the attributes that affect the appearance of our drawing. As we saw before, fill color and stroke color, weight, caps, and joins are all style attributes. As our sketches grow in complexity, especially when changing style attributes multiple times when drawing different objects, it can be easy to lose track of the current style.

Processing includes two functions, pushStyle() and popStyle(), that can be handy to manage the style of our shapes, especially when we need to change style attributes at many different places in our code. These functions work in a similar way to pushMatrix() and popMatrix(), which we saw in Chapter 2 when discussing geometry transformations. We can save the current values of all style attributes with pushStyle() and restore all previously saved values with popStyle(). So if we set a completely new style between consecutive pushStyle() and popStyle() calls, we can be certain that two different styles will not get mixed up. Listing 4-8 provides am example of this technique, with the output shown in Figure 4-10.

Listing 4-8. Saving and restoring styles with pushStyle() and popStyle()

```
Circle[] circles = new Circle[100];

void setup() {
  size(800, 800);
  for (int i = 0; i < circles.length; i++) {
    circles[i] = new Circle();
  }
}

void draw() {
  translate(width/2, height/2);
  for (int i = 0; i < circles.length; i++) {
    circles[i].display();
  }
}

class Circle {
  float centerX, centerY, radius, weight;
  color fillColor, strokeColor;
  float rotAngle, rotSpeed;
  Circle() {
    centerX = random(-width/2, width/2);
    centerY = random(-height/2, height/2);
    radius = random(10, 100);
    weight = random(2, 15);
    rotSpeed = random(0.005, 0.02);
    rotAngle = 0;
    fillColor = color(random(255), random(255), random(255));
    strokeColor = color(random(255), random(255), random(255));
  }
  void display() {
    pushMatrix();
      rotate(rotAngle);
```

```
    pushStyle();
      stroke(strokeColor);
      strokeWeight(weight);
      fill(fillColor);
      ellipse(centerX, centerY, radius, radius);
    popStyle();

  popMatrix();
  rotAngle += rotSpeed;
  }
}
```

Since this example draws many instances of the same entity, in this case, a circle with varying style attributes, we used another programming tool that is available in Java, and therefore in Processing, to organize the code more clearly: objects. We will not introduce object-oriented programming here; for those who are not familiar with the topic, the following Processing tutorial is a recommended resource: https://processing.org/tutorials/objects. Very briefly, we declare a class named Circle that contains both the data for each circle object (position, radius, color, etc.) and the function display() that draws each circle using its own data. As we can see in the implementation of the display() function, we call pushStyle() before setting the specific attributes of the circle and then popStyle() to restore the style. We also make use of pushMatrix() and popMatrix() to assign a different rotation angle to each circle, since they rotate at different speeds. We indented the code in display() at different levels depending on whether it falls inside the pushMatrix/popMatrix blocks, but this is only for clarity and is not required.

Figure 4-10. *Output of sketch demonstrating pushStyle() and popStyle()*

Drawing Images

We often need to load and display image files in our sketches, and Processing allows us to do this very easily. Processing supports the following image formats: GIF, JPG, TGA, and PNG, and offers a built-in class, PImage, to handle images inside a sketch. PImage contains all the information of an image, including width, height, and individual pixels. Loading and displaying an image can be accomplished with two functions, loadImage() and image(), as shown in Listing 4-9.

Listing 4-9. Loading and displaying an image

```
fullScreen();
PImage img = loadImage("paine.jpg");
image(img, 0, 0, width, height);
```

The image() function accepts up to four parameters: the x, y coordinates where the image will be placed on the screen and the width and height to display the image. These width and height parameters do not need to be the same as the original resolution of the image, which can be obtained from the PImage. width and PImage.height variables in the PImage object. Calling image() without width and height arguments results in the image drawn at its original resolution, which is equivalent to call image(img, 0, 0, img.width, img.height).

We can apply a tint to the entire image using the tint() function and remove it afterward with noTint() (otherwise, all images displayed subsequently will have the same tint, as tint is another style attribute). Listing 4-10 demonstrates the use of tint() and noTint(), with its output in Figure 4-11.

Listing 4-10. Tinting an image

```
PImage img;
void setup() {
  size(800, 533);
  img = loadImage("paine.jpg");
}

void draw() {
  image(img, 0, 0, width/2, height/2);
  tint(255, 0, 0);
  image(img, width/2, 0, width/2, height/2);
  tint(0, 255, 0);
  image(img, 0, height/2, width/2, height/2);
  tint(0, 0, 255);
  image(img, width/2, height/2, width/2, height/2);
  noTint();
}
```

■ **Note** We should always load images and any other media files such as videos inside the setup() function, because it is only called when the sketches start up. If we do it in draw(), the files will be loaded repeatedly in each frame, slowing down the sketch even to the point of making unusable.

Figure 4-11. *Output of displaying an image with three different tints and no tinting*

Drawing Text

Displaying text is another common task in graphics programming. Processing provides several functions we can use to draw text in our sketches and to control its appearance by using different fonts and adjusting its attributes such as size and alignment. We will overview some of these functions in the next few sections.

Loading and Creating Fonts

The first step to draw text in a Processing sketch is to load a bitmap font. The font will be stored in a PFont variable, and we can switch back and forth between different PFont variables in the same sketch to draw with different fonts at different times. The built-in font creator tool (available under "Tools ➤ Create Font...") allows us to generate a new bitmap font from the available fonts in the PC or Mac computer we are running Processing on. The interface of this tool is shown in Figure 4-12. Once we selected the font, desired size, and file name, we hit "OK" and the tool will generate a font file, with vlw extension, inside the data directory of our sketch and ready to use.

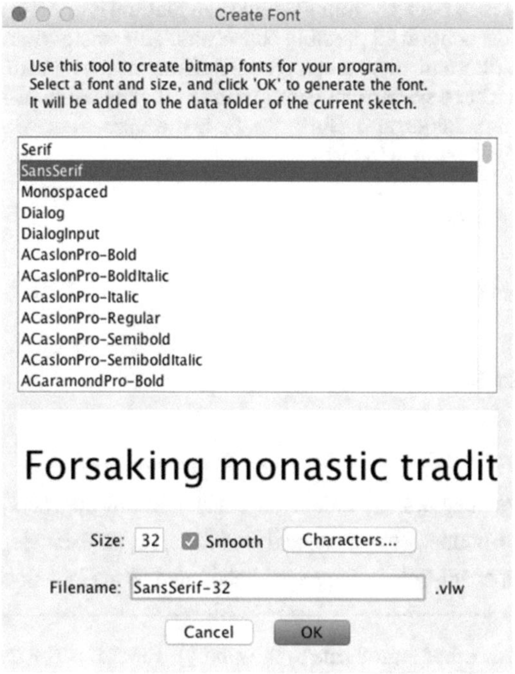

Figure 4-12. *The font creator tool in the PDE*

We have the loadFont() and textFont() functions to load our new font and to set it as the current, respectively. Once we have set the desired font, we can draw text anywhere on the screen using the text() function. All these functions are demonstrated in Listing 4-11.

Listing 4-11. Loading a bitmap font generated with the font creator tool

```
size(450, 100);
PFont font = loadFont("SansSerif-32.vlw");
textFont(font);
fill(120);
text("On Exactitude in Science", 40, 60);
```

The x and y arguments in the text(str, x, y) call let us set the screen location of the text. They represent, with the default text alignment options, the position of the lower left corner of the first character. Figure 4-13 shows the output of our text drawing sketch.

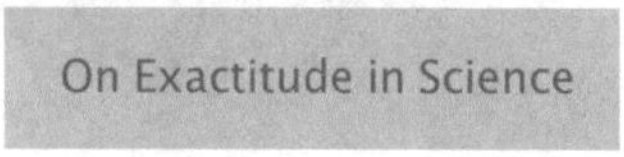

Figure 4-13. *Text output in Processing*

One disadvantage of creating a vlw font file and then loading it into the sketch is that, since the font is created beforehand, it must contain all possible characters. This wastes memory, especially if we end up using only a few of them. Alternatively, we can create the font on the fly with the createFont(name, size) function, which accepts either a system-wide font name or the file name of a TrueType (.ttf) or OpenType (.otf) font in the sketch's data folder, and a font size. Only the characters we use in the sketch will be created and stored in memory. This is shown in Listing 4-12.

Listing 4-12. Creating a font on the fly

```
size(450, 100);
PFont font = createFont("SansSerif", 32);
textFont(font);
fill(120);
text("On Exactitude in Science", 40, 60);
```

■ **Note** Android provides three system-wide fonts available to any app: serif, sans-serif, and monospaced. Each one has four variants: normal, bold, italic, and bold italic, so, for example, the font names for the sans-serif fonts are "SansSerif", "SansSerif-Bold", "SansSerif-Italic", and "SansSerif-BoldItalic".

If we don't provide any other arguments to the text() function, the text string will continuously extend to the right, until it falls out of the screen, or goes to the next line if the string includes a line break character ("\n"). We can set a rectangular area with four parameters, x, y, w, and h, and Processing will automatically accommodate the text within that rectangle by breaking it up in several lines if needed, as shown in Listing 4-13 and Figure 4-14.

Listing 4-13. Placing text inside a rectangular area

```
size(900, 300);
PFont font = createFont("Monospaced", 32);
textFont(font);
fill(120);
text("...In that Empire, the Art of Cartography attained such Perfection " +
     "that the map of a single Province occupied the entirety of a City, " +
     "and the map of the Empire, the entirety of a Province.", 20, 20,
     width - 40, height - 40);
```

Figure 4-14. *Text output in Processing fitted inside a rectangular area*

Text Attributes

In addition to the font name and its size, we can control text alignment (LEFT, RIGHT, CENTER, BOTTOM, TOP) and leading spacing between lines of text (Listing 4-14). Figure 4-15 shows the result of setting these attributes. Even though in this example we set the alignment only for the horizontal direction, we can also set the vertical alignment by providing a second argument to textAlign(), which can be CENTER, BOTTOM, or TOP.

Listing 4-14. Setting text alignment and leading

```
size(900, 300);
PFont titleFont = createFont("Serif", 32);
PFont textFont = createFont("Serif", 28);
textFont(titleFont);
textAlign(CENTER);
fill(120);
text("On Exactitude in Science", width/2, 60);
textFont(textFont);
textAlign(RIGHT);
textLeading(60);
text("...In that Empire, the Art of Cartography attained such Perfection " +
     "that the map of a single Province occupied the entirety of a City, " +
     "and the map of the Empire, the entirety of a Province.",
     20, 100, width - 40, height - 20);
```

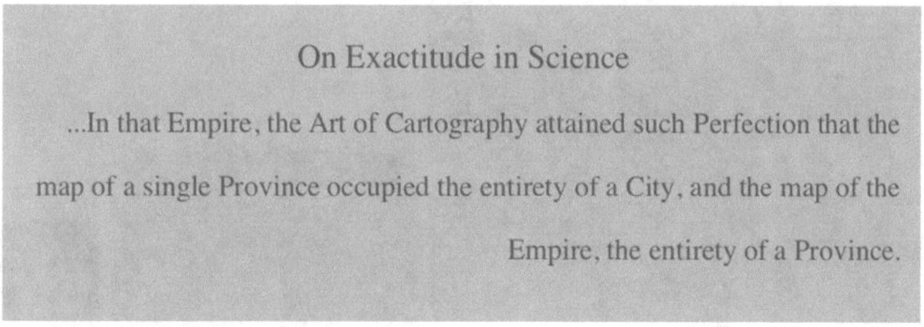

Figure 4-15. *Drawing text with different fonts and attributes*

Scaling Text

In Chapter 3, we saw how to scale the graphics in our sketch according to the device's DPI using the displayDensity variable. This technique allows us to maintain a consistent visual output across devices with different resolutions and screen sizes, and we can use it when drawing text as well. All we need to do is to multiply the font size by displayDensity, as shown in Listing 4-15. We see in Figure 4-16 that the size of the text on the screen remains the same on three devices with different DPIs. An additional function we introduced in this example is loadStrings(), which reads a text file in the data folder and returns an array of strings containing all the lines of text in the file.

Listing 4-15. Scaling font size by the display density

```
fullScreen();
orientation(PORTRAIT);
PFont titleFont = createFont("Serif-Bold", 25 * displayDensity);
PFont bodyFont = createFont("Serif", 18 * displayDensity);
PFont footFont = createFont("Serif-Italic", 15 * displayDensity);
String[] lines = loadStrings("borges.txt");
String title = lines[0];
String body = lines[1];
String footer = lines[2];
textFont(titleFont);
textAlign(CENTER, CENTER);
fill(120);
text(title, 10, 10, width - 20, height * 0.1 - 20);
textFont(bodyFont);
text(body, 10, height * 0.1, width - 20, height * 0.8);
textAlign(RIGHT, BOTTOM);
textFont(footFont);
text(footer, 10, height * 0.9 + 10, width - 20, height * 0.1 - 20);
```

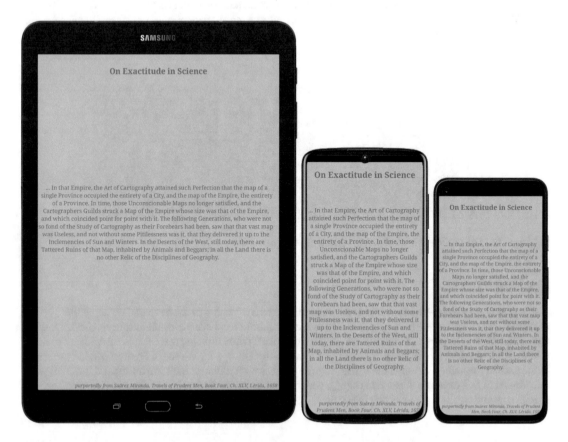

Figure 4-16. *From left to right, text output on a Samsung Galaxy Tab S3 (9.7", 20480×1536 px, 264 dpi), a Moto Z4 (6.4", 2340×1080 px, 403 dpi), and a Pixel 4a (5.81", 2340×1080 px, 433 dpi)*

Renderers in Processing

We have learned that the basic structure of interactive Processing sketches consists of a setup() function in charge of initialization and a draw() function that updates the screen in each frame. As part of the initialization, we need to indicate the size of the output area with the size() function, as shown in Listing 4-16. We also saw that the fullScreen() function allows us to use the entire area of the device's screen, irrespective of its resolution.

Both the size() or fullScreen() functions accept a "renderer" option. The renderer is the module in Processing that "transforms" the drawing commands in our sketch into a final image on the device's screen. The Processing renderer does this by communicating with the graphics hardware through an interface provided by the Android system (https://source.android.com/docs/core/graphics). There are different renderers in Processing, which rely on different interfaces to communicate with the hardware.

The default renderer (JAVA2D), enabled when no additional option is given to size() or fullScreen(), uses the Canvas interface in Android and offers high-quality 2D rendering, but performance can be limited, especially when drawing many shapes and other graphic elements. The other two renderers, P2D and P3D, use the Graphics Processing Unit (GPU) through the OpenGL interface, which gives higher performance, but at the expense of increased battery consumption. The P3D renderer also enables us to draw 3D shapes. These renderers can be selected by calling size() or fullScreen() with the appropriate parameter; for example, size(w, h) or size(w, h, JAVA2D) will result in the sketch using the default renderer, while size(w, h, P2D) or fullScreen(P2D) will enable the P2D renderer, as we do in Listing 4-16.

The output of this sketch, shown in Figure 4-17, is the same whether we use JAVA2D or P2D, but it should run much faster with P2D. Processing has a built-in variable called frameRate that tells us the current number of frames that our sketch is able to draw per second; in this example, we print the value of frameRate to the screen so we could compare performance with and without P2D. In the remaining sections of this chapter, we will see some other advantages of using P2D, in addition to the higher frame rate. We will cover the use of the P3D renderer to draw 3D graphics in Chapter 13.

Listing 4-16. Using full screen output with the P2D renderer

```
void setup() {
  fullScreen(P2D);
  orientation(LANDSCAPE);
  rectMode(CENTER);
  PFont font = createFont("Monospaced", 40);
  textFont(font);
}

void draw() {
  background(255);
  fill(150, 10);
  for (int i = 0; i < 100; i++) {
    float w = 2 * (width/2 - random(0, width));
    rect(width/2, height/2, w, w/width * height);
  }
  fill(255, 0, 0);
  text("Framerate " + frameRate, 10, 50);
}
```

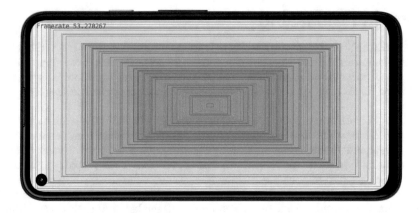

Figure 4-17. *Output of the full screen P2D sketch*

Another new function in this example is `orientation(LANDSCAPE)` in `setup()`, which locks the sketch to run in landscape orientation no matter the orientation of the device. We can also lock the orientation to portrait by calling `orientation(PORTRAIT)`.

The PShape Class

As we have seen so far, drawing shapes involves calling `beginShape()`, `vertex()`, and `endShape()` repeatedly in each frame. If our shapes are very complex, this could make our code run slowly and hard to understand. However, Processing offers a built-in class to hold shape data, called PShape. This class could not only help us to keep the code more organized and readable but also allows us to read shapes from vector graphics files (SVGs) and, when using the P2D renderer, to increase the performance of our sketch.

Creating PShapes

A PShape object can be created with a call to the `createShape()` function, passing the appropriate parameters to it in three different ways:

1. If no arguments are provided, `createShape()` returns an empty PShape, which we can use to construct a custom shape using `beginsShape()`, `vertex()` and `endShape()`.

2. Providing a primitive type (`ELLIPSE`, `RECT`, etc.) and the additional parameters needed to initialize the primitive shape.

3. Specifying a single `GROUP` argument, which results in a PShape that can be used to contain other shapes, either custom or primitive.

Once we have created and properly initialized the PShape object, we can draw it as many times as we want using the `shape()` function, as shown in Listing 4-17 and Figure 4-18.

Listing 4-17. Creating and drawing PShape objects

```
size(650, 200, P2D);
PShape circle = createShape(ELLIPSE, 100, 100, 100, 100);
PShape poly = createShape();
poly.beginShape(QUADS);
poly.vertex(200, 50);
poly.vertex(300, 50);
poly.vertex(300, 150);
poly.vertex(200, 150);
poly.endShape();
PShape group = createShape(GROUP);
group.addChild(circle);
group.addChild(poly);
shape(circle);
shape(poly);
translate(300, 0);
shape(group);
```

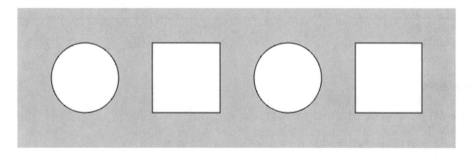

Figure 4-18. *Primitive, custom, and group PShape objects*

We can use all the shape drawing functionality we learned in the first sections of this chapter for custom shapes; the only difference is that we need to call the functions on the corresponding PShape object.

Group shapes are useful when we need to deal with a very large piece of geometry that does not change while the sketch is running. Without PShape, the vertices are sent to the GPU in each frame, which can slow down the frame rate. However, if we pack all these vertices inside a PShape, this transfer happens once (when we use P2D), which could result in much better performance. This is particularly important for mobile devices, which have performance constraints due to the use of battery power. As an example of this, we can compare the frame rate of the CubicGridImmediate (no PShape) and CubicGridRetained (PShape) under the Demos ➤ Performance examples that are bundled with the mode. Both sketches create the same geometry, a 3D grid of semitransparent cubes; however, the first sketch barely exceeds 10 frames per second (fps), while the second should run at 60 fps on most devices.

Even though the PShape geometry must be, in principle, static to enable these performance improvements, it is still possible to modify vertex color and position without losing the speed-up. For example, if our modifications are applied only to a subset of children shapes inside a larger group, then performance should remain high. Let's look at this scenario in Listing 4-18, which generates the output depicted in Figure 4-19.

Listing 4-18. Modifying attributes of child shapes after creation

```
PShape grid, sel;

void setup() {
  fullScreen(P2D);
  orientation(LANDSCAPE);
  grid = createShape(GROUP);
  for (int j = 0; j < 4; j++) {
    float y0 = map(j, 0, 4, 0, height);
    float y1 = map(j+1, 0, 4, 0, height);
    for (int i = 0; i < 8; i++) {
      float x0 = map(i, 0, 8, 0, width);
      float x1 = map(i+1, 0, 8, 0, width);
      PShape sh = createShape(RECT, x0, y0, x1 - x0, y1 - y0, 30);
      grid.addChild(sh);
    }
  }
}

void draw() {
  background(180);
  shape(grid);
}

void mousePressed() {
  int i = int(float(mouseX) / width * 8);
  int j = int(float(mouseY) / height * 4);
  int idx = j * 8 + i;
  sel = grid.getChild(idx);
  sel.setFill(color(#FA2D45));
}

void mouseReleased() {
  sel.setFill(color(#C252FF));
}
```

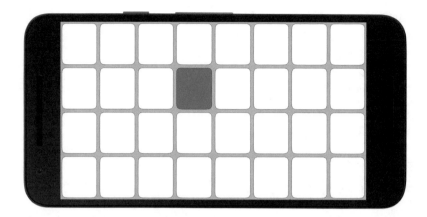

Figure 4-19. *Modifying the fill color of a child shape inside a group*

Here, only one child shape is modified at a time, setting a new fill color. This results in only the updated information being transferred to the GPU, keeping performance steady. However, this gain will diminish as more shapes are modified *simultaneously*, until performance becomes equivalent to drawing without any PShape objects.

■ **Note**   Most of the attributes of a PShape object can be modified after creating it. All the available setter functions can be found in the online reference at `https://processing.org/reference/PShape.html`.

Loading Shapes from SVG

We can also use a PShape object to load geometry stored in a file using the `loadShape()` function. This function accepts the formats SVG and OBJ, the latter being supported in the P3D renderer. SVG stands for Scalable Vector Graphics, and a file in SVG format contains the specification of a shape or group of shapes in a way that it is very close to how Processing handles geometry: either as a list of vertices, splines, or Bézier curves.

To load an SVG file in our sketch, we first need to place it inside the data directory of the sketch. When we run the sketch on the device or emulator, all the contents of the data folder will be properly packaged so they can be accessed from the app.

■ **Note**   The data directory can be created manually inside the sketch's folder. It is also created automatically if one drags a media file into the PDE.

Once the SVG is loaded into a PShape object, we can apply any transformations on it, like translations or rotations, or even change its style attributes, as we do in Listing 4-19, where we load three SVG files into separate shapes (output in Figure 4-20).

Listing 4-19. Loading SVG files into PShape objects

```
size(450, 200, P2D);
PShape cc = loadShape("cc.svg");
PShape moz = loadShape("mozilla.svg");
PShape ruby = loadShape("ruby.svg");
translate(30, 50);
cc.setFill(color(170, 116, 0));
cc.setStroke(color(255, 155, 0));
shape(cc);
translate(cc.width + 30, 0);
shape(moz);
translate(moz.width + 30, 0);
shape(ruby);
```

Figure 4-20. *Loading, modifying, and displaying SVGs*

SVG files can be useful to draw complex geometry, which would otherwise be hard to generate through code alone. Another advantage of complex SVGs is that they can be organized in a hierarchical fashion with children shape inside groups, allowing manipulation of the subshapes individually. Let's look at an example using a world map SVG that also contains names of countries in Listing 4-20. Running it should result in Figure 4-21.

Listing 4-20. Selecting a child shape by name and setting its attributes

```
PShape world;

void setup() {
  size(950, 620, P2D);
  orientation(LANDSCAPE);
  world = loadShape("World-map.svg");
  for (PShape child: world.getChildren()) {
    if (child.getName().equals("algeria")) child.setFill(color(255, 0, 0));
  }
}

void draw() {
  background(255);
  shape(world);
}
```

Figure 4-21. *Loading a map from an SVG file and selecting a country by its name attribute*

We iterate over all the children shapes, which can be retrieved as an array of PShape objects from the parent group using the getChildren() function.

Texturing Shapes

When we run our sketch with the P2D or P3D renderer, we can also use image files to texture shapes. Texturing essentially means "wrapping" an image around the shape so it is no longer drawn with a flat color. But this process requires specifying which parts of the image correspond to each vertex of the shape. Applying a texture on a shape can be difficult, especially if we are drawing irregular shapes in 3D. Listing 4-21 illustrates the simplest case, texturing a rectangular shape.

Listing 4-21. Texturing a rectangle with an image loaded from file

```
PImage img;
size(800, 533, P2D);
img = loadImage("paine.jpg");
beginShape();
texture(img);
vertex(100, 0, 0, 0);
vertex(width - 100, 0, img.width, 0);
vertex(width, height, img.width, img.height);
vertex(0, height, 0, img.height);
endShape();
```

As we see in this example, we need to provide two additional arguments to the vertex() function. These parameters in the vertex(x, y, u, v) call correspond to UV coordinates for the texture mapping, which indicate that pixel (u, v) in the image will go to the vertex (x, y) in the shape. The renderer will determine all the other pixel-vertex correspondences based on this information. In the case of our simple texturing code, the result is shown in Figure 4-22.

Figure 4-22. *Textured 2D shape*

We can also texture PShape objects by passing the image to the PShape.texture(image) function and then adding the additional (u, v) arguments to the PShape.vertex() function.

Summary

This was a long chapter, but we covered a lot of important concepts and techniques. Building up on the introduction to the Processing language in Chapter 2, we have now seen the details of drawing shapes using various types of geometry, including Bézier curves, adjusting their appearance with different attributes, and optimizing the code with the PShape class. In addition to all of that, we have also learned how to draw images and text in our sketches. By putting these resources into practice, we should be able to create virtually any visual composition we can think of and turn it into an Android app to run on phones, tablets, and even watches, as we will see in later chapters.

CHAPTER 5

Touchscreen Interaction

This chapter goes into the details of the touchscreen support in Processing for Android. We will learn how to capture single- and multi-touch events in our sketch; how to process these events to implement touch-based interactions such as selection, scrolling, swipe, and pinch; as well as how to use the virtual keyboard.

Touch Events in Android

With this chapter, we finally reached a topic that is very specific to mobile devices. Since the introduction of the iPhone in 2007, the touchscreen quickly became the main mechanism of interaction with smartphones, tablets, and wearable devices. Older phones often included a physical keyboard, but today, keyboard input is implemented through "virtual" or "software" keyboards with almost no exception.

Touchscreen interaction is characterized for being very immediate and intuitive, and useful in applications that involve gesturing as central part of the experience (e.g., note-taking and drawing apps.) The physicality of touch makes it the ideal interaction for creative applications of mobile devices.

The Android system provides full support for touchscreen interaction, ranging from single-touch events to multi-touch gestures triggered by our fingers, to pen stylus input (https://developer.android.com/develop/ui/views/touch-and-input/input). Because it is very general and flexible, the touch API in Android could be hard to use, Processing for Android wraps this complexity with a simpler API that. While it may not cover all touchscreen functions, Processing's touch API still makes possible to create a wide range of touch-based interactions.

Basic Touch Events

Since its earliest versions, the Java mode in Processing has included variables and functions to handle interaction with the mouse. All these variables and functions are available in the Android mode, and they work very similarly to their original Java mode counterparts, at least for single-touch events. The main difference is that the events are triggered by our fingers pressing the touchscreen, instead of by the movement of a mouse. We have used some of this mouse API in previous chapters, in particular, the mouseX and mouseY variables that allowed us to track the position of the touch point. Listing 5-1 shows a basic example of this API, where we control the position of some shapes (Figure 5-1).

Listing 5-1. Simple touch event handling using the mouse variables

```
void setup() {
  fullScreen();
  strokeWeight(20);
  fill(#3B91FF);
}
```

```
void draw() {
  background(#FFD53B);
  stroke(#3B91FF);
  line(0, 0, mouseX, mouseY);
  line(width, 0, mouseX, mouseY);
  line(width, height, mouseX, mouseY);
  line(0, height, mouseX, mouseY);
  noStroke();
  ellipse(mouseX, mouseY, 200, 200);
}
```

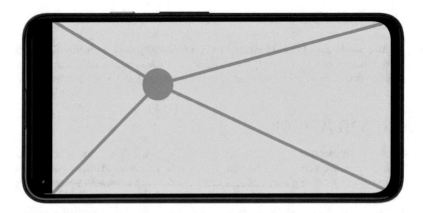

Figure 5-1. *Simple use of mouseX and mouseY variables to track touch position*

An important difference with a touchscreen is that an actual mouse may be in the "pressed" state: we can move the mouse without pressing any button, and when we do, a "drag" event is triggered until we release the button. But with a touchscreen, the "mouse" is always in the pressed state while it is moving. This difference also invalidates a typical mouse-based interaction: the hovering, which occurs when we move the mouse inside a predefined area of the screen but without pressing any button.

We can perform specific tasks exactly when a touch starts/ends, or a touch point changes position. The functions mousePressed(), mouseDragged(), and mouseReleased() are called automatically by Processing whenever any of these events take place so we can implement our event handling functionality in them. For example, in Listing 5-2, we draw a growing ellipse at the mouse position, as long as we keep dragging the finger across the screen. Also, notice the use of displayDensity to scale the initial radius of the ellipse and its regular increments while dragging so that it appears with the same size irrespective of the device's DPI.

Listing 5-2. Detecting press, drag, and release "mouse" events

```
boolean drawing = false;
float radius;

void setup() {
  fullScreen();
  noStroke();
  fill(100, 100);
}
```

```
void draw() {
  background(255);
  if (drawing) {
    ellipse(mouseX, mouseY, radius, radius);
  }
}

void mousePressed() {
  drawing = true;
  radius = 70 * displayDensity;
}

void mouseReleased() {
  drawing = false;
}

void mouseDragged() {
  radius += 0.5 * displayDensity;
}
```

We can build on top of this simple example by keeping a list of all the ellipses we created so far and assigning random RGB colors to them. For this purpose, we create a class to store the ellipse's position, size, and color, as shown in Listing 5-3.

Listing 5-3. Drawing multiple growing ellipses with mouse events

```
ArrayList<Circle> circles;
Circle newCircle;

void setup() {
  fullScreen();
  circles = new ArrayList<Circle>();
  noStroke();
}

void draw() {
  background(255);
  for (Circle c: circles) {
    c.draw();
  }
  if (newCircle != null) newCircle.draw();
}

void mousePressed() {
  newCircle = new Circle(mouseX, mouseY);
}

void mouseReleased() {
  circles.add(newCircle);
  newCircle = null;
}
```

```
void mouseDragged() {
  newCircle.setPosition(mouseX, mouseY);
  newCircle.grow();
}

class Circle {
  color c;
  float x, y, r;
  Circle(float x, float y) {
    this.x = x;
    this.y = y;
    r = 70 * displayDensity;
    c = color(random(255), random(255), random(255), 100);
  }
  void grow() {
    r += 0.5 * displayDensity;
  }
  void setPosition(float x, float y) {
    this.x = x;
    this.y = y;
  }
  void draw() {
    fill(c);
    ellipse(x, y, r, r);
  }
}
```

In addition to the mouseX/Y variables, Processing also stores the previous position of the touch pointer in the pmouseX/Y variables. Using these variables, we can code a simple drawing sketch, where we connect the previous and current mouse positions with a line segment to draw a continuous path as long as the user keeps pressing the screen. We can determine if the user is pressing the screen or not with the built-in boolean variable mousePressed. This sketch is in Listing 5-4, and a drawing made with it is shown in Figure 5-2.

Listing 5-4. Simple drawing sketch using current and previous mouse positions

```
void setup() {
  fullScreen();
  strokeWeight(10);
  stroke(100, 100);
}

void draw() {
if (mousePressed) {
  line(pmouseX, pmouseY, mouseX, mouseY);
}
}
```

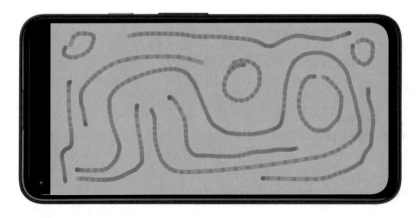

Figure 5-2. *Generating a line drawing with our sketch*

The difference between the previous and current touch positions tells us how fast we are swiping the finger across the screen. The faster we swipe, the larger this difference will be, so we could use it to drive the motion of some object, like the circles we had in Listing 5-3. For example, the "velocity" of the circles could be proportional to the swipe "speed." Let's implement this idea by adding a pair of velocity variables (vx for the x direction and vy for the y direction) and a setVelocity() method to the Circle class, as shown in Listing 5-5.

Listing 5-5. Calculating velocity of graphical elements using difference in touch positions

```
ArrayList<Circle> circles;
Circle newCircle;

void setup() {
  fullScreen();
  circles = new ArrayList<Circle>();
  noStroke();
}

void draw() {
  background(255);
  for (Circle c: circles) {
    c.draw();
  }
  if (newCircle != null) newCircle.draw();
}

void mousePressed() {
  newCircle = new Circle(mouseX, mouseY);
}

void mouseReleased() {
  newCircle.setVelocity(mouseX - pmouseX, mouseY - pmouseY);
  circles.add(newCircle);
  newCircle = null;
}
```

```
void mouseDragged() {
  newCircle.setPosition(mouseX, mouseY);
  newCircle.grow();
}

class Circle {
  color c;
  float x, y, r, vx, vy;
  Circle(float x, float y) {
    this.x = x;
    this.y = y;
    r = 70 * displayDensity;
    c = color(random(255), random(255), random(255), 100);
  }
  void grow() {
    r += 0.5 * displayDensity;
  }
  void setPosition(float x, float y) {
    this.x = x;
    this.y = y;
  }
  void setVelocity(float vx, float vy) {
    this.vx = vx;
    this.vy = vy;
  }
  void draw() {
    x += vx;
    y += vy;
    if (x < 0 || x > width) vx = -vx;
    if (y < 0 || y > height) vy = -vy;
    fill(c);
    ellipse(x, y, r, r);
  }
}
```

While in the original version of this sketch, the circles stop moving immediately after we release the touch, now they continue their displacement along the swipe direction, with a velocity proportional to the speed of our finger, since we keep adding vx and vy to their current positions. Also, with the if (x < 0 || x > width) vx = -vx; and if (y < 0 || y > height) vy = -vy; lines, we implemented a very simple "collision detection" algorithm, where if a circle moves past the edges of the screen, then its velocity gets inverted so that its movement reverses toward the interior of the screen. In other words, the circle bounces against the edges of the screen.

As a final addition to this example, we will implement a clear button. Now, we keep adding circles every time we touch the screen, so it eventually becomes cluttered. A "button" is just a rectangular area in the screen that triggers some action if we press on it, which in this case would be removing all the circles we have added since the beginning. In fact, we don't need much additional code to implement this button. Listing 5-6 shows what we need to incorporate in draw() and mouseReleased() to draw and trigger the button (Figure 5-3).

Listing 5-6. Implementation of a simple clear button

```
ArrayList<Circle> circles;
Circle newCircle;
float buttonHeight = 200 * displayDensity;
...
void draw() {
  background(255);
  for (Circle c: circles) {
    c.draw();
  }
  if (newCircle != null) newCircle.draw();
  fill(100, 180);
  rect(0, height - buttonHeight, width, buttonHeight);
  fill(80);
  text("Touch this area to clear", 0, height - buttonHeight, width, buttonHeight);
}
...
void mouseReleased() {
  newCircle.setVelocity(mouseX - pmouseX, mouseY - pmouseY);
  circles.add(newCircle);
  newCircle = null;
  if (height - buttonHeight < mouseY) circles.clear();
}
...
```

This example shows us how far we can go with single-touch events and how to use them to control movement and interaction in our app. We can extend these techniques to much more complex situations, with additional interface actions and object behaviors.

Figure 5-3. *Outcome of the circle drawing sketch, complete with a clear button*

Multi-touch Events

We have learned how to handle single-touch events using the mouse API inherited from Processing Java. However, touchscreens in Android devices can track several touch points at once, with a maximum determined by the capabilities of the screen. Some devices could track up to ten touch points simultaneously.

Processing includes the touches array to provide information about the touch points. Each element in this array contains a unique numerical identifier that allows us to track a pointer across successive frames and to retrieve its current X and Y coordinates, as well as the pressure and area of the pointer. The capacitive touchscreen in phones and tablets is not only capable of measuring the position of the touch point but also how much pressure we apply on the screen. The area is an approximate measure of the size of the pointer, which is related to the pressure, since the harder we press our finger against the screen, the larger the contact area.

Every time a new touch point is detected, Processing will trigger the startTouch() function. Conversely, endTouch() will be called when a touch point is released. Similarly with the mouseDragged() function for single-touch events, the touchMoved() function will be called every time any of the current touch points changes position. Also, analogous to mousePressed, there is a touchPressed logical variable that stores true or false depending on whether there is at least one touch point detected. All these functions are demonstrated in Listing 5-7, with its output showing multiple touch points in Figure 5-4.

■ **Note**   Pressure and area are given as normalized values between 0 and 1 and need to be scaled according to the screen resolution (pressure) and to the touchscreen calibration (area).

Listing 5-7. Accessing properties of multiple touch points

```
void setup() {
  fullScreen();
  noStroke();
  colorMode(HSB, 350, 100, 100);
textFont(createFont("SansSerif", displayDensity * 24));
}

void draw() {
  background(30, 0, 100);
  fill(30, 0, 20);
  text("Number of touch points: " + touches.length, 20, displayDensity * 50);
  for (int i = 0; i < touches.length; i++) {
    float s = displayDensity * map(touches[i].area, 0, 1, 30, 300);
    fill(30, map(touches[i].pressure, 0.6, 1.6, 0, 100), 70, 200);
    ellipse(touches[i].x, touches[i].y, s, s);
  }
}

void touchStarted() {
  println("Touch started");
}

void touchEnded() {
  println("Touch ended");
}

void touchMoved() {
  println("Touch moved");
}
```

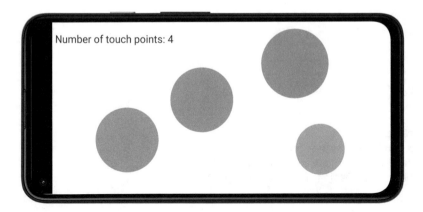

Figure 5-4. *Output of simple multi-touch example*

The mapping that converts the normalized area and pressure values is device specific. In this case, the size range goes from 0 to 0.1, which is the range observed in a Pixel 4a; however, other devices might have a different range. The situation is similar for the pressure, ranging from 0 to 0.5, on that same Pixel device.

Each touch point in the touches array has a unique ID that we can use to track its motion. The index of the touch point in the touches array should not be used as its identifier, since it may not be the same from one frame to the next (e.g., a touch point could be element 0 in one frame and element 3 in the next). The touch ID, on the other hand, is unique for each touch point since it is pressed until it is finally released.

We also introduced another way of specifying colors in Processing using the HSB (Hue, Saturation, and Brightness) mode. This mode is sometimes more convenient than the default RGB, because the first parameter is a value that ranges over all possible colors, while we can adjust the saturation and brightness independently with the two other parameters. The HSB mode can be set with the colorMode() function, which allows us to set the ranges for each component. In this example, we used the same hue for all the dots, but the saturation varies depending on the pressure. To learn more about color in Processing, read on the online tutorial: `https://processing.org/tutorials/color`.

In the next example, Listing 5-8, we will use the touch ID to create a multi-touch painting sketch. Each finger will control a brush that draws a circle with an HSB color determined by the index of the touch point. The idea is to store these brush objects in a hash map, which is a data structure also known as a dictionary (`https://developer.android.com/reference/java/util/HashMap.html`), which we can use to associate values (in this case, brushes) to unique keys (touch IDs).

In this code, we add a new brush to the hash table when a touch is detected in the touchStarted() function and remove an existing brush when its key (ID) is not found in the touches array when touchEnded() is called, and update all brushes every time a movement triggers the touchMoved() function. A typical output of this sketch is in Figure 5-5.

Listing 5-8. Painting with multiple brushes

```
import java.util.*;

HashMap<Integer, Brush> brushes;

void setup() {
  fullScreen();
  brushes = new HashMap<Integer, Brush>();
  noStroke();
```

```
  colorMode(HSB, 360, 100, 100);
  background(0, 0, 100);
}

void draw() {
  for (Brush b: brushes.values()) b.draw();
}

void touchStarted() {
  for (int i = 0; i < touches.length; i++) {
    if (!brushes.containsKey(touches[i].id)) {
      brushes.put(touches[i].id, new Brush(i));
    }
  }
}

void touchEnded() {
  Set<Integer> ids = new HashSet<Integer>(brushes.keySet());
  for (int id: ids) {
    boolean found = false;
    for (int i = 0; i < touches.length; i++) {
      if (touches[i].id == id) found = true;
    }
    if (!found) brushes.remove(id);
  }
}

void touchMoved() {
  for (int i = 0; i < touches.length; i++) {
    Brush b = brushes.get(touches[i].id);
    b.update(touches[i].x, touches[i].y, touches[i].area);
  }
}

class Brush {
  color c;
  float x, y, s;
  Brush(int index) {
    c = color(map(index, 0, 10, 0, 360), 60, 75, 100);
  }
  void update(float x, float y, float s) {
    this.x = x;
    this.y = y;
    this.s = map(s, 0, 1, 50, 500);
  }
  void draw() {
    fill(c);
    ellipse(x, y, s, s);
  }
}
```

Figure 5-5. *Multi-touch painting*

There are a couple of important things to pay attention to in this last code. First, we can be sure that `touchStarted()` and `touchEnded()` will be called only when a new touch point has gone down or up. So all we need to do in these functions is to identify which one is the incoming and outgoing pointer. In the case of a touch release, we iterate over all the current keys in the hash table until we find the one that does not correspond to a valid ID in the `touches` array. Since we are modifying the hash table as we iterate over its keys, we need to create a copy of the original set of keys with `Set<Integer> ids = new HashSet<Integer>(brushes.keySet());` and only then perform the search and delete operation.

Touch-Based Interaction

Creating an intuitive and engaging interface for a mobile app is not easy and requires understanding of user interface (UI) principles, practice, and a lot of testing and iteration. Processing for Android does not provide any built-in UI functionality beyond the low-level single- and multiple-touch handling functions, so we have a lot of freedom to define how our app will manage interaction with the user. We will review a few basic techniques in this section, which we could apply in many different situations.

Item Selection

Back in Chapter 4, we reviewed the use of PShape objects to store complex SVG shapes and increase frame rate with the P2D or P3D renderer. Since SVG shapes are composed of subshapes that we may want to select individually with a touch, it is useful to know how to perform a test to determine if a touch point falls inside a PShape object. If we are dealing with a primitive shape, such as a rectangle or a circle, we can write a simple test specific for that shape; however, with irregular shapes, such as countries in a map, we need a more general approach. The PShape class has a function called `getTessellation()`, which returns a new shape that is exactly the same as the source, but it is composed only of triangles (this collection of triangles determines what is called the "tessellation" of the more complex shape). Since it is easy to determine if a point falls inside a triangle (`http://blackpawn.com/texts/pointinpoly/default.html`), we can check if the mouse or touch position falls inside any of the triangles of the tessellation, and if so, we then conclude that the larger shape has been selected. This is what we do in Listing 5-9, with its result in Figure 5-6.

Listing 5-9. Selecting a child shape inside a group shape with touch events

```
PShape world, country;

void setup() {
  fullScreen(P2D);
  orientation(LANDSCAPE);
  world = loadShape("World-map.svg");
  world.scale(width / world.width);
}

void draw() {
  background(255);
  if (mousePressed) {
    if (country != null) country.setFill(color(0));
    for (PShape child: world.getChildren()) {
      if (child.getVertexCount() == 0) continue;
      PShape tess = child.getTessellation();
      boolean inside = false;
      for (int i = 0; i < tess.getVertexCount(); i += 3) {
        PVector v0 = tess.getVertex(i);
        PVector v1 = tess.getVertex(i + 1);
        PVector v2 = tess.getVertex(i + 2);
        if (insideTriangle(new PVector(mouseX, mouseY), v0, v1, v2)) {
          inside = true;
          country = child;
          break;
        }
      }
      if (inside) {
        country.setFill(color(255, 0, 0));
        break;
      }
    }
  }
  shape(world);
}

boolean insideTriangle(PVector pt, PVector v1, PVector v2, PVector v3) {
  boolean b1, b2, b3;
  b1 = sign(pt, v1, v2) < 0.0f;
  b2 = sign(pt, v2, v3) < 0.0f;
  b3 = sign(pt, v3, v1) < 0.0f;
  return ((b1 == b2) && (b2 == b3));
}

float sign (PVector p1, PVector p2, PVector p3) {
  return (p1.x - p3.x) * (p2.y - p3.y) - (p2.x - p3.x) * (p1.y - p3.y);
}
```

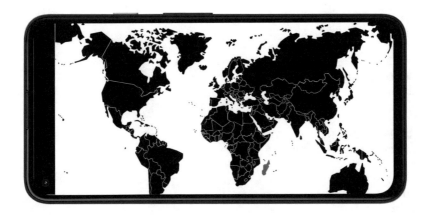

Figure 5-6. *Selecting a country inside an SVG shape with touch events*

Scrolling

Scrolling is another basic mode of interaction in mobile devices. Due to their small screen sizes relative to laptops and other computers, information often cannot be displayed all at once in one single page. A (horizontal or vertical) scroll bar controlled by the touch displacement across the edges of the screen is the most common scrolling functionality.

The next code example in Listing 5-10 includes a very simple vertical scrollbar class that keeps track of the displacement along the y axis to translate the graphical elements so the ones that should be visible are drawn on the screen. The key part of this scroll bar implementation is to calculate the total height of all the elements and use that to determine how much far down we can scroll with the bar until we reach the last element. The update() method in this class takes the amount of mouse/touch dragging and updates the variable translateY containing the vertical translation.

Listing 5-10. Implementing a scrolling bar

```
ScrollBar scrollbar;
int numItems = 20;

void setup() {
  fullScreen(P2D);
  orientation(PORTRAIT);
  scrollbar = new ScrollBar(0.2 * height * numItems, 0.1 * width);
  noStroke();
}

void draw() {
  background(255);
  pushMatrix();
  translate(0, scrollbar.translateY);
  for (int i = 0; i < numItems; i++) {
    fill(map(i, 0, numItems - 1, 220, 0));
    rect(20, i * 0.2 * height + 20, width - 40, 0.2 * height - 20);
  }
```

```
    popMatrix();
    scrollbar.draw();
}

public void mousePressed() {
    scrollbar.open();
}

public void mouseDragged() {
    scrollbar.update(mouseY - pmouseY);
}

void mouseReleased() {
    scrollbar.close();
}

class ScrollBar {
    float totalHeight;
    float translateY;
    float opacity;
    float barWidth;

    ScrollBar(float h, float w) {
        totalHeight = h;
        barWidth = w;
        translateY = 0;
        opacity = 0;
    }

    void open() {
        opacity = 150;
    }

    void close() {
        opacity = 0;
    }

    void update(float dy) {
        if (totalHeight + translateY + dy > height) {
            translateY += dy;
            if (translateY > 0) translateY = 0;
        }
    }

    void draw() {
        if (0 < opacity) {
            float frac = (height / totalHeight);
            float x = width - 1.5 * barWidth;
            float y = PApplet.map(translateY / totalHeight, -1, 0, height, 0);
            float w = barWidth;
            float h = frac * height;
```

```
      pushStyle();
      fill(150, opacity);
      rect(x, y, w, h, 0.2 * w);
      popStyle();
    }
  }
}
```

The condition `totalHeight + translateY + dy > height` makes sure that we don't scroll past the last element in our list, and `translateY > 0` avoids scrolling up after the top of the screen. We can use this class in any sketch as long as we can provide the total height of the elements we wish to display. Figure 5-7 shows our scrolling bar in action.

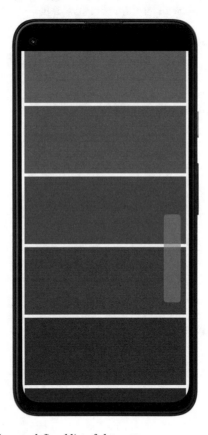

Figure 5-7. *Scrolling through a predefined list of elements*

Swipe and Pinch

The "swipe" and "pinch" gestures are two of the most used touchscreen interactions in smartphones and tablets. We typically use the swipe or fling to flip between consecutive elements, such as pages or images, and the pinch or scale is the default gesture to zoom in and out from an image or part of the screen.

Although Processing for Android does not trigger calls similar to mousePressed() or touchMoved() when a swipe or a pinch takes place, we can use the Android API inside our Processing sketch to add support for this event. The official Android Developers site from Google has a very detailed section on how to use touch gestures (https://developer.android.com/develop/ui/views/touch-and-input/gestures) via several gesture-detection classes.

Android offers a GestureDetector class that needs to be combined with a listener class. This listener contains a method that is called back when a swipe or scaling event is detected. We need to add a few imports from the Android SDK and then write the implementation for the gesture listener. The other important element when integrating event handling from Processing and Android is to pass the events objects from Processing to the gesture handler in the surfaceTouchEvent() function. This function is called every time there is a new touch event, but it also needs to call the parent implementation so Processing can carry out the default event handling (updating the mouse and touches variables, etc.) All of this is shown in Listing 5-11, where we do swipe detection, with its output in Figure 5-8.

Listing 5-11. Swipe detection using the Android API in Processing

```
import android.os.Looper;
import android.view.MotionEvent;
import android.view.GestureDetector;
import android.view.GestureDetector.OnGestureListener;

GestureDetector detector;
PVector swipe = new PVector();

void setup() {
  fullScreen();
  Looper.prepare();
  detector = new GestureDetector(surface.getActivity(),
                                 new SwipeListener());
  strokeWeight(20);
}

boolean surfaceTouchEvent(MotionEvent event) {
  detector.onTouchEvent(event);
  return super.surfaceTouchEvent(event);
}

void draw() {
  background(210);
  translate(width/2, height/2);
  drawArrow();
}

void drawArrow() {
  float x = swipe.x;
  float y = swipe.y;
  line(0, 0, x, y);
  swipe.rotate(QUARTER_PI/2);
  swipe.mult(0.85);
  line(x, y, swipe.x, swipe.y);
  swipe.rotate(-QUARTER_PI);
  line(x, y, swipe.x, swipe.y);
```

```
  swipe.rotate(QUARTER_PI/2);
  swipe.mult(1/0.85);
}

class SwipeListener extends GestureDetector.SimpleOnGestureListener {
  boolean onFling(MotionEvent event1, MotionEvent event2,
                  float velocityX, float velocityY) {
    swipe.set(velocityX, velocityY);
    swipe.normalize();
    swipe.mult(min(width/2, height/2));
    return true;
  }
}
```

Notice the call to Looper.prepare(), which we need to add to our sketch because Processing uses its own "thread" to drive the animation, and the gesture detected needs a looper from the app's main thread to recognize Processing's thread. We will take a closer look at threads in Chapter 9; at this moment, we do not need to worry about them beyond using the prepare() function.

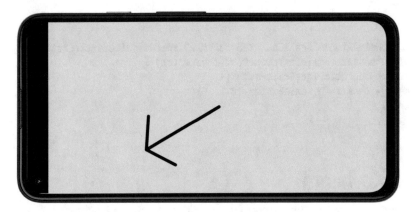

Figure 5-8. *Detecting swipe direction*

We can implement the scale detector in a similar way, and in Listing 5-12, we apply it to zoom in and out from an image.

Listing 5-12. Zooming in and out with a scale detector

```
import android.os.Looper;
import android.view.MotionEvent;
import android.view.ScaleGestureDetector;
import android.view.ScaleGestureDetector.SimpleOnScaleGestureListener;

ScaleGestureDetector detector;
PImage img;
float scaleFactor = 1;
```

```
void setup() {
  fullScreen();
  img = loadImage("jelly.jpg");
  Looper.prepare();
  detector = new ScaleGestureDetector(surface.getActivity(),
                                      new ScaleListener());
  imageMode(CENTER);
}

boolean surfaceTouchEvent(MotionEvent event) {
  detector.onTouchEvent(event);
  return super.surfaceTouchEvent(event);
}

void draw() {
  background(180);
  translate(width/2, height/2);
  scale(scaleFactor);
  image(img, 0, 0);
}

class ScaleListener extends ScaleGestureDetector.SimpleOnScaleGestureListener {
  public boolean onScale(ScaleGestureDetector detector) {
    scaleFactor *= detector.getScaleFactor();
    scaleFactor = constrain(scaleFactor, 0.1, 5);
    return true;
  }
}
```

Using the Keyboard

We conclude this chapter by describing some of the functions available in Processing for key input. Even though the keyboard and mouse are often distinct input devices on laptops and desktop computers, the touchscreen also functions as the keyboard by means of the "soft" or virtual keyboards.

Processing Java has several functions to handle keyboard events, as well as variables to inspect the last pressed key, as described in the online language reference (https://processing.org/reference/) and tutorials (https://processing.org/tutorials/interactivity/). All of these functions (with the exception of keyTyped) are available in the Android mode.

If the device has a physical keyboard, there is nothing special to do to use the keyboard API, but in the case of virtual keyboards, we need to open it first and close it once the user is done typing. The Android mode adds two functions to do this: openKeyboard() and closeKeyboard(). The final example in this chapter, Listing 5-13, exemplifies their use, together with some of the other functions.

Listing 5-13. Typing text with the virtual keyboard

```
String text = "touch the screen to type something";
boolean keyboard = false;

void setup() {
  fullScreen();
  textFont(createFont("Monospaced", 25 * displayDensity));
```

```
  textAlign(CENTER);
  fill(100);
}

void draw() {
  background(200);
  text(text, 0, 20, width, height - 40);
}

void keyReleased() {
  if (key == DELETE || key == BACKSPACE) {
    text = text.substring(text.length() - 1);
  } else {
    text += key;
  }
}

void mouseReleased() {
  if (!keyboard) {;
    text = "";
    openKeyboard();
    keyboard = true;
  } else {
    closeKeyboard();
    keyboard = false;
  }
}
```

Summary

We have learned how to handle single- and multiple-touch events in Processing, and from there, we moved on to examine different interaction techniques commonly used on mobile devices (selection, scroll, swipe, pinch, and zoom). With all these techniques at our fingertips, we can start implementing user interfaces that best fit the needs of our Processing for Android projects.

CHAPTER 6

■ ■ ■

Live Wallpapers

After exploring the details of drawing and interaction with Processing for Android, we will conclude the second part of the book with this chapter on live wallpapers. We will learn how to load images from the camera to create a gallery wallpaper and then how to use particle systems to implement an animated background for our phone or tablet.

Live Wallpapers

Live wallpapers are a special type of Android applications that run as the background of the home and lock screens. They were introduced back in version 2.1 of Android, so all of today's devices should support them. We can apply any of the drawing and interaction techniques we have seen so far in a live wallpaper. This enables us to create dynamic backgrounds for our devices while also accessing sensor and network data and reacting to user's input.

We can take any sketch from previous chapters and run it as a live wallpaper, but to design and implement a successful wallpaper, we should take into consideration their unique features and limitations, which we will discuss in the next sections.

Writing and Installing Live Wallpapers

Processing for Android lets us run our sketches as a live wallpaper very easily: all we need to do is to select the "Wallpaper" option under the "Android" menu in the PDE. Once the sketch is installed as a wallpaper, it won't start running immediately. It needs to be selected through Android's wallpaper selector. To do so, long-press on any free area in the home screen, choose the "Wallpaper & Style" option in the pop-up menu that appears next, select "Change wallpaper" after that, and finally look for the desired wallpaper under the "Live Wallpapers" category. The wallpaper will run first in a preview mode, where we can finally confirm the selection or continue browsing through the available wallpapers. Once selected, the wallpaper will be restarted to run in the background of the home screens, behind the launcher icons. These steps, shown in Figure 6-1 for a Pixel 4a phone running Android 13, may look different on other devices depending on the Android version or UI skin.

© Andrés Colubri 2023
A. Colubri, *Processing for Android*, https://doi.org/10.1007/978-1-4842-9585-4_6

Figure 6-1. *Selecting the wallpaper option in the PDE (left), opening the wallpaper selector on the device (center), and live wallpaper running in the home screen (right)*

Before going any further, let's look at a few important aspects of live wallpapers. First, they cover the entire area of the screen, so we should initialize them with the fullScreen() function. Second, live wallpapers run continuously in the background, and so, they can drain the battery faster. Because of this, it is a good idea that we don't use very heavy calculations in the sketches we are planning to run as wallpapers. This recommendation is valid for all mobile apps in general, but even more so for wallpapers. A simple "trick" to decrease the battery use of a live wallpaper is to set a lower frame rate with the frameRate() function. Using 30 or 25, instead of the default of 60, will keep the animation reasonably smooth without redrawing the screen at a very high rate and consuming more battery.

The code in Listing 6-1 generates a grid of ellipses of variable sizes, and we use both fullScreen() to ensure the wallpaper covers the entire screen and frameRate(25) since the screen does not need to be updated faster.

Listing 6-1. Simple live wallpaper

```
void setup() {
  fullScreen();
  frameRate(25);
  noStroke();
  fill(#FF03F3);
}

void draw() {
  background(#6268FF);
  float maxRad = 50 * displayDensity;
  for (int i = 0; i < width/maxRad; i++) {
    float x = map(i, 0, int(width/maxRad) - 1, 0, width);
    for (int j = 0; j < height/maxRad; j++) {
```

```
      float y = map(j, 0, int(height/maxRad) - 1, 0, height);
      float t = millis() / 1000.0;
      float r = maxRad * cos(t + 0.1 * PI * i * j);
      ellipse(x, y, r, r);
    }
  }
}
```

We just saw that we need to open a live wallpaper in the selector before placing it in the home or lock screen of our phone. In fact, the selector shows us a "preview" instance of the wallpaper, which we can set as the background, or cancel to preview another one. Right after we set the wallpaper, the preview instance is shut down by the system, replaced by a normal, non-preview instance. We can check if the wallpaper is running in preview mode by calling the previewWallpaper() function that returns true or false accordingly. This gives us the opportunity to perform special customizations for the preview mode, such as loading fewer resources since the wallpaper will not run for long or showing a representative output of the wallpaper.

■ **Note**   On recent versions of Android, live wallpapers are not listed in the app drawer that you open by swiping up the bottom edge of the home screen. So to uninstall a live wallpaper sketch, you need to open the Apps section in the system settings and there select "See all apps."

Using Multiple Home Screens

Before taking on more advanced wallpaper examples, we will learn a few important features of live wallpapers through a simpler application: showing a background image. We already saw how to load and display images in Processing. The same approach works for wallpapers: just copy an image file to the sketch's data folder (you can just drag and drop the image into the PDE; this will automatically copy it to the data folder), load it with loadImage(), and display it with image() so it covers the entire screen of the device, as shown in Listing 6-2.

Listing 6-2. Loading and displaying an image in full-screen mode

```
PImage pic;
fullScreen();
pic = loadImage("paine.jpg");
image(pic, 0, 0, width, height);
```

A problem with this code is that the image will look distorted if it does not have the same proportions as the screen. Also, the wallpaper is always displayed in portrait mode, so a picture taken in landscape orientation will be squeezed to fit the screen. We could set the height in the image() function so that the width-to-height ratio with which the image is displayed is the same as its original ratio, like in Listing 6-3.

Listing 6-3. Keeping the original ratio when drawing an image

```
PImage pic;
fullScreen();
pic = loadImage("paine.jpg");
imageMode(CENTER);
```

```
float r = float(pic.width) / float(pic.height);
float h = width / r;
image(pic, width / 2, height / 2, width, h);
```

Here, we set the image mode to CENTER, so the x and y arguments of the image() function are taken to be the center of the image, which makes it easier to place it exactly in the middle of the screen. Since we are drawing it with the width of the screen, we need to use a height of width / r, with r being the original width-to-height ratio of the image. Note that we used float(pic.width) / float(pic.height) to calculate the image ratio instead of just pic.width / pic.height. The reason for this is that the width and height variables in a PImage object are integer numbers, meaning that they don't have a fractional part. By default, Processing assumes that the division of two integer numbers will yield another integer number. While this assumption may be fine in many situations, in this case, it will give us incorrect results; for example, if we have an image with a size of 1200×800 pixels, even though 1200/800 is 1.5, the result as an integer number is 1. By telling Processing to handle the image's width and height as "floating-point" or "float" numbers with the addition of "float()" around the variable, we will get the correct result as a float number for the image's ratio.

However, with this approach, we could end up wasting a lot of the screen space, especially if the image is very wide. Android offers a functionality that can help in this situation: multiple home screens. The user can move through these screens by swiping left and right, and the wallpaper will know the current amount of horizontal displacement, in addition to the total number of screens available, to stretch the image across the home screens and adjust its position accordingly. Processing provides this information through two Android-specific functions: wallpaperHomeCount() and wallpaperOffset(). The first returns the current number of home screens (which could change during the lifetime of the wallpaper, as the user adds or removes home screens), while the second returns a float between 0 and 1 that corresponds to the horizontal displacement along the home screens: 0 when we are at the first screen and 1 at the last. Listing 6-4 shows how we can use these functions to create the image scroll interaction.

Listing 6-4. Image scrolling across home screens

```
PImage pic;
float ratio;

void setup() {
  fullScreen();
  pic = loadImage("paine.jpg");
  ratio = float(pic.width) / float(pic.height);
}

void draw() {
  background(0);
  float w = wallpaperHomeCount() * width;
  float h = w / ratio;
float x = map(wallpaperOffset(), 0, 1, 0, -(wallpaperHomeCount() - 1) * width);
float y = 0.5 * (height - h);
  image(pic, x, y, w, h);
}
```

To ensure that our image spans across all the home screens, we can use the width built-in variable, which stores the width of the home screen. By multiplying it with the value returned by wallpaperHomeCount(), we obtain the desired width for displaying our image. Then, we calculate the horizontal translation of the image to the left in the variable x as the user swipes to the right. In this way, the correct portion of the image is displayed in the current screen, in addition to moving smoothly from one screen to the next since wallpaperOffset() varies continuously between 0 and 1 (Figure 6-2).

Figure 6-2. *Visual explanation of the offset function in live wallpapers*

■ **Note**   We may notice choppy animation when swiping across screens, especially on devices with high-resolution screens. This is likely due to the default renderer not able to draw in full-screen mode at smooth frame rates. A solution is to switch to the P2D renderer, which uses the graphics processing unit (GPU) in the phone for higher frame rates, by using fullScreen(P2D).

Handling Permissions

We learned to load an image and display it as a wallpaper across multiple home screens. We can build upon this technique to create a photo gallery wallpaper that browses through the photos that have been taken with the camera in the phone or tablet. But to load these photos, our sketch needs to access the external storage of the device, and permission for reading the external storage must be explicitly granted by the user. We will see how to deal with permission requests in our Processing sketches, and although we will apply this in a wallpaper example, the functions we will see next can be used in any type of sketch.

Permissions are a very important aspect of Android development: mobile devices handle several different kinds of personal data (contacts, location, messages), and unauthorized access of such data could compromise the users' privacy. Therefore, Android makes sure that every app is granted permission from the user to access specific data and features in the device. Normal permissions (for instance, Wi-Fi and Bluetooth access) are granted once the user installs the app for the first time, while runtime (previously known as "dangerous") permissions (such as access to camera, location, microphone, storage, and body sensors) need to be granted (on devices with Android 6.0 or newer) when the user opens the app (https://developer.android.com/guide/topics/permissions/overview).

Any permissions required by our sketch, either normal or runtime, need to be added to the sketch from the PDE by using the Android Permissions Selector, which is available from the "Sketch Permissions" option under the "Android" menu (see Figure 6-3).

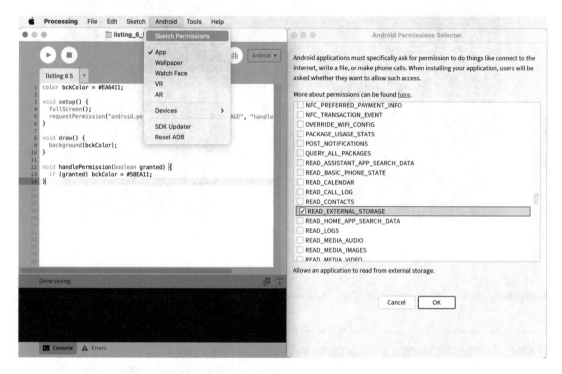

Figure 6-3. *The "Sketch Permissions" option (left) and the Android Permissions Selector dialog (right)*

For normal permissions, all we need to do is to select them with the Permission Selector. However, for runtime permissions, we also have to request them explicitly in the sketch code with the requestPermission() function. This function takes two arguments: the name of the permission to request (e.g., "android.permission.READ_EXTERNAL_STORAGE") and the name of a "callback" function in our sketch that will be called as soon as the user has granted (or denied) the permission. The callback function must have a boolean argument, where it will receive the result of the permission request. This mechanism is illustrated in Listing 6-5, where the background color turns green when the permission is granted. Notice that the callback function is not necessarily called from setup(), because the Android system will likely show the dialog to allow or deny the permission when the sketch is already in the draw() function. So it is very important that we deal with the situation of not having the permission yet when drawing elements that depend on it.

Listing 6-5. Requesting a runtime permission

```
color bckColor = #EA6411;

void setup() {
  fullScreen();
  requestPermission("android.permission.READ_EXTERNAL_STORAGE",
                                    "handlePermission");
}

void draw() {
  background(bckColor);
}

void handlePermission(boolean granted) {
  if (granted) bckColor = #58EA11;
}
```

■ **Note** A list of all permissions for each version of Android is available at `https://developer.android.com/reference/android/Manifest.permission.html`.

Returning to our image gallery wallpaper, besides requesting the permission to read the external storage, it also needs to list all the photos stored in the external storage. This functionality is not part of the Processing API, but we can access the Android SDK from our sketch and import the SDK packages that allow us to perform these more advanced tasks. In the case of listing files in the DCIM folder where pictures and videos taken with the camera are stored, we can use the `getExternalStoragePublicDirectory()` method in the `android.os.Environment` package (`https://developer.android.com/reference/android/os/Environment.html`). All we need to do to access this package is to import it at the beginning of our sketch.

Now we have all the pieces to put together our image gallery wallpaper, which is in Listing 6-6. We will now discuss the new code we have introduced in this example.

Listing 6-6. Photo gallery wallpaper

```
import android.os.Environment;

PImage defImage, currImage;
ArrayList<String> imageNames = new ArrayList<String>();
int lastChange;
int swapInterval = 10;

void setup() {
  fullScreen();
  defImage = loadImage("default.jpg");
  if (!wallpaperPreview()) {
    requestPermission("android.permission.READ_EXTERNAL_STORAGE", "scanForImages");
  }
  loadRandomImage();
}
```

```
void draw() {
  background(0);
  float ratio = float(currImage.width) / float(currImage.height);
  float w = wallpaperHomeCount() * width;
  float h = w / ratio;
  if (h < height) {
    h = height;
    w = ratio * h;
  }
  float x = map(wallpaperOffset(), 0, 1, 0, -(wallpaperHomeCount() - 1) * width);
  float y = 0.5 * (height - h);
  image(currImage, x, y, w, h);
  int t = millis();
  if (swapInterval * 1000 < t - lastChange) {
    loadRandomImage();
    lastChange = t;
  }
}

void loadRandomImage() {
  if (imageNames.size() == 0) {
    currImage = defImage;
  } else {
    int i = int(random(1) * imageNames.size());
    String fn = imageNames.get(i);
    currImage = loadImage(fn);
  }
}

void scanForImages(boolean grantedPermission) {
  if (grantedPermission) {
    File dcimDir = Environment.getExternalStoragePublicDirectory(
                   Environment.DIRECTORY_DCIM);
    String[] subDirs = dcimDir.list();
    if (subDirs == null) return;
    for (String d: subDirs) {
      if (d.charAt(0) == '.') continue;
      File fullPath = new File (dcimDir, d);
      File[] listFiles = fullPath.listFiles();
      for (File f: listFiles) {
        String filename = f.getAbsolutePath().toLowerCase();
        if (filename.endsWith(".jpg")) imageNames.add(filename);
      }
    }
  }
}
```

The logic of this code is the following: we have current and default PImage variables (currImage and defImage) and a list of image file names (imageNames). This list is initialized in the scanForImages() function when the READ_EXTERNAL_STORAGE permission is granted, by calling the method getExternalStoragePublicDirectory() from the Android API, which returns the folder in the external storage where Android saves the pictures from the camera. Then, the code iterates over all the subfolders in the external storage folder, queries the contents of each subfolder, and adds the image files to the list. Meanwhile, loadRandomImage() is called every ten seconds to pick a random file name from the list and load it as a new PImage in currImage. If imageNames is empty, either because the permission was not granted or no images were found, then the sketch uses a default image included with the sketch. Finally, we don't want to present the user with the permission dialog when previewing the wallpaper; that's why we only call requestPermission() if the sketch is not previewing; otherwise, it will show the default image.

■ **Note** We can use any method from the Android API in our sketches, such as getExternalStoragePublicDirectory(), which works with phones running older versions of Android. For newer APIs to retrieve media files, see Google's developer documentation: https://developer.android.com/training/data-storage/shared/media.

Drawing with Particle Systems

App developers often use live wallpapers to create animated graphics as an alternative to static background images. But these graphics should not be too overpowering because they could then distract the user from the relevant information presented on the device's screen (calls, messages, alerts from other apps). So our goal is to create a visually interesting wallpaper that does not take over the foreground. One idea could be to let a swarm of tiny brushes or "particles" move "organically" in the background, leaving soft traces behind that gradually build up to generate a drawing. We can find inspiration to realize this idea from impressionist painting to many code-based particle systems available on the Web (Figure 6-4).

Figure 6-4. From top to bottom: Starry Night by Vincent van Gogh (1889), Plate from "Processing Images and Video for an Impressionist Effect" by Peter Litwinowicz (1997), Particle Canvas by Dishun Chen (`https://openprocessing.org/sketch/1228217`)

The topic of particle systems has attracted much attention over the years, because they make it possible to simulate complex emergent behavior of large swarms of individual entities, with each one following a relatively simple movement or interaction rule. For the purpose of our wallpaper project, we don't need to dive into the depths of this fascinating topic, but for those who are interested to learn more, the book *The Nature of Code* by Daniel Shiffman (available online at `https://natureofcode.com/`) offers an excellent coverage of the topic (in particular, Chapters 4 and 6). The basic component of any particle system is, not surprisingly, the particle object. So we will start by creating a simple sketch that draws a bunch of circular particles on the screen. This is what we have in Listing 6-7.

Listing 6-7. Basic particle system with random positions and colors

```
Particle[] particles;

void setup() {
  fullScreen();
  particles = new Particle[50];
  for (int i = 0; i < particles.length; i++) {
    particles[i] = new Particle();
  }
```

```
    noStroke();
}

void draw() {
  background(255);
  for (int i = 0; i < particles.length; i++) {
    particles[i].display();
  }
}

class Particle {
  float x, y, r;
  color c;

  Particle() {
    x = random(0, width);
    y = random(0, height);
    r = 30 * displayDensity;
    c = color(random(0, 255), random(0, 255), random(0, 255));
  }

  void display() {
    fill(c);
    ellipse(x, y, r, r);
  }
}
```

In this example, we use the Particle class to encapsulate the attributes of each particle object, position, size, and color. With the help of this class, we only need to create an array of particle objects with as many elements as we want. The constructor of the class simply assigns random values to x, y, r, and c, which results in the output shown in Figure 6-5.

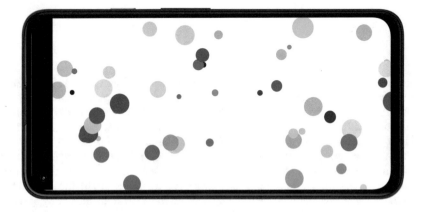

Figure 6-5. *Particles with random positions, sizes, and colors*

The next step would be to add motion to our particles. We do this by continuously modifying the values of x and y in each particle according to some simple rule. For example, we could add a constant displacement in each frame so that the particles move along a straight line. To make the output more varied, each particle could also follow a different direction that's selected randomly at the beginning. All of this can be done with some modifications to the Particle class shown in Listing 6-8.

Listing 6-8. Basic particle system with random positions and colors

```
class Particle {
  float x, y, r;
  float dx, dy;
  color c;

  Particle() {
    x = random(0, width);
    y = random(0, height);
    float a = random(0, TWO_PI);
    float s = random(-2, 2);
    dx = s * cos(a);
    dy = s * sin(a);
    r = random(10, 50) * displayDensity;
    c = color(random(0, 255), random(0, 255), random(0, 255));
  }

  void update() {
    x += dx;
    y += dy;
    if (x < 0 || width < x) x = random(0, width);
    if (y < 0 || height < y) y = random(0, height);
  }

  void display() {
    fill(c);
    ellipse(x, y, r, r);
  }
}
```

The constructor of the particle now picks a random angle between 0 and 2π and a speed between -2 and 2. With these two values, it calculates the direction of movement of the particle along the horizontal and vertical axes and stores it in the dx and dy variables. Then, in the update() method, the position variables x and y are incremented with dx and dy to move the particle to its next location on the screen. Also note that we have added two "if" conditions at the end of update() to make sure that the particle remains inside of the screen. If either coordinate goes outside of the screen range, it is placed back inside by choosing a new random value within (0, width) or (0, height). When running this code, we should see the colored random circles move in straight lines and randomly appear in new positions when they hit the edge of the screen. The particles do not leave a trace behind, since we call background(255) at the beginning of each frame. But if we move background() to the setup() function, then we will see the lines made by each particle across the screen, as shown in Figure 6-6.

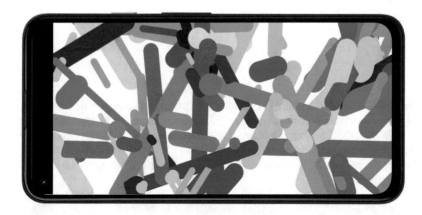

Figure 6-6. *Particles moving along randomly selected directions*

We could incorporate more variability if the particles randomly change their directions from time to time. This is easy to do; for example, we may put the code that picks the random direction of the particle into a separate method in the Particle class and call this method not only from the constructor to initialize the particle's movement but also at other random times while the sketch is running. This is done in Listing 6-9, where we only show the changes in the Particle class (the rest of the sketch is the same as in Listing 6-7).

Listing 6-9. Basic particle system with random positions and colors

```
class Particle {
  float x, y, r;
  float dx, dy;
  color c;

  Particle() {
    x = random(0, width);
    y = random(0, height);
    pickDirection();
    r = random(10, 50) * displayDensity;
    c = color(random(0, 255), random(0, 255), random(0, 255));
  }

  void update() {
    x += dx;
    y += dy;
    if (x < 0 || width < x) x = random(0, width);
    if (y < 0 || height < y) y = random(0, height);
    if (random(0, 1) < 0.03) pickDirection();
  }

  void pickDirection() {
    float a = random(0, TWO_PI);
    float s = random(-2, 2);
    dx = s * cos(a);
    dy = s * sin(a);
  }
}
```

115

```
void display() {
  fill(c);
  ellipse(x, y, r, r);
  }
}
```

You can see how we use the random() function again to trigger a change in direction: if a random draw between 0 and 1 is smaller than 0.03, then we call pickDirection() again. This means that particles change their direction only 3% of the time, but this is enough to introduce quite a bit of randomness in their motion, as shown in Figure 6-7. However, this randomness may seem a bit too jittery, not as smooth or "organic" as we were originally planning. In the next section, we will learn another technique to create random motion that changes more smoothly.

Figure 6-7. *Particles changing direction randomly*

Simulating Natural Motion

We have made extensive use of the random() function to generate random values for color and movement. While this is a simple approach to introduce randomness into our sketches, it may be "too random" for many applications, often resulting in changes that are jittery or sudden. An alternative to random()is the noise() function, which returns values from a smooth random landscape or "field" for a given position on that field. These values are still random, but they change smoothly as a function of the input position. More specifically, the noise() function in Processing uses the Perlin noise algorithm, developed by Ken Perlin in 1983 to make more natural-looking textures in computer graphics. Here, we will not get into the details of the Perlin noise; there are many online resources about it, including Daniel Shiffman's video on Perlin noise from his Coding Train channel on YouTube (https://youtu.be/8ZEMLCnn8vO).

For the purpose of our project, all we need to know at this time is that the Processing's noise() function can take one, two, or three input arguments to generate 1D, 2D, or 3D Perlin noise. These arguments represent the position in the random field the noise values come from. Figure 6-8 can help visualize the noise in two dimensions as a field of continuously changing random values represented by a grayscale and a particular selection from those values at a position (x, y). This brings up an important consideration when using Perlin noise: the scale of the position arguments. If the scale is too large compared with the variation in the noise field, we may end up with very large changes in the noise value. We can tweak this scale manually until we find a satisfactory level of smoothness. The next code example will demonstrate all these ideas.

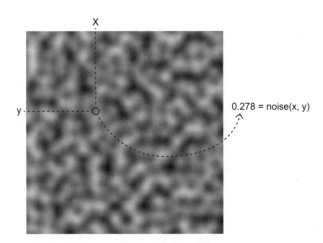

Figure 6-8. *Random values generated from 2D Perlin noise*

Using the code from the last listing as our starting point, we can replace random() with noise(). We will use the 3D noise, where the third argument represents time. We can visualize 3D Perlin noise as a sequence of 2D fields like the one shown in the previous figure, which change continuously from one to the next. The resulting code is in Listing 6-10.

Listing 6-10. Code that generates particles that move following the Perlin noise

```
Particle[] particles;
float noiseScale = 0.001;
float time = 0;
float timeStep = 0.01;

void setup() {
  fullScreen();
  particles = new Particle[50];
  for (int i = 0; i < particles.length; i++) {
    particles[i] = new Particle();
  }
  noStroke();
  background(255);
}

void draw() {
  for (int i = 0; i < particles.length; i++) {
    particles[i].update();
    particles[i].display();
  }
  time += timeStep;
}

class Particle {
  float x, y, r;
  float speed;
  color c;
```

```
Particle() {
  x = random(0, width);
  y = random(0, height);
  speed = random(-2, 2);
  r = random(5, 10) * displayDensity;
  c = color(random(0, 255), random(0, 255), random(0, 255));
}

void update() {
  float n = noise(noiseScale * x, noiseScale * y, time);
  float a = map(n, 0, 1, 0, TWO_PI);
  x += speed * cos(a);
  y += speed * sin(a);

  if (width < x) x = 0;
  if (x < 0) x = width - 1;
  if (height < y) y = 0;
  if (y < 0) y = height - 1;
}

void display() {
  fill(c);
  ellipse(x, y, r, r);
}
}
```

The changes are minor; the key difference is in the update() method, where we pick a noise value using the current position (x, y) of the particle and an additional "time" variable. This is a value between 0 and 1, so we map it to 0 and 2π to generate a random angle the particle will follow in the next frame of the animation. We also modified the way in which we handle particles moving outside of the screen; before we just placed them back inside at a random position; with the new conditions, we make them wrap around the screen so, for example, if they go out from the right side, then they come back in from the left. We can tweak the values of the noiseScale and timestep variables defined at the top of the sketch to increase or decrease the randomness. You can see a typical output of this sketch in Figure 6-9.

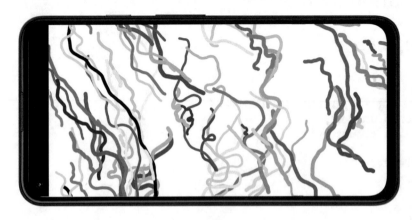

Figure 6-9. *Particle field generated with the noise function*

In all the particle system examples so far, we assigned a random color to each particle. This was sufficient while we were investigating the use of noise() to generate a more natural-looking flow of particles, but now it's time to think about how to use color in a way that's closer to our original idea of generating a drawing as the traces of the particles build up in the background. Earlier in this chapter we learned how to load pictures from the external storage of the phone, and these images could provide exactly what we need: a different pixel color at each position in the screen that the particle moving over that position could use as its fill color. By doing this, the particles would eventually reveal the underlying picture, but not in its original form, but as the result of their moving traces. Let's test this approach in Listing 6-11 using a single image included in the sketch's data folder.

Listing 6-11. Particles painting the screen with the colors of an underlying image

```
Particle[] particles;
float noiseScale = 0.001;
float time = 0;
float timeStep = 0.01;
PImage img;

void setup() {
  fullScreen();
  img = loadImage("paine_cropped.jpg");
  img.loadPixels();
...
background(0);
}
...
class Particle {
  ...
  void update() {
    ...
    getColor();
  }

  void getColor() {
    int i = int(map(x, 0, width, 0, img.width - 1));
    int j = int(map(y, 0, height, 0, img.height - 1));
    c = img.get(i, j);
  }

  void display() {
    fill(red(c), green(c), blue(c), 10);
    ellipse(x, y, r, r);
  }
}
```

In the new listing, we only show the code that's new from Listing 6-10: in setup(), we load a PImage object from the included image file and then load its pixels with img.loadPixels(). This step is needed so we can later access the color of each individual pixel in the image. We do this with the getColor() method in the Particle class. The pixels in an image object are accessed by their position (i, i), where i represents the pixel's column (horizontal direction between 0 and width-1) and j the pixel's row (vertical direction between 0 and height-1). We use the Processing's map() function to convert the particle's position into the corresponding pixel position and finally retrieve the color with PImage's get() function. Once we have this color in the class variable c, we use it in the display() method to set the fill color. But we don't use it as is; we extract its green, red, and blue components to then set its alpha to a very low opacity. This in combination with a black background should result in a more gradual build-up of the colors of the image. Figure 6-10 shows a few captures of this sketch running with different particle sizes. As you can see, we can get very different "styles" from our particle system by tweaking this and other parameters.

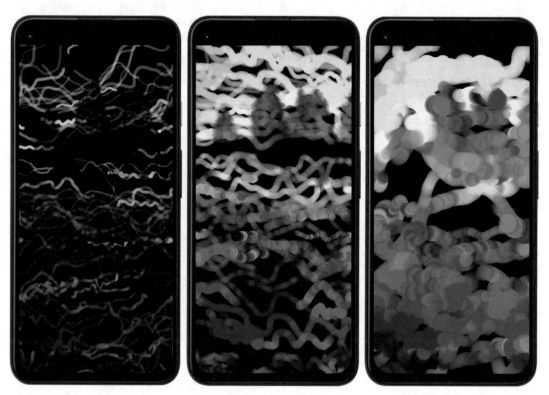

Figure 6-10. *Particle field colored by the pixels of an image using different particle sizes*

An Image-Flow Wallpaper

We now know how to simulate particles that move randomly but smoothly using the noise function and paint the particles with the pixels of an image. We could add a fixed list of images to our sketch and cycle through them to produce variable motion patterns. Even better, we could also apply the technique we learned with the photo gallery example to load pictures taken with the device's camera and use them as the source of our flow fields. This would add unique and endless variability to our wallpaper. However, there are still some important details to solve to implement this wallpaper, which we will consider in the following sections.

Loading, Resizing, and Cropping Images

One problem we can face is that the main camera of the phone typically takes pictures at very high resolutions. When we load these pictures into a PImage object and then load the pixels array with loadPixels(), we might run out of memory (wallpapers have fewer resources allocated to them to avoid affecting other apps in the foreground). But we don't need an image at full high resolution to color particles, since we can always map the positions to the pixel indices using the map() function, irrespective of the image resolution. We can in fact resize and crop images to the desired size before loading their pixels. In Listing 6-12, we demonstrate how to first resize the image to a desired height while keeping its original ratio and then crop the center portion of the resized image so that the cropped image has the same ratio as the phone's screen. In this way, we don't need to load any pixels that will not be visible.

Listing 6-12. Resizing and cropping images

```
PImage img;

void setup() {
  fullScreen();
  img = resizeAndCenterCrop("paine.jpg", 1080);
}

void draw() {
  image(img, 0, 0, width, height);
  image(img, 0, 0);
}

PImage resizeAndCenterCrop(String fn, int h) {
  PImage src = loadImage(fn);
  float imgRatio = float(src.width) / float(src.height);
  int w = int(imgRatio * h);
  src.resize(w, h);

  float screenRatio = float(width) / float(height);
  int wCrop = int(screenRatio * h);
  return src.get(w / 2 - wCrop / 2, 0, wCrop, h);
}
```

For the resizing portion, we apply the same ratio calculation we discussed before and then use the new width and height as the arguments for the resize() method in PImage. For the cropping, we first calculate the ratio of the screen and determine what's the width that corresponds to that ratio using the new height of the image after resize. The get() method in PImage returns the crop region of the image determined by the rectangle with top left corner (w / 2 - wCrop / 2, 0) and bottom right corner (w / 2 + wCrop / 2, h).

Putting Everything Together

After going in detail through the code to load images from the external storage (Listing 6-6), creating a particle system that gets its colors from an image (Listing 6-11), and resizing and cropping the images (Listing 6-12), we are ready to implement our image flow wallpaper in Listing 6-13.

Listing 6-13. Image flow wallpaper

```
import android.os.Environment;

PImage currImage;
ArrayList<String> imageNames = new ArrayList<String>();
String defImageName = "default.jpg";
```

```
int numParticles = 100;
Particle[] particles;
float noiseScale = 0.001;
float time = 0;
float timeStep = 0.01;

int lastChange;
int swapInterval = 30;

void setup() {
  fullScreen();
  if (!wallpaperPreview()) {
    requestPermission("android.permission.READ_EXTERNAL_STORAGE", "scanForImages");
  }
  loadRandomImage();
  particles = new Particle[numParticles];
  for (int i = 0; i < particles.length; i++) {
    particles[i] = new Particle();
  }
  noStroke();
  background(0);
}

void draw() {
  for (int i = 0; i < particles.length; i++) {
    particles[i].update();
    particles[i].display();
  }
  time += timeStep;
  int t = millis();
  if (swapInterval * 1000 < t - lastChange) {
    loadRandomImage();
    lastChange = t;
  }
}

void loadRandomImage() {
  if (imageNames.size() == 0) {
    currImage = resizeAndCenterCrop(defImageName, 800);
  } else {
    int i = int(random(1) * imageNames.size());
    String fn = imageNames.get(i);
    currImage = resizeAndCenterCrop(fn, 800);
  }
}

void scanForImages(boolean grantedPermission) {
  if (grantedPermission) {
    File dcimDir = Environment.getExternalStoragePublicDirectory(Environment.
    DIRECTORY_DCIM);
    String[] subDirs = dcimDir.list();
```

```
    if (subDirs == null) return;
    for (String d: subDirs) {
      if (d.charAt(0) == '.') continue;
      File fullPath = new File (dcimDir, d);
      File[] listFiles = fullPath.listFiles();
      for (File f: listFiles) {
        String filename = f.getAbsolutePath().toLowerCase();
        if (filename.endsWith(".jpg")) imageNames.add(filename);
      }
    }
  }
}

PImage resizeAndCenterCrop(String fn, int h) {
  PImage src = loadImage(fn);
  float imgRatio = float(src.width) / float(src.height);
  int w = int(imgRatio * h);
  src.resize(w, h);
  float screenRatio = float(width) / float(height);
  int wCrop = int(screenRatio * h);
  return src.get(w / 2 - wCrop / 2, 0, wCrop, h);
}

class Particle {
  float x, y, r;
  float speed;
  color c;

  Particle() {
    x = random(0, width);
    y = random(0, height);
    speed = random(-2, 2);
    r = random(5, 10) * displayDensity;
  }

  void update() {
    float n = noise(noiseScale * x, noiseScale * y, time);
    float a = map(n, 0, 1, 0, TWO_PI);
    x += speed * cos(a);
    y += speed * sin(a);

    if (width < x) x = 0;
    if (x < 0) x = width - 1;
    if (height < y) y = 0;
    if (y < 0) y = height - 1;

    getColor();
  }
```

```
void getColor() {
  int i = int(map(x, 0, width, 0, currImage.width - 1));
  int j = int(map(y, 0, height, 0, currImage.height - 1));
  c = currImage.get(i, j);
}

void display() {
  fill(red(c), green(c), blue(c), 10);
  ellipse(x, y, r, r);
  }
}
```

Our final sketch follows the general structure of the particle system from Listing 6-11, including the Particle class, and adds the image loading, resizing, and cropping from the other two examples. One minor tweak is that the default image is not loaded in setup with its original resolution, but it's also resized and cropped as all the pictures found in the external storage. In the end, we can see the sketch running as a background wallpaper in Figure 6-11.

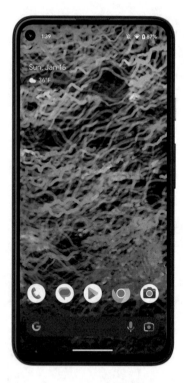

Figure 6-11. *Final version of the image flow wallpaper running in the background*

Wrapping the Project Up

As a final stage in this project, we should create icons for all the required resolutions (36×36, 48×48, 72×72, 96×96, 144×144, and 192×192 pixels), shown in Figure 6-12, and set a unique package name and version number for our wallpaper in the manifest file.

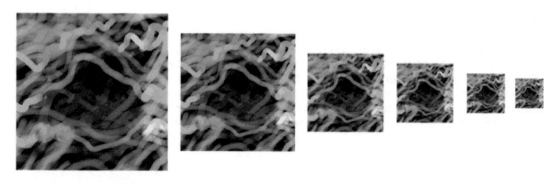

Figure 6-12. *Icon set for the image flow wallpaper*

The manifest file already has most of the required values already filled in if we ran the sketch at least once on the device or in the emulator. We should also set the android:label attribute both in the application and service tags so the wallpaper is identified with a more readable title in the wallpaper selector and app listing.

```
<?xml version="1.0" encoding="UTF-8"?>
<manifest xmlns:android="http://schemas.android.com/apk/res/android"
          android:versionCode="1"android:versionName="1.0"
          package="com.example">
    <uses-feature android:name="android.software.live_wallpaper"/>
    <application android:icon="@drawable/icon"
                 android:label="Image Flow">
        <service android:label="Image Flow"
                 android:name=".MainService"
                 android:permission="android.permission.BIND_WALLPAPER">
            <intent-filter>
                <action
                 android:name="android.service.wallpaper.WallpaperService"/>
            </intent-filter>
            <meta-data android:name="android.service.wallpaper"
                       android:resource="@xml/wallpaper"/>
        </service>
        <activity android:name="processing.android.PermissionRequestor"/>
    </application>
    <uses-permission android:name="android.permission.READ_EXTERNAL_STORAGE"/>
</manifest>
```

After editing the manifest, we are ready to export the sketch as a signed bundle for upload to the Google Play Store, as we learned in Chapter 3.

Summary

Live wallpapers give us a unique medium to create animated graphics that users can experience as backgrounds on their devices. We can take advantage of the drawing API in Processing to create original wallpapers, and as we learned in this chapter, it is also possible to use the Android API to carry out further Android-specific tasks that are not included in the Processing API, such as loading files from the external storage. This chapter also introduced the concept of normal and runtime permissions and how to request them from our sketches, which we will revisit again in the next chapters.

PART III

Sensors

CHAPTER 7

▪ ▪ ▪

Reading Sensor Data

Android devices are capable of capturing data from the physical world using many different sensors, including accelerometer, gyroscope, and GPS. In this chapter, we will learn how to access this data from our Processing sketch using the Android SDK and the Ketai library.

Sensors in Android Devices

Mobile devices, from smartphones to smartwatches and fitness trackers, are equipped with a wide range of hardware sensors to capture data from the movement, environment, and location of the device (and, by extension, of ourselves). Sensors we can find in Android devices are accelerometers, gyroscopes, and magnetometers, in addition to location sensors. These sensors give us access to a large amount of data we can use in our Processing sketches in multiple different ways, from controlling the behavior of graphical elements on the screen and creating user interfaces that are not limited to the touch gestures to inferring and visualizing our own patterns of motion.

Let's begin this chapter by going over the most typical sensors available on an Android phone, tablet, or watch (for more in-depth details, check Google's official developer on sensors at `https://developer.android.com/guide/topics/sensors/sensors_overview`).

Accelerometer

An accelerometer sensor measures acceleration (the rate of change of velocity) along the three directions in space, as shown in Figure 7-1. We would expect a phone lying flat on a table to have zero acceleration, but Android will always add a positive acceleration along the vertical direction due to the force of gravity. There are a couple of basic facts about acceleration: since it is the rate of change of velocity, an object moving at constant velocity has zero acceleration; the acceleration of an object is related to the forces acting upon the object according to Newton's second law of motion, force = mass x acceleration, with acceleration typically measured in meters/second^2. Acceleration data has many uses, for example, determining orientation in space (thanks to the presence of gravity's acceleration, which always points down) and detecting sudden motions such as shocks or vibrations as they cause short spikes in the acceleration of the device. To learn more about forces and motion, with many Processing examples, check out Chapter 2 from Daniel Shiffman's book *Nature of Code*: `https://natureofcode.com/book/chapter-2-forces/`.

A. Colubri, *Processing for Android*, https://doi.org/10.1007/978-1-4842-9585-4_7

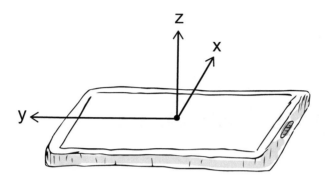

Figure 7-1. *Physical axes that Android uses to describe acceleration and other sensor data*

Gyroscope

The gyroscope measures the angular velocity of the device, which is the rate of rotation (in radians/second) around each of the same three axes as defined for the accelerometer sensor in Figure 7-1. Although it is similar to the accelerometer in that both can be used to determine position or orientation of the device, the main difference between them is that the gyroscope can sense rotation whereas the accelerometer cannot. Because of this, the gyroscope is very useful when we need to measure rotational movement, such as spinning, turning, etc.

Magnetometer

The magnetometer is a sensor that measures the strength and direction of the geomagnetic field of the Earth with respect to the device, also using the coordinate system described in Figure 7-1. The measurements provide the raw components of the geomagnetic field along each axis in µT (microtesla). A typical application of this sensor, which we will examine in more detail in the next chapter, is to implement a compass to represent the angle of the device with the direction pointing toward the magnetic north pole of the Earth.

Location

The device's location does not come from a single sensor, but Android calculates it by combining data collected from different sources (Global Positioning System or GPS, cell-ID, and Wi-Fi) that allows to determine the device's geographical location (in latitude/longitude) at different levels of resolution (coarse or fine). GPS data is obtained from a network of satellites orbiting the Earth and has an accuracy of around 4.9 meters (16 feet) under open sky (`www.gps.gov/systems/gps/performance/accuracy/`). Location information derived from cellular tower or Wi-Fi access point IDs has much lower accuracy (between hundreds of feet and 1 mile) but uses very little energy as it works passively, in contrast to GPS' active location fixing.

Accessing Sensors from Processing

The Processing language does not have specialized functions to read sensor data, but there are two easy ways we can use to access this data from our code. The first is to rely on the Android SDK API, which we can call from Processing by importing all the relevant Android packages, as we did in Chapter 4 to read files from the external storage. The second is to use a contributed library called Ketai that extends the functionality of the Android mode. We will learn both ways of accessing sensor data, starting by using the Android SDK from our sketch.

Creating a Sensor Manager

The first step for us to use the Android sensor API is to obtain the "context" of the app containing the sketch. We can think of the context as a special object that contains useful information about our app. For instance, once we got a hold of the context, we can retrieve a sensor manager from it. This manager will allow us to initialize any sensor we need in our sketch.

Let's write a concrete example by accessing the accelerometer. In Listing 7-1, we put all the initialization of the sensor manager inside the setup() function, where we obtain the sensor object encapsulating the accelerometer.

Listing 7-1. Accessing the accelerometer

```
import android.content.Context;
import android.hardware.Sensor;
import android.hardware.SensorManager;

Context context;
SensorManager manager;
Sensor sensor;

void setup() {
  fullScreen();
  context = getContext();
  manager = (SensorManager)context.getSystemService(Context.SENSOR_SERVICE);
  sensor = manager.getDefaultSensor(Sensor.TYPE_ACCELEROMETER);
}

void draw() {
}
```

As we can see in this code, we need to import several packages from the Android SDK to get access to the Context, SensorManager, and Sensor classes.

Adding a Sensor Listener

In our next step (Listing 7-2), we add an object called the "listener" because it will continuosly listen to the sensor and will notify our sketch when new data is available. We have to derive a listener class specific to our sketch from the base SensorEventListener class in the Android SDK by implementing two methods: onSensorChanged() and onAccuracyChanged(), which will get called when new data is available and when the accuracy of the sensor changes, respectively. Once we have an instance of the listener class, we can register this instance with the manager so it's ready to produce data.

Listing 7-2. Creating a listener

```
import android.content.Context;
import android.hardware.Sensor;
import android.hardware.SensorManager;
import android.hardware.SensorEvent;
import android.hardware.SensorEventListener;
```

```
Context context;
SensorManager manager;
Sensor sensor;
AccelerometerListener listener;

void setup() {
  fullScreen();
  context = getActivity();
  manager = (SensorManager)context.getSystemService(Context.SENSOR_SERVICE);
  sensor = manager.getDefaultSensor(Sensor.TYPE_ACCELEROMETER);
  listener = new AccelerometerListener();
manager.registerListener(listener, sensor,
                         SensorManager.SENSOR_DELAY_NORMAL);
}

void draw() {
}

class AccelerometerListener implements SensorEventListener {
  public void onSensorChanged(SensorEvent event) {
  }
  public void onAccuracyChanged(Sensor sensor, int accuracy) {
  }
}
```

You may have noticed the SensorManager.SENSOR_DELAY_NORMAL argument in the listener registration. This argument sets the rate at which the sensor is updated with new data. Faster rates mean not only more responsiveness but also more battery consumption. The default SENSOR_DELAY_NORMAL sets a rate fast enough for screen orientation changes, while SENSOR_DELAY_GAME and SENSOR_DELAY_UI are suitable for use in games and user interfaces, respectively. Finally, SENSOR_DELAY_FASTEST allows us to get sensor data as fast as possible.

Reading Data from the Sensor

As we just saw, the event listener has two methods: onSensorChanged() and onAccuracyChanged(). We only need to use onSensorChanged() to get the data from the sensor. In the case of the accelerometer, the data consists of three float numbers, representing the acceleration along the X, Y, and Z directions.

In Listing 7-3, we simply print these values to the screen. We can verify that if we place the phone flat on the table with the screen facing up, then we see a Z acceleration of 9.81 m/s^2, corresponding to the acceleration of gravity.

Listing 7-3. Reading the accelerometer

```
import android.content.Context;
import android.hardware.Sensor;
import android.hardware.SensorManager;
import android.hardware.SensorEvent;
import android.hardware.SensorEventListener;

Context context;
SensorManager manager;
```

```
Sensor sensor;
AccelerometerListener listener;
float ax, ay, az;

void setup() {
  fullScreen();
  context = getContext();
  manager = (SensorManager)context.getSystemService(Context.SENSOR_SERVICE);
  sensor = manager.getDefaultSensor(Sensor.TYPE_ACCELEROMETER);
  listener = new AccelerometerListener();
  manager.registerListener(listener, sensor,
                           SensorManager.SENSOR_DELAY_NORMAL);

  textFont(createFont("SansSerif", displayDensity * 24));
  textAlign(CENTER, CENTER);
}

void draw() {
  background(157);
  text("X: " + ax + "\n" + "Y: " + ay + "\n" + "Z: " + az, width/2, height/2);
}

public void resume() {
  if (manager != null) {
    manager.registerListener(listener, sensor,
                             SensorManager.SENSOR_DELAY_NORMAL);
  }
}

public void pause() {
  if (manager != null) {
    manager.unregisterListener(listener);
  }
}
class AccelerometerListener implements SensorEventListener {
  public void onSensorChanged(SensorEvent event) {
    ax = event.values[0];
    ay = event.values[1];
    az = event.values[2];
  }
  public void onAccuracyChanged(Sensor sensor, int accuracy) {
  }
}
```

Additionally, we unregister the listener when the sketch is paused and re-register when it resumes. Figure 7-2 shows the output of our first sensor sketch, which is just a printout of the X, Y, and Z acceleration.

■ **Note** As a best practice for using sensors, we should unregister the associated listeners when the sketch's activity is paused to reduce battery usage and then register it again when the activity resumes.

Figure 7-2. *Output of the accelerometer sensor example*

Reading Data from Other Sensors

The structure we put together in the previous example can be reused with few changes for other types of sensors. For example, if we want to read the rotation angles around each axis using the gyroscope, all we need to do is to request a TYPE_GYROSCOPE sensor, which is demonstrated in Listing 7-4.

Listing 7-4. Reading the gyroscope

```
import android.content.Context;
import android.hardware.Sensor;
import android.hardware.SensorManager;
import android.hardware.SensorEvent;
import android.hardware.SensorEventListener;

Context context;
SensorManager manager;
Sensor sensor;
GyroscopeListener listener;
float rx, ry, rz;

void setup() {
  fullScreen();
  context = getContext();
  manager = (SensorManager)context.getSystemService(Context.SENSOR_SERVICE);
  sensor = manager.getDefaultSensor(Sensor.TYPE_GYROSCOPE);
  listener = new GyroscopeListener();
  manager.registerListener(listener, sensor,
                         SensorManager.SENSOR_DELAY_NORMAL);

  textFont(createFont("SansSerif", displayDensity * 24));
  textAlign(CENTER, CENTER);
}
```

```
void draw() {
  background(157);
  text("X: " + rx + "\n" + "Y: " + ry + "\n" + "Z: " + rz, width/2, height/2);
}

public void resume() {
  if (manager != null) {
    manager.registerListener(listener, sensor,
                             SensorManager.SENSOR_DELAY_NORMAL);
  }
}

public void pause() {
  if (manager != null) {
    manager.unregisterListener(listener);
  }
}

class GyroscopeListener implements SensorEventListener {
  public void onSensorChanged(SensorEvent event) {
    rx = event.values[0];
    ry = event.values[1];
    rz = event.values[2];
  }
  public void onAccuracyChanged(Sensor sensor, int accuracy) {
  }
}
```

The Ketai Library

In the previous sections, we learned to access sensor data by calling the Android SDK API directly from our sketch. The advantage of this approach is we can always access the Android SDK, but a downside is the additional code we need to create for sensor managers and listeners. Also, this extra code does not follow the conventions of the Processing API, so it may be difficult for new users to understand.

We had to use sensor API from the Android SDK since Processing for Android does not include one. However, we can add new functionality to Processing using contributed libraries. As we learned in Chapter 1, contributed libraries are modules that package extra functions and classes that are not part of the Processing core. We can "import" these libraries into our sketch to access their features and functionality. It turns out that there is a library precisely aimed at working with Android sensors in a simplified, Processing-like manner, called Ketai (http://ketai.org/), created by Daniel Sauter and Jesus Duran.

Installing Ketai

Contributed libraries, such as Ketai, can be easily installed in Processing using the "Contribution Manager" or CM. To open the CM, we can go to the Sketch menu and then select "Import Library ➤ Add Library…". We already used the CM to install the Android mode itself, but it is also the main interface to install libraries, tools, and examples as well.

135

After opening the CM, we select the "Libraries" tab, and there we can search for the library of our interest either by scrolling down the list or by searching the name. Once we find the entry for Ketai, all we need to do is to click on the Install button (Figure 7-3).

Figure 7-3. *Installing the Ketai library through the Contribution Manager*

Using Ketai

The Ketai library provides a simple interface to the sensors in our Android device, following the style of the core Processing API. We don't need to write much additional code in order to read sensor values. It's enough with importing the library, initializing a KetaiSensor object, and implementing an "event handler" function that Ketai will call automatically every time there is a new value available from the sensor, similar to how the built-in mousePressed() or touchMoved() function works.

A simple sketch reading the accelerometer and showing the values as text, like we did in Listing 7-3, is presented in Listing 7-5. Its output is in Figure 7-4.

Listing 7-5. Reading the accelerometer data with Ketai

```
import ketai.sensors.*;

KetaiSensor sensor;
float accelerometerX, accelerometerY, accelerometerZ;

void setup() {
  fullScreen();
  sensor = new KetaiSensor(this);
  sensor.start();
```

```
  textAlign(CENTER, CENTER);
  textSize(displayDensity * 36);
}

void draw() {
  background(78, 93, 75);
  text("Accelerometer: \n" +
    "x: " + nfp(accelerometerX, 1, 3) + "\n" +
    "y: " + nfp(accelerometerY, 1, 3) + "\n" +
    "z: " + nfp(accelerometerZ, 1, 3), 0, 0, width, height);
}

void onAccelerometerEvent(float x, float y, float z) {
  accelerometerX = x;
  accelerometerY = y;
  accelerometerZ = z;
}
```

Figure 7-4. *Output of the Ketai accelerometer example*

Data from other sensors is accessed in the same way; we only need to add a different event handler. For example, Listing 7-6 demonstrates how to read the values from the gyroscope using onGyroscopeEvent().

Listing 7-6. Reading the gyroscope with Ketai

```
import ketai.sensors.*;

KetaiSensor sensor;
float rotationX, rotationY, rotationZ;

void setup() {
 fullScreen();
  sensor = new KetaiSensor(this);
  sensor.start();
  textAlign(CENTER, CENTER);
  textSize(displayDensity * 24);
}
```

```
void draw() {
  background(78, 93, 75);
  text("Gyroscope: \n" +
    "x: " + nfp(rotationX, 1, 3) + "\n" +
    "y: " + nfp(rotationY, 1, 3) + "\n" +
    "z: " + nfp(rotationZ, 1, 3), 0, 0, width, height);
}

void onGyroscopeEvent(float x, float y, float z) {
  rotationX = x;
  rotationY = y;
  rotationZ = z;
}
```

Event Handlers in Ketai

Ketai lets us choose what sensor data to read by adding the corresponding event handler function. Some handlers supported by Ketai are shown in the following, and the complete list is available in the reference of the library (http://ketai.org/reference/sensors). The book *Rapid Android Development* by Daniel Sauter, available online at www.mobileprocessing.org, is another good resource to learn all the details about Ketai.

- void onSensorEventChanged(SensorEvent e): This handler returns a "raw" Android sensor event object, which contains all the relevant information describing the event, including type, values, etc. The SensorEvent class is fully documented in the official Android reference: https://developer.android.com/reference/android/hardware/SensorEvent.html.

- void onAccelerometerEvent(float x, float y, float z, long a, int b): We receive accelerometer data, with (x, y, z) being the acceleration along the three axes in m/s^2, a the timestamp of the event (in nanoseconds), and b the current accuracy level.

- void onAccelerometerEvent(float x, float y, float z): Same as before but does not give the timestamp or the accuracy.

- void onGyroscopeEvent(float x, float y, float z, long a, int b): Provides the (x, y, z) angular velocity in radians/second, the event timestamp a, and the accuracy level b.

- void onGyroscopeEvent(float x, float y, float z): Only angular velocity.

- void onPressureEvent(float p): Current ambient pressure p in hectopascals (hPa).

- void onTemperatureEvent(float t): Current temperature t in degrees Celsius.

We can use several sensors at once just by adding all the required event handlers. However, a device may not include a specific sensor. In order to handle such situation properly, we can check the availability of any supported sensors using the isXXXAvailable() function in KetaiSensor. Let's combine our previous examples into a single sketch that reads and displays accelerometer and gyroscope data, but only if the device has these sensors. All Android phones should come with an accelerometer, but cheaper entry-level devices may lack a gyro.

Listing 7-7 includes the sensor availability in the setup() function and displays the accelerometer and gyroscope values graphically (Figure 7-5) instead of using text as we did before. It is inspired by a more comprehensive sensor example by Tiago Martins, who also wrote several other sketches illustrating the use of sensors in Processing (https://github.com/tms-martins/processing-androidExamples).

Listing 7-7. Checking sensor availability with Ketai

```
import ketai.sensors.*;

KetaiSensor sensor;
boolean hasAccel = false;
boolean hasGyro = false;
PVector dataAccel = new PVector();
PVector dataGyro = new PVector();

void setup() {
  fullScreen();
  sensor = new KetaiSensor(this);
  sensor.start();

  if (sensor.isAccelerometerAvailable()) {
    hasAccel = true;
    println("Device has accelerometer");
  }
  if (sensor.isGyroscopeAvailable()) {
    hasGyro = true;
    println("Device has gyroscope");
  }

  noStroke();
}

void draw() {
  background(255);
  float h = height/6;
  float y = 0;
  translate(width/2, 0);
  if (hasAccel) {
    fill(#C63030);
    rect(0, y, map(dataAccel.x, -10, +10, -width/2, +width/2), h);
    y += h;
    rect(0, y, map(dataAccel.y, -10, +10, -width/2, +width/2), h);
    y += h;
    rect(0, y, map(dataAccel.z, -10, +10, -width/2, +width/2), h);
    y += h;
  }
  if (hasGyro) {
    fill(#30C652);
    rect(0, y, map(dataGyro.x, -10, +10, -width/2, +width/2), h);
    y += h;
    rect(0, y, map(dataGyro.y, -10, +10, -width/2, +width/2), h);
    y += h;
    rect(0, y, map(dataGyro.z, -10, +10, -width/2, +width/2), h);
  }
}
```

```
void onAccelerometerEvent(float x, float y, float z) {
  dataAccel.set(x, y, z);
}

void onGyroscopeEvent(float x, float y, float z) {
  dataGyro.set(x, y, z);
}
```

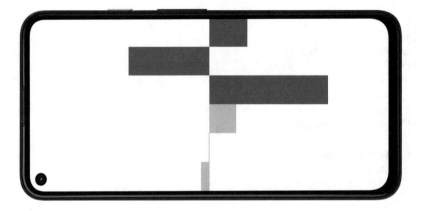

Figure 7-5. *Showing values from the accelerometer and the gyroscope*

Summary

This chapter gave us the basics to start using sensor data in our Processing sketches, either through the Android SDK or with the Ketai library. In the next chapters, we will build on top of these techniques to read sensor data, to create graphics and interactions that are driven by the movement or location of our device.

■ ■ ■

CHAPTER 8

Driving Graphics and Sound with Sensor Data

With the basics of reading sensor data already covered in the previous chapter, we will now learn how to use data from the accelerometer, magnetometer, and gyroscope to generate interactive graphics and sound in our Processing sketches.

Using Ketai to Read Sensor Data

The sensors available in an Android device give us plenty of data about the surroundings of the device. We saw how we can retrieve this data by using either the Android API or the Ketai library, with the latter making sensor handling easier. Once the data is available as numerical values inside our sketch, we can use it in any way we want to drive the animations and interactions in the code.

In this chapter, we will focus on three specific sensors that provide immediate feedback on the movement and position state of our device: the accelerometer (and the derived step counter), the magnetic field sensor, and the gyroscope. With the data from these sensors, our Android sketches will be able to react to a wide range of movements detected by the device: sudden shaking, walking, rotation in space, and orientation with respect to the Earth's magnetic field.

We will use Ketai to read the sensor data, since it simplifies the code by eliminating the need to define event listeners and sensor managers. However, all the examples in this chapter can be adapted to use the Android API without much difficulty.

Measuring Acceleration

Acceleration is the rate of change of velocity with respect to time, but the acceleration values returned by Android also include the acceleration due to gravity, which is directed toward the ground and has a magnitude of 9.8 m/s^2. If our phone is placed completely at rest on a table, with its screen facing up, its acceleration would read $a = (0, 0, 9.8)$, since it includes the gravity along the positive direction of the z axis (remember Figure 7-1). But if we rotate our phone around, the acceleration from gravity will be distributed along the three axes, depending on the orientation of the phone with respect to the vertical direction.

© Andrés Colubri 2023
A. Colubri, *Processing for Android*, https://doi.org/10.1007/978-1-4842-9585-4_8

Shake Detection

When we shake the phone, we cause its velocity to change quickly between zero and a high value in a very short time, which results in a sudden increase in the acceleration. We can detect this increase by calculating the magnitude of the acceleration vector and triggering a "shake event" if it is greater than some threshold. However, we also need to take into consideration that the gravity is already contributing to the device's acceleration, so this threshold should be at least larger than the gravity's magnitude, 9.8 m/s^2. We can do this by comparing the magnitude of the acceleration vector as obtained from Ketai with gravity's constant and deciding that a shake takes place if this magnitude is greater than the predefined threshold. This is what we do in Listing 8-1.

Listing 8-1. Simple shake detection code

```
import ketai.sensors.*;
import android.hardware.SensorManager;

KetaiSensor sensor;
PVector accel = new PVector();
int shakeTime;

color bColor = color(78, 93, 75);

void setup() {
  fullScreen();
  sensor = new KetaiSensor(this);
  sensor.start();
  textAlign(CENTER, CENTER);
  textSize(displayDensity * 36);
}

void draw() {
  background(bColor);
  text("Accelerometer: \n" +
    "x: " + nfp(accel.x, 1, 3) + "\n" +
    "y: " + nfp(accel.y, 1, 3) + "\n" +
    "z: " + nfp(accel.z, 1, 3), 0, 0, width, height);
}

void onAccelerometerEvent(float x, float y, float z) {
  accel.set(x, y, z);
  int now = millis();
  if (now - shakeTime > 250) {
    if (1.2 * SensorManager.GRAVITY_EARTH < accel.mag()) {
      bColor = color(216, 100, 46);
      shakeTime = now;
    } else {
      bColor = color(78, 93, 75);
    }
  }
}
```

The condition that detects a shake is 1.2 * SensorManager.GRAVITY_EARTH < accel.mag()). We use a factor of 1.2 to make sure the acceleration of the device is larger than gravity, and we can use a smaller or larger factor to detect weaker or stronger shakes. The SensorManager class from the Sensor API in Android becomes handy as it contains a constant, GRAVITY_EARTH, that represents the Earth's gravity acceleration (there are similar constants for all the planets in the Solar System, plus the moon, the Sun, and the fictional Death Star from *Star Wars*!). The time condition is in place so consecutive shake events cannot happen faster than 250 milliseconds apart.

Step Counter

With the case of the shake detection, we only had to recognize a single event characterized by the magnitude of the acceleration. In the case of detecting the steps when walking or running, the problem is harder: it is not enough to recognize a single change in acceleration when we make one step, but a regular pattern through time, as shown in Figure 8-1.

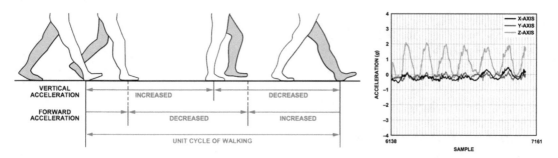

Figure 8-1. *Acceleration pattern during the walking stages (left) and acceleration data corresponding to a series of steps (right). Image adapted from "Full-Featured Pedometer Design Realized with 3-Axis Digital Accelerometer" by Neil Zhao*

However, this pattern does not follow a perfect curve, as it is affected by signal noise and irregularities in the walking pace. In addition to that, it is different from person to person, depending on their gait. While it is not impossible to figure out an algorithm capable of detecting steps from the raw accelerometer data, Android takes care of this problem by providing a "derived" sensor: the step counter. This sensor does the analysis of the accelerometer input for us. It triggers an event with each step, so we can count steps in any interval of time we wish. A very simple example of a step detection sketch in Processing is described in Listing 8-2. An important aspect to consider is that starting with Android 10, accessing the step counter requires the user to explicitly grant a runtime permission called ACTIVITY_RECOGNITION, and as we saw in Chapter 6, we need to use the requestPermission() function in the code of the sketch to do so and also to select the ACTIVITY_RECOGNITION in the Android Permissions Selector in the PDE.

Listing 8-2. Using Android's step counter

```
import ketai.sensors.*;

KetaiSensor sensor;
color bColor = color(78, 93, 75);
int stepTime = 0;
int stepCount = 0;
```

```
void setup() {
  fullScreen();
  orientation(PORTRAIT);
  textAlign(CENTER, CENTER);
  textSize(displayDensity * 24);
  requestPermission("android.permission.ACTIVITY_RECOGNITION", "handlePermission");
}

void draw() {
  if (millis() - stepTime > 500) {
    bColor = color(78, 93, 75);
  }
  background(bColor);
  text("Number of steps = " + stepCount, 0, 0, width, height);
}

void onStepDetectorEvent() {
  bColor = color(216, 100, 46);
  stepTime = millis();
  stepCount++;
}

void handlePermission(boolean granted) {
  if (granted) {
    sensor = new KetaiSensor(this);
    sensor.start();
  }
}
```

Note that we are initializing Ketai inside the function that handles the permission result, only if the permission has been granted by the user. If we create the KetaiSensor object in setup(), before the ACTIVITY_RECOGNITION permission has been granted, then the step counter will not work. Also note that Ketai has another function, onStepCounterEvent(float n), where we receive in the variable n the total number of steps since the device was rebooted. This can be useful if we need to track the total number of steps throughout the day without missing the activity while the app is not running.

Audio-visual Mapping of Step Data

We saw that counting individual steps using the step detector event in Ketai is very easy. How to use this step count data in our Processing sketch is a separate question that we can answer only after considering what our final goal is, for example, showing a practical visualization of physical activity, creating a more abstract representation of this activity, driving some background graphics (and/or audio) that we can use as a live wallpaper, etc.

It is up to us to determine how we would map the sensor data into visual or sound elements. To illustrate how to carry out this mapping, we will work on a sketch where each new step triggers a simple animation of a colored circle showing up on the screen and fading back into the background, so the result would be a geometric pattern that responds to our walking.

We could start writing some initial sketches in the Java mode, to refine the visual concept before moving on to the phone. One possible approach would be to work with a rectangular grid where we place the colored dots at random. It can be useful to define a class to hold the animation logic of the dots, as well as to use an array list to keep track of a variable number of dots while the sketch is running. All these ideas are implemented in Listing 8-3.

144

Listing 8-3. Random colored dots

```
float minSize = 50;
float maxSize = 100;
ArrayList<ColorDot> dots;

void setup() {
  size(800, 480);
  colorMode(HSB, 360, 100, 100, 100);
  noStroke();
  dots = new ArrayList<ColorDot>();
}

void draw() {
  background(0, 0, 0);

  if (random(1) < 0.1) {
    dots.add(new ColorDot());
  }

  for (int i = dots.size() - 1; i >= 0 ; i--) {
    ColorDot d = dots.get(i);
    d.update();
    d.display();
    if (d.colorAlpha < 1) {
      dots.remove(i);
    }
  }
}

class ColorDot {
  float posX, posY;
  float rad, maxRad;
  float colorHue, colorAlpha;

  ColorDot() {
    posX = int(random(1, width/maxSize)) * maxSize;
    posY = int(random(1, height/maxSize)) * maxSize;
    rad = 0.1;
    maxRad = random(minSize, maxSize);
    colorHue = random(0, 360);
    colorAlpha = 70;
  }

  void update() {
    if (rad < maxRad) {
      rad *= 1.5;
    } else {
      colorAlpha -= 0.3;
    }
  }
```

```
  void display() {
    fill(colorHue, 100, 100, colorAlpha);
    ellipse(posX, posY, rad, rad);
  }
}
```

Here, we used the HSB space to pick a random color along the entire spectrum while keeping the saturation and brightness fixed. The dots animate by quickly becoming larger (with the rad *= 1.5 update of the radius) and then fade out by decreasing the alpha with colorAlpha -= 0.3 until they became completely transparent, which is the moment when they are removed. New dots are added with a probability of 0.1 in each frame. After tweaking these values, we should get an output similar to Figure 8-2.

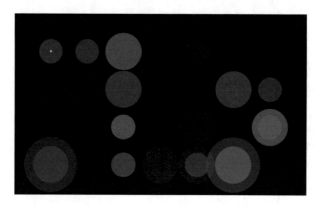

Figure 8-2. *Output of the initial sketch that generates random dots*

The next step is connecting the dot animation with the step detection. A simple way to achieve this could be to create a new dot every time a step detector event is triggered. So we would need to add the Ketai library to our previous code and then to create the dots in the onStepDetectorEvent() event, which is shown in Listing 8-4.

Listing 8-4. Using steps to animate the dots

```
import ketai.sensors.*;

KetaiSensor sensor;

float minSize = 150 * displayDensity;
float maxSize = 300 * displayDensity;
ArrayList<ColorDot> dots;

void setup() {
  fullScreen();
  orientation(LANDSCAPE);
  colorMode(HSB, 360, 100, 100, 100);
  noStroke();
  dots = new ArrayList<ColorDot>();
  requestPermission("android.permission.ACTIVITY_RECOGNITION", "handlePermission");
}
```

```
void draw() {
  background(0, 0, 0);
  for (int i = dots.size() - 1; i >= 0 ; i--) {
    ColorDot d = dots.get(i);
    d.update();
    d.display();
    if (d.colorAlpha < 1) {
      dots.remove(i);
    }
  }
}

class ColorDot {
  float posX, posY;
  float rad, maxRad;
  float colorHue, colorAlpha;

  ColorDot() {
    posX = int(random(1, width/maxSize)) * maxSize;
    posY = int(random(1, height/maxSize)) * maxSize;
    rad = 0.1;
    maxRad = random(minSize, maxSize);
    colorHue = random(0, 360);
    colorAlpha = 70;
  }

  void update() {
    if (rad < maxRad) {
      rad *= 1.5;
    } else {
      colorAlpha -= 0.1;
    }
  }

  void display() {
    fill(colorHue, 100, 100, colorAlpha);
    ellipse(posX, posY, rad, rad);
  }
}

void onStepDetectorEvent() {
  dots.add(new ColorDot());
}

void handlePermission(boolean granted) {
  if (granted) {
    sensor = new KetaiSensor(this);
    sensor.start();
  }
}
```

Notice how the minimum and the maximum size of the dots are now scaled by displayDensity, so the output of our sketch preserves its proportions irrespective of the DPI of the screen's device. We can run this sketch either as a regular app or as a live wallpaper in case we want to have it running the entire time and driving the background image in our home screen.

It is possible to refine this sketch in different ways. For example, we could decrease randomness in the size and color of the dots by linking these parameters to the time and the walking speed. To calculate the latter, we could reset the step count variable to zero at some fixed interval, say, every five seconds, and divide the count value by the time elapsed since the last reset (since speed = change in value / time difference). Listing 8-5 includes the additional variables we need to store the current walking speed, the time of the last update, and the step count, and the differences in the calculation of the dot radius and hue (the rest being identical to Listing 8-4).

Listing 8-5. Using time and walking speed to control animation

```
import ketai.sensors.*;

KetaiSensor sensor;

float minSize = 150 * displayDensity;
float maxSize = 300 * displayDensity;
ArrayList<ColorDot> dots;

int stepCount = 0;
int updateTime = 0;
float walkSpeed = 0;
...
class ColorDot {
  float posX, posY;
  float rad, maxRad;
  float colorHue, colorAlpha;

  ColorDot() {
    posX = int(random(1, width/maxSize)) * maxSize;
    posY = int(random(1, height/maxSize)) * maxSize;
    rad = 0.1;
    float speedf = constrain(walkSpeed, 0, 2)/2.0;
    maxRad = map(speedf, 1, 0, minSize, maxSize);
    colorHue = map(second(), 0, 60, 0, 360);
    colorAlpha = 70;
  }
  ...
}

void onStepDetectorEvent() {
  int now = millis();
  stepCount++;
  if (5000 < now - updateTime) {
    walkSpeed = stepCount/5.0;
    stepCount = 0;
    updateTime = now;
  }
  dots.add(new ColorDot());
}
```

If we examine the calculation of the radius in the constructor of the ColorDot class, we can see that the value in walkSpeed is not used directly, but it is first constrained to the 0–2 steps/second range with the function constrain() and then normalized so we have a value between 0 and 1 that we can consistently map onto the radius range maxSize-minSize. This implies that the faster we walk, the smaller the dots should appear. The hue of the dots is also the result of a mapping calculation, in this case of the current second obtained with the second() function, to the 0-360 hue range.

Playing Audio

So far, all our examples in the book have been purely visual, with no audio component. However, the dots sketch could make use of sound to complement the walk-driven animation. One option is to just play random audio clips each time a step is detected, but perhaps we can do something a little more interesting instead by playing notes from a musical scale.

To keep things simple, let's use a pentatonic scale (https://en.wikipedia.org/wiki/Pentatonic_scale) with notes A, G, E, D, and C. If we always play these notes in their natural order, we will hear the original scale repeatedly, and the result would be quite monotonous. On the other extreme, choosing a note at random would be too chaotic and noisy. So we could try an intermediate solution that has enough variability while retaining the harmony of the scale, for example, by playing either the previous or next note to the current one, giving each choice a predefined probability. How do we go about implementing this idea?

Processing does not include any built-in functions for audio playback, but we can use the Android API to create a minimal AudioPlayer class that extends Android's MediaPlayer. We then need to obtain audio clips for our five notes and copy them into the sketch's data folder.

■ **Note** Android supports several audio formats, including MP3, WAVE, MIDI, and Vorbis. Refer to the media formats page in the development site for a full list of media formats and codecs: https://developer. android.com/guide/topics/media/platform/supported-formats.

Listing 8-6 combines our previous colored dot sketch with an AudioPlayer class and the simple logic we discussed previously to pick which note to play (only the parts in the code that differ from Listing 8-5 are shown).

Listing 8-6. Playing a pentatonic scale by walking around

```
import ketai.sensors.*;
import android.media.MediaPlayer;
import android.content.res.AssetFileDescriptor;
import android.media.AudioManager;

KetaiSensor sensor;
...
int numNotes = 5;
AudioPlayer [] notes = new AudioPlayer[numNotes];
int lastNote = int(random(1) * 4);

void setup() {
  fullScreen();
  orientation(LANDSCAPE);
  colorMode(HSB, 360, 100, 100, 100);
```

```
    noStroke();
    for (int i = 0; i < numNotes; i++) notes[i] = new AudioPlayer();
    notes[0].loadFile(this, "5A.wav");
    notes[1].loadFile(this, "4G.wav");
    notes[2].loadFile(this, "4E.wav");
    notes[3].loadFile(this, "4D.wav");
    notes[4].loadFile(this, "4C.wav");
    dots = new ArrayList<ColorDot>();
    requestPermission("android.permission.ACTIVITY_RECOGNITION", "handlePermission");
}
...
class ColorDot {
    float posX, posY;
    float rad, maxRad;
    float colorHue, colorAlpha;
    int note;

    ColorDot() {
        posX = int(random(1, width/maxSize)) * maxSize;
        posY = int(random(1, height/maxSize)) * maxSize;
        rad = 0.1;
        float speedf = constrain(walkSpeed, 0, 2)/2.0;
        maxRad = map(speedf, 1, 0, minSize, maxSize);
        selectNote();
        colorHue = map(note, 0, 4, 0, 360);
        colorAlpha = 70;
    }

    void selectNote() {
        float r = random(1);
        note = lastNote;
        if (r < 0.4) note--;
        else if (r > 0.6) note++;
        if (note < 0) note = 1;
        if (4 < note) note = 3;
        notes[note].play();
        lastNote = note;
    }
    ...
}
...
class AudioPlayer extends MediaPlayer {
    boolean loadFile(PApplet app, String fileName) {
        AssetFileDescriptor desc;
        try {
            desc = app.getActivity().getAssets().openFd(fileName);
        } catch (IOException e) {
            println("Error loading " + fileName);
            println(e.getMessage());
            return false;
        }
```

```
  if (desc == null) {
    println("Cannot find " + fileName);
    return false;
  }

  try {
    setDataSource(desc.getFileDescriptor(), desc.getStartOffset(),
                  desc.getLength());
    setAudioStreamType(AudioManager.STREAM_MUSIC);
    prepare();
    return true;
  } catch (IOException e) {
    println(e.getMessage());
    return false;
  }
}

void play() {
  if (isPlaying()) seekTo(0);
  start();
}
}
```

Some discussion about this sketch: we load each note in a separate instance of the AudioPlayer class and store the five AudioPlayer objects in the notes array. We initialize this array in setup() and implement the selection logic in the new selectNote() method in the ColorDot class, using 0.4 as the probability for selecting the preceding note in the scale and 0.6 for the next. Figure 8-3 shows the output of this sketch, but of course, we need to run it on a device to appreciate its sounds as we walk around.

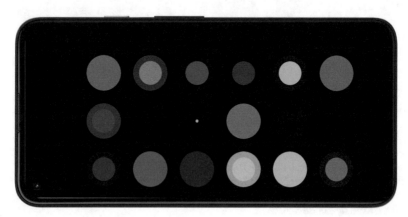

Figure 8-3. *Dots sketch running on the device*

Using the Magnetic Sensor

The magnetic sensor (or magnetometer) is another very common sensor we can find in Android devices, and it is useful for several applications. For example, Listing 8-7 shows how we can use it to detect the proximity of a metal object by comparing the measured magnitude of the magnetic field with the expected magnitude of the Earth's magnetic field at our present location. If we run this sketch on our phone, we will be effectively turning it into a metal detector!

Listing 8-7. Detecting the strength of the magnetic field

```
import ketai.sensors.*;
import android.hardware.GeomagneticField;

KetaiSensor sensor;
float expMag, obsMag;

void setup() {
  fullScreen();
  sensor = new KetaiSensor(this);
  sensor.start();
  GeomagneticField geoField = new GeomagneticField(14.0093, 120.996147, 300,
                      System.currentTimeMillis());
  expMag = geoField.getFieldStrength()/1000;
}

void draw() {
  println(obsMag, expMag);
  if (obsMag < 0.7 * expMag || 1.3 * expMag < obsMag) {
    background(255);
  } else {
    background(0);
  }
}

void onMagneticFieldEvent(float x, float y, float z) {
  obsMag = sqrt(sq(x) + sq(y) + sq(z));
}
```

Note that we have to provide the geographical coordinates of our current location expressed as latitude and longitude in degrees and altitude in meters, as well as the so-called "Epoch Time" (current time expressed as milliseconds since January 1, 1970), to the GeomagneticField() constructor in order to obtain the field due solely to the Earth's magnetic field. We can then perform the comparison with the actual magnetic field measured by the device.

Creating a Compass App

Besides implementing a handy metal detector, another application that results from combining the magnetic field data with the acceleration is to determine the orientation of the device with respect to the Earth's North Magnetic Pole – in other words, a compass.

The gravity and geomagnetic vectors encode all the information required to determine the orientation of the device in relation to the Earth's surface. Using Ketai, we can get the components of the acceleration and magnetic field vectors, and with those, we can obtain the rotation matrix that transforms coordinates from the device system (Figure 7-1) to a world's coordinate system that we can imagine attached to our location on the surface of the Earth, as illustrated in Figure 8-4.

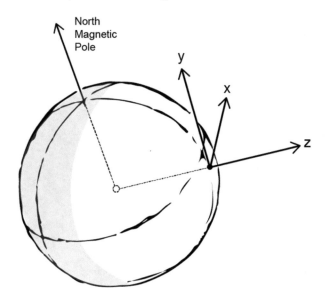

Figure 8-4. *World coordinate system, with X pointing east, Y pointing north, and Z away from the Earth's center*

The final step is to derive, from the rotation matrix, the orientation angles with respect to these XYZ axes: azimuth (the angle around Z), pitch (the angle around X), and roll (the angle around Y). To implement a compass, we only need the azimuth angle, since it gives us the deviation with respect to the y axis pointing north at our location. The SensorManager class from the Android SDK contains several utility methods to carry out all these calculations, which we perform in Listing 8-8.

Listing 8-8. A compass sketch

```
import ketai.sensors.*;
import android.hardware.SensorManager;

KetaiSensor sensor;

float[] gravity = new float[3];
float[] geomagnetic = new float[3];
float[] I = new float[16];
float[] R = new float[16];
float orientation[] = new float[3];
```

```
float easing = 0.05;
float azimuth;

void setup() {
  fullScreen(P2D);
  orientation(PORTRAIT);
  sensor = new KetaiSensor(this);
  sensor.start();
}

void draw() {
  background(255);

  float cx = width * 0.5;
  float cy = height * 0.4;
  float radius = 0.8 * cx;

  translate(cx, cy);

  noFill();
  stroke(0);
  strokeWeight(2);
  ellipse(0, 0, radius*2, radius*2);
  line(0, -cy, 0, -radius);

  fill(192, 0, 0);
  noStroke();
  rotate(-azimuth);
  beginShape();
  vertex(-30, 40);
  vertex(0, 0);
  vertex(30, 40);
  vertex(0, -radius);
  endShape();
}

void onAccelerometerEvent(float x, float y, float z) {
  gravity[0] = x; gravity[1] = y; gravity[2] = z;
  calculateOrientation();
}

void onMagneticFieldEvent(float x, float y, float z) {
  geomagnetic[0] = x; geomagnetic[1] = y; geomagnetic[2] = z;
  calculateOrientation();
}

void calculateOrientation() {
  if (SensorManager.getRotationMatrix(R, I, gravity, geomagnetic)) {
    SensorManager.getOrientation(R, orientation);
    azimuth += easing * (orientation[0] - azimuth);
  }
}
```

By using the acceleration and magnetic field vectors to the getRotationMatrix() and getOrientation() methods in SensorManager, we will obtain an orientation vector containing the azimuth, pitch, and roll angles. In this example, we only use the azimuth to draw the compass, and we can install it as a live wallpaper to have always available as background (shown in Figure 8-5).

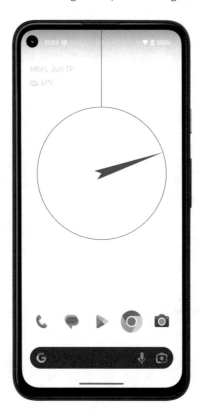

Figure 8-5. *Compass sketch running as a live wallpaper*

The values from both the accelerometer and the magnetometer are noisy, so that's the reason to apply some "easing" of the values with the line azimuth += easing * (orientation[0] - azimuth). With this formula, we update the current azimuth value with a fraction of the new value, so changes are softer, and noise is smoothed out. The closer to 0 the easing constant is, the stronger the smoothing and the softer the movement of the compass' hand. On the other end, an easing value of 1 will result in no smoothing at all, since it is equivalent to assigning the new sensor value azimuth = orientation[0].

Alternatively, we can get the orientation vector directly from Ketai, without having to rely on the SensorManager class from Android. To do so, we first have to enable the accelerometer and the magnetic field sensors explicitly in setup() (since we will not be using Ketai's event functions), and we can then just call getOrientation() from the KetaiSensor object in draw(), as shown in Listing 8-9. The output of this modified version of the sketch should be the same as before.

Listing 8-9. Compass using Ketai's getOrientation() function

```
import ketai.sensors.*;

float orientation[] = new float[3];
float easing = 0.05;
float azimuth;

KetaiSensor sensor;

void setup() {
  fullScreen(P2D);
  orientation(PORTRAIT);
  sensor = new KetaiSensor(this);
  sensor.enableAccelerometer();
  sensor.enableMagenticField();
  sensor.start();
}

void draw() {
...
ellipse(0, 0, radius*2, radius*2);
line(0, -cy, 0, -radius);

  sensor.getOrientation(orientation);
  azimuth += easing * (orientation[0] - azimuth);

  fill(192, 0, 0);
  noStroke();
  ...
}
```

The Gyroscope

The gyroscope could complement the accelerometer and magnetometer but could also be used in situations where those other sensors would not be very useful. The accelerometer and the magnetometer give us data about the movement and orientation of the device in space; however, they have limitations. The accelerometer, on one hand, is not able to detect movements at constant speed, since in such cases the acceleration is zero, while the magnetic sensor, on the other hand, only gives a very coarse variable related to the location (i.e., orientation with respect to the Earth's magnetic field). Both are also quite noisy due to the physical processes that generate their data.

The gyroscope, in contrast, gives us a quite precise reading of the angular velocity at which the device is rotating around in space. With this velocity, it is possible to infer the orientation of the device with respect to an arbitrary initial state. This is to say it cannot give us an absolute description of its orientation with respect to a system such as the world coordinates that we discussed before. However, this information can be inferred from the accelerometer and magnetometer.

Let's look into a few simple examples to get a sense of how the gyroscope works. Since it provides values that we can use to control 3D movement in our Processing sketch, it makes sense to write a very simple 3D sketch. Using Ketai, it is easy to obtain the rotational angles from the gyroscope, as we did for the other sensors before. We will use the P3D renderer in Listing 8-10 to draw a simple 3D scene, a cube that is rotated around its center according to the angular velocity measured by the gyroscope. The output of this sketch is shown in Figure 8-6.

Listing 8-10. Rotating a box with the gyroscope

```
import ketai.sensors.*;

KetaiSensor sensor;
float rotationX, rotationY, rotationZ;
void setup() {
  fullScreen(P3D);
  orientation(LANDSCAPE);
  sensor = new KetaiSensor(this);
  sensor.start();
  rectMode(CENTER);
  fill(180);
}

void draw() {
  background(255);
  translate(width/2, height/2);
  rotateZ(rotationZ);
  rotateY(rotationX);
  rotateX(rotationY);
  box(height * 0.3);
}

void onGyroscopeEvent(float x, float y, float z) {
  rotationX += 0.1 * x;
  rotationY += 0.1 * y;
  rotationZ += 0.1 * z;
}
```

A few important aspects to note in this example: since the x, y, and z values are (angular) velocities, we don't use them directly to apply the rotations to the objects in our scene but instead add them up to the rotation variables (scaled by a constant that in this case is 0.1 but can be adjusted to make the movement on the screen slower or faster). Moreover, we apply the rotationX angle with the rotateY() function (meaning that we are rotating the cube around the y axis) and rotationY with rotateX(). The reason for this switch is that the orientation of the device is locked in LANDSCAPE, meaning that the x axis in the Processing screen corresponds to the horizontal direction of the device, which runs along the y axis of the device's coordinate system we saw in Figure 7-1.

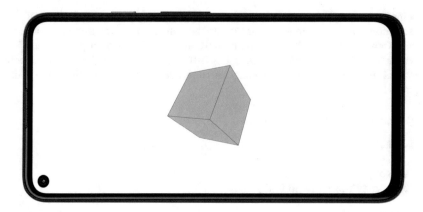

Figure 8-6. *Sketch using the gyroscope to control rotation of a cube*

Another important aspect of using the gyroscope is that any rotation involving the device will be measured by the sensor, for example, when the person holding the phone turns around while walking (even if the relative orientation of the phone with respect to the user does not change). In such cases, we can keep the initial orientation by subtracting an offset value at any moment we want to "re-center" the scene in our phone. For instance, we can store the current rotation angles as our offset when touching the screen, as it is done in Listing 8-11 (only showing the differences with Listing 8-10).

Listing 8-11. Re-centering the gyroscope data

```
...
void draw() {
  background(255);
  translate(width/2, height/2);
  rotateZ(rotationZ - offsetZ);
  rotateY(rotationX - offsetX);
  rotateX(rotationY - offsetY);
  box(height * 0.3);
}
...
void mousePressed() {
  offsetX = rotationX;
  offsetY = rotationY;
  offsetZ = rotationZ;
}
```

We are not limited to working with 3D geometry when using the gyroscope. If we are drawing in 2D, all we need to do is to keep track of the Z rotation, like in Listing 8-12.

Listing 8-12. Rotation in 2D with the gyroscope

```
import ketai.sensors.*;

KetaiSensor sensor;
float rotationZ, offsetZ;
void setup() {
```

```
  fullScreen(P2D);
  orientation(LANDSCAPE);
  sensor = new KetaiSensor(this);
  sensor.start();
  rectMode(CENTER);
  fill(180);
}

void draw() {
  background(255);
  translate(width/2, height/2);
  rotate(rotationZ - offsetZ);
  rect(0, 0, height * 0.3, height * 0.3);
}

void onGyroscopeEvent(float x, float y, float z) {
  rotationZ += 0.1 * z;
}

void mousePressed() {
  offsetZ = rotationZ;
}
```

The gyroscope can be useful to implement input in a game app. We will see how to do that in the final section of this chapter.

Controlling Navigation with the Gyroscope

In the last few examples dealing with the gyroscope sensor, we used the rotation angles to control 2D and 3D shapes that remained fixed in the center of the screen. This would be enough if we need to control only the rotation of the shapes, but if we want to determine their translation as well, we need to come up with other methods.

In fact, one approach is not to translate the shapes in question, but the rest of the scene in the opposite direction, after applying the rotation transformation measured with the gyroscope. This is inspired by the classic arcade game Asteroids by Atari, a screenshot of which is shown in Figure 8-7 to help to explain the idea. In this game, the player controls a spaceship moving through space and avoiding multiple dangers, including asteroids and UFOs. Even though the spaceship is capable of translating across the screen, the player could also remain stationary and only rotate the spaceship around its current position to aim for their foes. Here, we will write a sketch to navigate a spaceship (a triangle shape, just like in Asteroids) through an endless field of asteroids (ellipses). The key part is to properly code for the translation of all the ellipses to convey the relative movement in (2D) space of the spaceship with respect to the asteroids.

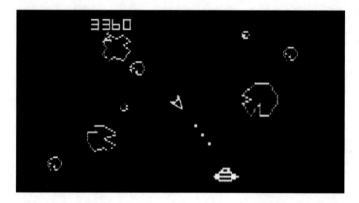

Figure 8-7. *Screenshot of the original Asteroids game (Atari 1979) showing a ship in the center of the screen and surrounding asteroid shapes*

The math to achieve this effect is as follows: if our shape is initially moving toward the top edge of the screen, the forward vector describing this movement would be `v = new PVector(0, -1)`, since the y axis in Processing points down. We can calculate a matrix that represents the rotation that should be applied on this vector. The rotated vector can be used to translate all the other shapes in the scene to create the relative motion.

The Processing API includes a PMatrix2D class that does these calculations for us. If our rotation angle is, for example, QUARTER_PI, we can then generate a rotation matrix corresponding to this rotation by doing `mat.rotate(QUARTER_PI)`, with mat being an object of type PMatrix3D. Once we have done this, we can apply the matrix to the PVector object representing the translation, for example, `mat.mult(v, rv)`, where v is the original PVector and rv is the resulting rotated PVector. Let's use this API in Listing 8-13.

Listing 8-13. Controlling a spaceship with the gyroscope

```
import ketai.sensors.*;

KetaiSensor sensor;
float rotationZ, offsetZ;
PMatrix2D rotMatrix = new PMatrix2D();
PVector forward = new PVector(0, -1);
PVector forwardRot = new PVector();
ArrayList<Asteroid> field;
float speed = 2;

void setup() {
  fullScreen(P2D);
  orientation(LANDSCAPE);
  sensor = new KetaiSensor(this);
  sensor.start();
  ellipseMode(CENTER);
  noStroke();
  field = new ArrayList<Asteroid>();
  for (int i = 0; i < 100; i++) {
    field.add(new Asteroid());
  }
}
```

```
void draw() {
  background(0);

  boolean hit = false;
  float angle = rotationZ - offsetZ;
  rotMatrix.reset();
  rotMatrix.rotate(angle);
  rotMatrix.mult(forward, forwardRot);
  forwardRot.mult(speed);
  for (Asteroid a: field) {
    a.update(forwardRot);
    a.display();
    if (a.hit(width/2, height/2)) hit = true;
  }

  pushMatrix();
  translate(width/2, height/2);
  rotate(angle);
  if (hit) {
    fill(252, 103, 43);
  } else {
    fill(67, 125, 222);
  }
  float h = height * 0.2;
  triangle(0, -h/2, h/3, +h/2, -h/3, +h/2);
  popMatrix();
}

void onGyroscopeEvent(float x, float y, float z) {
  rotationZ += 0.1 * z;
}

void mousePressed() {
  offsetZ = rotationZ;
}

class Asteroid {
  float x, y, r;
  color c;
  Asteroid() {
    c = color(random(255), random(255), random(255));
    r = height * random(0.05, 0.1);
    x = random(-2 * width, +2 * width);
    y = random(-2 * height, +2 * height);
  }
  void update(PVector v) {
    x -= v.x;
    y -= v.y;
    if (x < -2 * width || 2 * width < x ||
        y < -2 * height || 2 * height < y) {
      x = random(-2 * width, +2 * width);
      y = random(-2 * height, +2 * height);
```

```
    }
  }
  void display() {
    fill(c);
    ellipse(x, y, r, r);
  }
  boolean hit(float sx, float sy) {
    return dist(x, y, sx, sy) < r;
  }
}
```

As we can see in this code, the spaceship is always drawn at the center of the screen, and it is the asteroids the items that get translated by the rotated forward vector, as we discussed before. The Asteroid class contains all the logic that handles placing each asteroid at a random position, updating its position using the rotated forward vector, displaying it at the current position, and determining if it is hitting the center of the screen where the spaceship is.

Each asteroid is placed in a rectangular area of dimensions [-2 * width, +2 * width] · [-2 * height, +2 * height], and as soon as it moves out of this area (which is determined by the boundary check in the update() function), it is placed back inside again. Also, notice the minus sign in the translations along x and y, -v.x, and -v.y, which ensures the correct relative motion. We can think of the forward vector as the velocity of our spaceship, and in fact by scaling it by the speed factor (set to 2 in this sketch), we can make the spaceship move faster or slower.

Finally, we implemented a simple collision detection so that the spaceship changes color when an asteroid gets close enough to its position at the center of the screen. We could imagine multiple ways to turn this early prototype into a proper game by adding interactions to control the speed, better graphics with images and SVG shapes, and even lasers to destroy the asteroids! The output of our initial prototype should look like Figure 8-8.

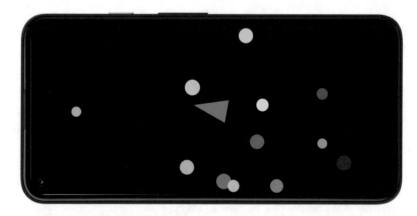

Figure 8-8. Controlling the navigation through a field of obstacles with the gyroscope

Summary

Building upon the basic techniques to read sensor data from Processing, we have now learned some advanced applications of three types of hardware sensors: the accelerometer, the magnetometer, and the gyroscope. These sensors are particularly important because they provide instant feedback on the movement and position of our device and so enable us to create interactive apps based on physical gestures and actions. We will find these interactions very useful in a wide range of projects, from visualizing physical activity to coding up our own game experiences with graphics and sound.

CHAPTER 9

■ ■ ■

Geolocation

Geolocation sensors give us the ability to know where our devices are with high accuracy and to use this information in location-aware apps. In this chapter, we will see how to create this type of apps in Processing and will develop a final project combining location with images from Google Street View.

Location Data in Android

We use location-aware apps in our smartphones all the time to find places of interest around us, to plan travel directions in advance, or to play location-based games like Pokémon GO. All these uses are enabled by the same underlying geolocation technologies, mainly Global Positioning System (GPS), but also cell-tower triangulation, Bluetooth proximity detection, and Wi-Fi access points. GPS is the technology that most people immediately associate with geolocation: it is based on a network of satellites, owned by the United States and operated by the United States Air Force, that send geolocation information to a GPS receiver on the Earth's surface, including those in a mobile phone.

■ **Note**   Other countries have also developed similar systems, such as GLONASS (Russia), BeiDou (China), NavIC (India), and Galileo (Europe). By default, the Android system only uses GPS satellites, but some manufacturers introduced changes to get geolocation data from these other systems as well, which can provide better coverage and accuracy. The app called GPS Test in the Play Store shows the systems in use by our phone.

One drawback of using GPS or a comparable navigation satellite system to get location data is that it uses a lot of battery to power the GPS antenna. Also, the phone needs to have an unobstructed line of sight to the sky. To deal with these issues, we can take advantage of other location sources, such as Cell-ID, Bluetooth, and Wi-Fi, which are less precise but consume less energy. As a reference, the accuracy of GPS location ranges around 16 feet (4.9 meters), while the accuracy of Wi-Fi is 40 meters. Cell-ID has a much higher degree of variability, depending on cell size, which can range from some meters to kilometers.

However, we don't need to worry (too much) about when and how to choose a particular location system, as Android will automatically switch between the best location providers given an app-specific configuration in the settings of the phone, seen in Figure 9-1. Starting with Android 7, we only need to set whether we want high-accuracy location by combining all possible sources, battery saving without GPS, or GPS only.

© Andrés Colubri 2023
A. Colubri, *Processing for Android*, https://doi.org/10.1007/978-1-4842-9585-4_9

Figure 9-1. *App-specific location settings in Android 13*

Using Location API in Processing

Android provides a comprehensive API to access the location services available in the system (https://developer.android.com/training/location). We can also use the Ketai library to get location values without having to worry about this API, as we did for motion sensors. However, in this chapter, we will use the location API directly from our Processing sketch. The reason for doing this is that there are a number of important aspects to consider when using location services, specifically permission handling and concurrency, and it is a good idea to familiarize ourselves with them even if we later use Ketai.

■ **Note** The Google Play services location API (https://developers.google.com/android/reference/com/google/android/gms/location/package-summary) is a newer and more feature-rich alternative to the standard Android location API we will learn in this chapter. However, Processing only supports the latter when coding from the PDE. We can export our sketch as an Android project and then import it from Android Studio to use Google Play services (see Appendix A for details).

Location Permissions

The use of specific functionality in our Android app, such as accessing the Internet, requires adding the appropriate permission to our sketch using the Android Permissions Selector. However, we saw in Chapter 6 that this is not enough for runtime permissions, which need an additional explicit request during runtime in devices running Android 6 or newer. The permissions to access location data fall within this category, and they are ACCESS_COARSE_LOCATION and ACCESS_FINE_LOCATION. The first grants access to approximate location derived from cell towers and Wi-Fi, while the second enables obtaining location from the GPS. In order to use these permissions in our sketch, we need to check them in the Permissions Selector (Figure 9-2) and then use the requestPermission() function in the code of our sketch.

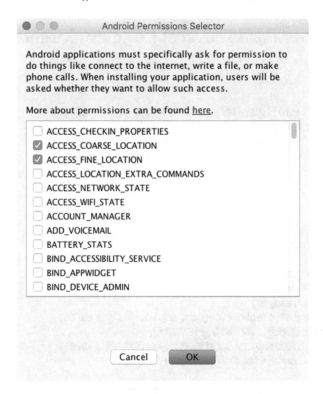

Figure 9-2. *Selecting coarse and fine location permissions*

Listing 9-1 demonstrates the basic setup of a location-enabled sketch, where we define a location manager, and the associated listener, in a similar manner as we did with other sensors before, including setting up the permissions required by the sketch.

Listing 9-1. Getting location data

```
import android.content.Context;
import android.location.Location;
import android.location.LocationListener;
import android.location.LocationManager;
import android.os.Bundle;
```

```
LocationManager manager;
SimpleListener listener;
String provider;

double currentLatitude;
double currentLongitude;
double currentAltitude;

void setup () {
  fullScreen();
  textFont(createFont("SansSerif", displayDensity * 24));
  textAlign(CENTER, CENTER);
  requestPermission("android.permission.ACCESS_FINE_LOCATION", "initLocation");
}

void draw() {
  background(0);
  if (hasPermission("android.permission.ACCESS_FINE_LOCATION")) {
    text("Latitude: " + currentLatitude + "\n" +
         "Longitude: " + currentLongitude + "\n" +
         "Altitude: " + currentAltitude, 0, 0, width, height);
  } else {
    text("No permissions to access location", 0, 0, width, height);
  }
}

void initLocation(boolean granted) {
  if (granted) {
    Context context = getContext();
    listener = new SimpleListener();
    manager = (LocationManager)
              context.getSystemService(Context.LOCATION_SERVICE);
    provider = LocationManager.NETWORK_PROVIDER;
    if (manager.isProviderEnabled(LocationManager.GPS_PROVIDER)) {
      provider = LocationManager.GPS_PROVIDER;
    }
    manager.requestLocationUpdates(provider, 1000, 1, listener);
  }
}

public void resume() {
  if (manager != null) {
    manager.requestLocationUpdates(provider, 1000, 1, listener);
  }
}

public void pause() {
  if (manager != null) {
    manager.removeUpdates(listener);
  }
}
```

```
class SimpleListener implements LocationListener {
  public void onLocationChanged(Location loc) {
    currentLatitude = loc.getLatitude();
    currentLongitude = loc.getLongitude();
    currentAltitude = loc.getAltitude();
  }
  public void onProviderDisabled(String provider) { }
  public void onProviderEnabled(String provider) { }
  public void onStatusChanged(String provider, int status, Bundle extras) { }
}
```

The location object received in onLocationChanged() contains several pieces of information, the most important of which are the latitude and longitude values that indicate our position on the surface of the Earth, along the lines parallel to the Equator, and the meridian lines that connect the geographical poles, respectively.

■ **Note**   Android provides latitude and longitude as double-precision numbers, and the significant digits reflect the precision of the location reading: five significant digits are needed for meter precision, while six or more for submeter detail.

There are a few more things that we should pay attention to. First, we requested the fine location permission, which will give us the highest resolution available, but also access to less accurate sources, so there is no need to request separate permission for coarse location. Second, we configured the location manager with the requestLocationUpdates() by indicating our preferred provider (network or GPS). Android will determine the actual provider by considering the combination of requested permissions, the location mode of the device, and the available source of location data at each moment. In the code, we set the network provider as the default, which determines location using data from cell towers and Wi-Fi access points, and switch to the more accurate GPS if the corresponding provider is enabled. We also set the minimum time interval between location updates, in milliseconds (here, 1000 means that updates cannot happen more often than once every second), and the minimum distance, in meters, to trigger location updates.

Finally, we implemented the resume and pause events as we did with other sensors before, so no location updates are generated while the app is paused and requesting them again after resuming. This is very important to save battery when the app is in the background.

Accessing Data from Multiple Threads

In all sensor examples we saw earlier, we read the sensor data in the corresponding listener without any issues. If we are just storing the last received data in float variables, then we will be fine. However, problems will start as soon as we save sensor information in data structures in our code, such as an array to keep track of values measured so far. The problem with location data is that there are situations where the same data may be accessed simultaneously from different "threads." But what is a thread? According to the Processing reference (https://processing.org/reference/thread_.html), "Processing sketches follow a specific sequence of steps: setup() first, followed by draw() over and over and over again in a loop. A thread is also a series of steps with a beginning, a middle, and an end. A Processing sketch is a single thread, often referred to as the Animation thread." But we can have sketches with multiple threads running in parallel, and conflicts might arise if two threads try to read from or write to the same variables simultaneously (e.g., if a thread tries to get the last element in an array while another thread adds a new element at the end of the array, what should be the correct output?). This can happen in our location sketches, for example, if data is read in the draw() function, which is called from the animation thread, while the event handling methods, like onLocationChanged() in the case of location, are called from a different thread (typically, the so-called "event" thread). This can lead to unexpected behaviors in our app and even sudden crashes.

Solving these "threading" issues requires some extra work. One solution is to store the location data obtained in each call of onLocationChanged() in a "queue" and then retrieve the events from the queue during drawing. The queue is "synchronized," meaning that when new data is being added or existing data is removed in one thread, any other thread must wait until the operation is concluded. This technique would not fix all concurrency problems, but it should be enough in our case. Listing 9-2 shows how we can implement a queue of latitude/longitude locations.

Listing 9-2. Storing locations in a queue

```
import android.content.Context;
import android.location.Location;
import android.location.LocationListener;
import android.location.LocationManager;
import android.os.Bundle;

LocationManager manager;
SimpleListener listener;
String provider;
LocationQueue queue = new LocationQueue();
ArrayList<LocationValue> path = new ArrayList<LocationValue>();

void setup () {
  fullScreen();
  textFont(createFont("SansSerif", displayDensity * 24));
  textAlign(CENTER, CENTER);
  requestPermission("android.permission.ACCESS_FINE_LOCATION", "initLocation");
}

void draw() {
  background(0);
  while (queue.available()) {
    LocationValue loc = queue.remove();
    path.add(0, loc);
  }
  String info = "";
  for (LocationValue loc: path) {
    info += loc.latitude + ", " + loc.longitude + "\n";
  }
  text(info, 0, 0, width, height);
}

void initLocation(boolean granted) {
  if (granted) {
    Context context = getContext();
    listener = new SimpleListener();
    manager = (LocationManager)
                context.getSystemService(Context.LOCATION_SERVICE);
    provider = LocationManager.NETWORK_PROVIDER;
```

```
      if (manager.isProviderEnabled(LocationManager.GPS_PROVIDER)) {
        provider = LocationManager.GPS_PROVIDER;
      }
      manager.requestLocationUpdates(provider, 1000, 1, listener);
    }
  }

  class SimpleListener implements LocationListener {
    public void onLocationChanged(Location loc) {
      queue.add(new LocationValue(loc.getLatitude(), loc.getLongitude()));
    }
    public void onProviderDisabled(String provider) { }
    public void onProviderEnabled(String provider) { }
    public void onStatusChanged(String provider, int status, Bundle extras) { }
  }

  public void resume() {
    if (manager != null) {
      manager.requestLocationUpdates(provider, 1000, 1, listener);
    }
  }

  public void pause() {
    if (manager != null) {
      manager.removeUpdates(listener);
    }
  }

  class LocationValue {
    double latitude;
    double longitude;
    LocationValue(double lat, double lon) {
      latitude = lat;
      longitude = lon;
    }
  }

  class LocationQueue {
    LocationValue[] values = new LocationValue[10];
    int offset, count;

    synchronized void add(LocationValue val) {
      if (count == values.length) {
        values = (LocationValue[]) expand(values);
      }
      values[count++] = val;
    }

    synchronized LocationValue remove() {
      if (offset == count) {
        return null;
      }
```

```
    LocationValue outgoing = values[offset++];
    if (offset == count) {
      offset = 0;
      count = 0;
    }
    return outgoing;
  }

  synchronized boolean available() {
    return 0 < count;
  }
}
```

The permission and listener setup code are the same as in Listing 9-1, but now we have two new classes: LocationValue and LocationQueue. LocationValue is very simple; it just stores a single pair of latitude/longitude values in double precision. Let's look at LocationQueue more closely. It has three methods: add(), remove(), and available(), all of which are synchronized so they cannot be called simultaneously from different threads. When a new location is received in onLocationChanged(), we create a new LocationValue and add it to the queue. As new locations keep coming in from the event thread, they get stored in the values array inside the queue, which is expanded by doubling its size if needed. On the animation thread, we remove locations from the queue and add them to the path array list, so we can print in every frame all the latitude/longitude values received so far, in reverse order from last to first. Notice that we remove the locations from the queue not by looking at how many are left, since this number could change as new locations may arrive while we are still drawing a new frame, but simply by checking if the queue has available elements.

■ **Note**   We may experience some delay until the app starts receiving location values. This delay is caused by the device searching for the signal from a GPS satellite, or from a local cell tower or Wi-Fi access point.

We can now draw the path as a line strip connecting the successive locations. Listing 9-3 shows the new draw() function to do this, with the rest of the sketch being the same. Since we map the latitude and longitude values to positions on the screen, we need to determine the minimum and maximum values in order to define the mapping. Also, we convert the double-precision values into single-precision floats we can use as arguments in the min(), max(), and map() functions. Figure 9-3 shows a typical output of this sketch as one walks around.

Listing 9-3. Drawing the locations along a line strip

```
float minLat = 90;
float maxLat = -90;
float minLon = 180;
float maxLon = -180;
...
void draw() {
  background(255);
  while (queue.available()) {
    LocationValue loc = queue.remove();
    minLat = min(minLat, (float)loc.latitude);
    maxLat = max(maxLat, (float)loc.latitude);
    minLon = min(minLon, (float)loc.longitude);
```

```
    maxLon = max(maxLon, (float)loc.longitude);
    path.add(0, loc);
  }
  stroke(70, 200);
  strokeWeight(displayDensity * 4);
  beginShape(LINE_STRIP);
  for (LocationValue loc: path) {
    float x = map((float)loc.longitude, minLon, maxLon,
                                    0.1 * width, 0.9 * width);
    float y = map((float)loc.latitude, minLat, maxLat,
                                    0.1 * height, 0.9 * height);
    vertex(x, y);
  }
  endShape();
}
```

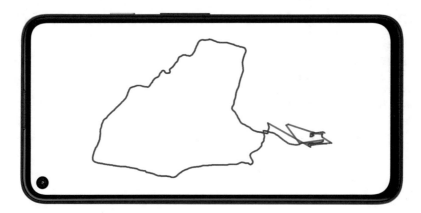

Figure 9-3. *Output of the path tracking sketch*

Location with Ketai

The advantage of using the Ketai sensor library is that all the details we discussed in the previous section (permissions, threads) are automatically taken care of by Ketai, so we can focus on using the location values. The previous example, rewritten using Ketai, is much shorter, as we can see in Listing 9-4.

Listing 9-4. Getting location data with Ketai

```
import ketai.sensors.*;

KetaiLocation location;
ArrayList<LocationValue> path = new ArrayList<LocationValue>();

float minLat = 90;
float maxLat = -90;
float minLon = 180;
float maxLon = -180;
```

```
void setup () {
  fullScreen();
  location = new KetaiLocation(this);
}

void draw() {
  background(255);
  stroke(70, 200);
  strokeWeight(displayDensity * 4);
  beginShape(LINE_STRIP);
  for (LocationValue loc: path) {
    float x = map((float)loc.longitude, minLon, maxLon,
                                0.1 * width, 0.9 * width);
    float y = map((float)loc.latitude, minLat, maxLat,
                                0.1 * height, 0.9 * height);
    vertex(x, y);
  }
  endShape();
}

void onLocationEvent(double lat, double lon) {
  path.add(new LocationValue(lat, lon));
  minLat = Math.min(minLat, (float)lat);
  maxLat = Math.max(maxLat, (float)lat);
  minLon = Math.min(minLon, (float)lon);
  maxLon = Math.max(maxLon, (float)lon);
}

class LocationValue {
  double latitude;
  double longitude;
  LocationValue(double lat, double lon) {
    latitude = lat;
    longitude = lon;
  }
}
```

The onLocationEvent() is triggered by Ketai in the same thread as the draw() function, so there is no risk of running into concurrency issues.

Using Additional Location Data

When our location listener receives a new location in the onLocationChanged() handler method, it is not only the latitude and longitude of the location that become available to us but also other relevant information, such as altitude, accuracy, and bearing (https://developer.android.com/reference/android/location/Location.html). The accuracy value is important as it reflects the location precision of the current provider. It will not make sense to store consecutive location values if they differ by less than the current accuracy. We can modify our previous location queue example (Listing 9-3) to incorporate this check. The changes are shown in Listing 9-5.

Listing 9-5. Using location accuracy

```
...
void draw() {
background(255);
while (queue.available()) {
    LocationValue loc = queue.remove();
    minLat = min(minLat, (float)loc.latitude);
    maxLat = max(maxLat, (float)loc.latitude);
    minLon = min(minLon, (float)loc.longitude);
    maxLon = max(maxLon, (float)loc.longitude);
    if (0 < path.size()) {
      LocationValue last = path.get(path.size() - 1);
      if (last.distanceTo(loc) < loc.accuracy + last.accuracy) continue;
    }
    path.add(0, loc);
}
stroke(70, 200);
strokeWeight(displayDensity * 4);
beginShape(LINE_STRIP);
for (LocationValue loc: path) {
    float x = map((float)loc.longitude, minLon, maxLon, 0.1 * width, 0.9 * width);
    float y = map((float)loc.latitude, minLat, maxLat,  0.1 * height, 0.9 * height);
    vertex(x, y);
}
endShape();
}
...
class SimpleListener implements LocationListener
  public void onLocationChanged(Location loc) {
    queue.add(new LocationValue(loc.getLatitude(), loc.getLongitude(),
                                loc.getAccuracy())

  ...
}
...
class LocationValue
  double latitud
  double longitude;
double accuracy;

LocationValue(double lat, double lon, double acc) {
  latitude = lat;
  longitude = lon;
  accuracy = acc;

  double distanceTo(LocationValue dest) {
    double a1 = radians((float)latitude);
    double a2 = radians((float)longitude);
    double b1 = radians((float)dest.latitude);
    double b2 = radians((float)dest.longitude);
```

```
    double t1 = Math.cos(a1) * Math.cos(a2) * Math.cos(b1) * Math.cos(b2);
    double t2 = Math.cos(a1) * Math.sin(a2) * Math.cos(b1) * Math.sin(b2);
    double t3 = Math.sin(a1) * Math.sin(b1);
    double tt = Math.acos(t1 + t2 + t3);

    return 6366000 * t
  }
}
```

We obtain the location accuracy from the `Location` argument in the `onLocationChanged()` event and store it in the `LocationValue` object alongside its latitude and longitude. Then, we use the accuracy of the latest and previous locations to determine if the latest is different enough to be added to the path. This involves calculating the distance between two locations, which is the length of the arc connecting them on the surface of the Earth. There are several formulas to approximate this distance (https://en.wikipedia. org/wiki/Great-circle_distance#Computational_formulae); in the code, we used the so–called "Law of Cosines" that assumes a perfectly spherical Earth (not entirely accurate since our planet is slightly flattened along its South-North axis, but good enough for this simple application).

A Street View Collage

At this point, we have added many techniques in our toolkit to create a more elaborate geolocation project. As mentioned at the beginning, we use location-aware apps constantly, probably dozens or even hundreds of times a day. Tools such as Google Street View are so popular that it is often that we first see a new place not when we visit it in person but when we view it on Street View in our phone. Our experience in the city is so mediated by these apps that could be worth trying to use imagery from Street View in combination with the locations we visit during the day to create some kind of visual collage from this data.

Thanks to the always-on nature of the smartphone and the possibility of real-time location updates, we could build a dynamic collage that uses Street View images downloaded from the Internet as we move around. From the point of view of the visual output, the most important question to solve is how to combine urban imagery into an engaging composition. As inspiration, Figure 9-4 shows two panoramic photo collages created by artists Masumi Hayashi and Annalisa Casini, the first made with images from a custom-made system for capturing 360° strips of scenery and the second from hand-curated Street View images.

We will start by solving the problem of retrieving Street View images from our Processing sketch, as this step is a prerequisite for any further work to realize our concept. Once we have solved this technical challenge, we will investigate ways of combining the images to create the collage.

Figure 9-4. *Top: OSERF Building Broad Street View, Columbus, Ohio, by Masumi Hayashi (2001). Bottom: Urban Sprawl New York by Annalisa Casini (2011)*

Using Google Street View Image API

Google Street View is a popular feature of Google Maps and Google Earth that provides panoramic views of many places around the world, primarily streets in cities and towns, but also sites like building interiors, coral reefs, and even space (`https://tinyurl.com/yc6hwav8`)! Street View can be accessed from Android apps using different APIs; one of them allows to create interactive panoramas inside a specialized view component. However, this API is not suitable to use in our Processing sketch, since the panorama view cannot be integrated with Processing's surface view that renders the sketch output.

Fortunately, Google also offers an image API where one can download Street View static images corresponding to a latitude/longitude coordinate using an HTTP request (`https://developers.google.com/maps/documentation/streetview/overview`). To use this API, we first have to set up a new project in the Google Cloud console (`https://console.cloud.google.com/apis/dashboard`) and enable the "Street View Static API" for the project, and then you should get an API key ready to use. It is important to note that you also need to enable billing in your account since the Google Cloud services are not free; however, Google offers a $200 monthly credit at no charge for Google Maps APIs, which includes the Street View Static API. This should be sufficient for testing our app. Completing all these steps is very important; otherwise, our Processing sketches will not be able to request Street View images. We can check if everything is working as expected by creating a Google Street View Image API request in the web browser with the following format:

```
https://maps.googleapis.com/maps/api/streetview?size=WIDTHxHEIGHT&location=LAT,LONG&sensor=
SENSOR_STATUS&heading=HEADING&fov=FOV&pitch=PITCH&key=API_KEY
```

Most of the parameters in the request are optional, except for the location, size, and API key. The Google Street View Image API page linked to in the previous paragraph describes all these URL parameters in detail. The request should return an image that we can then save in our computer. We can use the same request syntax in a Processing sketch to request a PImage. This is achieved with the simple code in Listing 9-6, where you need to provide your own API key and to add the Internet permission to the sketch.

Listing 9-6. Requesting a Street View image

```
PImage streetImage;
String apiKey = "<your API key>";

void setup() {
  size(512, 512);
  streetImage = requestImage("https://maps.googleapis.com/maps/api/streetview?" +
                    "size=512x512&location= 42.3742025,-71.1292058&+
                    "fov=100&heading=230&key=" + apiKey);
}

void draw() {
  if (0 < streetImage.width && 0 < streetImage.height) {
    image(streetImage, 0, 0, width, height);
  }
}
```

The requestImage() function returns a PImage object that will be downloaded in a separate thread to avoid freezing our sketch while the image data is transferred. We will know that the image is ready when its width and height are greater than zero. If for some reason the request failed, the width and height will both be set to -1.

By combining the ability to request images from Google Street View Image API with our previous path tracking sketch from Listing 9-5, we should be able to display a street image of the latest position received from the location services. Let's see how to do this in Listing 9-7.

Listing 9-7. Showing Street View of our last location

```
...
ArrayList<LocationValue> path = new ArrayList<LocationValue>();
ArrayList<PImage> images = new ArrayList<PImage>();
String apiKey = "<your API key>";
...
void draw() {
  background(255);
  while (queue.available()) {
    LocationValue loc = queue.remove();
    if (0 < path.size()) {
      LocationValue last = path.get(path.size() - 1);
      if (last.distanceTo(loc) < loc.accuracy + last.accuracy) continue;
    }
    path.add(0, loc);
    String url = "https://maps.googleapis.com/maps/api/streetview?location=" +
                loc.latitude + "," + loc.longitude +
                "&size=512x512&fov=90&pitch=-10&sensor=false&key=" + apiKey;
```

```
    images.add(requestImage(url));
  }
  if (0 < images.size()) {
    PImage img = images.get(images.size() - 1);
    if (0 < img.width && 0 < img.height) {
      image(img, 0, 0, width, height);
    }
  }
}
...
```

We add the requested images for each new location to the street array list and then draw the last one in the list when it has finished downloading, like we did in Listing 9-6.

■ **Note** If you use a version control service, such as GitHub, to store your code projects, be careful of not uploading your API keys to public repositories that anyone can access. If you committed sensitive data into a public Git repository, this article explains how to completely remove it: `https://docs.github.com/en/ authentication/keeping-your-account-and-data-secure/removing-sensitive-data-from- a-repository`.

Making a Simple Image Collage

Our previous sketch shows an image from Google Street View corresponding to the last location of the phone. As we move around with our phone, the image keeps changing. A simple way to combine these images, inspired by the collages in Figure 9-4, could be to take a vertical strip from each new image and put them next to each other to form a long panorama-style composite. In Chapter 6, we learned how to crop an image with PImage.get(), and this function will become handy here as well. Let's look at the code in Listing 9-8, where we load five images into a PImage array and then use get() to crop a rectangular piece of each image to create our first collage.

Listing 9-8. Cropping images to create a collage

```
PImage[] images;

void setup () {
  size(1000, 400);
  images = new PImage[5];
  for (int i = 0; i < 5; i++) {
    images[i] = loadImage("streetview" + (i + 1) + ".jpg");
  }
}

void draw() {
  background(0);
  for (int i = 0; i < 5; i++) {
    PImage crop = images[i].get(200, 56, 200, 400);
    image(crop, i * 200, 0);
  }
}
```

We can see the output of this code in Figure 9-5, as generated on a desktop (we should see a similar result with the Android mode). We can play with this collage by adding more images or by cropping thinner strips from the original images.

Figure 9-5. *Output of the code in Listing 9-8, a panorama stitching five images together*

However, there is one problem with the code in Listing 9-8. Because we are running the cropping in the draw() function, if we load many images or they have high resolutions, our sketch may slow down. Besides, nothing is really changing in our collage, so it would be much more efficient if we generate the collage once in setup() and we just display it in draw() instead of regenerating it in every frame. But how can we do this? One way is to use an off-screen drawing buffer. We can think of this buffer as a piece of paper where we make our drawing outside of the screen. Once we have completed the drawing, we can show the piece of paper onscreen as many times as we want.

Processing allows to create such offscreen buffers with the createGraphics(width, height) function, which returns a PGraphics object (https://processing.org/reference/PGraphics.html). This object represents a buffer with the requested resolution, and a great feature of the PGraphics objects is that we can use all the APIs we have learned so far to draw onto them. There are two important things to remember while using a PGraphics object as a drawing surface: first, to enclose all calls to draw on a PGraphics buffer between beginDraw() and endDraw(), and second, the calls must be done on the object itself. Listing 9-9 illustrates these concepts by re-implementing the collage we had in the previous listing, but this time using offscreen rendering with PGraphics.

Listing 9-9. Using PGraphics to create the collage during setup

```
PGraphics collage;

void setup () {
  size(1000, 400);
  collage = createGraphics(1000, 400);
  collage.beginDraw();
   for (int i = 0; i < 5; i++) {
    PImage source = loadImage("streetview" + (i + 1) + ".jpg");
    PImage crop = source.get(200, 56, 200, 400);
    collage.image(crop, i * 200, 0);
  }
  collage.endDraw();
}
```

```
void draw() {
  image(collage, 0, 0);
}
```

Putting Everything Together

In the last section, we generated a collage with a set of predefined Street View images. We can now combine that code with our earlier sketches that retrieved the device's location from the available location services. We will use the latitude and longitude values to assemble the HTTPS request to obtain a new Street View image, as we did in Listing 9-7, and append this image to a list of images from which we can generate a dynamic collage as the location changes. With these considerations in mind, let's look at the full code in Listing 9-10.

Listing 9-10. Street View collage

```
import android.content.Context;
import android.location.Location;
import android.location.LocationListener;
import android.location.LocationManager;
import android.os.Bundle;

LocationManager manager;
SimpleListener listener;
String provider;
LocationQueue queue = new LocationQueue();
ArrayList<LocationValue> path = new ArrayList<LocationValue>();
ArrayList<PImage> images = new ArrayList<PImage>();
PGraphics collage;
String apiKey = "<your API key>";

void setup () {
  fullScreen();
  orientation(LANDSCAPE);
  collage = createGraphics(width, height);
  collage.beginDraw();
  collage.background(0);
  collage.endDraw();
  requestPermission("android.permission.ACCESS_FINE_LOCATION", "initLocation");
}

void draw() {
  updateCollage();
  image(collage, 0, 0);
}

void updateCollage() {
  while (queue.available()) {
    LocationValue loc = queue.remove();
    if (0 < path.size()) {
      LocationValue last = path.get(path.size() - 1);
```

```
      if (last.distanceTo(loc) < loc.accuracy + last.accuracy) continue;
    }
    path.add(0, loc);
    String url = "https://maps.googleapis.com/maps/api/streetview?location=" +
                  loc.latitude + "," + loc.longitude +
                  "&size=512x512&fov=90&pitch=-10&sensor=false&key=" + apiKey;
    images.add(requestImage(url));
    if (10 < images.size()) {
      images.remove(0);
    }

    for (int i = 0; i < images.size(); i++) {
      collage.beginDraw();
      PImage source = images.get(i);
      PImage crop = source.get(200, 56, 200, 400);
      float w = float(width) / 10;
      collage.image(crop, i * w, 0, w, height);
      collage.endDraw();
    }
  }
}

void initLocation(boolean granted) {
  if (granted) {
    Context context = getContext();
    listener = new SimpleListener();
    manager = (LocationManager) context.getSystemService(Context.LOCATION_SERVICE);
    provider = LocationManager.NETWORK_PROVIDER;
    if (manager.isProviderEnabled(LocationManager.GPS_PROVIDER)) {
      provider = LocationManager.GPS_PROVIDER;
    }
    manager.requestLocationUpdates(provider, 1000, 1, listener);
  }
}

class SimpleListener implements LocationListener {
  public void onLocationChanged(Location loc) {
    queue.add(new LocationValue(loc.getLatitude(), loc.getLongitude(), loc.getAccuracy()));
  }
  public void onProviderDisabled(String provider) { }
  public void onProviderEnabled(String provider) { }
  public void onStatusChanged(String provider, int status, Bundle extras) { }
}

public void resume() {
  if (manager != null) {
    manager.requestLocationUpdates(provider, 1000, 1, listener);
  }
}
```

```
public void pause() {
  if (manager != null) {
    manager.removeUpdates(listener);
  }
}

class LocationValue {
  double latitude;
  double longitude;
  double accuracy;

  LocationValue(double lat, double lon, double acc) {
    latitude = lat;
    longitude = lon;
    accuracy = acc;
  }

  double distanceTo(LocationValue dest) {
    double a1 = radians((float)latitude);
    double a2 = radians((float)longitude);
    double b1 = radians((float)dest.latitude);
    double b2 = radians((float)dest.longitude);

    double t1 = Math.cos(a1) * Math.cos(a2) * Math.cos(b1) * Math.cos(b2);
    double t2 = Math.cos(a1) * Math.sin(a2) * Math.cos(b1) * Math.sin(b2);
    double t3 = Math.sin(a1) * Math.sin(b1);
    double tt = Math.acos(t1 + t2 + t3);

    return 6366000 * tt;
  }
}

class LocationQueue {
  LocationValue[] values = new LocationValue[10];
  int offset, count;

  synchronized void add(LocationValue val) {
    if (count == values.length) {
      values = (LocationValue[]) expand(values);
    }
    values[count++] = val;
  }

  synchronized LocationValue remove() {
    if (offset == count) {
      return null;
    }
    LocationValue outgoing = values[offset++];
```

```
    if (offset == count) {
      offset = 0;
      count = 0;
    }
    return outgoing;
  }

  synchronized boolean available() {
    return 0 < count;
  }
}
```

Most of this sketch should be familiar from Listing 9-7, so let's focus on the new code in the `updateCollage()` function. The first part is very similar to what we had before: removing new locations from the queue, skipping them if they are too close to the previous depending on the accuracy of the location values, and otherwise adding them to the path. We also generate the corresponding Street View request and append the resulting `PImage` object at the end of the images array list. If this list grows over ten elements, we remove its first element, so it always contains the Street View images of the latest ten locations. We finally crop a rectangle of 200 by 400 pixels from the left edge of each image and draw it on the collage PGraphics buffer. Since we update the collage only when a new location is received, the sketch should run smoothly.

We can run this sketch as a regular app or as a live wallpaper (in the second case, we may want to use the `wallpaperPreview()` function so the location permission is requested only after the wallpaper is selected). Some examples of the output are shown in Figure 9-6. If we plan to distribute it via the Play Store, we will also have to create a full set of icons; write down the full package and name of the app, as well as the version, in its manifest file; and export a release package, as we did for the final projects in Chapters 3 and 6.

Figure 9-6. *A Street View collage generated with the final sketch*

Summary

In this chapter, we explored the possibilities offered by the Android location API in detail and how we can use it in the Android mode in Processing to experiment with geolocation in combination with other technologies such as Google Street View. As we just saw, Processing gives us a lot of freedom to access different data sources (GPS, images, etc.) but also provides a solid framework to successfully integrate these sources so we can turn our ideas into concrete apps.

PART IV

■ ■ ■

Wearables and Watch Faces

CHAPTER 10

Wearable Devices

In this chapter, we will learn how to use Processing to create watch faces for Android smartwatches. We will go through the specific features and limitations of wearable devices that we should take into consideration when writing apps to use on these devices.

From Activity Trackers to Smartwatches

We may think of phones and tablets first when considering mobile development, but wearable devices have been used by many people since the introduction of fitness trackers such as the Fitbit back in 2009 and more recently with digital smartwatches from Apple and several Android manufacturers. With the rapid advance of sensing technology and decrease in size of the electronic components, these devices can perform a wide array of functions, well beyond counting steps and heartbeats. In fact, a smartwatch in 2023 has most of the capabilities of a smartphone (2D and 3D graphics, touchscreen, location and movement sensors, Wi-Fi connectivity). Due to small size and weight, one defining feature of these devices is their portability, which makes them "wearable" in the full sense of the word.

The Android platform provides support for all these devices through Wear OS (`https://developer.android.com/training/wearables`), formerly called Android Wear. Devices running Wear 1.x need to be paired with an Android phone running Android 4.3 and higher (or with an iPhone with iOS 8.2 and higher) to enable all the functionality in the device (e.g., displaying email and message notifications from the phone), but since Wear 2.x, it is possible to run stand-alone apps that don't require pairing the watch with a phone. Wear OS 3, launched in 2022, represents a major update in the platform, and most older watches cannot be updated to version 3. Many types of apps are available for smartwatches, including watch faces, which are a special kind of app that runs as the background of the watch, like live wallpapers, and are meant to display the time and other relevant information, such as physical activity.

Processing for Android allows us to run a sketch as a watch face on Android smartwatches, but not as a general Wear OS app. All the drawing, interaction, and sensing API discussed in previous chapters is applicable for watch faces, with a few additions that allow to handle some unique aspects of smartwatches.

▓ **Note** Version 4.5 and newer of the Android mode can be used to create watch faces for smartwatches running Android Wear 3.0 or higher. It does not support Wear 1.x or 2.x devices.

© Andrés Colubri 2023
A. Colubri, *Processing for Android*, https://doi.org/10.1007/978-1-4842-9585-4_10

Smartwatches

Several electronics companies sell Android smartwatches, and because of that, there is a wide range of models with different specifications and styles. Figure 10-1 shows a small selection of Android watches released since 2022.

Figure 10-1. *A selection of Android smartwatches, from left to right: Google Pixel Watch, Samsung Galaxy Watch 5, Fossil Gen 6, and TicWatch Pro 3*

Even though there is a wide selection of Wear OS watches, all of them must conform to a minimum baseline of technical specifications. Starting with Android Wear 1.x, compatible watches are required to have (round or square) displays with density between 200 and 300 dpi (within the hdpi range), Wi-Fi and Bluetooth connectivity, accelerometer, gyroscope, and typically heart rate sensors, with 4GB of internal storage, and a battery time of up to two days of mixed use (fully active vs. battery-saving "ambient" mode). Wear OS 3 increased the minimum bar specially on the CPU front to ensure that the newer devices are more performant and have longer battery life. Also, it only works with phones running Android 6.0+ or iOS 13.0+.

Running Watch Face Sketches

Just like Processing sketches that we can run as regular apps either on an actual device or in the emulator, we can also run our watch face sketches on a watch or in the emulator. The process of debugging on a physical device is generally more convenient, since the emulator is typically slower and not capable of simulating all sensor data that we might need to debug our watch face, but the emulator gives us the possibility of running our watch face in case we don't have an Android watch yet, or to test different display configurations.

Using a Watch

To run a Processing sketch on an Android watch, we first need to enable "Developer Options" on the watch. The steps to do so are the following (they may differ slightly between watches from different manufacturers):

1. Open the Settings menu on the watch.

2. Scroll to the bottom of the menu and tap "System ➤ About".

3. Tap the "Build number" seven times.

4. From the Settings menu, tap Developer Options.

5. Confirm that "ADB debugging" is enabled.

Once we have enabled the Developer Options, we have two alternatives to run and debug our watch face sketches on a Wear OS 3 watch: Wi-Fi and Bluetooth. The developer guide from Google on debugging Wear apps goes through all the details (`https://developer.android.com/training/wearables/get-started/debugging`), and here, we will review the most important steps.

With Bluetooth, the watch must be paired with the phone. So first we need to enable Bluetooth debugging on both devices. On the watch, by opening the "Settings ➤ Developer Options" and enabling "Debug Over Bluetooth". On the phone, we would need to install and open the corresponding companion app from the watch's manufacturer, since the earlier "Wear OS by Google Smartwatch" companion app that used to work with any watch is not compatible with Wear OS 3 devices. Once you have installed the companion app, you would need to find the option to enable debugging over Bluetooth. Refer to the manufacturer's instructions on how to do this. Once we have completed these steps, Processing should be able to connect to the watch via its Bluetooth pairing with the phone.

■ **Note** If the watch is paired with a phone over Bluetooth and this phone is the only device plugged to the computer through USB, then Processing will be able to connect to the watch automatically. But if there is more than one phone, then you need to connect the watch manually with the adb command "./adb -s ID forward tcp:4444 localabstract:/adb-hub" providing the ID of the phone the watch is paired to and followed by "adb connect 127.0.0.1:4444".

In the case of Wi-Fi, both the computer we are running Processing on and the watch must be connected to the same Wi-Fi network. Then, we need to enable Wi-Fi debugging on the watch by going to "Settings ➤ Developer Options" and enabling "Debug over Wi-Fi". Next, we would get the watch's IP address on the Wi-Fi network (e.g., 192.168.0.12) by navigating to "Settings ➤ Connections" and selecting the active Wi-Fi connection to see the details, including the assigned IP address. Once we have obtained the IP address of the watch, we will open a terminal and from there, change to the platform-tools folder inside the Android SDK and run the command "adb connect <id address of watch>", shown here with an IP address of 192.168.0.228:

```
$ cd ~/Documents/Processing/android/sdk/platform-tools
$ ./adb connect 192.168.0.228
```

Once we have connected the watch either via Wi-Fi or Bluetooth, we should see it in the list of devices under the "Android" menu. Also, we need to make sure to select the "Watch Face" option, since Processing will not allow to run other type of sketch on a watch (Figure 10-2).

Figure 10-2. *Running a sketch as watch face and listing a connected watch*

After connecting to our watch either via Bluetooth or Wi-Fi, we can try Listing 10-1 to run an animated watch face.

Listing 10-1. Simple animated watch face

```
void setup() {
  fullScreen();
  strokeCap(ROUND);
  stroke(255);
  noFill();
}

void draw() {
  background(0);
  if (wearAmbient()) strokeWeight(1);
  else strokeWeight(10);
  float angle = map(millis() % 60000, 0, 60000, 0, TWO_PI);
  arc(width/2, height/2, width/2, width/2, 0, angle);
}
```

Once Processing has installed the sketch on the device as a watch face, we need to select it as the active watch face. To do this, long-press the main screen to access the list of favorite watch faces. If ours does not show up in this list, tap on "Add more watch faces" at the rightmost end of the list, and there you should find the sketch, possibly among other available watch faces. Select it there first, and once it is added to the favorite list, you can tap on it to set it as the current background. The output would look like the one shown in Figure 10-3.

Figure 10-3. *Output of the first watch face example*

We may notice that the watch face will likely not look like in this figure all the time. After a few seconds, the watch will enter "ambient mode," where the display is updated only once every minute. The purpose of this mode is to save battery when we are not looking at the watch. As soon as the watch detects (using its accelerometer) the typical gesture of turning the wrist to look at the time, then it will return to the interactive mode. The developer guides from Google recommend setting most of the screen to a black background when in ambient mode while drawing the remaining graphic elements with thin white lines. As we can see in the code, Processing gives us the wearAmbient() function to detect whether the watch is in ambient mode or not and update the graphics accordingly.

Using the Emulator

We saw in Chapter 1 that we need to install a system image to run a phone Android Virtual Device (AVD) in the emulator, as well as decide whether we want to use ARM or x86 images. In the case of watch faces, we can also use the emulator, and to do so, we need to install a separate watch AVD for the emulator to use. The first time we run sketch as a watch face in the emulator, we should see a dialog asking us to download the watch system image (Figure 10-4), followed by the ARM/x86 selection. Once the image (and the HAXM software for x86 images, as we also discussed in Chapter 1) is downloaded and installed, Processing will continue by copying the sketch into the emulator and informing us once the sketch has been installed successfully as a watch face.

Figure 10-4. *Dialog to download the watch system image*

Similarly with physical devices, we need to select our watch face to set it as the current background, following an identical series of steps, which are shown in Figure 10-5: adding the watch face to the list of favorites and then selecting it from that list.

Figure 10-5. *Selecting a watch face in the emulator*

Processing by default creates a square watch AVD, with a 280×280 resolution. However, in Chapter 3, we also learned that we could create other AVDs with the avdmanager command-line tool. Processing will run our sketches on these AVDs, if we launch them with the emulator tool on the right port. For instance, let's create a round watch AVD with the "wear_round_360_300dpi" device definition and launch it on port 5576 so we can use it from Processing. The commands to do this are shown in the following (after creating the AVD, remember to add the skin parameter to its config.ini file, as we saw in Chapter 3). The resulting emulator running our sketch in the round watch AVD is shown in Figure 10-6.

```
$ cd ~/Documents/Processing/android/sdk
$  cmdline-tools/latest/bin/avdmanager create avd -n round-watch -k "system-
images;android-30;android-wear;x86" -d "wear_round_360_300dpi" -p ~/Documents/Processing/
android/avd/round-watch
$ emulator/emulator -avd round-watch -gpu auto -port 5576
```

Figure 10-6. *Running our watch face sketch in the custom AVD*

Displaying Time

The display of time is one of the basic functions of a watch, and with Processing, we would be able to create any visual representation of time we could imagine. Processing offers a number of functions to obtain the current time and date: year(), month(), day(), hour(), minute(), and second(), which will allow us to generate our own time visualizations. As a simple example, in Listing 10-2, we show the time using text.

Listing 10-2. Displaying the time as text

```
void setup() {
  fullScreen();
  frameRate(1);
  textFont(createFont("Serif-Bold", 48));
  textAlign(CENTER, CENTER);
  fill(255);
}
```

```
void draw() {
  background(0);
  if (wearInteractive()) {
    String str = hour() + ":" + nfs(minute(), 2) + ":" + nfs(second(), 2);
    text(str, width/2, height/2);
  }
}
```

Notice that we use frameRate(1). Since we are showing the time down to seconds, there is no need to run the sketch at a higher frame rate, which also helps at saving battery. The nfs() function conveniently adds zeros to the right of the number so the resulting string always has two digits. Finally, wearInteractive() simply returns the opposite of the wearAmbient() function, which we used in our first watch face.

Counting Steps

We can access the sensors available in our watch with the same techniques we saw in the previous chapters, either through the Android API or with the Ketai library. We will investigate the possibilities of body sensing in Chapter 12, but here in Listing 10-3, we have a simple step counter example with the Android sensor API.

Listing 10-3. Simple step counter

```
import android.content.Context;
import android.hardware.Sensor;
import android.hardware.SensorManager;
import android.hardware.SensorEvent;
import android.hardware.SensorEventListener;

Context context;
SensorManager manager;
Sensor sensor;
SensorListener listener;

int offset = -1;
int steps;

void setup() {
  fullScreen();
  frameRate(1);
  textAlign(CENTER, CENTER);
  fill(255);
  requestPermission("android.permission.ACTIVITY_RECOGNITION", "handlePermission");
}

void draw() {
  background(0);
  if (wearInteractive()) {
    String str = steps + " steps";
    float w = textWidth(str);
    text(str, width/2, height/2);
  }
}
```

```
void resume() {
if (manager != null)
  manager.registerListener(listener, sensor,
                           SensorManager.SENSOR_DELAY_NORMAL);
}

void pause() {
  if (manager != null) manager.unregisterListener(listener);
}

class SensorListener implements SensorEventListener {
  public void onSensorChanged(SensorEvent event) {
    if (offset == -1) offset = (int)event.values[0];
    steps = (int)event.values[0] - offset;
  }
  public void onAccuracyChanged(Sensor sensor, int accuracy) { }
}

void handlePermission(boolean granted) {
  if (granted) {
    Context context = (Context) surface.getComponent();
    manager = (SensorManager)context.getSystemService(Context.SENSOR_SERVICE);
    sensor = manager.getDefaultSensor(Sensor.TYPE_STEP_COUNTER);
    listener = new SensorListener();
    manager.registerListener(listener, sensor, SensorManager.SENSOR_DELAY_NORMAL);
  }
}
```

Since the values returned by the step counter sensor (which is not an actual hardware sensor but a "derived" sensor that uses information from the accelerometer to compute the steps) are cumulative from the time the watch booted up, we store the first value to start the counting since the moment that watch face is open. And as we discussed in Chapters 6 and 8, accessing step counter data requires requesting the user to grant the ACTIVITY_RECOGNITION permission using the requestPermission() function and to select the ACTIVITY_RECOGNITION in the Android Permissions Selector in the PDE.

Designing for Smartwatches

The possibility of using Processing's drawing API to create watch faces opens countless directions for representation of time in combination with contextual and sensor data. However, the limited size of smartwatch displays presents us with some challenges in terms of visual design and information density. We will look more deeply into these challenges in the next two chapters.

The official Google developer site includes a section specifically on face watch design and development (https://developer.android.com/training/wearables/watch-faces), which provides some useful guidance on design concepts and language, as well as how to handle aspects unique to smartwatches.

Adjusting for Screen Shape

A first important aspect to consider is adapting the graphics of the watch face to both round and square displays so that our visual design works effectively under both scenarios.

■ **Note** Even if the display is round, the width and height values refer to the largest extent of the display along the horizontal and vertical directions.

You can determine the shape of the screen by calling the wearRound() or the wearSquare() function, which will return true for round/square screens and false otherwise, as demonstrated in Listing 10-4.

Listing 10-4. Adjusting graphics to the screen shape

```
void setup() {
  fullScreen();
  if (wearSquare()) rectMode(CENTER);
}

void draw() {
  background(0);
  if (wearAmbient()) {
    stroke(255);
    noFill();
  } else {
    noStroke();
    fill(255);
  }
  float scale = map(second(), 0, 59, 0, 1);
  if (wearRound()) {
    ellipse(width/2, height/2, scale * width, scale * width);
  } else {
    rect(width/2, height/2, scale * width, scale * height);
  }
}
```

Watch Face Preview Icons

In addition to the regular app icons that we discussed in Chapter 3, Wear OS requires a set of preview icons to show the watch face in the selection list. The regular icons will be used in other parts of the UI, such as the app info/uninstall menu.

Since the watch can be either round or square, we need to provide only two preview icons: one for the round case (with 320×320 pixels resolution) and the other for the square case (with 280×280 pixels resolution). Both icons need to be copied into the sketch's folder and must have the names preview_circular. png and preview_rectangular.png.

Only the area covered by the largest circle enclosed in the 320×320 square in the circular icon will be displayed in the watch face selector (Figure 10-7), whereas the entire rectangular image will be used in the selector. When exporting the sketch as a signed package, Processing will not let us complete the export until all eight icons – six regular icons for ldpi, mdpi, hdpi, xhdpi, xxhdpi, and xxxhdpi resolutions and two preview icons – are included in the sketch folder.

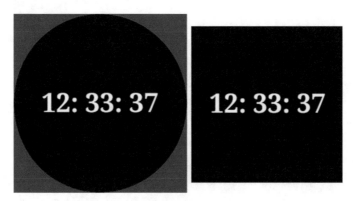

Figure 10-7. *Preview images for round (left) and square (right) devices. The red portion in the round preview will be ignored*

Summary

In this first chapter about Android smartwatches, we learned the basics about wearable devices and apps and how to create watch faces for these small but powerful devices. We also looked in detail at the setup required to connect Processing either to actual watches or the emulator to test our watch face sketches across different display configurations.

CHAPTER 11

■ ■ ■

Visualizing Time

The display of time is one of the main functions of any clock, including smartwatches, and in this chapter, we will learn how to apply Processing's drawing API to experiment with different visual representations of time.

From Sundials to Smartwatches

The visual representation of time dates to the beginnings of civilization, when sundials were used to keep track of the time during the day hours. Mechanical pocket and then smaller wristwatches have been in use since the 16th century. In the digital era, electronic watches with multiple features became popular only a few decades ago. The long history of the machines for the measuring and display of time (Figure 11-1) gives us a rich technical and cultural background to draw inspiration from, or to re-interpret the representation of time with the nearly boundless possibilities of the digital canvas of the smartwatch.

Figure 11-1. *From left to right: Sundial at the Imperial Palace in Beijing (8th century AC), design for a ring watch from Livre d'Aneaux d'Orfevrerie (1561), a late Victorian silver open faced pocket watch (~1890), and Casio DBC 600 digital calculator watch (1985)*

Although we can already find hundreds of different watch faces on the Google Play Store, many of them translate physical watch faces into realistic digital representations. This is a perfectly fine approach, but the digital canvas also allows us to represent time in entirely new ways. Figure 11-2 shows some examples of Android watch faces, all available on the Google Play Store, which demonstrate some interesting ideas: from eyes staring back to the user and abstract patterns, to whimsical animations representing the passage of time, and re-interpretations of an analog watch face using animated digital dials.

© Andrés Colubri 2023
A. Colubri, *Processing for Android*, https://doi.org/10.1007/978-1-4842-9585-4_11

Figure 11-2. *From left to right: Gaze Effect (by Fathom Information Design), Domino (by ustwo), Space and Time (by Geng Gao), and Radii (by The Design Cycle)*

■ **Note**   In order to take a screenshot of a watch face, we can use the adb tool in the Android SDK, first to save the screen grab to an image file on the watch: "adb -s 127.0.0.1:4444 shell screencap -p /sdcard/screenshot.png", and then to download the resulting image to the computer: "adb -s 127.0.0.1:4444 pull -p /sdcard/screenshot.png".

Using Time to Control Motion

Processing includes a time API that allows us to obtain the current time and date. Let's begin by using hours, minutes, and seconds to control a simple animation. If we were to work with a digital implementation of an analog concept, such as rotating hands, the transformation between time and angular values is straightforward: we can map the values between their respective ranges, for instance, between 0 and 60 for minutes and seconds, and 0 to 2π for angles. This mapping is demonstrated in Listing 11-1.

Listing 11-1. Concentric circles for seconds, minutes, and hours

```
void setup() {
  noStroke();
  strokeWeight(2);
}

void draw() {
  background(0);

  float hAngle = map(hour() % 12, 0, 12, 0, TWO_PI);
  float mAngle = map(minute(), 0, 60, 0, TWO_PI);
  float sAngle = map(second(), 0, 60, 0, TWO_PI);

  translate(width/2, height/2);
  fill(ambientMode ? 0 : #F0DB3F);
  ellipse(0, 0, width, width);
  drawLine(hAngle, width/2);

  fill(ambientMode ? 0 : #FFB25F);
  ellipse(0, 0, 0.75 * width, 0.75 * width);
  drawLine(mAngle, 0.75 * width/2);
```

```
  fill(ambientMode ? 0 : #ED774D);
  ellipse(0, 0, 0.5 * width, 0.5 * width);
  drawLine(sAngle, 0.5 * width/2);

  fill(0);
  ellipse(0, 0, 0.25 * width, 0.25 * width);
}

void drawLine(float a, float r) {
  pushStyle();
  stroke(wearAmbient() ? 255 : 0);
  pushMatrix();
  rotate(a);
  line(0, 0, 0, -r);
  popMatrix();
  popStyle();
}
```

The output of this sketch (Figure 11-3) is three concentric circles, where the lines correspond to the hands for hour, minute, and second. Since the lines are drawn from the center of the screen pointing upward, which is the typical reference position in an analog watch, the rotation can be applied directly between 0 and TWO_PI.

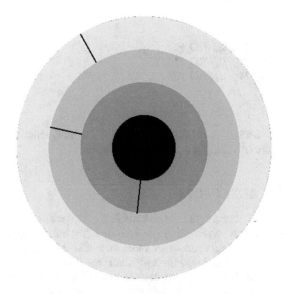

Figure 11-3. *Concentric circles watch face*

Once we run this simple watch face on the device or in the emulator, we should be able to notice that the animation of the hands is not smooth. The innermost circle jumps from one second to the next, and the reason is that we are not interpolating the intermediate angles between two consecutive seconds. One solution to this problem is to use the millis() function. This function returns the milliseconds elapsed since the sketch started running. We can calculate the difference between consecutive millis() calls to obtain the difference in milliseconds between two points in time and use it to create a smoother animation.

More concretely, if we add two new variables to our previous sketch, for example, s0 and m0, we can keep track of the moment when the value of the second changes (either by incrementing by one or resetting to zero), store the milliseconds at that moment, and then use it to compute the fraction of the second we are at each successive moment. This is in fact easier done than said, and Listing 11-2 shows the additions to our previous sketch to make this work.

Listing 11-2. Concentric circles with second animation

```
void draw() {
  background(0);

  int h = hour() % 12;
  int m = minute();
  int s = second();

  if (s0 != s) {
    m0 = millis();
    s0 = s;
  }
  float f = (millis() - m0)/1000.0;

  float sf = s + f;
  float mf = m + sf/60.0;
  float hf = h + mf/60.0;

  float hAngle = map(hf, 0, 12, 0, TWO_PI);
  float mAngle = map(mf, 0, 60, 0, TWO_PI);
  float sAngle = map(sf, 0, 60, 0, TWO_PI);
...
}
```

The sf, mf, and hf are the decimal second, minute, and hour values, which we can map to the angular ranges as we did before, but now resulting in a continuous rotation.

Square vs. Round Watch Faces

Android smartwatches can have either a square or a round frame, and we need to accommodate our watch face design to work with both, or at least prioritize one over the other, but still providing a usable experience with either one. The preference of round over square watches, and vice versa, is a contested topic in watch UI design: "In my experience, round-faced watches sell better than square-faced watches. I don't know exactly why that is [...] It's most likely purely psychological; people's semantic notion of what a clock or a watch should look like" (www.wareable.com/smartwatches/round-v-square-smartwatches-which-is-best), while on the opposite side: "I think that Round's days are numbered. We underestimate people's ability to get used to new things, to new paradigms. I think the experience of using a more squared watch will make more sense to people when they use both, and they will come around" (https://birchtree.me/blog/data-is-square).

Regardless of which format ends up being preferred by people, Android supports both (although it seems to promote the round format more strongly, probably as a differentiator from the square Apple Watch), and it is up to us to come up with designs that contemplate square and round watches. As an illustration on this problem, let's go ahead with a simple design for a square watch face: a rectangular grid with 24 squares, split into 6 rows and 4 columns. Each square corresponds to one hour, hours that already have passed are entirely grayed out, and the current hour is grayed out up to the percentage given by the current minute. An implementation of this design is presented in Listing 11-3.

Listing 11-3. Rectangular hour grid

```
void setup() {
  textFont(createFont("Monospaced", 15 * displayDensity));
  textAlign(CENTER, CENTER);
  noStroke();
}

void draw() {
  background(0);
  int h = hour();
  int m = minute();
  float cellW = 0.9 * width/4.0;
  float cellH = 0.9 * height/6.0;
  translate(0.05 * cellW, 0.05 * cellH);
  for (int n = 0; n < 24; n++) {
    int i = n % 4;
    int j = n / 4;
    float x = map(i, 0, 4, 0, width);
    float y = map(j, 0, 6, 0, height);
    float w = n == h ? map(m, 0, 60, 0, cellW) : cellW;

    if (!wearAmbient()) {
      fill(#578CB7);
      rect(x, y, cellW, cellH);
    }

    fill(255);
    text(str(n), x, y, cellW, cellH);

    if (n <= h) {
      fill(0, 170);
      rect(x, y, w, cellH);
    }
  }
}
```

Since in this watch face we are working with text, we create a monospaced font at a size that is scaled by the `displayDensity` system variable, as we did in other examples before to ensure the consistent appearance of the text across devices with different DPIs. Screen resolution of Android watches is typically between only 300 and 400 pixels, but due to the small screen size, the DPIs are in the xhdpi range (~320dpi).

This design will clearly not work very well on a round-faced watch. We could replace this rectangular grid with a polar one, but in that case, each cell will have a different size, as shown in the left panel of Figure 11-4, and it will also be harder to implement the partial graying out the cell according to the current minute ot the hour. Another alternative could be to still use a rectangular grid, this time of 6×6, and remove the six corner cells that are either entirely or mostly outside of the circumscribed circle (right panel in Figure 11-4).

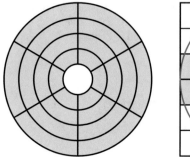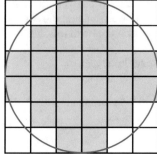

Figure 11-4. Adapting a 6×4 rectangular grid to fit inside a round watch face, either as a polar grid (left) or as a larger 6×6 grid with some elements removed (right)

The option here will depend on the desired visual result, and in certain cases, the polar grid might be a better choice, while the trimmed rectangular grid in others. Since our priority is to keep all the elements with the same size, here, we chose the latter in Listing 11-4.

Listing 11-4. Rectangular grid for a circular watch

```
import java.util.Arrays;
import java.util.List;
List<Integer> corners = Arrays.asList(1, 2, 5, 6, 7, 12, 25,
                                      30, 31, 32, 35, 36);

void setup() {
  textFont(createFont("Monospaced", 15 * displayDensity));
  textAlign(CENTER, CENTER);
  noStroke();
}

void draw() {
  background(0);
  int h = hour();
  int m = minute();
  float cellW = 0.9 * width/6.0;
  float cellH = 0.9 * height/6.0;
  translate(0.05 * cellW, 0.05 * cellH);
  int n = 0;
  for (int n0 = 0; n0 < 36; n0++) {
    if (corners.contains(n0 + 1)) continue;

    int i = n0 % 6;
    int j = n0 / 6;
    float x = map(i, 0, 6, 0, width);
    float y = map(j, 0, 6, 0, height);
    float cw = n == h ? map(m, 0, 60, 0, cellW) : cellW;
```

```
  if (!wearAmbient()) {
    fill(#578CB7);
    rect(x, y, cellW, cellH);
  }

  fill(255);
  text(str(n), x, y, cellW, cellH);

  if (n <= h) {
    fill(0, 170);
    rect(x, y, cw, cellH);
  }
  n++;
 }
}
```

The output of these two watch faces can be seen in Figure 11-5. The code of the two sketches can be combined into a single watch face that selects the appropriate visualization depending on the value returned by the wearRound() or wearSquare() function.

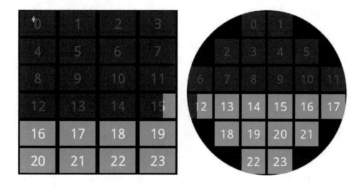

Figure 11-5. *Hour grid for square (left) and round (right) watches*

Working with a Watch Face Concept

Creating a watch face involves balancing several factors. As we mentioned at the beginning of this chapter, there is an established visual language that people expect to communicate time. Smartwatches give us the opportunity to expand upon this existing language, as well as to come up with entirely new concepts. In addition to that, watch faces can be interactive, configurable, and augmented with additional information (physical activity, calendar events, etc.) Some of these considerations are covered in the design guide from Google (https://developer.android.com/training/wearables/watch-faces/designing), but playful experimentation can lead us to new ideas for displaying time.

As we saw with the development of other types of apps, one methodology that remains equally powerful when designing watch faces is sketching and iteration. A concept might be original and attractive but is unlikely that it will be successful in its first implementation. In the next sections, we will carry one concept through several iterations until reaching a final version.

Elapsed/Remaining Time

The concept for this watch face is not so much to serve as a functional timepiece but rather to provide a reminder of the amount of time elapsed since the beginning of the day and the remaining time until it ends. To accentuate this progression, we can measure time in total seconds since and from midnight and display it as it changes continuously from and toward zero.

As a visual representation of this progression, the waxing crescent of the moon could work as a metaphor for the diminishing day (Figure 11-6). Of course, this is not the only visual representation possible (and one could argue that it would mislead users to think the watch face is displaying the actual phases of the moon), but it should be fine as our first design.

Figure 11-6. *Crescent moon*

Bézier curves become handy to create the shape of the waxing crescent, by partially covering an ellipse with a shape containing the edge of the dark region, which is illustrated by the diagrams in Figure 11-7.

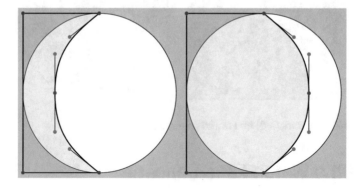

Figure 11-7. *Drawing a waxing crescent moon with Bézier curves*

As the elapsed seconds increase from 0 to 86,400 (24*60*60), the control vectors of the Bézier curve at the top and bottom of the shape should transition from being completely horizontal, pointing toward the left side of the screen, to completely horizontal but pointing toward the left and going through the vertical direction exactly at midday. So we could map the seconds to an angular value from PI to 0 and then use it to calculate the control points.

The code in Listing 11-5 implements this idea. It also shows the remaining seconds as text, which is scaled up or down according to the space left in the visible crescent.

Listing 11-5. Moon watch face

```
int totSec = 24 * 60 * 60;
PFont font;

void setup() {
  font = createFont("Serif", 62);
  textAlign(LEFT, CENTER);
}

void draw() {
  background(0);
  int sec = 60 * 60 * hour() + 60 * minute() + second();
  float a = map(sec, 0, totSec, PI, 0);
  float x = map(sec, 0, totSec, 0, width);
  float r = sec < totSec/2 ? map(sec, 0, totSec/2, 90, 50) :
                             map(sec, totSec/2, totSec, 50, 90);

  int t = totSec - sec;
  String strt = str(t);
  int n = strt.length();
  float d = (width - x) / n;
  textFont(font, 1.75 * d);

  float rad = 0.5 * width;
  float diam = width;
  if (wearAmbient()) {
    fill(255);
    text(strt, x, rad);
  } else {
    fill(255);
    ellipse(rad, rad, diam, diam);
    noStroke();
    fill(0);
    beginShape();
    vertex(0, 0);
    vertex(rad, 0);
    float cx = r * cos(a);
    float cy = r * sin(a);
    bezierVertex(rad + cx, cy, x, rad - r, x, rad);
    vertex(x, rad);
    bezierVertex(x, rad + r, rad + cx, diam - cy, rad, diam);
    vertex(0, diam);
    endShape(CLOSE);

    fill(0, 170);
    text(strt, x, rad);
  }
}
```

In this code, we are using a large, non-scaled font size when creating the font for the numbers in the watch face. Since the numbers change size as the space grows and shrinks, we set the original font size as the largest possible so that the text still looks good when resizing it to a smaller value (fuzzy-looking text happens when we create the font with a certain size but then set a larger size for drawing).

Adding Interaction

Watch faces can receive touch events via the touchscreen just as any regular apps in phones and tablets. We can handle these events in Processing using the mousePressed() and mouseReleased() functions. However, dragging events are not supported on watch faces, since they are used by the Android system to drive the swipes that give access to the different menus in the UI. Multi-touch events are not supported either.

Given the small size of the watch screen, touch events are typically meant to toggle between different views in the watch face, and not to drive precise interaction using the X and Y coordinates associated to the touch. In the case of our watch face, we can use a single touch to toggle between showing the elapsed vs. the remaining seconds. The entire code including the new interaction handling is in Listing 11-6.

Listing 11-6. Moon watch face with interaction

```
int totSec = 24 * 60 * 60;
boolean showElapsed = false;
PFont font;

void setup() {
  font = createFont("Serif", 62);
  textAlign(LEFT, CENTER);
}

void draw() {
  background(0);
  int sec = 60 * 60 * hour() + 60 * minute() + second();
  float a = map(sec, 0, totSec, PI, 0);
  float x = map(sec, 0, totSec, 0, width);
  float r = sec < totSec/2 ? map(sec, 0, totSec/2, 90, 50) :
                             map(sec, totSec/2, totSec, 50, 90);

  int t = showElapsed ? sec : totSec - sec;
  String strt = str(t);
  int n = strt.length();
  float d = showElapsed ? x / n : (width - x) / n;
  textFont(font, 1.75 * d);

  float rad = 0.5 * width;
  float diam = width;
  if (wearAmbient()) {
    fill(255);
    text(strt, x, rad);
  } else {
    fill(255);
    ellipse(rad, rad, diam, diam);
    noStroke();
    fill(0);
```

```
    beginShape();
    vertex(0, 0);
    vertex(rad, 0);
    float cx = r * cos(a);
    float cy = r * sin(a);
    bezierVertex(rad + cx, cy, x, rad - r, x, rad);
    vertex(x, rad);
    bezierVertex(x, rad + r, rad + cx, diam - cy, rad, diam);
    vertex(0, diam);
    endShape(CLOSE);

    if (showElapsed) fill(255, 170);
    else fill(0, 170);
    text(strt, x, rad);
  }
}

void mousePressed() {
  showElapsed = !showElapsed;
  if (showElapsed) textAlign(RIGHT, CENTER);
  else textAlign(LEFT, CENTER);
}
```

Loading and Displaying Images

Images are supported in watch faces in the same way as with the rest of Android app types. We can use the loadImage() function to load an image file into our sketch and the image() function to display the image on the screen. With the help of this functionality, we can complete our watch face in Listing 11-7 with an actual image of the moon as the background. Different outputs of the watch face, with and without the background image, are included in Figure 11-8.

Listing 11-7. Moon watch face with background image

```
int totSec = 24 * 60 * 60;
boolean showElapsed = false;
PFont font;
PImage moon;

void setup() {
  moon = loadImage("moon.png");
  font = createFont("Serif", 62);
  textAlign(LEFT, CENTER);
}

void draw() {
  background(0);
  int sec = 60 * 60 * hour() + 60 * minute() + second();
  float a = map(sec, 0, totSec, PI, 0);
  float x = map(sec, 0, totSec, 0, width);
  float r = sec < totSec/2 ? map(sec, 0, totSec/2, 90, 50) :
                             map(sec, totSec/2, totSec, 50, 90);
```

```
    int t = showElapsed ? sec : totSec - sec;
    String strt = str(t);
    int n = strt.length();
    float d = showElapsed ? x / n : (width - x) / n;
    textFont(font, 1.75 * d);

    float rad = 0.5 * width;
    float diam = width;
    if (wearAmbient()) {
      fill(255);
      text(strt, x, rad);
    } else {
      image(moon, 0, 0, 2*rad, 2*rad);
      noStroke();
      fill(0);
      beginShape();
      vertex(0, 0);
      vertex(rad, 0);
      float cx = r * cos(a);
      float cy = r * sin(a);
      bezierVertex(rad + cx, cy, x, rad - r, x, rad);
      vertex(x, rad);
      bezierVertex(x, rad + r, rad + cx, diam - cy, rad, diam);
      vertex(0, diam);
      endShape(CLOSE);

      if (showElapsed) fill(255, 170);
      else fill(200, 230);
      text(strt, x, rad);
    }
}

void mousePressed() {
  showElapsed = !showElapsed;
  if (showElapsed) textAlign(RIGHT, CENTER);
  else textAlign(LEFT, CENTER);
}
```

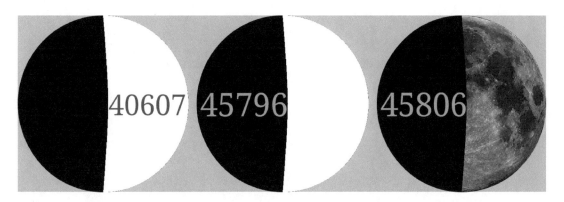

Figure 11-8. *Versions of the "moon" watch face showing remaining seconds in the day, elapsed, and moon texture*

One small change we made in this new version of our watch face was to use a different color for the text of the remaining seconds. In the version without background image, we had a dark gray (0, 170) that offered good contrast with the white background. Now, the moon image is too dark to ensure that the text is readable enough, so we switched to a much brighter gray, set with the color values (200, 230).

Summary

We introduced the topic of watch faces for the display of time. As part of this introduction, we discussed some of the issues one needs to be aware of, starting with the use of time values to implement dynamic visualizations of time, how to adjust our designs to round and square watches, and concluding with an example that showed the importance of iteration in watch face design. These materials should provide readers a first foray into the topic, and many possibilities await to those interested in delving deeper in the development of time watch faces.

CHAPTER 12

Visualizing Physical Activity

In this chapter, we will go over some of the body sensors available on smartwatches, and wearable devices in general, and will learn a few techniques that we have at our disposal to read and use data from these sensors in real time.

Body Sensors

We can find body sensors in many kinds of wearable devices, especially in fitness trackers designed for personal monitoring of physical activity. These devices are often complemented with mobile apps that help the users track their progress over time. Most Android smartwatches come with at least two kinds of body sensors: a pedometer or step counter and a heart rate sensor. This shows some overlap between activity trackers (which also include clock functions) and proper smartwatches.

In the last two chapters, we learned how to use Processing to create animated watch faces, and before that, we went through the details of accessing sensor data using the Android SDK and the Ketai library. We should now be able to combine all this knowledge to create watch faces that read the data from the body sensors on the watch and present this data to the user through a dynamic visualization.

Step Counter

The step counter is the most common sensor of physical activity. It uses data from the accelerometer to infer movement patterns of the person wearing the device and specifically data produced by walking or running. Step count is a proxy for overall physical activity, although of limited accuracy, as it is not able to measure other forms of activity that do not involve walking or running, or the intensity of the movement.

A daily step count of 10,000 is a typically accepted goal for an adequate level of physical activity, but there has been some controversy surrounding this number as a universal target for fitness (https://www.scientificamerican.com/article/you-dont-really-need-10-000-daily-steps-to-stay-healthy/).

Heart Rate

Heart rate is a very precise indicator of physical exertion, and the heart rate monitor on a smartwatch allows us to access this information in real time. We should be aware that optical heart rate monitors, like the ones used in smartwatches, are generally less reliable than other types of monitors. Optical monitors measure heart rate in a process called photoplethysmography, where they shine light, typically from an LED, into the skin and detect the differences in light diffraction due to the changes in blood flow. The watch processes this data to generate a pulse reading that can be displayed back to the user.

© Andrés Colubri 2023
A. Colubri, *Processing for Android*, https://doi.org/10.1007/978-1-4842-9585-4_12

On the other hand, electrocardiogram (ECG) sensors measure the electrical signals from heart activity directly, but they require electrodes attached to different parts of the body, as the first electrocardiographs in the early 20th century (Figure 12-1). Medical ECG sensors can use up to 12 electrodes, but sport chest straps rely on a single ECG sensor placed near the heart. However, optical monitors in smartwatches and other wearables have evolved to be able to monitor heart rate accurately enough and continuously throughout the day with minimal inconvenience.

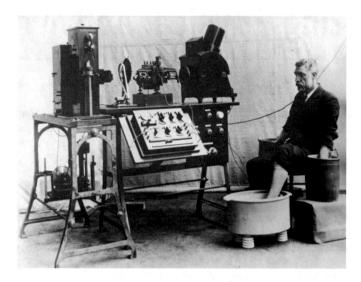

Figure 12-1. *An early electrocardiograph from 1911; the patient had to immerse the arms and one leg in buckets, which contain a saline solution to conduct the body's current. Modern ECG sensors are still based on this three-point principle, but optical sensors rely on a completely different physical process to measure heart rate*

Visualizing Physical Activity in Real Time

Implementing a watch face that displays step count of heart rate data in Processing is not difficult. We can retrieve the sensor data in the same way we did with other sensors before, like the accelerometer and the gyroscope. All we need is to create a sensor manager, get the corresponding sensor object from it, and attach a listener that will return the actual values as they are measured by the hardware.

Simple Step Counter

As discussed in previous chapters, the step counter sensor requires the user to explicitly grant the ACTIVITY_RECOGNITION runtime permission. This sensor runs continuously, even if our watch face does not access it. One particularity is that it returns the number of steps since the last startup of the watch, and it is reset to zero only on a system reboot. Because of this, if we want to show the number of steps since we launched the watch face, we should store the first step count value we receive from the listener and subtract it from all subsequent values, as shown in Listing 12-1.

Listing 12-1. Displaying the step count

```
import android.content.Context;
import android.hardware.Sensor;
import android.hardware.SensorManager;
import android.hardware.SensorEvent;
import android.hardware.SensorEventListener;

Context context;
SensorManager manager;
Sensor sensor;
SensorListener listener;

int offset = -1;
int steps;

void setup() {
  fullScreen();
  frameRate(1);
  textFont(createFont("SansSerif", 28 * displayDensity));
  textAlign(CENTER, CENTER);
  requestPermission("android.permission.ACTIVITY_RECOGNITION", "handlePermission");
}

void draw() {
  background(0);
  text(steps + " steps", 0, 0, width, height);
}

void handlePermission(boolean granted) {
  if (granted) {
    initCounter();
  }
}

void initCounter() {
  Context context = getContext();
  manager = (SensorManager)context.getSystemService(Context.SENSOR_SERVICE);
  sensor = manager.getDefaultSensor(Sensor.TYPE_STEP_COUNTER);
  listener = new SensorListener();
  manager.registerListener(listener, sensor,
                           SensorManager.SENSOR_DELAY_NORMAL);
}

class SensorListener implements SensorEventListener {
  void onSensorChanged(SensorEvent event) {
    if (offset == -1) offset = (int)event.values[0];
    steps = (int)event.values[0] - offset;
  }
  void onAccuracyChanged(Sensor sensor, int accuracy) { }
}
```

Here, we use the offset variable, initialized to -1, to store the initial step count. Also, if we are planning to create a watch face that keeps track of daily step counts, we should implement our own "overnight reset," since Android will not do that automatically for us.

Accessing the Heart Rate Sensor

The heart rate requires the BODY_SENSORS permission, which is classified as a runtime permission due to the personal nature of the data. Like with the step counter before, it is not enough to select the permission through the Android Permissions Selector in the PDE (Figure 12-2), and we have to manually request the permission in the code with the requestPermission() function, providing the name of the function that will be called upon the result of the permission request. This is shown in Listing 12-2.

Listing 12-2. Displaying the heart rate

```
import android.content.Context;
import android.hardware.Sensor;
import android.hardware.SensorManager;
import android.hardware.SensorEvent;
import android.hardware.SensorEventListener;

Context context;
SensorManager manager;
Sensor sensor;
SensorListener listener;

int bpm;

void setup() {
  fullScreen();
  frameRate(1);
  textFont(createFont("SansSerif", 28 * displayDensity));
  textAlign(CENTER, CENTER);
  requestPermission("android.permission.BODY_SENSORS", "initMonitor");
}

void draw() {
  background(0);
  text(bpm + " beats/min", 0, 0, width, height);
}

void initMonitor(boolean granted) {
  if (granted) {
    Context context = getContext();
    manager = (SensorManager)context.
              getSystemService(Context.SENSOR_SERVICE);
    sensor = manager.getDefaultSensor(Sensor.TYPE_HEART_RATE);
    listener = new SensorListener();
    manager.registerListener(listener, sensor,
                        SensorManager.SENSOR_DELAY_NORMAL);
  }
}
```

```
class SensorListener implements SensorEventListener {
  void onSensorChanged(SensorEvent event) {
    bpm = int(event.values[0]);
  }
  void onAccuracyChanged(Sensor sensor, int accuracy) { }
}
```

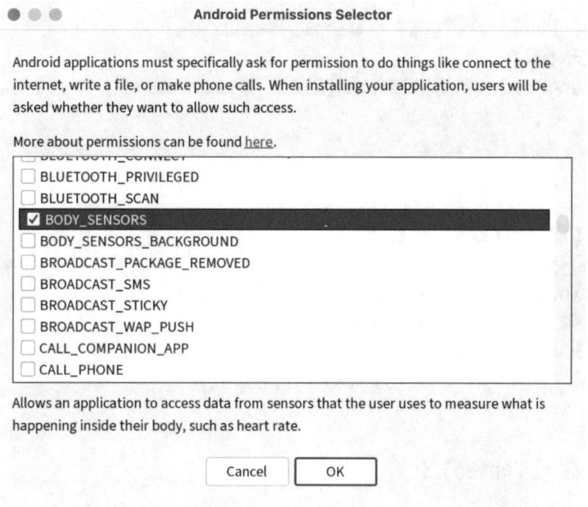

Figure 12-2. *The BODY_SENSORS permission in the selector*

When we open the watch face for the first time, we should see a dialog like the one in Figure 12-3 asking us to allow or deny accessing body sensor data.

Figure 12-3. *Permission request when launching the watch face*

Visualizing Step Count Data

A simple way of visualizing activity data could be a radial representation depicting the progression toward a set goal. We already used the arc() function to display elapsed time, and we can adapt it easily to show step count toward a desired value, for example, 100, as in Listing 12-3.

Listing 12-3. Radial step count visualization

```
...
void setup() {
  frameRate(1);
  strokeCap(ROUND);
  stroke(255);
  noFill();
  textFont(createFont("SansSerif", 18 * displayDensity));
  textAlign(CENTER, CENTER);
  requestPermission("android.permission.ACTIVITY_RECOGNITION", "initCounter");
}

void draw() {
  background(0);
  if (wearAmbient()) strokeWeight(1);
  else strokeWeight(10);
  float angle = map(min(steps, 100), 0, 100, 0, TWO_PI);
  arc(width/2, height/2, width/2, width/2,
  PI + HALF_PI, PI + HALF_PI + angle);
  if (steps == 0) text("0 steps", 0, 0, width, height);
}

void initCounter(boolean granted) {
  if (granted) {
    Context context = getContext();
    manager = (SensorManager)context.getSystemService(Context.SENSOR_SERVICE);
    sensor = manager.getDefaultSensor(Sensor.TYPE_STEP_COUNTER);
    listener = new SensorListener();
    manager.registerListener(listener, sensor, SensorManager.SENSOR_DELAY_NORMAL);
  }
}
...
```

The rest of the sketch is identical to Listing 12-1. Next, we can add a multiplier to show how many times the user has reached the goal already by simply dividing the number of steps by the target, in this case, 100, and drawing that value as text in the center of the screen. The updated draw() function is in Listing 12-4, and the output of this new watch face is in Figure 12-4.

Listing 12-4. Adding a multiplier to the step counter

```
void draw() {
  background(0);
  if (wearAmbient()) strokeWeight(1);
  else strokeWeight(10);
  int mult = int(steps / 100);
  float angle = map(steps - mult * 100, 0, 100, 0, TWO_PI);
  noFill();
  arc(width/2, height/2, width/2, width/2, PI + HALF_PI, PI + HALF_PI + angle);
  fill(255);
  if (0 < steps) {
    text("x" + (mult + 1), 0, 0, width, height);
```

```
  } else {
    text("0 steps", 0, 0, width, height);
  }
}
```

Figure 12-4. *Step count watch face, with multiplier counter*

A Beating Heart

For a visual representation of the heart rate data, we can rely on a very direct translation: a beating heart, or as first approximation, a beating ellipse. We already know how to obtain the beats-per-minute value from the sensor; the problem is how to animate the ellipse based on this rate, so it is accurate enough to convey the motion and rhythm of the heartbeat. An actual ECG signal is depicted in Figure 12-5, where we see that a single beat has two peaks in proximity, the first much higher than the second, followed by a relatively flat line.

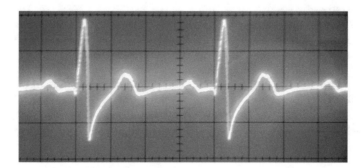

Figure 12-5. *A typical ECG signal*

We can approximate this pattern with an "impulse" curve that presents a rapid initial increase, followed by a decay until the next beat (Figure 12-6). A simple mathematical function that generates this impulse curve is as follows:

```
float impulse(float k, float t) {
  float h = k * t;
  return h * exp(1.0 - h);
}
```

217

In this formula, the constant k determines how quickly the impulse reaches its peak (the position of the peak is exactly t = 1/k). From inspecting the ECG signal in Figure 12-5, we could conclude that the first peak in a heartbeat occurs at around 25% of the entire duration of the beat. As an example, if our heart is beating at 80 beats per minute (bpm), then a single beat would last 60,000/80 = 750 milliseconds, and its first peak should occur at approximately 0.25*750 = 187.5 milliseconds. From this, we calculate k since t = 187.5 = 1/k, giving in this case k ~ 0.0053. In general, if we call x the measured bpm value, the constant k will be equal to x/(0.25*60,000).

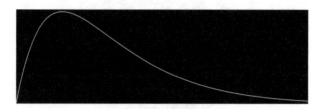

Figure 12-6. *An impulse function, plotted with the Graphtoy tool by Inigo Quilez (*`www.iquilezles.org/apps/graphtoy/index.html`*)*

We can control the animation of any shape in Processing using this impulse formula. Of course, this formula is not exact, and its peak does not necessarily coincide with the exact moment when the heart beats but should be enough as an approximation to convey the beating pace. Listing 12-5 extends our previous heart rate watch face from Listing 12-2 by incorporating an ellipse whose radius follows the impulse function. As before, we need to add the BODY_SENSORS permission through the PDE and grant this permission once the watch face launches on the device or in the emulator.

Listing 12-5. Creating a heartbeat animation

```
import android.content.Context;
import android.hardware.Sensor;
import android.hardware.SensorManager;
import android.hardware.SensorEvent;
import android.hardware.SensorEventListener;

Context context;
SensorManager manager;
Sensor sensor;
SensorListener listener;

int bpm;

void setup() {
  fullScreen();
  noStroke();
  textFont(createFont("SansSerif", 28 * displayDensity));
  textAlign(CENTER, CENTER);
  requestPermission("android.permission.BODY_SENSORS", "initMonitor");
}

void draw() {
  background(0);
  if (wearAmbient()) {
```

```
    fill(255);
    text(bpm + " bpm", 0, 0, width, height);
  } else {
    int duration = 750;
    if (0 < bpm) duration = 60000 / bpm;
    float x = millis() % duration;
    float k = 1/(0.25 * duration);
    float a = impulse(k, x);
    float r = map(a, 0, 1, 0.75, 0.9) * width;
    translate(width/2, height/2);
    fill(247, 47, 47);
    ellipse(0, 0, r, r);
  }
}

float impulse(float k, float x) {
  float h = k * x;
  return h * exp(1.0 - h);
}

void initMonitor(boolean granted) {
  if (!granted) return;
  Context context = getContext();
  manager = (SensorManager)context.getSystemService(Context.SENSOR_SERVICE);
  sensor = manager.getDefaultSensor(Sensor.TYPE_HEART_RATE);
  listener = new SensorListener();
  manager.registerListener(listener, sensor,
                           SensorManager.SENSOR_DELAY_NORMAL);
}

class SensorListener implements SensorEventListener {
  void onSensorChanged(SensorEvent event) {
    bpm = int(event.values[0]);
  }
  void onAccuracyChanged(Sensor sensor, int accuracy) { }
}
```

The ellipse is drawn only when the watch is in interactive mode. We calculate the duration of a single beat at the current bpm and store it in the duration variable, which we use in all the other parameters needed to evaluate the impulse function. Since the impulse ranges between 0 and 1, we map it to the (0.75, 0.9) interval so that the size of ellipse varies between contracted and expanded states that are either too small or too big. We can tweak these parameters until we are satisfied with the final result.

Sensor Debugging

Testing a watch face that makes use of sensors can be difficult, as we may need to move around to get enough data from the step counter or heart rate sensor to make sure that we evaluate the different instances in our code. Since Processing allows us to easily switch back and forth between modes, and the great majority of the Processing API remains the same between the Java and Android modes, we could use the Java mode to test the parts of the code that do not depend on the actual sensors, particularly the rendering code.

However, we often need to inspect the actual sensor data to determine if something is wrong either with our assumptions about this data or in the way we are processing it in our code. One way we could do this is by recording the values from the sensors into a text file and then pulling this file from the watch to look for any patterns of interest. Listing 12-6 demonstrates this approach to save the data from the heart rate sensor. Since we write the data to a file in the external storage, we need to add the WRITE_EXTERNAL_ STORAGE permission to the sketch and the corresponding request in the sketch code since it is also a runtime permission.

Listing 12-6. Saving sensor data to a file

```
import android.content.Context;
import android.hardware.Sensor;
import android.hardware.SensorManager;
import android.hardware.SensorEvent;
import android.hardware.SensorEventListener;
import android.os.Environment;

Context context;
SensorManager manager;
Sensor sensor;
SensorListener listener;

int bpm;
String[] data = { "time,rate" };

void setup() {
  fullScreen();
  frameRate(1);
  textFont(createFont("SansSerif", 28 * displayDensity));
  textAlign(CENTER, CENTER);
  requestPermission("android.permission.BODY_SENSORS", "initMonitor");
  requestPermission("android.permission.WRITE_EXTERNAL_STORAGE");
}

void draw() {
  background(0);
  text(bpm + " beats/min", 0, 0, width, height);
}

void mousePressed() {
  background(200, 40, 40);
  File sd = Environment.getExternalStorageDirectory();
  String path = sd.getAbsolutePath();
  File directory = new File(path, "out");
  File file = new File(directory, "sensor-data.csv");
  saveStrings(file, data);
}

void initMonitor(boolean granted) {
  if (granted) {
    Context context = getContext();
    manager = (SensorManager)
```

```
                context.getSystemService(Context.SENSOR_SERVICE);
    sensor = manager.getDefaultSensor(Sensor.TYPE_HEART_RATE);
    listener = new SensorListener();
    manager.registerListener(listener, sensor,
                             SensorManager.SENSOR_DELAY_NORMAL);
  }
}

class SensorListener implements SensorEventListener {
  void onSensorChanged(SensorEvent event) {
    bpm = int(event.values[0]);
    data = (String[]) append(data, millis() + "," + bpm);
  }
  void onAccuracyChanged(Sensor sensor, int accuracy) { }
}
```

First, notice how the request for the WRITE_EXTERNAL_STORAGE permission does not include a function to call after the permission has been granted (or denied). This is so because there is no additional initialization required to write to the external storage.

In this sketch, every time we receive a new sensor value, we append it to the string array data, together with the time in milliseconds. We save this array as a CSV (comma-separated values) file into the device's external storage when touching the screen using the saveStrings() function. The external storage in a watch is emulated in its internal storage, as they don't include SD cards. To download the file to the development computer, we can run the following command from the terminal:

```
adb -s 127.0.0.1:4444 pull /storage/emulated/0/out/sensor-data.csv
```

Once we have downloaded the data file, we can read it from a text editor or a spreadsheet software. We could also use it as the input in a Processing sketch, like the one in Listing 12-7, where we read the CSV file with the loadTable() function (https://processing.org/reference/loadTable_.html). This function returns a Table object containing all the data organized in rows and columns. In this case, we simply draw a line plot with a LINE_STRIP shape, connecting the values in each consecutive row. A typical outcome of this sketch is depicted in Figure 12-7.

Listing 12-7. Plotting sensor data in Processing

```
size(700, 200, P2D);
Table table = loadTable("sensor-data.csv", "header");
background(90);
stroke(247, 47, 47);
strokeWeight(4);
beginShape(LINE_STRIP);
for (int i = 0; i < table.getRowCount(); i++) {
  TableRow row = table.getRow(i);
  int r = row.getInt("rate");
  float x = map(i, 0, table.getRowCount() - 1, 0, width);
  float y = map(r, 0, 100, height, 0);
  vertex(x, y);
}
endShape();
```

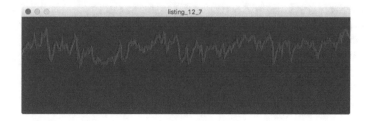

Figure 12-7. *Line plot of heart rate data*

In these two examples, our goal was to record the sensor data to examine the data later to identify any issues. A different, but related, aim is to debug our data-processing code in a more controlled fashion. We could do this by generating "synthetic" data resembling what would come out from the sensors. For example, Listing 12-8 shows the heart rate example from before, modified to print random bpm values generated continuously with a "thread" running in parallel with the face watch animation.

Listing 12-8. Generating synthetic sensor data

```
int bpm;

void setup() {
  fullScreen();
  frameRate(1);
  textFont(createFont("SansSerif", 28 * displayDensity));
  textAlign(CENTER, CENTER);
  thread("generateData");
}

void draw() {
  background(0);
  text(bpm + " beats/min", 0, 0, width, height);
}

void generateData() {
  while (true) {
    bpm = int(random(60, 100));
    delay(2000);
  }
}
```

The thread() function in Processing launches a calculation in the provided user function and keeps running it in parallel to the main drawing animation in our sketch to avoid slowing down the frame rate. Here, we launch the generateData() function at the end of setup(). In this function, we keep generating random bpm values between 60 and 100, with a delay of two seconds between each consecutive value, which approximates the behavior of the real heart rate sensor well enough for testing (the delay interval could also be random to add even more variability).

Grow a Tree As You Exercise!

So far, our physical activity watch faces have been relatively simple. Can we make an activity tracker more interesting (and maybe more rewarding) by offering a visual output that not only tracks the activity level but also introduces some visual variation? If we think of the step count as a value that starts at 0 and grows until reaching a set goal, say, 10,000 steps, would it be possible to use it to drive the "growth" of some organic element in our sketch, for example, a plant or a tree?

Generating a naturally looking tree with code is a problem that can take us to fascinating ideas in mathematics, like self-similarity and fractals (https://en.wikipedia.org/wiki/Self-similarity). We can find several techniques to do it, some of them shown in Figure 12-8.

Figure 12-8. *Different algorithms for tree generation. Left: fractal recursion (by Daniel Shiffman, https:// processing.org/examples/tree.html). Center: branching tree (by Ryan Chao, www.openprocessing.org/ sketch/186129). Right: particle system tree (by Asher Salomon, www.openprocessing.org/sketch/144159)*

Most importantly, we need an algorithm that lets us grow our tree as the step count increases. Both the fractal recursion and the particle system algorithms referred in Figure 12-8 can be unfolded through time, particularly the latter, as it gradually grows until it reaches its full size and gives a more "organic look" than the fractal recursion. Furthermore, its code is available on OpenProcessing, so we can use it as the starting point for our project.

■ **Note** OpenProcessing (www.openprocessing.org/) is an online library of Processing sketches, most of which can be run inside the browser, available for modification and sharing under a Creative Commons license.

Generating a Tree with a Particle System

We already made use of particle systems in Chapter 6 to generate an animation that reads the pixels in an image to color the screen as the particles follow a Perlin noise field. Particle systems can be used in many different scenarios to create organic movement, and it is the case again here. Making some changes to the OpenProcessing sketch by Asher Salomon, we arrive to the code in Listing 12-9, which gives us the output in Figure 12-9 when running it in the Java mode.

Listing 12-9. A growing tree

```
ArrayList<Branch> branches = new ArrayList<Branch>();

void setup() {
  size(500, 500);
  noStroke();
  branches.add(new Branch());
  background(155, 211, 247);
}

void draw() {
  for (int i = 0; i < branches.size(); i++) {
    Branch branch = branches.get(i);
    branch.update();
    branch.display();
  }
}

class Branch {
  PVector position;
  PVector velocity;
  float diameter;

  Branch() {
    position = new PVector(width/2, height);
    velocity = new PVector(0, -1);
    diameter = width/15.0;
  }
  Branch(Branch parent) {
    position = parent.position.copy();
    velocity = parent.velocity.copy();
    diameter = parent.diameter / 1.4142;
    parent.diameter = diameter;
  }
  void update() {
    if (1 < diameter) {
      position.add(velocity);
      float opening = map(diameter, 1, width/15.0, 1, 0);
      float angle = random(PI - opening * HALF_PI,
                                      TWO_PI + opening * HALF_PI);
      PVector shake = PVector.fromAngle(angle);
      shake.mult(0.1);
      velocity.add(shake);
      velocity.normalize();
      if (random(0, 1) < 0.04) branches.add(new Branch(this));
    }
  }
  void display() {
    if (1 < diameter) {
      fill(175, 108, 44, 50);
```

```
    ellipse(position.x, position.y, diameter, diameter);
    }
  }
}
```

To understand this code, we should look at how the Branch class is used to represent a swarm of moving particles that, as they leave a trail on the screen, generate the branches of the tree. The basic idea is this: each particle is a small ellipse with a position, velocity, and diameter. Initially, there is a single particle, placed at the bottom of the screen, with a diameter of width/15 (more about this choice later) and an upwards velocity of 1. From time to time, a new particle branches out from an existing one, so we eventually get many branches coming out from a single trunk. For this to work properly, we have to be careful to call background() only in setup() so the trails of the particles are not erased at the start of each new frame.

Every time the update() method of a particle is called in draw(), its position is updated according to the current velocity, and the velocity is slightly "jolted" by the shake vector. This vector has a magnitude of 0.1 and a random direction determined by the angle variable. However, there is one important detail in the way this angle is calculated, which makes it not completely random. The reason for this is that we want to avoid the tree to swing to the sides early on, so we map the branches' diameter, ranging from width/15 at the beginning to 1 at the end, to the opening variable between 0 and 1. If the diameter of a branch approaches 1, it means that the tree is already well grown, so the branch does not need to be straight and the angle of the shake vector can be anywhere between PI - opening * HALF_PI and TWO_PI + opening * HALF_PI. If opening is exactly 1, then the angle is chosen from the entire circle range. On the other hand, when opening is close to 0 at the beginning, the angle can only range between PI and TWO_PI, which represents the upper half of the circle. In this way, the branches are forced to move upward when the tree is just sprouting up.

The other key aspect of the algorithm is the branching mechanism: every time a particle is updated, it creates a new branch at the current position if a random draw between 0 and 1 is smaller than 0.04. The new branch is just another particle object, which is initialized from its parent by having the same position and velocity, but a diameter scaled down by a factor of $1/\sqrt{2}$. As a result of the branching, the parent particle also gets its diameter reduced by the same factor.

We just reviewed the main elements of the algorithm. As we see in the code, there are several numerical parameters we could modify to tweak the appearance of the tree. One such choice is the initial diameter of the branches, here set to width/15 because it gives reasonably sized trees. Also, as the result of this parameter selection, the algorithm will take a well-defined number of iterations to reach a fully grown tree, which in this case is around 300 (we will come back to this number soon).

Figure 12-9. *Output of the tree generation algorithm*

Incorporating Step Count Data

We have a working version of the tree generation algorithm, but it is not tied to the step count sensor yet. Inspecting the values returned by this sensor, we would realize that steps are not detected one by one, but we instead get a number that increases at irregular amounts. So we could compute the difference in the step count between the current and the last onSensorChanged() event and update our particles as many times as needed. Let's try this approach in Listing 12-10.

Listing 12-10. Driving the growth of the tree with the step count

```
import android.content.Context;
import android.hardware.Sensor;
import android.hardware.SensorManager;
import android.hardware.SensorEvent;
import android.hardware.SensorEventListener;

Context context;
SensorManager manager;
Sensor sensor;
SensorListener listener;

int offset = -1;
int psteps, steps;
int stepInc = 0;

ArrayList<Branch> branches = new ArrayList<Branch>();
PGraphics canvas;

void setup() {
  fullScreen();
  noStroke();
  branches.add(new Branch());
  initCanvas();
  requestPermission("android.permission.ACTIVITY_RECOGNITION", "initCounter");
}

void draw() {
  background(0);
  if (wearInteractive()) growTree();
  image(canvas, 0, 0);
}

synchronized void growTree() {
  canvas.beginDraw();
  for (int s = 0; s < stepInc; s++) {
    for (int i = 0; i < branches.size(); i++) {
      Branch branch = branches.get(i);
      branch.update();
      branch.display();
    }
  }
```

```
    canvas.endDraw();
    stepInc = 0;
}

synchronized void updateSteps(int value) {
    if (offset == -1) offset = value;
    steps = value - offset;
    stepInc += steps - psteps;
    psteps = steps;
}

void initCanvas() {
    canvas = createGraphics(width, height);
    canvas.beginDraw();
    canvas.background(155, 211, 247);
    canvas.noStroke();
    canvas.endDraw();
}

class Branch {
    PVector position;
    PVector velocity;
    float diameter;

    Branch() {
        position = new PVector(width/2, height);
        velocity = new PVector(0, -1);
        diameter = width/15.0;
    }
    Branch(Branch parent) {
        position = parent.position.copy();
        velocity = parent.velocity.copy();
        diameter = parent.diameter / 1.4142;
        parent.diameter = diameter;
    }
    void update() {
        if (1 < diameter) {
            position.add(velocity);
            float opening = map(diameter, 1, width/15.0, 1, 0);
            float angle = random(PI - opening * HALF_PI,
                                 TWO_PI + opening * HALF_PI);
            PVector shake = PVector.fromAngle(angle);
            shake.mult(0.1);
            velocity.add(shake);
            velocity.normalize();
            if (random(0, 1) < 0.04) branches.add(new Branch(this));
        }
    }
    void display() {
        if (1 < diameter) {
            canvas.fill(175, 108, 44, 50);
```

```
    canvas.ellipse(position.x, position.y, diameter, diameter);
    }
  }
}

void initCounter(boolean granted) {
  if (granted) {
    Context context = getContext();
    manager = (SensorManager)context.getSystemService(Context.SENSOR_SERVICE);
    sensor = manager.getDefaultSensor(Sensor.TYPE_STEP_COUNTER);
    listener = new SensorListener();
  manager.registerListener(listener, sensor,
                        SensorManager.SENSOR_DELAY_NORMAL);
  }
}

class SensorListener implements SensorEventListener {
  void onSensorChanged(SensorEvent event) {
    updateSteps(int(event.values[0]));
  }
  void onAccuracyChanged(Sensor sensor, int accuracy) { }
}
```

We reused most of the code from Listing 12-9 and added the standard Android event handlers. But there are several new things we should consider. First, we are drawing the branches into an offscreen PGraphics surface, which we used already in Chapter 9. The reason is the following: as a watch face, our sketch will have to present a different output for the ambient mode. Since this would require erasing the entire screen, we would then lose the particle trails defining the tree. Drawing them into a separate surface, which we can display at any time, is one easy way to solve this problem.

Note that the functions growTree() and updateSteps() have the keyword "synchronized" at the beginning. This is because both access and modify the stepInc variable, which contains the number of steps counted since the last onSensorChanged() event, from different threads running in parallel: growTree() is called from Processing's drawing thread and updateSteps() from onSensorChanged(), which in turn is triggered from the app's main thread handling input events. We introduced threads and synchronization in Chapter 9, when we had a similar problem of multiple threads accessing location data at the same time.

Tweaking the Watch Face

We still have two issues with our first version of the tree watch face. One is that, since one step equates to one branch update cycle, the tree will grow too quickly, especially if we want it to reach full size only when the step count hits our target value, say, 10,000. The second problem is due to the nature of the step counter sensor: the onSensorChanged() may be called at irregular intervals, with a large step increase at one moment and a small change at another. In particular, if the increase is very large, the growTree() function may take a long time to run, freezing the watch face, because it updates all particles as many times as steps were counted since the last sensor changed event.

To solve the first problem, let's recall our earlier observation that the algorithm, with this current parameter selection, takes around 300 updates to completely grow the tree. This means that one step should represent only a fraction of an update iteration. More precisely, if our goal is to complete the tree at 10,000 steps, then the contribution of one single step toward one update iteration would be 300/10,000.

For the second problem of the freezing animation, a simple solution could be to remove the first loop in the growTree() function and run just one update per particle while decreasing the value of stepInc by exactly one. In this way, we do a single update per frame so the watch face does not freeze but will keep growing the tree until stepInc reaches zero. Listing 12-11 shows the changes needed in the code to implement these tweaks.

Listing 12-11. Controlling growth rate

```
...
int offset = -1;
int psteps, steps;
float stepInc = 0;
int stepGoal = 10000;
float stepScale = stepGoal / 300.0;
...
synchronized void growTree() {
  if (1 <= stepInc) {
    canvas.beginDraw();
    for (int i = 0; i < branches.size(); i++) {
      Branch branch = branches.get(i);
      branch.update();
      branch.display();
    }
    canvas.endDraw();
    stepInc--;
  }
}

synchronized void updateSteps(int value) {
  if (offset == -1) offset = value;
  steps = value - offset;
  stepInc += (steps - psteps) / stepScale;
  psteps = steps;
}
...
```

Blooming the Tree

We are very close to completing our watch face! We still need some improvements: an ambient mode, which could simply be a text message informing of the total step count and the time, an extra animation when approaching the desired step count goal, the typical 10,000 steps for example, and a restart after reaching the goal. Listing 12-12 adds all these improvements, which we will discuss right after the code.

Listing 12-12. Adding flowers, time, and step count

```
import android.content.Context;
import android.hardware.Sensor;
import android.hardware.SensorManager;
import android.hardware.SensorEvent;
import android.hardware.SensorEventListener;
```

```
Context context;
SensorManager manager;
Sensor sensor;
SensorListener listener;

int offset = -1;
int tsteps, psteps, steps, phour;
float stepInc = 0;
int stepGoal = 10000;
float stepScale = stepGoal / 300.0;

ArrayList<Branch> branches = new ArrayList<Branch>();
PGraphics canvas;
color bloomColor = color(230, 80, 120, 120);

void setup() {
  fullScreen();
  noStroke();
  textFont(createFont("SansSerif-Bold", 28 * displayDensity));
  branches.add(new Branch());
  initCanvas();
  requestPermission("android.permission.ACTIVITY_RECOGNITION", "initCounter");
}

void draw() {
  background(0);
String str = hour() + ":" + nfs(minute(), 2) + ":" +
                                    nfs(second(), 2) + "\n" +
                                    tsteps + " steps";

  if (wearInteractive()) {
    growTree();
    if (stepGoal <= steps) clearTree();
    image(canvas, 0, 0);
    textAlign(CENTER, BOTTOM);
    textSize(20 * displayDensity);
    fill(0, 80);
  } else {
    textAlign(CENTER, CENTER);
    textSize(28 * displayDensity);
    fill(200, 255);
  }
  text(str, 0, 0, width, height);
}

synchronized void growTree() {
  if (1 <= stepInc) {
    canvas.beginDraw();
    for (int i = 0; i < branches.size(); i++) {
      Branch branch = branches.get(i);
      branch.update();
      branch.display();
```

```
      branch.bloom();
    }
    canvas.endDraw();
    stepInc--;
  }
}

synchronized void updateSteps(int value) {
  if (hour() < phour) tsteps = steps;
  if (offset == -1) offset = value;
  steps = value - offset;
  tsteps += steps - psteps;
  stepInc += (steps - psteps) / stepScale;
  psteps = steps;
  phour = hour();
}

synchronized void clearTree() {
  canvas.beginDraw();
  canvas.background(155, 211, 247);
  canvas.endDraw();
  branches.clear();
  branches.add(new Branch());
  offset = -1;
  steps = psteps = 0;
  bloomColor = color(random(255), random(255), random(255), 120);
}

void initCanvas() {
  canvas = createGraphics(width, height);
  canvas.beginDraw();
  canvas.background(155, 211, 247);
  canvas.noStroke();
  canvas.endDraw();
}

class Branch {
  PVector position;
  PVector velocity;
  float diameter;

  Branch() {
    position = new PVector(width/2, height);
    velocity = new PVector(0, -1);
    diameter = width/15.0;
  }
  Branch(Branch parent) {
    position = parent.position.copy();
    velocity = parent.velocity.copy();
    diameter = parent.diameter / 1.4142;
    parent.diameter = diameter;
  }
```

```
  void update() {
    if (1 < diameter) {
      position.add(velocity);
      float opening = map(diameter, 1, width/15.0, 1, 0);
      float angle = random(PI - opening * HALF_PI,
                                        TWO_PI + opening * HALF_PI);
      PVector shake = PVector.fromAngle(angle);
      shake.mult(0.1);
      velocity.add(shake);
      velocity.normalize();
      if (random(0, 1) < 0.04) branches.add(new Branch(this));
    }
  }
  void display() {
    if (1 < diameter) {
      canvas.fill(175, 108, 44, 50);
      canvas.ellipse(position.x, position.y, diameter, diameter);
    }
  }
  void bloom() {
    if (0.85 * stepGoal < steps && random(0, 1) < 0.001) {
      float x = position.x + random(-10, +10);
      float y = position.y + random(-10, +10);
      float r = random(5, 20);
      canvas.fill(bloomColor);
      canvas.ellipse(x, y, r, r);
    }
  }
}

void initCounter(boolean granted) {
  if (granted) {
    Context context = getContext();
    manager = (SensorManager)context.getSystemService(Context.SENSOR_SERVICE);
    sensor = manager.getDefaultSensor(Sensor.TYPE_STEP_COUNTER);
    listener = new SensorListener();
  manager.registerListener(listener, sensor,
                        SensorManager.SENSOR_DELAY_NORMAL);
  }
}

class SensorListener implements SensorEventListener {
  void onSensorChanged(SensorEvent event) {
    updateSteps(int(event.values[0]));
  }
  void onAccuracyChanged(Sensor sensor, int accuracy) { }
}
```

The implementation of the ambient mode is easy: screen-centered text drawing (but it could be something more involved too). The tree blooming is also relatively simple: once we reach 85% of the total step goal, we place an ellipse near the current position of each branch particle, with a probability of 0.001.

One other function we need in the final watch face is a reset after reaching the goal so the canvas is cleared and all particles are removed to start a new tree. This is done in the clearTree() function, synchronized since it modifies the offset, pstep, and step variables that are also altered in every sensor changed event. Also, we added a "midnight reset" so that the total step count, tstep, is set to the current step value when the hour wraps around back to zero, with the line if (hour() < phour) tsteps = steps in updateSteps().

Figure 12-10 shows a sequence of three screen captures with a tree at different growth stages, from early in the step tracking until blooming when nearing the step count goal. In Figure 12-11, we can see how the watch face looks like in ambient and interactive modes on an actual watch.

Figure 12-10. *Three stages in the growth of our tree*

Testing and debugging this watch face can be challenging because we need to walk around long enough to observe changes in the growth of the tree. However, we can easily generate synthetic data that resembles the output of the step count sensor. Listing 12-13 illustrates the changes needed in the code to use a "step count generator" instead of the step count listener. These changes are in fact minimal, essentially launching a thread that runs the data-generation loop. We can adjust the values in the loop to increase or decrease the frequency of the updates, as well as the range of the values. This gives us enough flexibility to evaluate our code under different scenarios that would be hard to test with real step count data.

Listing 12-13. Testing with synthetic data

```
...
void setup() {
...
  branches.add(new Branch());
  initCanvas();
  thread("generateData");
}
...
void generateData() {
  int total = 0;
  while (true) {
    total += int(random(10, 20));
    updateSteps(total);
    delay(500);
  }
}
```

The final step in the development process would be to upload our watch face to the Google Play Store. Android devices running Wear 3.x can install stand-alone apps and watch faces without the need of a "companion" mobile app, as indicated in the online developer documentation on packaging and distributing Wear apps: https://developer.android.com/training/wearables/packaging. To get the signed package for the watch face from the PDE, we can follow the same steps for regular apps described in Chapter 3.

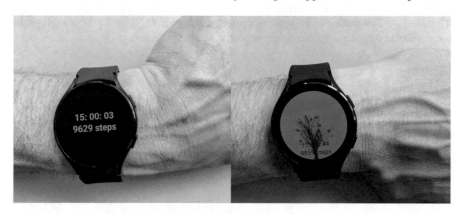

Figure 12-11. *Final version of the tree watch face, in ambient (left) and interactive (right) modes*

First, we need to write a package name in the manifest file inside the sketch's folder. A label for the service and the application are optional, but highly recommended, as it will be used throughout the watch UI to identify the watch face. Then, we have to create a full icon set including the six app icons for all DPI levels (xxxhdpi through ldpi) and the circular and rectangular preview icons (Figure 12-12).

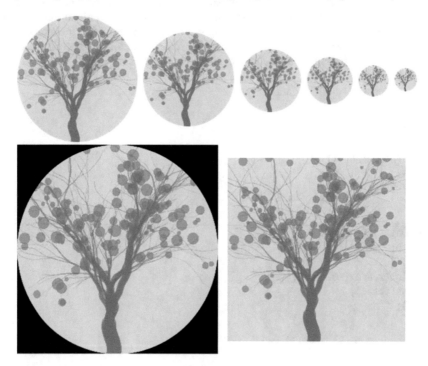

Figure 12-12. *Icon set needed to export the signed package*

Summary

This chapter concludes the section on wearable devices and watch faces. Although wearable development is an entire field on its own right, we were able to apply most of the techniques we learned in previous chapters to create interactive graphics and dynamic visualizations of sensor data, while considering some of the unique features of wearable devices in terms of screen size, resolution, and battery life.

PART V

3D and Shaders

CHAPTER 13

3D in Processing

We start this new part in the book with an introduction to the basic concepts in 3D programming with Processing: coordinate systems, 3D transformations, lighting, texturing, and creation of 3D shapes, which we can apply not only in VR and AR apps but in any situation where we may need interactive 3D graphics.

The P3D Renderer

So far, we have used Processing drawing functions to make "flat" or 2D shapes, using either the default or the P2D renderer, but sometimes, we need to step into the third dimension! For example, working in VR and AR requires knowing how to create interactive 3D graphics. Even though 2D rendering is a special case of 3D, there are many aspects of motion and interaction that are specific to 3D graphics that we need to become familiar with.

Processing includes a renderer for drawing 3D scenes, appropriately called P3D. It supports basic 3D features, such as lighting and texturing objects, but also more advanced functionality, including GLSL shaders and retained-mode rendering. We can use P3D by providing the renderer argument in the size() or fullScreen() function during setup(), e.g., size(width, height, P3D) or fullScreen(P3D). After doing that, we can not only use all the 3D rendering functions available in Processing but continue to create 2D drawings as we did before.

Hello World in 3D

Let's start by writing a simple sketch that demonstrates the basics of 3D in Processing: a rotating cube. Listing 13-1 includes translation and rotation transformations, as well as default lighting.

Listing 13-1. Basic 3D sketch

```
float angle = 0;

void setup() {
  fullScreen(P3D);
  fill(#AD71B7);
}

void draw() {
  background(#81B771);
  lights();
  translate(width/2, height/2);
  rotateY(angle);
```

© Andrés Colubri 2023

A. Colubri, *Processing for Android*, https://doi.org/10.1007/978-1-4842-9585-4_13

```
  rotateX(angle*2);
  box(300);
  angle += 0.01;
}
```

We will look at these functions more closely in the next sections, but here there is an overview of what happens in draw(): we first "turn on" a set of default lights with lights(), then translate the entire scene to the center of the screen with translate(width/2, height/2), and apply two rotations: one along the y axis with rotateY(angle) and a second along the x axis with rotateX(angle*2). Just like in 2D drawing before, these transformations affect all shapes we draw afterward, in this case, the cube drawn with box(300). We end by increasing the rotation angle by a small amount, so we have a continuous animation. Figure 13-1 shows the output of this sketch.

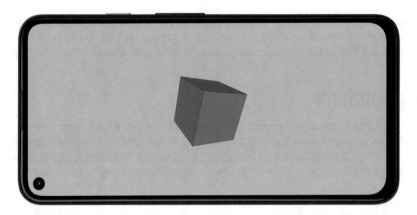

Figure 13-1. *Simple 3D rendering in Processing*

3D Transformations

We will now learn how to move our objects around in 3D space. We have three types of 3D transformations: translations (moving from point A to B), rotations (turning around an axis), and scaling (contracting or expanding uniformly or along one direction). Listings 13-2 through 13-4 exemplify each type of transformation on their own.

Listing 13-2. Applying a translation

```
void setup() {
  fullScreen(P3D);
  fill(120);
}

void draw() {
  background(157);
  float x = map(cos(millis()/1000.0), -1, +1, 0, width);
  translate(x, height/2);
  box(200);
}
```

For the rotation, we need to do a translation to the center of the screen first, since the box() function places the cube at (0, 0, 0).

Listing 13-3. Applying a rotation

```
void setup() {
  fullScreen(P3D);
  fill(120);
}

void draw() {
  background(157);
  translate(width/2, height/2);
  rotateY(millis()/1000.0);
  box(200);
}
```

It is the same with scaling, we apply the translation to (width/2, height/2) first so the box appears in the center of screen.

Listing 13-4. Applying a scaling

```
void setup() {
  fullScreen(P3D);
  fill(120);
}

void draw() {
  background(157);
  translate(width/2, height/2);
  float f = map(cos(millis()/1000.0), -1, +1, 0.1, 5);
  scale(f);
  box(200);
}
```

■ **Note**   The relative size of the shapes in all these examples will be different depending on the device's DPI. We can use the densityDisplay Processing constant to scale them up or down so they look consistent across screens with different resolutions and sizes.

Combining Transformations

The previous examples demonstrated how to use 3D transformations separately (although in the case of rotation and scaling, there was the initial translation to the center of the screen). But in most situations, we need to combine translations, rotations, and scaling, typically by defining a "chain of transformations" that put an object in the desired spot in 3D space and with the intended proportions.

Transformations can be combined to create very complex movements, we should only keep in mind a few "rules" for our transformations to work as intended: (1) the order of transformations cannot be exchanged (e.g., applying a rotation and then a translation is not equivalent to translate first and rotate later, as we discussed it in the context of 2D drawing in Chapter 4), and (2) a chain of transformations can be manipulated with pushMatrix() and popMatrix(), with pushMatrix() preserving the current combination of transformations, thus "isolating" the effect of additional transformations that happen between it and the matching popMatrix(). We saw some examples of this in Chapter 2. Listing 13-5 implements a chain of 3D transformations with the goal of animating an articulated "arm" with multiple segments, which we can see in Figure 13-2.

Listing 13-5. Chaining 3D transformations to animate an object

```
float[] r1, r2;

void setup() {
  fullScreen(P3D);
  noStroke();
  r1 = new float[100];
  r2 = new float[100];
  for (int i = 0; i < 100; i++) {
    r1[i] = random(0, 1);
    r2[i] = random(0, 1);
  }
}

void draw() {
  background(157);
  lights();
  translate(width/2, height/2);
  scale(4);
  for (int i = 0; i < 100; i++) {
    float tx = 0, ty = 0, tz = 0;
    float sx = 1, sy = 1, sz = 1;
    if (r1[i] < 1.0/3.0) {
      rotateX(millis()/1000.0);
      tz = sz = 10;
    } else if (1.0/3.0 < r1[i] && r1[i] < 2.0/3.0) {
      rotateY(millis()/1000.0);
      tz = sz = 10;
    } else {
      rotateZ(millis()/1000.0);
      if (r2[i] < 0.5) {
        tx = sx = 10;
      } else {
        ty = sy = 10;
      }
    }
    translate(tx/2, ty/2, tz/2);
    pushMatrix();
    scale(sx, sy, sz);
    box(1);
    popMatrix();
    translate(tx/2, ty/2, tz/2);
  }
}
```

The important points in this example are as follows: first, we use random numbers (r1 and r2) to decide which axis at each joint we rotate the next segment around and also which axis we extend the segment along, and second, the use of scale() in two different places: right after centering the scene, to increase the size of the entire arm, and before drawing each arm and only along the displacement axis, so the segments are properly connected with each other. Also, notice that the random numbers are pre-calculated in setup() and stored in float arrays; otherwise, the geometry will change completely from frame to frame, resulting in a very chaotic animation.

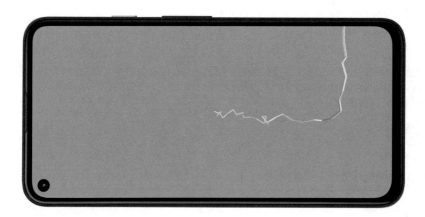

Figure 13-2. *Animated arm with combined 3D transformations*

3D Shapes

Just like we do in 2D, we can generate primitive shapes using Processing's functions. All the 2D primitives (triangle, ellipse, rectangle, and quads) can be used in 3D, with the addition of two new 3D primitives (box and sphere). Listing 13-6 draws all these primitives in a single sketch, whose output is in Figure 13-3.

Listing 13-6. Drawing 2D and 3D primitives in 3D

```
float[] r1, r2;
void setup() {
  fullScreen(P3D);
}

void draw() {
  background(157);

  translate(width/2, height/2);

  pushMatrix();
  translate(-width/3, -height/4);
  rotateY(millis()/2000.0);
  ellipse(0, 0, 200, 200);
  popMatrix();
```

```
pushMatrix();
translate(0, -height/4);
rotateY(millis()/2000.0);
triangle(0, +150, -150, -150, +150, -150);
popMatrix();

pushMatrix();
translate(+width/3, -height/4);
rotateY(millis()/2000.0);
rect(-100, -100, 200, 200, 20);
popMatrix();

pushMatrix();
translate(-width/3, +height/4);
rotateY(millis()/2000.0);
quad(-40, -100, 120, -80, 120, 150, -80, 150);
popMatrix();

pushMatrix();
translate(0, +height/4);
rotateY(millis()/2000.0);
box(200);
popMatrix();

pushMatrix();
translate(+width/3, +height/4);
rotateY(millis()/2000.0);
sphere(150);
popMatrix();
}
```

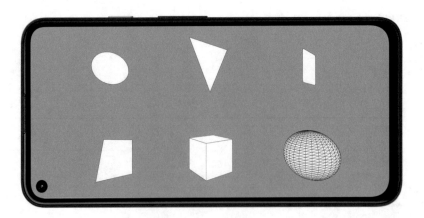

Figure 13-3. *2D and 3D primitives rendered with P3D*

Custom Shapes

We saw already in Chapter 4 that it is possible to create custom shapes using the beginShape()/vertex()/endShape() function, with the appropriate shape kind (POINTS, LINES, TRIANGLES, etc.) All the code we learned for 2D rendering can be reused in P3D without any changes, but now with the possibility of adding a Z coordinate. For instance, let's create in Listing 13-7 a terrain with QUADS and some randomness in the heights from the noise() function.

Listing 13-7. Creating a custom shape with QUADS

```
void setup() {
  fullScreen(P3D);
}

void draw() {
  background(150);
  lights();
  translate(width/2, height/2);
  rotateX(QUARTER_PI);
  beginShape(QUADS);
  float t = 0.0001 * millis();
  for (int i = 0; i < 50; i++) {
    for (int j = 0; j < 50; j++) {
      float x0 = map(i, 0, 50, -width/2, width/2);
      float y0 = map(j, 0, 50, -height/2, height/2);
      float x1 = x0 + width/50.0;
      float y1 = y0 + height/50.0;
      float z1 = 200 * noise(0.1 * i, 0.1 * j, t);
      float z2 = 200 * noise(0.1 * (i + 1), 0.1 * j, t);
      float z3 = 200 * noise(0.1 * (i + 1), 0.1 * (j + 1), t);
      float z4 = 200 * noise(0.1 * i, 0.1 * (j + 1), t);
      vertex(x0, y0, z1);
      vertex(x1, y0, z2);
      vertex(x1, y1, z3);
      vertex(x0, y1, z4);
    }
  }
  endShape();
}
```

The noise is generated using the (i, j) indices of the vertices defining the mesh, so it ensures that the height displacement is consistent at the vertices shared between contiguous quads (we learned about the basics of the noise function back in Chapter 6). We can see the result in Figure 13-4.

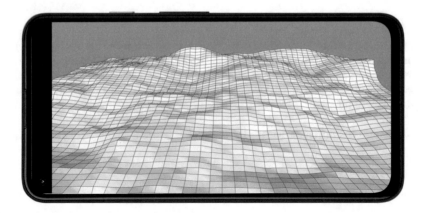

Figure 13-4. *Terrain generated with a QUADS shape*

The Camera

So far, we have let Processing handle how we peek into the 3D world from our screen, but we will now learn to do that ourselves. When we draw any 3D scene, there is a "camera" looking into the virtual space. We can think of the screen as the viewport of that camera. Processing includes some functions to manipulate the position and "virtual" lenses of the camera. In VR and AR sketches, on the other hand, the Processing camera will be controlled automatically by the movement of the phone in space. In either case, Processing's camera is defined by three vectors: the eye position, the center of the scene, and the "up" vector, illustrated in Figure 13-5.

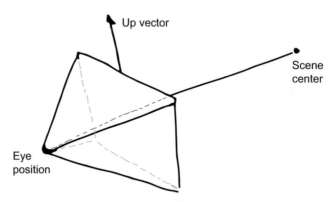

Figure 13-5. *Vectors defining position and orientation of the camera*

These vectors can be set using the camera() function: camera(eyeX, eyeY, eyeZ, centerX, centerY, centerZ, upX, upY, upZ). Calling camera() without any argument will set the default camera's position and orientation, in which the center is the (0, 0, 0) point, the eye is placed along the z axis, and the up direction is the positive Y vector. By continuously changing the eye's position, we can look at the scene from any vantage point. Listing 13-8 illustrates how to set these parameters.

Listing 13-8. Setting the parameters of the Processing camera

```
void setup() {
  fullScreen(P3D);
  fill(#AD71B7);
}

void draw() {
  background(#81B771);
  float t = millis()/1000.0;
  float ex = width/2 + 500 * cos(t);
  float ey = height/2 + 500 * sin(t);
  float ez = 1000 + 100 * cos(millis()/1000.0);
  camera(ex, ey, ez, width/2, height/2, 0, 0, 1, 0);
  lights();
  translate(width/2, height/2);
  box(300);
}
```

We can set not only the camera's position and orientation but also choose how the scene is projected onto the camera's viewport (which can be thought of as choosing the camera "lenses"). There are two types of projections available in P3D: perspective and orthographic. They are illustrated in Figure 13-6. Perspective projection, the default setting in P3D, is the one that corresponds to how images are formed in the physical world: the objects are projected onto the viewport plane following lines of view that converge into the "eye" position behind the viewport. This simulates the effect of perspective, where distant objects look smaller. In fact, Processing uses default perspective parameters so that a rectangle of dimensions (0, 0, width, height) at Z = 0 exactly covers the output window. Thanks to these settings, we can draw 2D shapes in P3D without any changes in the code.

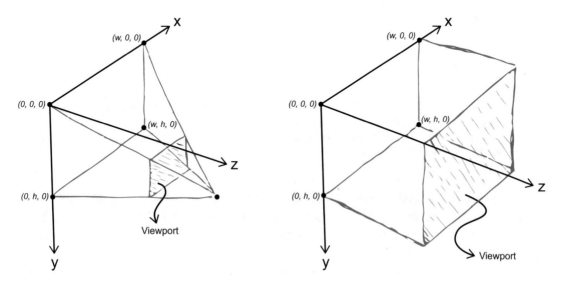

Figure 13-6. *Perspective (left) and orthographic (right) projections in Processing*

In orthographic projection, on the other hand, the objects are projected onto the viewport following lines perpendicular to it, so there is no decrease or increase in size as objects move away from or toward the camera eye. The default settings of the orthographic projection in Processing are such that the points of 3D coordinates (0, 0) and (width, height) fall exactly on the upper right and lower left corners of the output window.

We can easily switch back between these two projection modes with the perspective() and ortho() functions. These functions have the default settings as described previously, but we can also use them with additional arguments to adjust the field of vision, the position of the camera eye and other parameters: perspective(fovy, aspect, zNear, zFar) and ortho(left, right, bottom, top, near, far). In Listing 13-9, we link the field of vision with time through a cosine function so it oscillates back and forth between an angle of 10° (very narrow field of vision; object blows up to occupy almost the entire screen) and 80° (very wide; object looks smaller than normal).

Listing 13-9. Setting the perspective parameters

```
float angle = 0;

void setup() {
  fullScreen(P3D);
  fill(#AD71B7);
}

void draw() {
  background(#81B771);
  float fov = radians(map(cos(millis()/1000.0), -1, +1, 10, 80));
  float ratio = float(width)/height;
  perspective(fov, ratio, 1, 2000);
  lights();
  translate(width/2, height/2);
  rotateY(angle);
  rotateX(angle*2);
  box(300);
  angle += 0.01;
}
```

A couple of additional things to note here are the setting of the width-to-height aspect ratio, which in most situation should simply be the width/height, and the clipping planes. These planes determine the visible volume along the Z direction by having a near and a far value: anything closer than the former or farther than the latter is clipped out from view.

■ **Note**   The camera() and perspective() functions are not particularly intuitive to use, especially if one would like to think of camera movements and adjustment in physical space (like zooming, panning, and rolling), but there are libraries that simplify camera handling, among them PeasyCam, Obsessive Camera Direction, and nub. Appendix B includes a list of libraries that we can use from the Android mode.

Immediate vs. Retained Rendering

One important aspect about how we were handling the 3D scene until now is that we were creating a new 3D object from scratch in every frame and discarding it right afterward. This way of drawing 3D (and 2D) graphics, known as "immediate rendering," is adequate if we have relatively few objects in our scene but might slow down our sketch if we have a more complex scene with many shapes. This is particularly relevant with our goal of writing XR apps, as we will discuss further in the final part of the book, because the rendering animation should be as smooth as possible to ensure that the viewer does not experience motion sickness due to low or uneven frame rates in VR, or stuttering while interacting with objects in the physical space when running AR sketches.

Processing provides another way of drawing geometry, called "retained rendering," to improve performance. With retained rendering, we create our shapes once, and then we redraw them as many times as needed. We already used this technique in Chapter 4, and it can be much faster when drawing complex scenes. Retained rendering will become very handy later when we learn VR and AR.

Using retained rendering is simple; we only need to store our shapes in a PShape object. Processing provides a few predefined 3D shapes like boxes and spheres that we can create with a single call, as shown in Listing 13-10.

Listing 13-10. Using retained rendering

```
float angle = 0;
PShape cube;

void setup() {
  fullScreen(P3D);
  perspective(radians(80), float(width)/height, 1, 1000);
  PImage tex = loadImage("mosaic.jpg");
  cube = createShape(BOX, 400);
  cube.setTexture(tex);
}

void draw() {
  background(#81B771);
  lights();
  translate(width/2, height/2);
  rotateY(angle);
  rotateX(angle*2);
  shape(cube);
  angle += 0.01;
}
```

In this code, once we get our box object from the createShape() function, we can still make changes to it. Here, we apply a texture, so the faces of the box are covered with the image for a more interesting look. The final output is depicted in Figure 13-7.

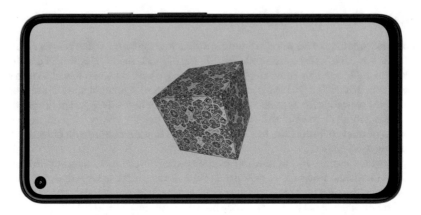

Figure 13-7. *Drawing a textured PShape*

Custom PShape Objects

As we saw in the preceding section, we can use predefined PShape objects to draw boxes, spheres, and other basic geometric shapes in 3D. The main advantage of using PShapes is increased performance, thanks to retained rendering. We can create virtually any kind of 3D shape and store it in a PShape object for faster retained rendering, as shown in Listing 13-11.

Listing 13-11. Storing a custom shape inside a PShape object

```
PShape terrain;

void setup() {
  fullScreen(P3D);
  terrain = createShape();
  terrain.beginShape(QUADS);
  for (int i = 0; i < 50; i++) {
    for (int j = 0; j < 50; j++) {
      float x0 = map(i, 0, 50, -width/2, width/2);
      float y0 = map(j, 0, 50, -height/2, height/2);
      float x1 = x0 + width/50.0;
      float y1 = y0 + height/50.0;
      float z1 = 200 * noise(0.1 * i, 0.1 * j, 0);
      float z2 = 200 * noise(0.1 * (i + 1), 0.1 * j, 0);
      float z3 = 200 * noise(0.1 * (i + 1), 0.1 * (j + 1), 0);
      float z4 = 200 * noise(0.1 * i, 0.1 * (j + 1), 0);
      terrain.vertex(x0, y0, z1);
      terrain.vertex(x1, y0, z2);
      terrain.vertex(x1, y1, z3);
      terrain.vertex(x0, y1, z4);
    }
  }
  terrain.endShape();
}
```

```
void draw() {
  background(150);
  lights();
  translate(width/2, height/2);
  rotateX(QUARTER_PI);
  shape(terrain);
}
```

We can still modify a PShape object after we have created it. For example, the code in Listing 13-12 wiggles the vertices in each frame up and down with the setVertex() function (the setup is identical to Listing 13-11).

Listing 13-12. Modifying a PShape object after creation

```
...
void draw() {
  background(150);
  lights();
  translate(width/2, height/2);
  rotateX(QUARTER_PI);
  updateShape();
  shape(terrain);
  println(frameRate);
}

void updateShape() {
  float t = 0.0001 * millis();
  int vidx = 0;
  for (int i = 0; i < 50; i++) {
    for (int j = 0; j < 50; j++) {
      float x0 = map(i, 0, 50, -width/2, width/2);
      float y0 = map(j, 0, 50, -height/2, height/2);
      float x1 = x0 + width/50.0;
      float y1 = y0 + height/50.0;
      float z1 = 200 * noise(0.1 * i, 0.1 * j, t);
      float z2 = 200 * noise(0.1 * (i + 1), 0.1 * j, t);
      float z3 = 200 * noise(0.1 * (i + 1), 0.1 * (j + 1), t);
      float z4 = 200 * noise(0.1 * i, 0.1 * (j + 1), t);
      terrain.setVertex(vidx++, x0, y0, z1);
      terrain.setVertex(vidx++, x1, y0, z2);
      terrain.setVertex(vidx++, x1, y1, z3);
      terrain.setVertex(vidx++, x0, y1, z4);
    }
  }
}
```

However, by modifying all the vertices of the PShape object, we will likely see the performance of the sketch return to the levels of immediate rendering. We can also modify only some vertices, in which case, performance would still be higher.

We can group PShape objects of different types as child objects into a single parent PShape. Processing will render them all together as a single entity, which will also result in higher frame rates than if they were drawn either with immediate rendering or as a separate PShape objects. In Listing 13-13, we read the 3D coordinates of 1,000 points from a text file using loadStrings() and then draw them as boxes or spheres.

Listing 13-13. Creating a group shape

```
PVector[] coords;
PShape group;

void setup() {
  fullScreen(P3D);
  textFont(createFont("SansSerif", 20 * displayDensity));
  sphereDetail(10);
  group = createShape(GROUP);
  String[] lines = loadStrings("points.txt");
  coords = new PVector[lines.length];
  for (int i = 0; i < lines.length; i++) {
    String line = lines[i];
    String[] valores = line.split(" ");
    float x = float(valores[0]);
    float y = float(valores[1]);
    float z = float(valores[2]);
    coords[i] = new PVector(x, y, z);
    PShape sh;
    if (random(1) < 0.5) {
      sh = createShape(SPHERE, 20);
      sh.setFill(#E8A92A);
    } else {
      sh = createShape(BOX, 20);
      sh.setFill(#4876B2);
    }
    sh.translate(x, y, z);
    sh.setStroke(false);
    group.addChild(sh);
  }
  noStroke();
}

void draw() {
  background(255);
  fill(0);
  text(frameRate, 50, 50);
  fill(255, 0, 0);
  lights();
  translate(width/2, height/2, 0);
  rotateY(map(mouseX, 0, width, 0, TWO_PI));
  shape(group);
}
```

We applied a few optimization tricks to this code to reduce the complexity of the scene: we set the sphere detail to 10 (the default is 30) and disable the stroke. Stroke lines can add a lot of extra geometry to a shape, thus slowing down the rendering. The result should look something like the one shown in Figure 13-8, with a reasonable performance even on low-end phones (a frame rate over 30 frames per second).

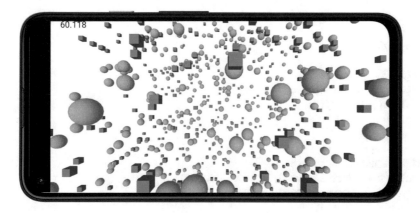

Figure 13-8. *Group shape containing shapes of different kinds*

■ **Note**   Performance in 3D can be affected by several factors, but one of the most important ones is the total vertex count in the scene. It is important that we do not add unnecessarily vertices to a scene, keeping in mind that users will look at our sketches on a (relatively) small phone's screen. We can take advantage of other useful optimizations, such as using PShape objects to store static geometry.

Loading OBJ Shapes

The OBJ file format (http://paulbourke.net/dataformats/obj) is a simple text-based format to store 3D geometry and material definitions, created back in the 1980s by Wavefront Technologies, a company that developed 3D animation software used in movies and other industries. Although it is very basic in terms of the information it can contain, it is supported by most 3D modeling tools, and there are many online repositories that include free 3D models in this format. Processing's API includes the loadShape() function, which we have used to load SVG shapes in 2D, and would read OBJ shapes in P3D, as demonstrated in Listing 13-14.

Listing 13-14. Loading an OBJ file

```
PShape model;
PVector center;

void setup() {
  fullScreen(P3D);
  model = loadShape("deer.obj");
  center = getShapeCenter(model);
  float dim = max(model.getWidth(), model.getHeight(), model.getDepth());
```

```
  float factor = width/(3 * dim);
  model.rotateX(PI);
  model.scale(factor);
  center.mult(factor);
  center.y *= -1;
}

void draw() {
  background(157);
  lights();
  translate(width/2, height/2);
  translate(-center.x, -center.y, -center.z);
  rotateY(millis()/1000.0);
  shape(model);
}

PVector getShapeCenter(PShape sh) {
  PVector bot = new PVector(+10000, +10000, +10000);
  PVector top = new PVector(-10000, -10000, -10000);
  PVector v = new PVector();
  for (int i = 0; i < sh.getChildCount(); i++) {
    PShape child = sh.getChild(i);
    for (int j = 0; j < child.getVertexCount(); j++) {
      child.getVertex(j, v);
      bot.x = min(bot.x, v.x);
      bot.y = min(bot.y, v.y);
      bot.z = min(bot.z, v.z);
      top.x = max(top.x, v.x);
      top.y = max(top.y, v.y);
      top.z = max(top.z, v.z);
    }
  }
  return PVector.add(top, bot).mult(0.5);
}
```

In this code, we start by loading the OBJ shape from the file, followed by calculating some parameters so that Processing can place it correctly on the scene. First, we compute the center position of the shape with the getShapeCenter() function, where we go over all the vertices in the shape and get the maximum and minimum values across each axis. The two vectors holding the minimum and maximum values, bot and top, are the opposite corners of the bounding box enclosing the entire shape. The middle point of the bounding box is the center of the shape, which we want to coincide with the center of the screen, as seen in Figure 13-9.

Also, the coordinates in an OBJ model could have a very different range of values from what we use in Processing (typically 0 – width and 0 – height), so by getting the dimensions of the model along each axis (using getWidth(), getHeight(), and getDepth()), we can calculate a factor to scale the shape up or down to fit the screen. The shape also needs to be rotated 180° around X, since it is upside down. This is often the case when loading OBJ files since a common convention in 3D graphics is to have the y axis pointing upward, while Processing uses a y axis pointing down, a more typical setting in vector graphics design tools. Note that we need to scale and invert the center vector separately, since it is computed from the input coordinates of the shape, which are not affected by the shape transformations.

Notice how we retrieve the shape's coordinates with a getVertex() call, where we reuse the same PVector object v. The reason is the following: if we were to create a new temporary PVector for each vertex, all these objects would need to be discarded from memory at the end. This memory-release operation, although very fast, could add up to a noticeable delay when freeing thousands of PVector objects, potentially resulting in a jittery animation.

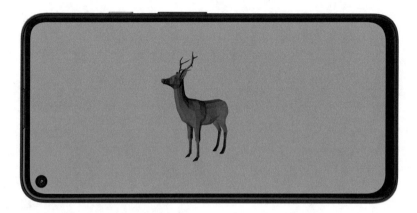

Figure 13-9. *3D shape loaded from an OBJ file*

Summary

With the help of the techniques that we have learned in this chapter, we will be able to create interactive 3D graphics in Android apps using Processing, including lighting, texturing, objects created on the fly and loaded from OBJ models, and performance tricks. Irrespective of whether we will be applying them to XR or not, these techniques are a useful toolkit for any 3D development we may want to do for games, visualizations, and other types of applications.

CHAPTER 14

■ ■ ■

Lighting and Texturing

In this chapter, we will build on the basics of 3D graphics by learning how to incorporate lights and textures to our Processing sketches. This will allow us to create more visually vivid scenes and set the stage for VR and AR apps where we need more realistic rendering for immersive and interactive experiences.

Making 3D Scenes more Realistic with Lights and Textures

Lights and textures are two key aspects we need to consider when creating a 3D scene. Without them, most objects in it will look just like flat shapes without providing any sense of depth or surface complexity. Lighting and texturing algorithms simulate in the computer how lights and materials interact with each other in the physical world so that 3D graphics are realistic enough to convey a plausible space. We might not need photo-realism, but still a combination of lights and materials that approximates reality to some extent is necessary to engage our users. Lights and textures become even more critical when working with VR and AR, where users are surrounded by our synthetic 3D scene, or they manipulate digital objects embedded in the physical world.

Processing has several functions to create light sources and set the material properties of 3D shapes, including textures. The lighting model that underlies these functions in the P3D renderer is a first approximation to more complex models. As such, it is not capable of generating shadows or rendering rugged or bumpy surfaces, but it can handle phenomena such as brightness and emissivity of a material, light falloffs, directional light sources, and spotlights. In the next chapter, we will learn how to implement our own, more realistic, lighting models through custom shaders.

Light Sources and Material Properties

The final color of a shape in a 3D scene in Processing is determined by the interplay between its material properties and the characteristics of the light sources. Very briefly, the color of a light source will "affect" a shape depending on whether the corresponding material property of the shape has been set to a color that matches to some degree the light's source color. The most important property is the fill color. For instance, if a light source has an RGB color of (200, 150, 150) and the fill color of the shape is (255, 255, 20), the shape will reflect the entirety of the red and green components of the light, but only a small fraction of its blue component.

© Andrés Colubri 2023

A. Colubri, *Processing for Android*, https://doi.org/10.1007/978-1-4842-9585-4_14

There are four types of light sources in Processing:

1) Ambient: Represents a light that doesn't come from a specific direction; the rays of light have bounced around so much that objects are evenly lit from all sides. The function that sets the ambient light is

```
ambientLight(c1, c2, c3);
```

The color of the ambient light is (c2, c2, c3), which is interpreted according to the current color mode.

2) Point light: It is a light that has a specific location in space and emits in all directions from that location as the center. Its function:

```
pointLight(c1, c2, c3, x, y, z);
```

The position of the point light is given by (x, y, z), while its color by (c1, c2, c3).

3) Directional light: Represents a light source that is far enough from the objects that all its rays follow the same direction (the Sun being an example of a directional light source). We configure it with

```
directionalLight(c1, c2, c3, nx, ny, nz);
```

The direction of the directional light is given by (nx, ny, nz), while its color by (c1, c2, c3).

4) Spotlight: It is a source that illuminates all objects within a cone volume centered at the light position. A spotlight has several parameters:

```
spotLight(c1, c2, c3, x, y, z, nx, ny, nz, angle, concentration)
```

As before, the position of the spotlight is given by (x, y, z) and its color by (c1, c2, c3). The additional parameters are (nx, ny, nz), the direction of the cone (not of the light rays, which are casted away from the origin as in a point light), the aperture angle of the cone, and the concentration toward the center of the cone.

Let's now consider Listing 14-1 to see how this works with a few shapes and a couple of objects.

Listing 14-1. Adding lights to a 3D scene

```
void setup() {
  fullScreen(P3D);
  noStroke();
}

void draw() {
  background(20);
translate(width/2, height/2);

  float pointX = map(mouseX, 0, width, -width/2, +width/2);
  float dirZ = map(mouseY, 0, height, 0, -1);
  pointLight(200, 200, 200, pointX, 0, 600);
  directionalLight(100, 220, 100, 0, 1, dirZ);

  rotateY(QUARTER_PI);
```

```
fill(255, 250, 200);
box(320);

translate(-400, 0);
fill(200, 200, 250);
sphere(160);

translate(0, +110, 360);
fill(255, 200, 200);
box(100);
}
```

In this example, we have two light sources: a bright gray point light and a green directional light. We can control the X position of the point light by swiping the touch pointer horizontally and the Z component of the directional light by swiping vertically. Since each object has its own fill color "reflecting" different components of the incoming lights, the final appearance of the scene can change quite significantly depending on the position and direction of the lights, as we can see in Figure 14-1. For example, the larger the component of the directional light along Z, the more directly it impacts the shapes with faces that are perpendicular to Z and so the increase of the overall green hue.

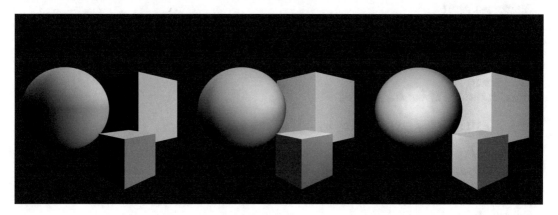

Figure 14-1. *Color of shapes in a scene change as light sources move around*

■ **Note** We should set the lights in every call of the draw() function; otherwise, they won't be active. We can set a default lighting configuration, sometimes enough for quick tests, by calling the lights() function.

The fill color, which determines how the surface reflects the incoming light color, is not the only material property we can adjust. We have the following additional properties:

1) Emissivity: The capacity of emitting light on its own. It is controlled by the following function:

   emissive(c1, c2, c2)

   where (c1, c2, c3) is the emissive color of the material.

2) Shininess: The amount of gloss in the surface of shapes. We only need to set a single parameter with

```
shininess(s)
```

with s being the level of gloss, starting from 0 (no shininess) to 1 (maximum shininess).

3) Specularity: The capacity to create specular reflections. The way it works is by calling the following function:

```
specular(c1, c2, c2)
```

with the color (c1, c2, c3) of the specular highlights.

By adjusting these three material properties, we can generate a wide range of material surfaces, even if the fill color is the same across the materials, as demonstrated in Listing 14-2, with its output shown in Figure 14-2.

Listing 14-2. Material properties

```
void setup() {
  fullScreen(P3D);
  noStroke();
}

void draw() {
  background(0);
  translate(width/2, height/2);

  directionalLight(255, 255, 255, 0, 0, -1);

  pushMatrix();
  translate(-width/3, 0);
  fill(250, 100, 50);
  specular(200, 250, 200);
  emissive(0, 0, 0);
  shininess(10.0);
  sphere(200);
  popMatrix();

  pushMatrix();
  fill(250, 100, 50);
  specular(255);
  shininess(1.0);
  emissive(0, 20, 0);
  sphere(200);
  popMatrix();

  pushMatrix();
  translate(+width/3, 0);
  fill(250, 100, 50);
  specular(255);
  shininess(2.0);
```

```
  emissive(50, 10, 100);
  sphere(200);
  popMatrix();
}
```

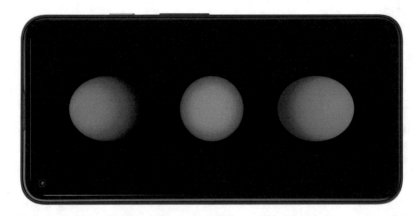

Figure 14-2. *Spheres with different material properties*

As with other properties in Processing, the emissive(), specular(), and shininess() functions set the corresponding properties for all shapes drawn afterward. Calling pushStyle() and popStyle() also acts on the material properties, including the fill, emissivity, specular colors, and shininess factor.

Texture Mapping

The use of fill color and other material properties gives us plenty of room to define how a specific shape will look like under different lighting scenarios, ranging from no lights (in which case the fill color is used to paint shapes uniformly) to more complex situations with multiple light sources. However, shapes are still relatively "flat" in the sense that they look like they are made of a single material. Texture mapping allows us to address that uniformity and to create more complex-looking surfaces with ease by simply "wrapping" the 3D shapes with a texture image, illustrated in the case of a sphere in Figure 14-3.

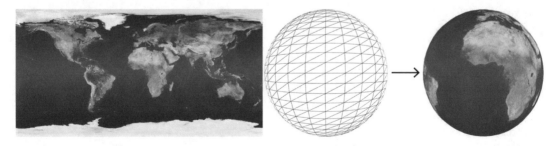

Figure 14-3. *Texture mapping a sphere with an image of the Earth*

Primitive shapes, such as boxes and spheres, can be textured right away by providing a suitable image, which is done in Listing 14-3.

Listing 14-3. Texturing a sphere

```
PShape earth;
PImage texmap;

void setup() {
  fullScreen(P3D);
  texmap = loadImage("earthmap1k.jpg");
  earth = createShape(SPHERE, 300);
  earth.setStroke(false);
  earth.setTexture(texmap);
}

void draw() {
  background(255);
  translate(width/2, height/2);
  rotateY(0.01 * frameCount);
  shape(earth);
}
```

When we create custom shapes, we need to provide some extra information to apply a texture successfully: texture coordinates. These coordinates indicate which pixel (u, v) in the image goes to which vertex (i, j) in the shape, and using those specifications, P3D is able to apply all the pixels in the image onto the entire shape.

The simplest texture mapping would be that of a rectangle, illustrated in Listing 14-4, where we only need to match the corners of the image with the four vertices of the quad.

Listing 14-4. Texturing a rectangle

```
PImage texmap;

void setup() {
  fullScreen(P3D);
  texmap = loadImage("woodstock.png");
  noStroke();
}

void draw() {
  background(255);
  translate(width/2, height/2);
  rotateY(0.01 * frameCount);
  scale(displayDensity);
  beginShape(QUAD);
  texture(texmap);
  vertex(-150, -150, 0, 0);
  vertex(-150, 150, 0, texmap.height);
  vertex(150, 150, texmap.width, texmap.height);
  vertex(150, -150, texmap.width, 0);
  endShape();
}
```

Oftentimes, we might find more convenient to specify the image pixels using normalized coordinates. This allows us to set texture mapping with a portion of an image without having to use the width and height values. We switch between default (IMAGE) and normalized (NORMAL) mode using the textureMode() function. Once we select the normal mode, the (u, v) values should range between 0 and 1, as in Listing 14-5. The output of this sketch is shown in Figure 14-4.

Listing 14-5. Using normalized texture coordinates

```
PImage texmap;

void setup() {
  fullScreen(P3D);
  texmap = loadImage("woodstock.png");
  textureMode(NORMAL);
  noStroke();
}

void draw() {
  background(255);
  translate(width/2, height/2);
  rotateY(0.01 * frameCount);
  beginShape(QUAD);
  texture(texmap);
  vertex(-150, -150, 0, 0);
  vertex(-150, 150, 0, 1);
  vertex(150, 150, 1, 1);
  vertex(150, -150, 1, 0);
  endShape();
}
```

Figure 14-4. Applying a texture image using normalized coordinates

With more complex shapes, we need to make sure that the texture coordinates are correctly calculated so the final textured object looks as we intended. For example, if we go back to the terrain example from Listing 13-11, we have the (i, j) indices of the grid, and we can use them to obtain the corresponding normalized texture coordinates with the map() function. Listing 14-6 shows how to do it, and the corresponding output is shown in Figure 14-5.

Listing 14-6. Texturing a complex shape

```
PShape terrain;

void setup() {
  fullScreen(P3D);
  PImage dirt = loadImage("dirt.jpg");
  textureMode(NORMAL);
  terrain = createShape();
  terrain.beginShape(QUADS);
  terrain.noStroke();
  terrain.texture(dirt);
  for (int i = 0; i < 50; i++) {
    for (int j = 0; j < 50; j++) {
      float x0 = map(i, 0, 50, -width/2, width/2);
      float y0 = map(j, 0, 50, -width/2, width/2);
      float u0 = map(i, 0, 50, 0, 1);
      float v0 = map(j, 0, 50, 0, 1);
      float u1 = map(i + 1, 0, 50, 0, 1);
      float v1 = map(j + 1, 0, 50, 0, 1);
      float x1 = x0 + width/50.0;
      float y1 = y0 + width/50.0;
      float z1 = 200 * noise(0.1 * i, 0.1 * j, 0);
      float z2 = 200 * noise(0.1 * (i + 1), 0.1 * j, 0);
      float z3 = 200 * noise(0.1 * (i + 1), 0.1 * (j + 1), 0);
      float z4 = 200 * noise(0.1 * i, 0.1 * (j + 1), 0);
      terrain.vertex(x0, y0, z1, u0 ,v0);
      terrain.vertex(x1, y0, z2, u1 ,v0);
      terrain.vertex(x1, y1, z3, u1 ,v1);
      terrain.vertex(x0, y1, z4, u0 ,v1);
    }
  }
  terrain.endShape();
}

void draw() {
  background(150);
  lights();
  translate(width/2, height/2);
  rotateX(QUARTER_PI);
  shape(terrain);
}
```

It is worth noting that (u, v) texture coordinates, in the same way as (x, y, z) coordinates, don't have to be static. Even in a PShape object we can modify the texture coordinates dynamically using the setTextureUV() function in PShape, and this allows for very interesting visual effects.

Figure 14-5. *Terrain shape with a dirt texture applied to it*

Putting Everything Together

Let's wrap up this chapter by working on an example that combines different lighting settings, texturing, and 3D transformations to create a visually convincing (although not physically realistic) space scene with the Earth and moon orbiting around the Sun.

Creating the 3D objects will be easy; we only need three spheres to represent the solar bodies in our scene. We can use what we learned in the previous chapter on combining 3D transformations, so we set the Sun as the center of the scene, rotating around its axis, the Earth revolving around the Sun at some present distance, and finally the moon revolving around the Earth. This can be achieved by applying a sequence of transformations to translate the entire scene to the center of the screen, place the Sun there and then rotate it around its y axis, then rotate and translate the Earth to its location, and finally rotate and translate the moon with respect to the Earth's location. The other important element to consider is lighting; since the Sun can be considered as the source of light illuminating all the objects in the scene from its center, we could place a point light at the center of the scene (which is where the Sun is located) so the shadows of the moon and the Earth are correctly cast as they revolve around the Sun. Listing 14-7 puts these considerations into practice.

Listing 14-7. Lighting and texturing a space scene

```
PShape sun, earth, moon;
float sunAngle, earthAngle, moonAngle;

void setup() {
  fullScreen(P3D);
  orientation(LANDSCAPE);

  sun = createShape(SPHERE, 150);
  sun.setStroke(false);
  sun.setEmissive(color(255, 255, 255));
  sun.setTexture(loadImage("sun.jpg"));

  earth = createShape(SPHERE, 80);
  earth.setStroke(false);
  earth.setTexture(loadImage("earth.jpg"));
```

```
  moon = createShape(SPHERE, 30);
  moon.setStroke(false);
  moon.setTexture(loadImage("moon.jpg"));
}

void draw() {
  background(0);

  translate(width/2, height/2);
  rotateX(-QUARTER_PI);

  pointLight(255, 255, 255, 0, 0, 0);

  rotateY(sunAngle);
  shape(sun);

  pushMatrix();
  rotateY(earthAngle);
  translate(600, 0);
  shape(earth);

  pushMatrix();
  rotateY(moonAngle);
  translate(150, 0);
  shape(moon);
  popMatrix();

  popMatrix();

  earthAngle += 0.01;
  moonAngle += 0.005;
  sunAngle += 0.001;
}
```

In this code, notice how the three PShape objects for the Sun, Earth, and moon are initialized in the setup() function, where we load and set their corresponding textures. The pointLight(255, 255, 255, 0, 0, 0) call in draw() generates a point source that emits white light in all directions from its (0, 0, 0) location. Note that this location corresponds to the center of the screen (width/2, height/2, 0) due to the preceding translation. However, this light source will not illuminate the Sun because it is placed inside of it. Therefore, we set an emissive white color for the Sun alone so it appears fully lit from its own emissive property (which, by the way, does not illuminate any other object; only the point light does). We also applied a rotation of -QUARTER_PI around the X (horizontal) axis to make the whole scene slightly angled so it can be seen from above.

This is already quite good; however, we could still add a couple of improvements. First, the background is completely black, while it should be filled with stars. An apparently simple solution would be to draw the image of a star field to cover the entire screen. However, if we do this, we will run into the following issue: when we draw an image with P3D, Processing places a textured rectangle at Z = 0 with the coordinates we specify in the image() call, and so, the moving objects in our scene will go through this plane, breaking the illusion of a true background image. But there is a trick we can use to solve this issue. It's rather technical, and a quick explanation is the following: Processing keeps track of the distance to the screen of each object it draws so it can determine which objects are closer and hence occlude those that are behind. These distances get saved to an internal area of video memory called the "depth mask." We can disable updates to the depth mask temporarily, and if we draw objects while the updates to the depth mask are disabled, those objects will always be occluded even if they are in front of everything else. In this case, if we draw the star field background image while the updates to the depth mask are disabled, all spheres drawn afterwards will appear in front of the stars.

Finally, we can add a simple interaction by using the Y position of the pointer to set the angle of the entire scene so it can be seen from above, below, or perfectly from the side. These changes are shown in Listing 14-8, and the output of the sketch is shown in Figure 14-6.

Listing 14-8. Disabling the depth mask to draw a background image

```
void draw() {
  background(0);
  hint(DISABLE_DEPTH_MASK);
  image(stars, 0, 0, width, height);
  hint(ENABLE_DEPTH_MASK);

  translate(width/2, height/2);
  rotateX(map(mouseY, 0, height, HALF_PI, -HALF_PI));
  ...
}
```

Figure 14-6. *Space scene with the moon orbiting the Earth and Earth rotating around the Sun*

Summary

After incorporating lighting and texturing into our 3D toolkit, we are at a place where we should be able to make complex scenes with movement, lights, and textures using Processing. By carefully defining light sources, material properties, and texture images, our objects can look much more realistic and responsive to changes in the environment. This, in turn, will help us to create convincing 3D scenes as well as immersive VR and AR experiences.

CHAPTER 15

■ ■ ■

GLSL Shaders

We will conclude our journey through 3D graphics with an exciting topic: GLSL shaders. Shader programming has a fame of being the tool of choice for creating striking real-time computer graphics. While this is true, it is also true that coding shaders is not easy because they require an advanced understanding of how computers convert numbers into images on the screen, which often involves a great deal of mathematics. In this chapter, we will try to go through the basic concepts and applications of GLSL shaders step by step, so readers should end up with a good foundation to continue learning more about this powerful tool.

What Is a Shader?

This is a good question to start our chapter with! A quick answer could be that a shader is a piece of code that generates an image on the screen from input data representing a 2D or 3D scene. This code runs on the Graphics Processing Unit (GPU) of the computer (either desktop, laptop, phone, or watch). In the previous chapters, we already saw how to enter some of that data with the Processing API: vertices, colors, textures, lights, etc., but we did not need to write any shader code. But everything that Processing draws on the screen with the P2D and P3D renderers is the output of a specific default shader running behind the scenes. Processing handles these default shaders transparently so that we don't need to worry about them, and we can simply use the Processing's drawing functions to create all kinds of shapes, animations, and interactions.

Processing offers a set of advanced functions and variables that allows us to replace the default shaders with our own, written in a language called GLSL, from "OpenGL Shading Language" (OpenGL refers to a programming interface for 2D and 3D graphics; Processing uses OpenGL internally to talk to the GPU). This opens many exciting possibilities: rendering 3D scenes using more realistic lighting and texturing algorithms, applying image postprocessing effects in real time, creating complex procedural objects that would be very hard or impossible to generate with the regular drawing API, and sharing shader effects between desktop, mobile, and web platforms with minimal code changes. All of this surely sounds great, but to be able to write our own shaders, we first need to understand how they work and how they can be used to modify and extend the drawing capabilities of Processing. The next section will provide a brief overview of the inner workings of shaders before we jump into writing GLSL code.

The Graphics Pipeline: Vertex and Pixel Shaders

All modern GPUs in our computing devices implement a well-defined sequence of stages from input data to final output on the screen, called the "graphics pipeline." We will look at the main stages in the graphics pipeline from the perspective of a simple Processing sketch so we can understand how the data we enter in Processing goes through this pipeline. This sketch, shown in Listing 15-1, draws a quad with lights and some geometric transformations using the functions we learned in Chapters 13 and 14.

© Andrés Colubri 2023
A. Colubri, *Processing for Android*, https://doi.org/10.1007/978-1-4842-9585-4_15

Listing 15-1. Processing sketch that draws a lit rotating rectangle in 3D

```
float angle;

void setup() {
  size(400, 400, P3D);
  noStroke();
}

void draw() {
  background(255);
  perspective();
  camera();
  pointLight(255, 255, 255, 200, 200, -300);
  translate(200, 200);
  rotateY(angle += 0.01);
  beginShape(QUADS);
  normal(0, 0, 1);
  fill(50, 50, 200);
  vertex(-100, +100);
  vertex(+100, +100);
  fill(200, 50, 50);
  vertex(+100, -100);
  vertex(-100, -100);
  endShape();
}
```

The data we send to the graphics pipeline from the sketch consists of the global parameters of the scene (e.g., projection, camera, and lighting setup, model or geometry transformations applied on the shapes such as rotations and translations) and the attributes of each individual vertex that form our shapes (including position, color, normal vectors, and texture coordinates). Another important piece of information is the type of shape (in this case, QUAD), which tells the GPU how the vertices should be connected with each other (we saw all the different shape types supported by Processing in Chapter 4). The first stage in the pipeline is the "vertex shader." It calculates the position of each vertex in 3D space after applying setup and geometric transformations, as well as its color as the result of the lights in the scene and the material attributes of the vertex. The type of shape is also considered in this stage so that by connecting the vertices with each other according to the type, the output of the vertex shader will be the list of pixels that should be painted with a specific color to draw the desired shape on the screen. This output is called "fragment data," which comprises not only the coordinate of each pixel on the screen that should be painted but also its color (and potentially other attributes that are defined per pixel). This output from the vertex shader in turn represents the input of the "fragment shader" (called this way since it operates on fragments). The fragment shader outputs the final color for each pixel on the screen. This sequence of operations is depicted in Figure 15-1.

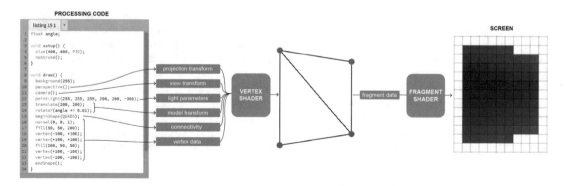

Figure 15-1. *Diagram of the vertex and fragment stages in the graphics pipeline*

■ **Note** This is a very simplified representation of the graphics pipeline; there are several other stages that are not shown here so we can focus on its most important elements. References to learn shader programming in more depth are provided at the end of this section.

A key feature that makes shaders so important in graphics programming is their speed. In principle, we could potentially draw any 2D or 3D scene without using shaders. For example, Processing allows us to set the color of each pixel on the screen directly from our sketch, simply by looping over all the pixels one by one, as we can see in Listing 15-2.

Listing 15-2. Processing sketch that sets the color of each pixel on the screen

```
fullScreen();
for (int x = 0; x < width; x++) {
  for (int y = 0; y < height; y++) {
    set(x, y, color(map(x, 0, width, 0, 255), map(y, 0, height, 0, 255), 255));
  }
}
```

While this code is perfectly valid and will generate a gradient of color covering the entire screen, it works sequentially, going one pixel at a time and setting its color. This will not run very fast, especially for devices with high-resolution screens. For example, a resolution of 2340×1080 pixels or more is very common for current Android devices, meaning that there is a total of at least 2,527,200 pixels to paint in every frame. If we now consider that a smooth animation often requires drawing 60 frames per second, this means that we should be able to calculate and set a color (at least) 15,1632,000 times per second, which, if we do sequentially one pixel at a time, may significantly slow down our sketch. On the other hand, vertex and fragment shaders are exceptionally fast, allowing real-time rendering even for very high vertex and pixel counts. This is because instead of processing vertices or fragments one by one, they work in parallel. Therefore, they can process many vertices or fragments simultaneously, even if the calculations on each vertex or fragment are quite complicated. We can think of shaders as little snippets of code that run on each vertex (or fragment), all at the same time. We don't need to worry about looping over all the vertices (or fragments); the GPU will do that for us and with the added benefit of doing it in parallel to ensure smooth real-time animations!

The remainder of this chapter will provide an overview of GLSL shaders within Processing. However, there are many other programming tools and environments that support shader programming, and thanks to the use of GLSL as the common language, shader code and techniques can be ported back and forth between these tools and Processing. For example, we can use shaders in web apps through WebGL, the JavaScript API for rendering interactive 2D and 3D graphics in any compatible web browser. *The Book of Shaders* (https://thebookofshaders.com), by Patricio Gonzalez Vivo and Jen Lowe, is an excellent learning resource on shaders, which focuses on the use of fragment shaders with WebGL. The p5.js library also supports GLSL shaders, and P5.js Shaders (https://itp-xstory.github.io/p5js-shaders), by Casey Conchinha and Louise Lessél, is another guide that can also be useful for Processing users. Online tools specifically designed for creating and sharing shaders are excellent places to learn and experiment, such as the following:

- Shadertoy: www.shadertoy.com/
- GLSL Sandbox: https://glslsandbox.com/
- Vertex Shader Art: www.vertexshaderart.com/

The Processing shader examples by Gene Kogan (https://github.com/genekogan/Processing-Shader-Examples) is a good collection of GLSL shaders specifically to be run inside Processing and shows how to adapt shader effects from online tools such as the GLSL Sandbox to be compatible with Processing's shader API. The shader examples for Processing by Adam Ferriss (https://github.com/aferriss/shaderExamples) is another useful resource for shader programming in Processing, with a version for p5.js (https://github.com/aferriss/p5jsShaderExamples).

The PShader Class

In the previous section, we saw that the two stages in the graphics pipeline are the vertex and fragment shaders. Both are needed to specify a complete, working pipeline. In Processing, we write the GLSL code for the fragment and vertex shaders in separate files, which then are combined to form a single "shader program" than can be run by the GPU. The word "program" is often skipped, with the assumption that when we say shader, we are referring to a complete shader program involving both fragment and vertex shaders.

A shader (program) is encapsulated in Processing by the PShader class. A PShader object is created with the loadShader() function that takes the file names of the vertex and fragment shaders as the arguments. If we only provide one file name, then Processing will expect that the file name corresponds to the fragment shader and will use a default vertex shader to complete the program. Listing 15-3 shows a sketch loading and using a basic shader that renders a shape using its current fill color, and includes the code of the fragment and vertex shaders after the sketch's code. The files frag.glsl and vert.glsl should be saved in the data folder of the sketch. The output of this code is shown in Figure 15-2.

Listing 15-3. Sketch that uses a shader to draw a shape using its fill color

```
PShader simple;
float angle;

void setup() {
  fullScreen(P3D);
  simple = loadShader("frag.glsl", "vert.glsl");
  shader(simple);
  noStroke();
}
```

```
void draw() {
  background(255);
  translate(width/2, height/2);
  rotateY(angle);
  beginShape(QUADS);
  normal(0, 0, 1);
  fill(50, 50, 200);
  vertex(-200, +200);
  vertex(+200, +200);
  fill(200, 50, 50);
  vertex(+200, -200);
  vertex(-200, -200);
  endShape();
  angle += 0.01;
}
```

frag.glsl

```
#ifdef GL_ES
precision mediump float;
precision mediump int;
#endif

varying vec4 vertColor;

void main() {
  gl_FragColor = vertColor;
}
```

vert.glsl

```
uniform mat4 transform;

attribute vec4 position;
attribute vec4 color;

varying vec4 vertColor;

void main() {
  gl_Position = transform * position;
  vertColor = color;
}
```

Notice how the shader is set using the shader() function, which takes the shader object we want to use as its argument. This function works like other Processing functions that set the style of the scene, in the sense that Processing will try to use this shader to render all subsequent shapes. We can set a new shader at any time by calling shader() again with the appropriate argument, and if we want Processing to go back to its built-in shaders, we just call resetShader(). In this example, the output of the custom shader is identical to what Processing would render without it. This is so because our shader is replicating the default shader that Processing uses to draw scenes without lights or textures. We will go through the details of this first custom shader in the next section and will learn how to make some changes to modify its output.

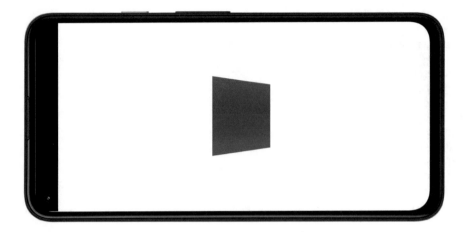

Figure 15-2. *Output of our first custom shader from Listing 15-3*

Anatomy of a Simple Shader

Listing 15-3 included the source code of the vertex and fragment shaders we used to arrive to the image in Figure 15-2. Let's look at them separately to start understanding the inputs, calculation, and outputs of each stage and how they work together to render the shapes in our Processing sketch. First, the vertex shader:

```
uniform mat4 transform;

attribute vec4 position;
attribute vec4 color;

varying vec4 vertColor;

void main() {
  gl_Position = transform * position;
  vertColor = color;
}
```

The vertex shader's code starts with the declaration of four variables: transform, position, color, and vertColor, followed by the instructions inside the main() function, which the GPU runs automatically on each vertex. The declared variables have types, in this case, mat4 and vec4, which mean that they hold either a matrix of 4×4 elements (in the case of transform) or vectors of four elements (in the case of position, color, and vertColor). Each one of these variables also has a "storage qualifier," which is uniform for the transform matrix, attribute for the position and color vectors, and varying for vertColor. We will explain what these qualifiers mean in a second. But first, we should note that by inspecting this code, we have encountered a defining feature of shaders: they operate on vectors and matrices, which are very convenient mathematical objects to represent and work with 3D data. The details of mathematics for computer graphics (mostly consisting of vector and matrix algebra) are beyond the scope of this chapter; here, we will only say that by multiplying the position vector by the transform matrix (which combines the effect of the geometry and camera transformations), we obtain the coordinates of the vector in screen space and then assign them to the gl_Position vector, which is a built-in GLSL variable that stores the result of this calculation and sends it down the pipeline:

$$gl\_Position = transform \cdot position = \begin{pmatrix} m_0 & m_4 & m_8 & m_{12} \\ m_1 & m_5 & m_9 & m_{13} \\ m_2 & m_6 & m_{10} & m_{14} \\ m_3 & m_7 & m_{11} & m_{15} \end{pmatrix} \cdot \begin{pmatrix} x \\ y \\ z \\ w \end{pmatrix}$$

In this formula, we can see that the transform matrix has 16 elements (since it's 4 rows by 4 columns) and that the position has x, y, z, and w coordinates (with x, y, and z coming from our sketch code and w being a normalization factor needed for perspective calculations and determined automatically by Processing). Unless we want to manipulate these numbers to do some advanced calculation ourselves, we don't need to worry about them at all; GLSL will carry out the matrix-vector multiplication for us. The only other line of code in the shader is the vertColor = color assignment; this is simply passing along the color vector (which contains the red, green, blue, and alpha values we set with the fill() function in our sketch) to the next stage in the pipeline, using the vertColor variable for this purpose.

As we briefly mentioned before, the shader variables have a storage qualifier, either uniform, attribute, or varying. Now that we have seen what each of these variables does, it will make more sense to describe what the qualifiers mean. The transform matrix, for example, has the uniform qualifier, which indicates that it is the constant for all the vertices going through the vertex shader. This is reasonable, since all vertices have the same transformation applied to them. Then, we have the position and color qualified as attributes; this means that these variables store values defined for each individual vertex that passes through the shader. Finally, variables qualified as varying are variables that communicate information between the vertex and the fragment shaders. Here, we only have one varying variable, vertColor, which will be used, immediately after the vertex stage, to calculate the color of the fragments going into the fragment shader. The gl_Position variable is also a varying, but since it is a built-in variable from GLSL, we don't need to declare it like the other variables at the top of the vertex shader's code.

Having dissected the elements of the vertex shader in our example, we can move on to the fragment shader:

```
#ifdef GL_ES
precision mediump float;
precision mediump int;
#endif

varying vec4 vertColor;

void main() {
  gl_FragColor = vertColor;
}
```

We can see that the vertColor varying variable that we had as the output in the vertex shader now appears in the declaration of the variables of the fragment shader, also as a varying variable. In general, any varying variable we declare in the vertex shader should also appear in the declaration section of the corresponding fragment shader. The implementation of the fragment shader, inside the main() function, is very simple; we just assign the vertColor variable, containing the color computed in the vertex stage, to the gl_FragColor, another built-in GLSL variable that sends the output of the fragment calculation to the corresponding pixel on the screen. The ifdef section at the top is required to make the shader compatible with mobile devices. It sets the precision of the float and integer numbers to medium, which should be fine for most devices. We need to remember to include this section in all our fragment shaders.

> ■ **Note** Knowledge of vector and matrix linear algebra is very important if we want to write our own shaders. There are many books on the topic; some good free online resources are the following: Linear Algebra section from Khan Academy (www.khanacademy.org/math/linear-algebra), Scratch Pixel (www.scratchapixel.com/), Immersive Linear Algebra (https://immersivemath.com), and the OpenGL tutorials from Song Ho Ahn (www.songho.ca/opengl/).

We already noted that our shader does not generate anything different from the default Processing output, but now that we have a basic understanding of the GLSL code, we should be able to make some small changes. For instance, we could try setting a constant color in the fragment shader, as shown in Listing 15-4 (the rest of the code, including sketch and vertex shader, is identical to that in Listing 15-3).

Listing 15-4. Fragment shader that sets green as the fragment color

```
#ifdef GL_ES
precision mediump float;
precision mediump int;
#endif

varying vec4 vertColor;

void main() {
  gl_FragColor = vec4(0, 1, 0, 1);
}
```

The output of this shader is shown in Figure 15-3. Even though we are sending the same fill colors from our sketch as before, the fragment shader is ignoring the value from vertColor and using a constant value for all fragments generated by the rectangle. We should also keep in mind that in GLSL, the components of a color are between 0 and 1, so that's why we use the (0, 1, 0, 1) value to output green (0 = red, 1 = green, 0 = blue, 1 = alpha).

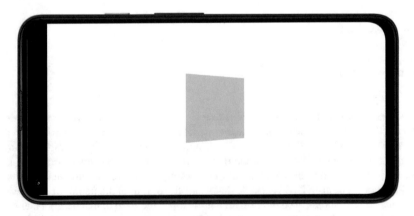

Figure 15-3. *Output of the shader in Listing 15-4, with constant fragment color*

One handy feature of shaders is the possibility of easy reuse. Since they implement graphics calculations at the level of each individual vertex or fragment, they are independent of the details of the geometry in our sketch, so we could apply the same shaders across different projects. For example, in Listing 15-5, we could load the same shaders from Listing 15-4, but this time the shape is a static rectangle that covers the entire screen.

Listing 15-5. Reusing our basic custom shader with a different shape

```
PShader simple;

void setup() {
  fullScreen(P3D);
  simple = loadShader("frag.glsl", "vert.glsl");
  shader(simple);
  noStroke();
}

void draw() {
  rect(0, 0, width, height);
}
```

The output of this sketch should be the entire screen of the device painted green, since the rectangle goes from (0, 0) to (width, height) and so it generates fragments for all the pixels on the screen.

Defining Custom Uniforms

As we have seen so far, shaders are a very powerful tool for graphics programming, but our learning needs to move forward by taking small steps; the downside is that shaders require very specialized knowledge in a new language, GLSL, as well as good understanding of vector and matrix algebra to fully take advantage of their capabilities. However, even at this initial stage, we can already try some interesting possibilities by defining custom uniform variables to pass parameters and user input to our shaders.

In Listing 15-6, we define two custom uniforms: `resolution` and `pointer`. In the first one, we will store the (width, height) values from Processing, while in the second, we will store the (mouseX, mouseY) coordinates. We can take advantage of another built-in varying variable available in the fragment shader, gl_FragCoord, which contains the (x, y) screen coordinates of the fragment. Using all these variables, we can construct a dynamic gradient that depends on the position of the mouse pointer on the screen.

Listing 15-6. Dynamic gradient using mouse pointer and screen resolution

```
PShader gradient;

void setup() {
  fullScreen(P3D);
  gradient = loadShader("frag.glsl", "vert.glsl");
  gradient.set("resolution", float(width), float(height)) ;
  noStroke();
}

void draw() {
  shader(gradient);
  fill(255);
```

```
    gradient.set("pointer", float(mouseX), float(mouseY));
    rect(0, 0, width, height);
    resetShader();
    fill(255);
    ellipse(mouseX, mouseY, 100, 100);
}
```

frag.glsl

```
#ifdef GL_ES
precision mediump float;
precision mediump int;
#endif

uniform vec2 resolution;
uniform vec2 pointer;

varying vec4 vertColor;

void main() {
  float maxr = pointer.x / resolution.x;
  float maxg = pointer.y / resolution.y;
  float gradx = gl_FragCoord.x / resolution.x;
  float grady = gl_FragCoord.y / resolution.y;
  gl_FragColor = vec4(maxr * gradx * vertColor.r, maxg * grady * vertColor.g,
  vertColor.b, 1);
}
```

vert.glsl

```
uniform mat4 transform;

attribute vec4 position;
attribute vec4 color;

varying vec4 vertColor;

void main() {
  gl_Position = transform * position;
  vertColor = color;
}
```

The output of this code is shown in Figure 15-4. By moving the pointer around, the shader calculates the maximum red and green component of the gradient by dividing the pointer coordinates by the resolution (let's remember that colors in GLSL need to be normalized between 0 and 1), while the position along the gradient in x and y is determined by dividing the fragment coordinates by the resolution, again resulting in a 0-1 number. The Processing function to set the value of a uniform is PShader.set(), and it is important to note that the (width, height) and (mouseX, mouseY) values are interpreted as float numbers so they are received by the shader as floating-point vectors. In fact, the gradient can get modulated by the fill color of the rectangle, since the varying vertColor that passes the color from the vertices is used to multiply each component in the gl_FragColor. Finally, we use the resetShader() function in the sketch to disable our custom gradient shader and draw an ellipse using the default Processing shader.

Even though this example is very simple, it demonstrates how we can perform per-pixel calculations using custom parameters we send from our sketch to the shaders. This same approach can be applied to generate much more complex shader effects.

Figure 15-4. *Output of the dynamic gradient shader*

Types of Shaders in Processing

In all the shader examples we have considered so far, we only run sketches without any lighting or texturing, so shapes always appear rendered with a flat color. Can we use those same shaders as soon as we incorporate lights in our scene and apply textures to the shapes? The answer is no, because a shader for rendering lit shapes requires additional attributes and uniform variables from Processing. These additional variables are not needed by shaders to render flat-colored shapes without lights or textures, so the source code of the shaders must be different. Similarly, a shader for rendering textured shapes needs its own uniforms and attributes that would not be required otherwise. In summary, we have four possible scenarios, each requiring its own type of shader:

- There are no lights and no textures: Use a color shader.

- There are lights but no textures: Use a light shader.

- There are textures but no lights: Use a texture shader.

- There are both textures and lights: Use a texlight shader.

So depending on the current configuration of our sketch (we could be drawing flat-colored shapes at some point and textured or lit shapes later), we need to provide a shader of the correct type at each moment. For example, if we are drawing textured shapes but we set a color shader, Processing will ignore it and use its default texture shader. Processing is also capable of autodetecting the type of shader we are trying to use depending on the type of uniforms and attributes defined in the shader code. We will learn more about each type in the next sections.

Color Shaders

We used color shaders in Listings 15-3 through 15-6, since in those sketches we had neither lights nor textures. A color shader only requires the transform uniform to convert the raw vertex positions into pixels and the position and color attributes per vertex. Since shaders are reusable, we could just drop the color shader from Listing 15-3 in the next listing, Listing 15-7, where we use a blue sphere shape to demonstrate the flat shading.

Listing 15-7. Applying a color shader to a sphere

```
PShape globe;
float angle;
PShader colorShader;

void setup() {
  fullScreen(P3D);
  colorShader = loadShader("colorfrag.glsl", "colorvert.glsl");
  globe = createShape(SPHERE, 300);
  globe.setFill(color(#4C92F2));
  globe.setStroke(false);
}

void draw() {
  background(0);
  shader(colorShader);
  translate(width/2, height/2);
  rotateY(angle);
  shape(globe);
  angle += 0.01;
}
```

We didn't need to list the fragment and vertex shaders, since they are identical to those in Listing 15-3. The output of this code is shown in Figure 15-5.

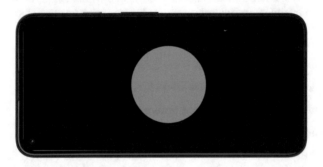

Figure 15-5. *Output of the color shader applied to a sphere*

Texture Shaders

Rendering textured shapes requires additional uniforms and attributes in the shader. Let's look at the sketch in Listing 15-8, together with the accompanying fragment and vertex shaders.

Listing 15-8. Sketch for textured rendering (no lights)

```
PImage earth;
PShape globe;
float angle;
PShader texShader;
```

```
void setup() {
  fullScreen(P3D);
  texShader = loadShader("texfrag.glsl", "texvert.glsl");
  earth = loadImage("earthmap1k.jpg");
  globe = createShape(SPHERE, 300);
  globe.setTexture(earth);
  globe.setStroke(false);
}

void draw() {
  background(0);
  shader(texShader);
  translate(width/2, height/2);
  rotateY(angle);
  shape(globe);
  angle += 0.01;
}
```

texfrag.glsl

```
#ifdef GL_ES
precision mediump float;
precision mediump int;
#endif

uniform sampler2D texture;

varying vec4 vertColor;
varying vec4 vertTexCoord;

void main() {
  gl_FragColor = texture2D(texture, vertTexCoord.st) * vertColor;
}
```

texvert.glsl

```
uniform mat4 transform;
uniform mat4 texMatrix;

attribute vec4 position;
attribute vec4 color;
attribute vec2 texCoord;

varying vec4 vertColor;
varying vec4 vertTexCoord;

void main() {
  gl_Position = transform * position;

  vertColor = color;
  vertTexCoord = texMatrix * vec4(texCoord, 1.0, 1.0);
}
```

In this listing, we have a new uniform in the vertex shader called texMatrix, which properly scales the texture coordinates of each vertex, passed in the additional attribute texCoord. In the fragment shader, we have another new uniform variable, of type sampler2D, called texture, and that gives the shader access to the texture data. The GLSL function texture2D() allows us to retrieve the content of the texture at the position specified by the texture coordinate vertTexCoord. The result of this sketch is shown in Figure 15-6.

Figure 15-6. *Output of the texture shader applied to a sphere*

The texture2D() function becomes very handy to implement many different kinds of effects using textures. For example, we can pixelate the texture very easily by modifying the texture coordinate values, vertTexCoord.st, so that they are binned within a given number of cells. We can make this number into a uniform parameter controlled by user input, as shown in Listing 15-9, with a typical rendering in Figure 15-7 (vertex shader is omitted as it is identical to the one in Listing 15-8).

Listing 15-9. Sketch for pixelated texture rendering

```
PImage earth;
PShape globe;
float angle;
PShader pixShader;

void setup() {
  fullScreen(P3D);
  pixShader = loadShader("pixelated.glsl", "texvert.glsl");
  earth = loadImage("earthmap1k.jpg");
  globe = createShape(SPHERE, 300);
  globe.setTexture(earth);
  globe.setStroke(false);
}

void draw() {
  background(0);
  shader(pixShader);
  pixShader.set("numBins", int(map(mouseX, 0, width, 0, 100)));
  translate(width/2, height/2);
  rotateY(angle);
  shape(globe);
  angle += 0.01;
}
```

pixelated.glsl

```
#ifdef GL_ES
precision mediump float;
precision mediump int;
#endif

uniform int numBins;
uniform sampler2D texture;

varying vec4 vertColor;
varying vec4 vertTexCoord;

void main() {
  int si = int(vertTexCoord.s * float(numBins));
  int sj = int(vertTexCoord.t * float(numBins));
  gl_FragColor = texture2D(texture, vec2(float(si) / float(numBins), float(sj) /
  float(numBins))) * vertColor;
}
```

Figure 15-7. *Output of the pixelated texture shader applied to a sphere*

Light Shaders

As we learned in Chapter 14, lighting a 3D scene involves placing one or more light sources in the virtual space, defining their parameters (http://www.learnopengles.com/android-lesson-two-ambient-and-diffuse-lighting/), such as type (point, spotlight) and color (diffuse, ambient, specular). It also requires using a mathematical model that takes in those parameters to generate convincing lit surfaces. This is a huge topic in computer graphics; without going into any details, we would only say that all lighting models we can implement with the help of GLSL shaders are approximations to how light works in the real world. The model we will use in this section is probably one of the simplest; it evaluates the light intensity at each vertex of the object as the dot product between the vertex normal and the direction vector between the vertex and light positions. This model represents a point light source that emits light equally in all directions, as illustrated in Figure 15-8.

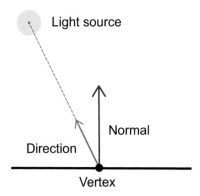

Figure 15-8. *Diagram illustrating the basic lighting model in the light shader*

Using the same geometry from the previous examples, we can now write a simple shader to render the scene with a single point light. To do so, we need some extra uniform variables in the vertex shader: lightPosition, which holds the position of the light source, and normalMatrix, which is a 3×3 matrix to convert the normal vector to the appropriate coordinates to perform the lighting calculations. The full sketch and shader code is provided in Listing 15-10.

Listing 15-10. Sketch with a simple lighting shader

```
PShape globe;
float angle;
PShader lightShader;

void setup() {
  fullScreen(P3D);
  lightShader = loadShader("lightfrag.glsl", "lightvert.glsl");
  globe = createShape(SPHERE, 300);
  globe.setStroke(false);
}

void draw() {
  background(0);
  shader(lightShader);
  pointLight(255, 255, 255, width, height/2, 500);
  translate(width/2, height/2);
  rotateY(angle);
  shape(globe);
  angle += 0.01;
}
```

lightfrag.glsl

```
#ifdef GL_ES
precision mediump float;
precision mediump int;
#endif
```

```
varying vec4 vertColor;

void main() {
  gl_FragColor = vertColor;
}
```

lightvert.glsl

```
uniform mat4 modelview;
uniform mat4 transform;
uniform mat3 normalMatrix;

uniform vec4 lightPosition;

attribute vec4 position;
attribute vec4 color;
attribute vec3 normal;

varying vec4 vertColor;

void main() {
  gl_Position = transform * position;
  vec3 ecPosition = vec3(modelview * position);
  vec3 ecNormal = normalize(normalMatrix * normal);

  vec3 direction = normalize(lightPosition.xyz - ecPosition);
  float intensity = max(0.0, dot(direction, ecNormal));
  vertColor = vec4(intensity, intensity, intensity, 1) * color;
}
```

In the vertex shader, the ecPosition variable is the position of the input vertex expressed in eye coordinates, not screen coordinates, since it is obtained by multiplying the vertex position by the modelview matrix, which encodes the camera (view) and geometry (model) transformations, but not the projection transformations. Similarly, by multiplying the input normal vector with the normalMatrix, we obtain its coordinates in the eye coordinates system. Once all the vectors are expressed in the same system, they can be used to calculate the intensity of the incident light at each vertex. From inspecting the formula used in the shader, we could see that the intensity is directly proportional to the angle between the normal and the vector between the vertex and the light source.

In this example, there is a single point light, but Processing can send to the shader up to eight different lights and their associated parameters. The full list of light uniforms that can be used to get this information in the shader is as follows:

- uniform int lightCount: Number of active lights

- uniform vec4 lightPosition[8]: Position of each light

- uniform vec3 lightNormal[8]: Direction of each light (only relevant for directional and spot lights)

- uniform vec3 lightAmbient[8]: Ambient component of light color

- uniform vec3 lightDiffuse[8]: Diffuse component of light color

- uniform vec3 lightSpecular[8]: Specular component of light color

- uniform vec3 lightFalloff[8]: Light falloff coefficients

- uniform vec2 lightSpot[8]: Light spot parameters (cosine of light spot angle and concentration)

The values in these uniforms completely specify any lighting configuration set in the sketch using the ambientLight(), pointLight(), directionalLight(), and spotLight() functions in Processing. However, a valid light shader doesn't need to declare all these uniforms; for instance, in the previous listing, we only needed the lightPosition uniform. The output of this listing is shown in Figure 15-9.

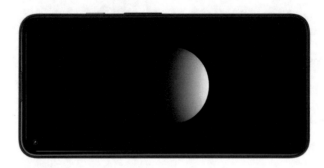

Figure 15-9. *Output of the light shader applied to a sphere*

Texlight Shaders

Finally, a textlight shader incorporates the uniforms from both light and texture shaders, and that's why it's called that way. We can integrate the code from the previous sections in the sketch shown in Listing 15-11. Its output is provided in Figure 15-10.

Listing 15-11. Sketch combining texturing and per-vertex lighting

```
PImage earth;
PShape globe;
float angle;
PShader texlightShader;

void setup() {
  fullScreen(P3D);
  texlightShader = loadShader("texlightfrag.glsl", "texlightvert.glsl");
  earth = loadImage("earthmap1k.jpg");
  globe = createShape(SPHERE, 300);
  globe.setTexture(earth);
  globe.setStroke(false);
}

void draw() {
  background(0);
  shader(texlightShader);
  pointLight(255, 255, 255, width, height/2, 500);
  translate(width/2, height/2);
  rotateY(angle);
```

```
  shape(globe);
  angle += 0.01;
}
```

texlightfrag.glsl

```
#ifdef GL_ES
precision mediump float;
precision mediump int;
#endif

uniform sampler2D texture;

varying vec4 vertColor;
varying vec4 vertTexCoord;

void main() {
  gl_FragColor = texture2D(texture, vertTexCoord.st) * vertColor;
}
```

texlightvert.glsl

```
uniform mat4 modelview;
uniform mat4 transform;
uniform mat3 normalMatrix;
uniform mat4 texMatrix;

uniform vec4 lightPosition;

attribute vec4 position;
attribute vec4 color;
attribute vec3 normal;
attribute vec2 texCoord;

varying vec4 vertColor;
varying vec4 vertTexCoord;

void main() {
  gl_Position = transform * position;
  vec3 ecPosition = vec3(modelview * position);
  vec3 ecNormal = normalize(normalMatrix * normal);

  vec3 direction = normalize(lightPosition.xyz - ecPosition);
  float intensity = max(0.0, dot(direction, ecNormal));
  vertColor = vec4(intensity, intensity, intensity, 1) * color;

  vertTexCoord = texMatrix * vec4(texCoord, 1.0, 1.0);
}
```

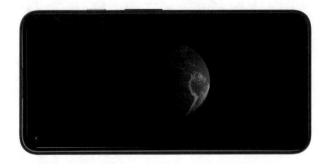

Figure 15-10. *Output of the texlight shader applied to a sphere*

■ **Note**   We cannot use a texlight shader to render a sketch only with textures or only with lights; in those cases, we will need a separate texture or light shader.

Image Postprocessing Filters

As we saw with the pixelated texture example from Listing 15-9, the fragment shader can be used to run image postprocessing effects very efficiently by taking advantage of the parallel nature of the GPUs. For example, let's imagine that we want to render a texture using only black and white colors: black if the luminance of the original color at a given pixel in the image is below a threshold and white if it is above. This can be implemented with the texture shader in Listing 15-12.

Listing 15-12. Sketch with a black and white shader

```
PImage earth;
PShape globe;
float angle;
PShader bwShader;

void setup() {
  fullScreen(P3D);
  bwShader = loadShader("bwfrag.glsl");
  earth = loadImage("earthmap1k.jpg");
  globe = createShape(SPHERE, 300);
  globe.setTexture(earth);
  globe.setStroke(false);
}

void draw() {
  background(0);
  shader(bwShader);
  translate(width/2, height/2);
  rotateY(angle);
  shape(globe);
  angle += 0.01;
}
```

bwfrag.glsl

```glsl
#ifdef GL_ES
precision mediump float;
precision mediump int;
#endif

uniform sampler2D texture;

varying vec4 vertColor;
varying vec4 vertTexCoord;

const vec4 lumcoeff = vec4(0.299, 0.587, 0.114, 0);

void main() {
  vec4 col = texture2D(texture, vertTexCoord.st);
  float lum = dot(col, lumcoeff);
  if (0.5 < lum) {
    gl_FragColor = vertColor;
  } else {
    gl_FragColor = vec4(0, 0, 0, 1);
  }
}

#ifdef GL_ES
precision mediump float;
precision mediump int;
#endif

uniform sampler2D texture;

varying vec4 vertColor;
varying vec4 vertTexCoord;

const vec4 lumcoeff = vec4(0.299, 0.587, 0.114, 0);

void main() {
  vec4 col = texture2D(texture, vertTexCoord.st);
  float lum = dot(col, lumcoeff);
  if (0.5 < lum) {
    gl_FragColor = vertColor;
  } else {
    gl_FragColor = vec4(0, 0, 0, 1);
  }
}
```

The fragment shader reads the texture at position vertTexCoord.st and uses the color value to compute the luminance and then the two alternative outputs based on the threshold, which in this case is 0.5, resulting in the black and white rendering in Figure 15-11. We can notice that this time the loadShader() function only receives the file name of the fragment shader. How does Processing complete the entire shader program? The answer is that it uses the default vertex stage for texture shaders. Because of this, and since the varying variables are first declared in the vertex stage, the fragment shader needs to follow the varying names adopted in the default shader. In this case, the varying variables for the fragment color and texture coordinate must be named vertColor and vertTexCoord, respectively.

Figure 15-11. *Output of the black and white shader applied to a sphere*

Convolution filters (https://lodev.org/cgtutor/filtering.html) can also be implemented easily in the fragment shader. Given the texture coordinates of a fragment, vertTexCoord, the neighboring pixels in the texture (also called "texels") can be sampled using the texOffset uniform. This uniform is set automatically by Processing and contains the vector (1/width, 1/height), with width and height being the resolution of the texture. These values are precisely the offsets along the horizontal and vertical directions needed to sample the color from the texels around vertTexCoord.st. For example, vertTexCoord.st + vec2(texOffset.s, 0) is the texel exactly one position to the right. Listing 15-13 shows the implementation of a standard emboss filter, and Figure 15-12 shows its output.

Listing 15-13. Sketch with an emboss shader

```
PImage earth;
PShape globe;
float angle;
PShader embossShader;

void setup() {
  fullScreen(P3D);
  embossShader = loadShader("embossfrag.glsl");
  earth = loadImage("earthmap1k.jpg");
  globe = createShape(SPHERE, 300);
  globe.setTexture(earth);
  globe.setStroke(false);
}

void draw() {
  background(0);
  shader(embossShader);
  translate(width/2, height/2);
  rotateY(angle);
  shape(globe);
  angle += 0.01;
}
```

embossfrag.glsl

```glsl
#ifdef GL_ES
precision mediump float;
precision mediump int;
#endif

uniform sampler2D texture;
uniform vec2 texOffset;

varying vec4 vertColor;
varying vec4 vertTexCoord;

const vec4 lumcoeff = vec4(0.299, 0.587, 0.114, 0);

void main() {
  vec2 tc0 = vertTexCoord.st + vec2(-texOffset.s, -texOffset.t);
  vec2 tc1 = vertTexCoord.st + vec2(            0.0, -texOffset.t);
  vec2 tc2 = vertTexCoord.st + vec2(-texOffset.s,             0.0);
  vec2 tc3 = vertTexCoord.st + vec2(+texOffset.s,             0.0);
  vec2 tc4 = vertTexCoord.st + vec2(            0.0, +texOffset.t);
  vec2 tc5 = vertTexCoord.st + vec2(+texOffset.s, +texOffset.t);

  vec4 col0 = texture2D(texture, tc0);
  vec4 col1 = texture2D(texture, tc1);
  vec4 col2 = texture2D(texture, tc2);
  vec4 col3 = texture2D(texture, tc3);
  vec4 col4 = texture2D(texture, tc4);
  vec4 col5 = texture2D(texture, tc5);

  vec4 sum = vec4(0.5) + (col0 + col1 + col2) - (col3 + col4 + col5);
  float lum = dot(sum, lumcoeff);
  gl_FragColor = vec4(lum, lum, lum, 1.0) * vertColor;
}
```

Figure 15-12. *Output of the emboss shader applied to a sphere*

All these postprocessing effects were implemented as texture shaders since they only require the texture image as an input. Another way of using them is through the filter() function in Processing (https://processing.org/reference/filter_.html). This function applies a filter effect on an image that we can select from a list of predefined effects (threshold, invert, posterize, etc.), or using a shader object. We can reuse any of our texture shaders to use in filter(); for example, Listing 15-14 shows the use of the black and white shader we had in Listing 15-12, but this time applied on a flat image drawn on the screen. The result is displayed in Figure 15-13.

Listing 15-14. Using the black and white shader as a filter

```
PImage earth;
PShader bwShader;

void setup() {
  fullScreen(P2D);
  bwShader = loadShader("bwfrag.glsl");
  earth = loadImage("earthmap1k.jpg");
}

void draw() {
  image(earth, 0, 0, width, height);
  filter(bwShader);
}
```

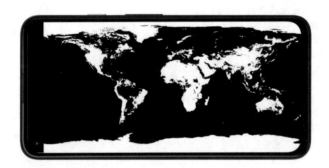

Figure 15-13. *Output of the black and white shader applied as a filter image*

Day-to-Night Earth Shader and Live Wallpaper

To conclude this chapter on shader programming and cap the section on 3D graphics, let's take on a final project where we put our newly gained GLSL skills to good use! We can continue with the Earth theme we had throughout the examples in the chapter while introducing a few advanced techniques. Let's start with an observation we could derive from the texture shader examples: the fragment shader always gets the color values from a single texture. However, we can read texels from several textures at the same time, and this feature enables shader programmers to implement very sophisticated effects (such as realistic lighting with shadows and other visual nuances). As we pointed out before, most of these effects would also require some advanced mathematics, so we will try to keep our code as simple as possible.

An idea for a shader that requires reading from two textures simultaneously would be to render the Earth so that the night lights caused by human activity become visible as the planet rotates around its axis. The site Solar System Scope contains equirectangular maps for many objects in the Solar System that can be freely shared under the Creative Commons Attribution 4.0 International license (`www.solarsystemscope.com/textures/`), including the Earth's Day and night maps (Figure 15-14) we will use for this project.

We know how to implement a shader in Processing to render a textured object (e.g., Listing 15-8) with a single texture, and we will now learn how to read more than one texture from our shader. It is not difficult; all we need to do is to declare two sampler2D uniform variables in the fragment shader and manually set those uniforms from the Processing code with the corresponding image object, as it is shown in Listing 15-15.

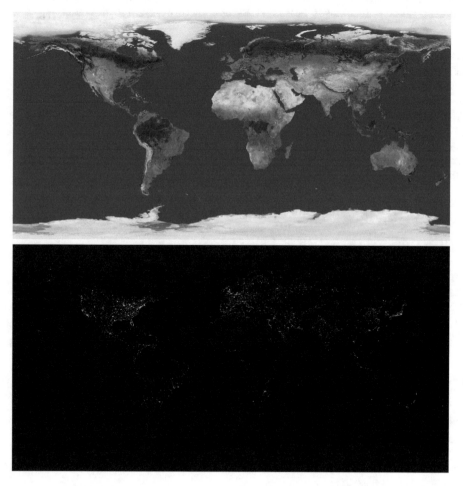

Figure 15-14. *Day and night maps of the Earth from the Solar System Scope repository*

Listing 15-15. Sketch with two images used for texturing a sphere

```
PShape earth;
PShader earthShader;

float viewRotation;

void setup() {
  fullScreen(P3D);

  PImage earthDay = loadImage("Solarsystemscope_texture_2k_earth_daymap.jpg");
  PImage earthNight = loadImage("Solarsystemscope_texture_2k_earth_nightmap.jpg");

  earthShader = loadShader("EarthFrag.glsl");
  earthShader.set("dayTexture", earthDay);
  earthShader.set("nightTexture", earthNight);

  earth = createShape(SPHERE, 400);
  earth.setStroke(false);
}

void draw() {
  background(0);

  earthShader.set("mixFactor",  map(mouseX, 0, width, 0, 1));
  viewRotation += 0.001;

  translate(width/2, height/2);

  shader(earthShader);
  pushMatrix();
  rotateY(viewRotation);
  shape(earth);
  popMatrix();
}
```

EarthFrag.glsl

```
#ifdef GL_ES
precision mediump float;
precision mediump int;
#endif

uniform sampler2D dayTexture;
uniform sampler2D nightTexture;

uniform float mixFactor;

varying vec4 vertColor;
varying vec4 vertTexCoord;
```

```
void main() {
  vec2 st = vertTexCoord.st;
  vec4 dayColor = texture2D(dayTexture, st);
  vec4 nightColor = texture2D(nightTexture, st);
  gl_FragColor = mix(dayColor, nightColor, mixFactor) * vertColor;
}
```

In the fragment shader, we also define another uniform variable, mixFactor, where we store a value between 0 and 1 to mix both textures in different proportions depending on the horizontal position of the mouse. GLSL provides a built-in function precisely called mix that allows us to create a linear interpolation between two values (in this case, the texels sampled from the day and night textures). Figure 15-15 shows the output of this code.

Figure 15-15. *Sphere textured with a mixture of day and night maps of the Earth*

However, for our day-to-night effect, we need to mix the two textures according to the angle around the Earth's sphere. The values corresponding to the sunrise and sunset are where the textures should transition into one another. These angles can be calculated in the vertex shader using the sphere's (x, y, z) coordinates we receive from Processing in the position attribute. By applying the formulas to convert between Cartesian and spherical coordinates (https://en.wikipedia.org/wiki/Spherical_coordinate_system#Cartesian_coordinates), we should be able to get the azimuthal angle θ, which corresponds to the longitude in the geographical coordinate system. We do this in Listing 15-16.

Listing 15-16. Calculation of spherical coordinates in the vertex shader

```
PShape earth;
PImage earthDay;PShape earth;
PShader earthShader;

float viewRotation;

void setup() {
  fullScreen(P3D);

  PImage earthDay = loadImage("Solarsystemscope_texture_2k_earth_daymap.jpg");
  PImage earthNight = loadImage("Solarsystemscope_texture_2k_earth_nightmap.jpg");
```

```
  PGraphicsOpenGL pgl = (PGraphicsOpenGL)g;
  pgl.textureWrap(REPEAT);

  earthShader = loadShader("EarthFrag.glsl", "EarthVert.glsl");
  earthShader.set("dayTexture", earthDay);
  earthShader.set("nightTexture", earthNight);
  earthShader.set("width", width);
  earthShader.set("height", height);

  earth = createShape(SPHERE, 400);
  earth.setStroke(false);
}

void draw() {
  background(0);

  float targetAngle = map(mouseX, 0, width, 0, TWO_PI);
  viewRotation += 0.05 * (targetAngle - viewRotation);

  translate(width/2, height/2);

  shader(earthShader);
  pushMatrix();
  rotateY(viewRotation);
  shape(earth);
  popMatrix();
}
PImage earthNight;
PShader earthShader;

float viewRotation;

void setup() {
  fullScreen(P3D);

  earthDay = loadImage("Solarsystemscope_texture_2k_earth_daymap.jpg");
  earthNight = loadImage("Solarsystemscope_texture_2k_earth_nightmap.jpg");

  earthShader = loadShader("EarthFrag.glsl");
  earthShader.set("dayTexture", earthDay);
  earthShader.set("nightTexture", earthNight);

  earth = createShape(SPHERE, 400);
  earth.setStroke(false);
}

void draw() {
  background(0);

  earthShader.set("mixFactor",  map(mouseX, 0, width, 0, 1));
  viewRotation += 0.001;
```

```
    translate(width/2, height/2);

    shader(earthShader);
    pushMatrix();
    rotateY(viewRotation);
    shape(earth);
    popMatrix();
}
```

EarthFrag.glsl

```
#ifdef GL_ES
precision mediump float;
precision mediump int;
#endif

#define TWO_PI 6.2831853076

uniform sampler2D dayTexture;
uniform sampler2D nightTexture;
varying vec4 vertColor;
varying vec4 vertTexCoord;
varying float azimuth;

void main() {
  vec2 st = vertTexCoord.st;
  vec4 dayColor = texture2D(dayTexture, st);
  vec4 nightColor = texture2D(nightTexture, st);
  gl_FragColor = mix(dayColor, nightColor, azimuth / TWO_PI) * vertColor;
}
```

EarthVert.glsl

```
uniform mat4 transform;
uniform mat4 modelview;
uniform mat4 texMatrix;

attribute vec4 position;
attribute vec4 color;
attribute vec2 texCoord;

varying vec4 vertColor;
varying vec4 vertTexCoord;
varying float azimuth;

uniform int width;
uniform int height;

#define PI 3.1415926538
```

```
void main() {
  gl_Position = transform * position;
  vec3 v = position.xyz - vec3(float(width)/2.0, float(height)/2.0, 0.0);
  azimuth = PI - sign(v.z) * acos(v.x / length(v.xz));
  vertColor = color;
  vertTexCoord = texMatrix * vec4(texCoord, 1.0, 1.0);
}
```

The calculation of the azimuth angle uses the vector v, which is the position minus (width/2, height/2, 0). The reason for this is because the formula assumes that the (x, y, z) coordinates are centered at zero, but in Processing, the origin of coordinates is located at the upper left corner, and a translation to (width/2, height/2, 0) is applied to have the Earth sphere rendered at the center of the screen. Because of this, the position coordinates are centered at (width/2, height/2, 0); the subtraction in vertex shader gets us the zero-centered coordinates that we can use to calculate the azimuth angle from the x and z values (since the equatorial plane of the Earth is the XZ plane in Processing). The calculation sign(v.z) * acos(v.x / length(v.xz)) returns an angle between -π and +π, and subtracting that from the PI constant (defined at the top of the vertex shader since GLSL does not include a built-in constant for π) gives us a value between 0 and 2π. This value is passed down to the fragment shader in the varying float azimuth, which is divided by the constant TWO_PI defined separately to have the mixing factor between 0 and 1 in mix(dayColor, nightColor, azimuth / TWO_PI). This is similar to what we had in the previous listing, but now the interpolation uses the azimuth angle, so the day and night textures are mixed following the longitude around the Earth. This takes us closer to our intended effect, as seen in Figure 15-16.

We need to add the rotation of the Earth, so the transition areas between day and night move around the sphere as time passes on. Instead of rotating the sphere, we could alternatively translate the texture coordinates along the horizontal direction, which would rotate the texture around the static object; rotating the vertices makes the calculations more involved because the azimuth angle would vary alongside the rotation. Listing 15-17 shows only the changes we need to make to our previous sketch to have this implemented; the vertex shader is not included since it remains the same from Listing 15-16.

Figure 15-16. *Interpolation between day and night Earth maps using the azimuth angle*

Listing 15-17. Calculation of spherical coordinates in the vertex shader

```
PShape earth;
PShader earthShader;

float viewRotation;
float earthRotation;

void setup() {
  ...
  PGraphicsOpenGL pgl = (PGraphicsOpenGL)g;
  pgl.textureWrap(REPEAT);
}

void draw() {
  background(0);

  earthShader.set("earthRotation", earthRotation % TWO_PI);
  earthRotation += 0.001;
  ...
}
```

EarthFrag.glsl

```
...
uniform float earthRotation;

void main() {
  float s = vertTexCoord.s;
  float t = vertTexCoord.t;
  vec2 st = vec2(s - earthRotation / TWO_PI, t);
  ...
}
```

We added a new variable in the sketch code, earthRotation, to store the rotation angle of the Earth as it revolves around its axis. We increase this angle by a small amount in each frame but make it vary only between 0 and TWO_PI when setting the value of the corresponding uniform in the shader by taking the modulus with earthRotation % TWO_PI. In this way, if, for example, earthRotation is 3π, the module would return π (which represents the same angle). Meanwhile, in the fragment shader, we add the earthRotation value, normalized to the 0–1 range by dividing it by TWO_PI, to the s coordinate of the vertex texture coordinate (the minus sign is to ensure that the rotation happens in the correct direction from east to west). We also use a new function in the shader code, textureWrap(REPEAT), so the texture coordinates wrap around (0, 1) as the values change along the s direction when adding earthRotation in the shader. Even though the angle is normalized, we could still have an s value outside (0, 1), for example, 0.5 + 07 = 1.2, but this would get wrapped around to 0.2, thanks to the textureWrap() setting. This is an advanced function that's not part of the regular Processing API, so to access it, we need the underlying renderer object g as a PGraphicsOpenGL variable, which is the renderer type when using P2D or P3D, and only then we can call the advanced functions available in the OpenGL renderers.

With all of this, we finally have our day-to-night effect fully working! We would need a few last touches to have the rotation of the Earth linked to the actual "real" time and the view of the Earth showing the geographical location of the user. For the first feature, linking the rotation to the real time, we can use the java.time package that provides utilities to retrieve the current Coordinated Universal Time (UTC). For the second feature, setting the view according to the users' location, we can use the Ketai library as we did in Chapter 9. None of this affects the shaders from the last listing; the changes in the sketch code are shown in Listing 15-18.

Listing 15-18. Calculation of spherical coordinates in the vertex shader

```
import java.time.Instant;
import java.time.ZoneOffset;
import ketai.sensors.*;
...

KetaiLocation location;
float longitude;

void setup() {
  ...
  location = new KetaiLocation(this);
}
void draw() {
background(0);

  Instant instant = Instant.now();
  int hour = instant.atZone(ZoneOffset.UTC).getHour();
  int minute = instant.atZone(ZoneOffset.UTC).getMinute();
  float utcTime = 60 * hour + minute;
  earthRotation = map(utcTime, 0, 1439, HALF_PI - PI, HALF_PI + PI);
  earthShader.set("earthRotation", earthRotation);
  earthShader.set("earthRotation", earthRotation % TWO_PI);

  viewRotation = longuitude - earthRotation;
  ...
}

void onLocationEvent(double lat, double lon) {
  longuitude = radians((float)lon + 210);
}
```

We see how we can retrieve the hour and minute of the current UTC using the instant. atZone(ZoneOffset.UTC).getHour() and getMinute() calls once we have the instant object from Instant. now(). Then, we convert the hour and minute values into the total amount of minutes since midnight with float utcTime = 60 * hour + minute and then map that value onto the Earth rotation angle. As the Earth revolves around itself, we want to view it from a vantage point flying over the user's geographical location. With Ketai, it is easy to get the (latitude, longitude) values from the GPS (remember to set the appropriate permissions with the sketch permissions tool) in the onLocationEventHandler() function. The latitude is not used since we only need the longitude to calculate the view rotation together with the Earth's rotation. By doing all of this, the output of our sketch is kind of a "world clock" since it visualizes the zone of daylight at the location of the user running the sketch and keeps updating it in real time. The only inaccuracy in this last version of the code is that it does not incorporate the declination angle that varies seasonally as the Earth tilts on its axis of rotation and the rotation of the Earth around the Sun (https://solarsena.com/solar-declination-angle-calculator/). Therefore, our rendering is only correct during the equinoxes, which is when the declination angle of the Earth is exactly zero. Adding this should not be too hard, and it is left as an exercise for the readers. ☺

We could even run our sketch as a live wallpaper, so it updates continuously in the background of our screen, showing the current time of the day or night. In this case, we could add a frameRate(1) call to setup, to make it refresh the screen just once every second to reduce battery usage. Running it faster than that would not be necessary in any case since the Earth's rotation is virtually unnoticeable in real time from second to second. Figure 15-17 shows some typical outputs of the wallpaper during different times of the day.

As the final step, we should create a set of icons for our day-to-night live wallpaper so it can be packaged and distributed on the Google Play Store!

Figure 15-17. *Final version of the day-to-night sketch, installed as a live wallpaper*

Summary

We only scratched the surface of a fascinating topic, shader programming, but we were able to cover the main types of shaders we can use in Processing. These shaders allow us to draw colored, textured, and lit scenes, and we apply them to create a live wallpaper that renders the Earth's day-to-night changes in real time. Writing GLSL shaders is not easy, it requires math skills especially in vector and matrix algebra, as well as a good understanding of how the graphics pipeline in modern GPUs works, but all of that can be gained with enough practice and dedication. Processing provides several functions to incorporate shaders into 2D and 3D sketches, which should be useful for those users who want to delve deeper into the world of shaders.

PART VI

Extended Reality: VR and AR

CHAPTER 16

Basics of VR

In this chapter, we will learn some of the basic techniques to create VR apps with Processing. These techniques cover object selection, interaction, and movement in VR space, and using eye coordinates to create static frames of reference to facilitate user experience.

Brief History of VR

Virtual reality has a much longer history than we may think. Stereoscopic photo viewers dating back to the first half of the 18th century already contain the basic idea behind VR, which is the use of two separate stereo images, one for each eye, to take the spectators into a "virtual world." The "Sensorama" immersive machine created in 1962 by filmmaker Morton Heilig is considered a direct precursor of VR. It looked like a 1980s era video arcade game and included a stereoscopic color display, stereo sound, fans, and even smell emitters, which allowed users to experience short multisensory films. The first head-mounted display that updated the graphics according to the users' movement was created in 1968 by Ivan Sutherland and his students at Harvard University. Between the 1970s and 1990s, VR technology advanced rapidly, but its use was restricted mostly to industry applications, such as flight simulation and automobile design. However, there are examples of early VR-based artistic explorations at that time. For example, digital artist David Em produced the first navigable virtual worlds in 1977 during a residence at the NASA's Jet Propulsion Laboratory. In the following years, many artists started to explore VR as a creative medium, like video game designer Brenda Laurel and artist Rachel Strickland, who created the groundbreaking multiplayer and multisensory VR installation Placeholder in 1994 at the Banff Centre for the Arts, as part of Canada's Art and Virtual Environment Project. There were several attempts to bring VR to gaming and entertainment in the late 1990s, although the technology was not yet ready for consumer-level use and interest in VR waned for a while. The recent resurgence of VR can be attributed to the introduction of the Oculus Rift headset in 2012, which brought features, such as 90 degree of vision, that were previously unavailable to consumers. Since then, many hardware manufacturers like HTC, Valve, and Sony have introduced newer VR headsets with increased display resolution and interaction capabilities, while software released by Google and other companies support the development of VR applications in different platforms.

Google Cardboard

Google's current VR platform is Google Cardboard (https://arvr.google.com/cardboard/), and in contrast to systems like the Vive or the Oculus, which require a dedicated desktop computer to drive the graphics, it can be experienced with just a smartphone attached to an inexpensive Cardboard viewer. This has advantages and disadvantages: on one hand, it is very accessible and easy to try out; on the other, the experience is not as rich as the one could have with a more sophisticated VR headset.

© Andrés Colubri 2023
A. Colubri, *Processing for Android*, https://doi.org/10.1007/978-1-4842-9585-4_16

■ **Note** Previously, Google offered another platform called Google VR (`https://developers.google.com/vr`), which supported both the Cardboard viewers and the more elaborated Daydream headset. Both Google VR and Daydream were discontinued by Google in 2019.

Hardware Requirements

To use Cardboard, we would need an Android phone running Android 4.1 or higher, with at least a gyroscope sensor so head motion can be properly tracked. These are very minimal requirements, since nearly all phones available today include a gyro and come with much newer versions of Android installed. In general, a smartphone with a fast processor is recommended; otherwise, the animation might not be smooth enough, affecting the quality of the VR experience (jittery VR graphics can result in headaches for the users). A Cardboard viewer is another requirement; Google lists a number of low-cost viewers available for purchase on the Cardboard site (`https://arvr.google.com/cardboard/get-cardboard/`), where it also provides instructions on how to build one ourselves using simple materials and everyday items that can be bought at a hardware store.

VR in Processing

Processing for Android includes a built-in VR library, which acts as a simplified interface to Google Cardboard and automatically configures Processing's 3D view based on the head tracking data from the phone's sensors. Using VR in Processing requires two steps. First, we need to select the VR option in the "Android" menu in the PDE, as seen in Figure 16-1.

Figure 16-1. Enabling the VR option in the Android menu

The second step is to import the VR library into our code and setting the STEREO renderer in the fullScreen() function. This renderer draws the 3D scene in our sketch with the appropriate camera transformations to follow the head movement in VR space and to account for the differences between each eye's point of view. Listing 16-1 shows a minimal VR sketch in Processing.

Listing 16-1. Basic VR sketch

```
import processing.vr.*;

void setup() {
  fullScreen(STEREO);
  fill(#AD71B7);
}

void draw() {
  background(#81B771);
  translate(width/2, height/2);
  lights();
  rotateY(millis()/1000.0);
  box(500);
}
```

We can see the result in Figure 16-2, a rotating cube in VR! If we place the phone in a Cardboard viewer, we would be able to see the cube from different angles as we turn our head around it. However, walking in physical space will not have any effect on the VR scene, as Cardboard viewers do not support positional tracking.

Figure 16-2. *Output of a simple VR sketch*

Stereo Rendering

As we saw in our first example, a VR sketch generates two copies of the scene: one for the left and the other for the right eye. They are slightly different since they correspond to how the scene is viewed from each eye. A consequence of this is that the draw() function is called twice in each frame (and we will talk more about this later).

All the techniques we saw in the previous chapter on 3D drawing using the P3D renderer translate over to VR with almost no modification. We can use shapes, textures, lights, and shaders in the same way as before. By default, the orientation of the XYZ axes is like in the P3D renderer, meaning that the origin is located at the upper left corner of the screen and the y axis points down. Listing 16-2 implements a simple scene to visualize those settings (Figure 16-3).

Listing 16-2. Coordinate axes in VR

```
import processing.vr.*;

void setup() {
  fullScreen(STEREO);
  strokeWeight(2);
}

void draw() {
  background(0);
  translate(width/2, height/2);
  lights();
  drawAxis();
  drawGrid();
}

void drawAxis() {
  line(0, 0, 0, 200, 0, 0);
  drawBox(200, 0, 0, 50, #E33E3E);
  line(0, 0, 0, 0, -200, 0);
  drawBox(0, -200, 0, 50, #3E76E3);
  line(0, 0, 0, 0, 0, 200);
  drawBox(0, 0, 200, 50, #3EE379);
}

void drawGrid() {
  beginShape(LINES);
  stroke(255);
  for (int x = -10000; x < +10000; x += 500) {
    vertex(x, +500, +10000);
    vertex(x, +500, -10000);
  }
  for (int z = -10000; z < +10000; z += 500) {
    vertex(+10000, +500, z);
    vertex(-10000, +500, z);
  }
  endShape();
}

void drawBox(float x, float y, float z, float s, color c) {
  pushStyle();
  pushMatrix();
  translate(x, y, z);
  noStroke();
  fill(c);
```

```
  box(s);
  popMatrix();
  popStyle();
}
```

Since the origin is located at the upper left corner of the screen, we need the `translate(width/2, height/2)` call to center the scene at the middle of the screen. Also, we can see that the blue box, placed at (0, -200, 0), is above the line of sight, which makes sense given the downward orientation of the y axis.

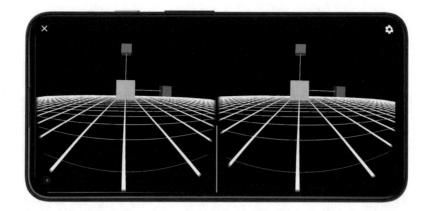

Figure 16-3. *Default coordinate axes in VR*

■ **Note**   Most frameworks for developing VR apps use a coordinate system where the origin is located at the center of the screen and the y axis points up. In Processing for Android, we can switch to this system by calling cameraUp() in setup().

Monoscopic Rendering

The Processing VR library includes another renderer that we can use to draw 3D scenes that respond to the phone's movement in physical space, but without entering the stereo mode. This can be useful if we simply want to peek into a 3D space without a VR headset. The only change we need in our code is to use the MONO renderer instead of STEREO, like we do in Listing 16-3. The result is shown in Figure 16-4.

Listing 16-3. Using the MONO renderer

```
import processing.vr.*;

float angle = 0;
PShape cube;

void setup() {
  fullScreen(MONO);
  PImage tex = loadImage("mosaic.jpg");
  cube = createShape(BOX, 400);
  cube.setTexture(tex);
}
```

```
void draw() {
  background(#81B771);
  translate(width/2, height/2);
  lights();
  rotateY(angle);
  rotateX(angle*2);
  shape(cube);
  angle += 0.01;
}
```

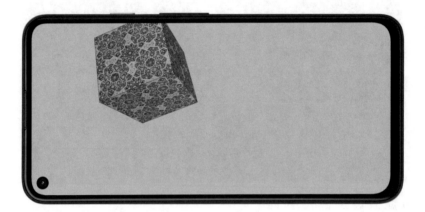

Figure 16-4. *Monoscopic rendering*

VR Interaction

The code examples so far show us that creating a VR scene in Processing is very easy: all we need is to select the VR mode in the PDE, import the VR library into our sketch, and use the STEREO renderer. With these steps, we can apply all the 3D rendering techniques we learned earlier. But as soon as we start thinking about user interaction in VR, we will find new challenges. First, Cardboard viewers do not include any controller, like more expensive VR headsets (Oculus, Vive) do. Manual input is limited to a button that triggers a touch on the screen, and some Cardboard viewers don't even have this button. So we need to solve some basic interaction problems in VR: How do we select 3D objects/UI elements, and how do we move around in VR space?

VR developers have been experimenting with various solutions to these problems, and an overview of VR apps on the Google Play Store can give us some hints. A common technique for interaction is gaze selection: the app detects which object we are looking at, and a touch press (or staring at it long enough) triggers the desired action. All VR apps use this technique in one way or another, in combination with other interesting ideas: head gestures (tilting, etc.), the use of special areas in VR space to place UI elements (i.e., looking up or down), and automation of certain actions (walking around, grabbing an item).

■ **Note** A successful VR experience needs to pay special attention to the interaction so that the users feel they are indeed inside of this space. Given the constraints of the VR headsets in terms of graphic realism and controls, we need to craft the interaction carefully so it makes sense in terms of the specific experience we are trying to convey.

Eye and World Coordinates

Before we start looking at interaction techniques for VR, we need to familiarize ourselves with the coordinate systems we will need to manipulate when developing our VR apps. There are two systems that we should keep in mind: the world coordinate system and the eye coordinate system, which are illustrated in Figure 16-5.

We have been using world coordinates all along, since Processing relies on these to characterize position and movement of shapes, both in 2D and 3D. Eye coordinates are new, though, and very specific to the way the VR view is constructed automatically for us from the head tracking information. The eye coordinate system is defined by three vectors: forward, right, and up (Figure 16-5). The forward vector represents the direction of our line of sight, and the right and up vectors complete the system. These vectors get updated automatically in each frame to reflect the movement of the head.

The eye coordinates are the natural choice to represent shapes and other graphical elements that always should be aligned with our view, such as a text message in front of our eyes, or a piece of geometry that provides a static frame of reference, for example, a helmet or the interior of a spaceship. The use of eye coordinates makes it very easy to draw those elements correctly; for example, a box right in front of our eyes would have coordinates (0, 0, 200).

The VR library in Processing lets us switch from world to eye coordinates simply by calling the eye() function, as illustrated in Listing 16-4. The quad, box, and text are always in front of our view, as we see in the output in Figure 16-6.

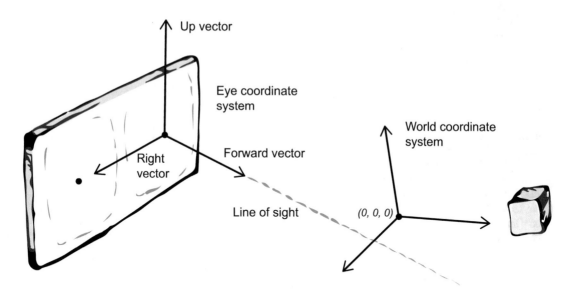

Figure 16-5. *Eye coordinate system with forward, right, and up vectors at the eye position*

Listing 16-4. Drawing in eye coordinates

```
import processing.vr.*;

public void setup() {
  fullScreen(STEREO);
  textFont(createFont("SansSerif", 30));
  textAlign(CENTER, CENTER);
}
```

```
public void draw() {
  background(255);
  translate(width/2, height/2);
  lights();
  fill(#EAB240);
  noStroke();
  rotateY(millis()/1000.0);
  box(300);
  drawEye();
}

void drawEye() {
  eye();

  float s = 50;
  float d = 200;
  float h = 100;

  noFill();
  stroke(0);
  strokeWeight(10);
  beginShape(QUADS);
  vertex(-s, -s, d);
  vertex(+s, -s, d);
  vertex(+s, +s, d);
  vertex(-s, +s, d);
  endShape();

  pushMatrix();
  translate(0, 0, d);
  rotateX(millis()/1000.0);
  rotateY(millis()/2000.0);
  fill(#6AA4FF);
  noStroke();
  box(50);
  popMatrix();

  fill(0);
  text("Welcome to VR!", 0, -h * 0.75, d);
}
```

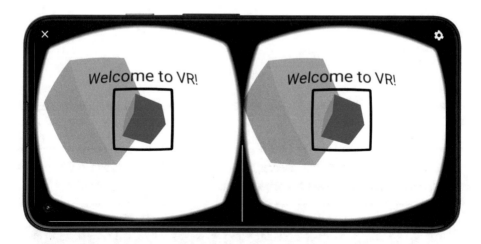

Figure 16-6. *Geometry defined in eye coordinates*

The Line of Sight

Simply looking around is probably the most immediate way of interacting in VR space. To implement gaze selection, we can refer to Figure 16-5, which shows the actual line of sight extending from the eye (or camera) position along the forward vector. If a 3D object is in the path of this line, we can conclude it is being looked at by the user (unless there is another object blocking the view). So how can we draw the line of sight? As we saw in the previous section, eye coordinates should be the answer, since this line starts at (0, 0, 0) and extends to (0, 0, L), where L is how far we want to go along the line.

In Listing 16-5, we draw the line of sight with an offset at the origin along X and Y so we can see where it intersects a box placed at the center of the world system (otherwise, it would be perfectly perpendicular to our view and thus hard to see).

Listing 16-5. Drawing the line of sight

```
import processing.vr.*;

PMatrix3D mat = new PMatrix3D();

void setup() {
  fullScreen(STEREO);
  hint(ENABLE_STROKE_PERSPECTIVE);
}

void draw() {
  background(120);
  translate(width/2, height/2);
  lights();

  noStroke();
  pushMatrix();
  rotateY(millis()/1000.0);
  fill(#E3993E);
  box(150);
  popMatrix();
```

313

```
  eye();
  stroke(#2FB1EA);
  strokeWeight(50);
  line(100, -100, 0, 0, 0, 10000);
}
```

In this code, we also use the ENABLE_STROKE_PERSPECTIVE hint so the line becomes thinner as it moves away from the eye (Figure 16-7).

■ **Note**   Hints are special settings for the renderer, which are enabled by passing an ENABLE_name constant to the hint() function and disabled by passing the corresponding DISABLE_name constant.

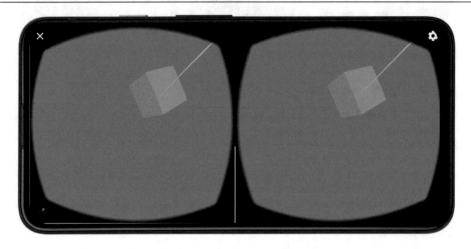

Figure 16-7. *Line of sight intersecting a box placed at the origin of coordinates*

We can also use a point stroke to show the exact location of the screen center, by drawing it at the eye coordinates (0, 0), like we do in Listing 16-6. Any 3D shape crossing the screen center is intersected by the line of sight, so this gives us another way of indicating what object the user might be looking at.

Listing 16-6. Drawing a circular aim

```
import processing.vr.*;

void setup() {
  fullScreen(STEREO);
}

void draw() {
  background(120);
  translate(width/2, height/2);

  lights();
```

```
  noStroke();
  fill(#E3993E);
  beginShape(QUAD);
  vertex(-75, -75);
  vertex(+75, -75);
  vertex(+75, +75);
  vertex(-75, +75);
  endShape(QUAD);

  eye();
  stroke(47, 177, 234, 150);
  strokeWeight(50);
  point(0, 0, 100);
}
```

The point stroke we draw with the function point() can be made as large as we need by setting the weight with strokeWeight() and serve the purpose of a "view aim" to point to objects in VR. Figure 16-8 shows the aim with a weight of 50. In the next section, we will see how to determine if a 3D point falls inside the aim.

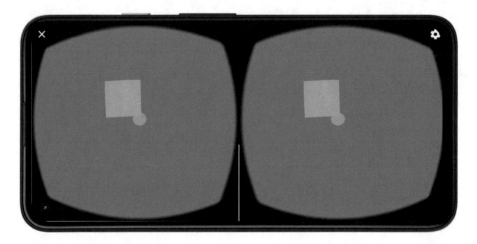

Figure 16-8. *View aim drawn with a point stroke*

Selecting a Shape with Screen Coordinates

As we just saw, an easy way to determine if a vertex in 3D space falls within our line of sight would be to determine if its "screen coordinates" are close enough to the center of the screen. This condition is simple to check visually by drawing a view aim at the exact center of the screen, like we did in Listing 16-6. However, we need a way to check the condition in our code. Processing has the functions screenX() and screenY() allowing us to do exactly that. These functions take as arguments the coordinates (x, y, z) of a point in 3D space and return the screen coordinates (sx, sy) of that point when projected onto the screen. If these screen coordinates are close enough to (width/2, height/2), then we could conclude that the shape is being selected by the user. Let's use this technique in Listing 16-7.

Listing 16-7. Gaze selection with button press

```
import processing.vr.*;

void setup() {
  fullScreen(STEREO);
}

void draw() {
background(120);
  translate(width/2, height/2);
  lights();
  drawGrid();
  drawAim();
}

void drawGrid() {
  for (int i = 0; i < 4; i++) {
    for (int j = 0; j < 4; j++) {
      beginShape(QUAD);
      float x = map(i, 0, 3, -315, +315);
      float y = map(j, 0, 3, -315, +315);
      float sx = screenX(x, y, 0);
      float sy = screenY(x, y, 0);
      if (abs(sx - 0.5 * width) < 50 && abs(sy - 0.5 * height) < 50) {
        strokeWeight(5);
        stroke(#2FB1EA);
        if (mousePressed) {
          fill(#2FB1EA);
        } else {
          fill(#E3993E);
        }
      } else {
        noStroke();
        fill(#E3993E);
      }
      vertex(x - 100, y - 100);
      vertex(x + 100, y - 100);
      vertex(x + 100, y + 100);
      vertex(x - 100, y + 100);
      endShape(QUAD);
    }
  }
}

void drawAim() {
  eye();
  stroke(47, 177, 234, 150);
  strokeWeight(50);
  point(0, 0, 100);
}
```

The mousePressed variable is set to true if we push the button in the Cardboard viewer, allowing to confirm the selection of the shape we are looking at and to get the entire rectangle highlighted like in Figure 16-9. However, if the viewer lacks a button, we need a different strategy. We can confirm the selection by looking at the shape for a specific duration of time, which we do in Listing 16-8 (only the differences with the previous listing are shown).

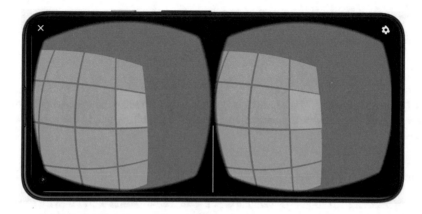

Figure 16-9. *Selecting a quad using screen coordinates*

Listing 16-8. Gaze selection with staring time

```
import processing.vr.*;

int seli = -1;
int selj = -1;
int startSel, selTime;
...
void drawGrid() {
  boolean sel = false;
  for (int i = 0; i < 4; i++) {
    for (int j = 0; j < 4; j++) {
      ...
      if (abs(sx - 0.5 * width) < 50 && abs(sy - 0.5 * height) < 50) {
        strokeWeight(5);
        stroke(#2FB1EA);
        if (seli == i && selj == j) {
          selTime = millis() - startSel;
        } else {
          startSel = millis();
          selTime = 0;
        }
        seli = i;
        selj = j;
        sel = true;
        if (2000 < selTime) {
          fill(#2FB1EA);
        } else {
```

```
        fill(#E3993E);
      }
  } else {
    ...
  }
  if (!sel) {
    seli = -1;
    selj = -1;
    selTime = 0;
  }
}
```

The idea here is to keep track of the indices of the currently selected rectangle and only confirm the selection when the selTime variable is greater than a desired threshold, which in this case is set to 2000 milliseconds.

Bounding Box Selection

The technique of selecting a 3D object by calculating its screen coordinates works well for simple shapes and can be useful to create a UI. However, it may not work as well for more complex objects with irregular silhouettes when projected onto the screen plane.

A common approach to determine object selection in 3D is bounding box intersection. A bounding box is a cube that completely encloses a given 3D object. If the line of sight does not intersect the bounding box of an object, we can be certain that the object is not being selected, and if it does, we could just select it, or perform a more detailed test. An axis-aligned bounding box (AABB) is a particular type of bounding box where the edges are aligned to the coordinate axes. This property makes our calculations simpler and faster, which is very important in the context of VR apps where we may have to test for hundreds or even thousands of bounding box intersections. The AABB of a 3D object can be calculated easily by taking the minimum and maximum over the xyz coordinates of the vertices and storing them in a pair of vectors, which completely determine the AABB.

There are many algorithms used to test intersection of a line with an AABB (www.realtimerendering.com/intersections.html); one that is efficient and simple to implement was proposed by Amy Williams and collaborators in 2005 (http://dl.acm.org/citation.cfm?id=1198748). In this algorithm, we need to provide the minimum and maximum vectors defining the AABB and a point where the line passes through and its direction vector (in the case of the intersection with the line of sight, these are the eye position and the forward vector). The problem is that if we apply transformations to the object, its bounding box may no longer be aligned to the axes. We can account for this by applying the inverse transformation to the line so that the relative orientation of the line and the AABB is the same as if we apply the transformations on the bounding box. This inverse transformation is encoded in the so-called "object matrix," which we can obtain with the getObjectMatrix() function.

As we already pointed out, this algorithm requires the eye position and the forward vector. These are part of the "eye matrix" that we have used before to switch to eye coordinates with the eye() function. In order to get a copy of this matrix, we also have the getEyeMatrix() in the Processing API. Listing 16-9 puts all this together by applying Williams' algorithm to a grid of boxes (see the result in Figure 16-10).

Listing 16-9. AABB line of sight intersection

```
import processing.vr.*;

PMatrix3D eyeMat = new PMatrix3D();
PMatrix3D objMat = new PMatrix3D();
```

```
PVector cam = new PVector();
PVector dir = new PVector();
PVector front = new PVector();
PVector objCam = new PVector();
PVector objFront = new PVector();
PVector objDir = new PVector();
float boxSize = 140;
PVector boxMin = new PVector(-boxSize/2, -boxSize/2, -boxSize/2);
PVector boxMax = new PVector(+boxSize/2, +boxSize/2, +boxSize/2);
PVector hit = new PVector();

void setup() {
  fullScreen(STEREO);
}

void draw() {
  getEyeMatrix(eyeMat);
  cam.set(eyeMat.m03, eyeMat.m13, eyeMat.m23);
  dir.set(eyeMat.m02, eyeMat.m12, eyeMat.m22);
  PVector.add(cam, dir, front);
  background(120);
  translate(width/2, height/2);
  lights();
  drawGrid();
  drawAim();
}

void drawGrid() {
  for (int i = 0; i < 4; i++) {
    for (int j = 0; j < 4; j++) {
      float x = map(i, 0, 3, -350, +350);
      float y = map(j, 0, 3, -350, +350);
      pushMatrix();
      translate(x, y);
      rotateY(millis()/1000.0);
      getObjectMatrix(objMat);
      objMat.mult(cam, objCam);
      objMat.mult(front, objFront);
      PVector.sub(objFront, objCam, objDir);
      boolean res = intersectsLine(objCam, objDir, boxMin, boxMax,
                                   0, 1000, hit);
      if (res) {
        strokeWeight(5);
        stroke(#2FB1EA);
        if (mousePressed) {
          fill(#2FB1EA);
        } else {
          fill(#E3993E);
        }
      } else {
```

```
      noStroke();
      fill(#E3993E);
    }
    box(boxSize);
    popMatrix();
  }
 }
}

void drawAim() {
  eye();
  stroke(47, 177, 234, 150);
  strokeWeight(50);
  point(0, 0, 100);
}

boolean intersectsLine(PVector orig, PVector dir,
  PVector minPos, PVector maxPos, float minDist, float maxDist, PVector hit) {
  PVector bbox;
  PVector invDir = new PVector(1/dir.x, 1/dir.y, 1/dir.z);

  boolean signDirX = invDir.x < 0;
  boolean signDirY = invDir.y < 0;
  boolean signDirZ = invDir.z < 0;

  bbox = signDirX ? maxPos : minPos;
  float txmin = (bbox.x - orig.x) * invDir.x;
  bbox = signDirX ? minPos : maxPos;
  float txmax = (bbox.x - orig.x) * invDir.x;
  bbox = signDirY ? maxPos : minPos;
  float tymin = (bbox.y - orig.y) * invDir.y;
  bbox = signDirY ? minPos : maxPos;
  float tymax = (bbox.y - orig.y) * invDir.y;

  if ((txmin > tymax) || (tymin > txmax)) {
    return false;
  }
  if (tymin > txmin) {
    txmin = tymin;
  }
  if (tymax < txmax) {
    txmax = tymax;
  }

  bbox = signDirZ ? maxPos : minPos;
  float tzmin = (bbox.z - orig.z) * invDir.z;
  bbox = signDirZ ? minPos : maxPos;
  float tzmax = (bbox.z - orig.z) * invDir.z;

  if ((txmin > tzmax) || (tzmin > txmax)) {
    return false;
  }
```

```
  if (tzmin > txmin) {
    txmin = tzmin;
  }
  if (tzmax < txmax) {
    txmax = tzmax;
  }
  if ((txmin < maxDist) && (txmax > minDist)) {
    hit.x = orig.x + txmin * dir.x;
    hit.y = orig.y + txmin * dir.y;
    hit.z = orig.z + txmin * dir.z;
    return true;
  }
  return false;
}
```

Each box in the grid has a different object matrix, since the transformations are different (same rotation but different translation). Once we obtain the object matrix, we apply it on the eye position and forward vector by matrix-vector multiplication. The eye position is transformed into object space directly; however, the forward direction needs to be added to the eye position to yield the position along the line (the forward vector is a direction, not a position, so it cannot be transformed directly) and then transformed, and finally the transformed direction is obtained by subtracting the transformed eye position.

The eye position and forward vector are encoded in the eye matrix as its third and fourth columns, so we can get the individual components of the matrix, (m02, m12, m22) and (m03, m13, m23), and then copy them into the dir and cam vectors, respectively.

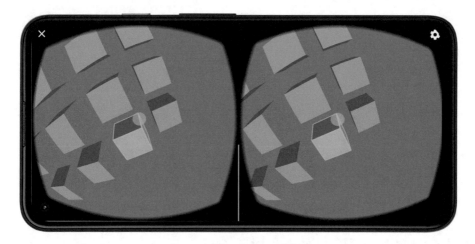

Figure 16-10. *Selecting a quad using screen coordinates*

The intersectsLine() function holds the implementation of Williams' algorithm. It is completely self-contained, so we can reuse it in other sketches. Note that besides returning true or false depending on whether the line intersects the AABB or not, it also returns the coordinates of the intersection point in the hit vector, which could be used to determine the closest intersection to the camera in case several are detected.

Movement in VR

Movement is a critical component of a VR experience that we need to consider carefully as it is subject to some constraints and requirements. On the one hand, we aim to convince the user to suspend their disbelief and immerse themselves into the virtual environment. Having some degree of freedom in this environment is important; on the other hand, this virtual movement will not completely match our senses and could cause "motion sickness," something to avoid at all costs in VR apps. Conversely, if we do move around in physical space while wearing a Cardboard viewer, we would experience another disconnect between our vision and physical senses.

Despite these constraints, we can still create convincing movement in VR space. One trick is to place some sort of reference object that remains fixed within the field of vision, matching our stationary condition in physical space. For example, in Listing 16-10, we load an OBJ shape for this purpose and place it at the camera position in eye coordinates. The shape is a dodecahedron (Figure 16-11), which acts as a cabin of sorts during our navigation through VR.

Listing 16-10. Drawing a stationary reference object

```
import processing.vr.*;

PShape frame;

void setup() {
  fullScreen(STEREO);
  frame = loadShape("dodecahedron.obj");
  prepare(frame, 500);
}

void draw() {
  background(180);
  lights();
  translate(width/2, height/2);
  eye();
  shape(frame);
}

void prepare(PShape sh, float s) {
  PVector min = new PVector(+10000, +10000, +10000);
  PVector max = new PVector(-10000, -10000, -10000);
  PVector v = new PVector();
  for (int i = 0; i < sh.getChildCount(); i++) {
    PShape child = sh.getChild(i);
    for (int j = 0; j < child.getVertexCount(); j++) {
      child.getVertex(j, v);
      min.x = min(min.x, v.x);
      min.y = min(min.y, v.y);
      min.z = min(min.z, v.z);
      max.x = max(max.x, v.x);
      max.y = max(max.y, v.y);
      max.z = max(max.z, v.z);
    }
  }
```

```
  PVector center = PVector.add(max, min).mult(0.5f);
  sh.translate(-center.x, -center.y, -center.z);
  float maxSize = max(sh.getWidth(), sh.getHeight(), sh.getDepth());
  float factor = s/maxSize;
  sh.scale(factor);
}
```

The function prepare() centers the shape at the origin and also scales it to have a size comparable to the dimensions of our scene. This step is important when loading OBJ files, since they may be defined using a different range of coordinate values, and so they could look either very small or very large. In this case, we place the dodecahedron shape centered at (cameraX, cameraY, cameraZ) so it provides a reference to our vision in VR. We will see next how to move around, having this reference in place.

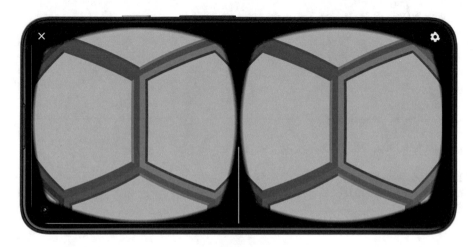

Figure 16-11. *Using an OBJ shape as a reference in our field of vision*

Automatic Movement

In some instances, we can create movement that is not controlled by the user, thus removing complexity from the interface. For example, this could be a good solution if the goal is taking the user through a predetermined path, or to transition between two checkpoints.

Once we have constructed the scene geometry, we can apply any transformations to it in order to create the movement, enclosing them between pushMatrix() and popMatrix() to keep the transformations from affecting any shapes that are fixed relative to the viewer. Listing 16-11 shows how to simulate a rotation around a circular track.

Listing 16-11. Moving along a predefined path

```
import processing.vr.*;

PShape frame;
PShape track;

public void setup() {
  fullScreen(STEREO);
```

```
  frame = loadShape("dodecahedron.obj");
  prepare(frame, 500);

  track = createShape();
  track.beginShape(QUAD_STRIP);
  track.fill(#2D8B47);
  for (int i = 0; i <= 40; i++) {
    float a = map(i, 0, 40, 0, TWO_PI);
    float x0 = 1000 * cos(a);
    float z0 = 1000 * sin(a);
    float x1 = 1400 * cos(a);
    float z1 = 1400 * sin(a);
    track.vertex(x0, 0, z0);
    track.vertex(x1, 0, z1);
  }
  track.endShape();
}

public void draw() {
  background(255);
  translate(width/2, height/2);

  directionalLight(200, 200, 200, 0, +1, -1);

  translate(1200, +300, 500);
  rotateY(millis()/10000.0);
  shape(track);

  eye();
  shape(frame);
}

void prepare(PShape sh, float s) {
  ...
}
```

In this code, we store the circular track in a PShape object; apply a translation to the right of the camera, so the user starts on top of the track; and then apply a rotation to create the desired movement around the track's center. The result of this sketch is shown in Figure 16-12.

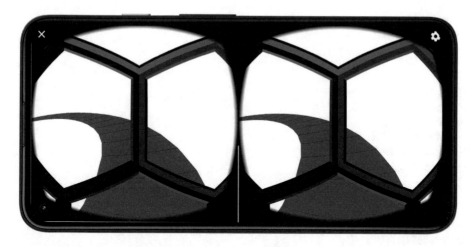

Figure 16-12. *Using an OBJ shape as a reference in our field of vision*

Unconstrained Movement

In contrast with the previous example, where movement is predefined and the user can only look around, we will now let the user roam freely in VR space. This is not that difficult to implement; all we need is to translate the objects in the scene along the forward vector, as it is done in Listing 16-12. However, here we make use of the calculate() function for the first time, an important function in VR sketches to run calculations that should be performed only once per frame.

Listing 16-12. Moving freely in VR space

```
import processing.vr.*;

PShape frame;
PShape cubes;
PMatrix3D eyeMat = new PMatrix3D();
float tx, ty, tz;
float step = 5;

public void setup() {
  fullScreen(STEREO);

  frame = loadShape("dodecahedron.obj");
  prepare(frame, 500);

  cubes = createShape(GROUP);
  float v = 5 * width;
  for (int i = 0; i < 50; i++) {
    float x = random(-v, +v);
    float y = random(-v, +v);
    float z = random(-v, +v);
    float s = random(100, 200);
    PShape sh = createShape(BOX, s);
    sh.setFill(color(#74E0FF));
```

```
    sh.translate(x, y, z);
    cubes.addChild(sh);
  }
}

void calculate() {
  getEyeMatrix(eyeMat);
  if (mousePressed) {
    tx -= step * eyeMat.m02;
    ty -= step * eyeMat.m12;
    tz -= step * eyeMat.m22;
  }
}

public void draw() {
  background(255);
  translate(width/2, height/2);

  directionalLight(200, 200, 200, 0, +1, -1);

  translate(tx, ty, tz);
  shape(cubes);

  eye();
  shape(frame);
}

void prepare(PShape sh, float s) {
  ...
}
```

The calculate() function is called just once in each frame, right before draw() gets called twice, once for each eye. This is useful in this example because if we were to put the translation code inside draw(), we would be increasing the translation by double of the intended amount, resulting in the incorrect movement. It is important we think about what operations should be done inside draw() – typically anything drawing related – and which ones in calculate() such as code that affect left and right views all the same.

A problem with fully unrestricted movement in VR space is that it could become disorienting for many people. A more manageable situation would involve restricting the motion to the XZ (floor) plane. This can still be accomplished with the forward vector as before, but only using its X and Z components to update the translation, which is illustrated in Listing 16-13.

Listing 16-13. Moving around in a 2D surface

```
import processing.vr.*;

PShape cubes;
PShape grid;
PMatrix3D eyeMat = new PMatrix3D();
float tx, tz;
float step = 10;
PVector planeDir = new PVector();
```

```
public void setup() {
  fullScreen(STEREO);

  grid = createShape();
  grid.beginShape(LINES);
  grid.stroke(255);
  for (int x = -10000; x < +10000; x += 500) {
    grid.vertex(x, +200, +10000);
    grid.vertex(x, +200, -10000);
  }
  for (int z = -10000; z < +10000; z += 500) {
    grid.vertex(+10000, +200, z);
    grid.vertex(-10000, +200, z);
  }
  grid.endShape();

  cubes = createShape(GROUP);
  float v = 5 * width;
  for (int i = 0; i < 50; i++) {
    float x = random(-v, +v);
    float z = random(-v, +v);
    float s = random(100, 300);
    float y = +200 - s/2;
    PShape sh = createShape(BOX, s);
    sh.setFill(color(#FFBC6A));
    sh.translate(x, y, z);
    cubes.addChild(sh);
  }
}

void calculate() {
  getEyeMatrix(eyeMat);
  if (mousePressed) {
    planeDir.set(eyeMat.m02, 0, eyeMat.m22);
    float d = planeDir.mag();
    if (0 < d) {
      planeDir.mult(1/d);
      tx -= step * planeDir.x;
      tz -= step * planeDir.z;
    }
  }
}

public void draw() {
background(0);
translate(width/2, height/2);
  pointLight(50, 50, 200, 0, 1000, 0);
  directionalLight(200, 200, 200, 0, +1, -1);
  translate(tx, 0, tz);
  shape(grid);
  shape(cubes);
}
```

In the `calculate()` function, we construct a plane direction vector from the `m02` and `m22` components of the eye matrix. We need to normalize this vector to ensure we keep making uniform strides as we move around, even if we are looking up and the forward vector has very small components along the X and Z axes. A view from this sketch is shown in Figure 16-13.

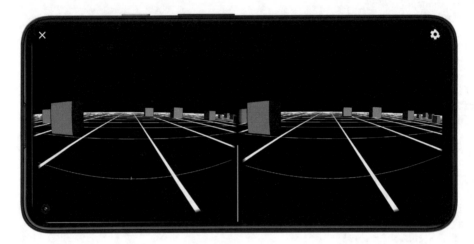

Figure 16-13. *Movement constrained to a 2D plane*

Summary

Virtual reality brings about exciting new possibilities to create immersive experiences as well as challenges to ensure those experiences are easy to navigate and enjoy by users. In this chapter, we learned several techniques in Processing to address some of these challenges and to explore where the possibilities of VR can take us. We paid particular attention to how intuitive interaction and movement are key to create engaging VR experiences.

CHAPTER 17

■ ■ ■

Basics of AR

After VR, the next stop in our journey through Extended Reality is AR. As with VR, Processing for Android includes a library allowing us to easily code AR apps for users to interact with virtual objects placed in real space.

A Brief History of AR

Virtual and augmented reality have shared origins and history. We cited in the previous chapter the head-mounted display created by Sutherland and students in 1968, which is often considered to be one of the first direct precursors of both VR and AR systems. But there are also differences between the two; the most important is probably related to immersion; whereas in VR the user is surrounded by a virtual environment, in AR, the user is still able to perceive the physical world, but with virtual elements "added" to it. Because there are different ways of creating AR experiences (e.g., head-mounted display vs. projection-based AR), practitioners have thought of how to define AR more precisely in relation to other interactive and immersive experiences. For example, back in 1997, computer scientist Ronald Azuma proposed that any AR system should include the following three characteristics: (1) combination of real and virtual elements, (2) real-time interaction, and (3) three-dimensional rendering. This is a widely accepted definition that allows several approaches to be considered AR, such as marker-based AR (where a user-defined image or "marker" activates the augmentation when detected by a camera) and projection-based AR (which has virtual objects rendered over the physical space using digital projectors). Superimposition-based AR is another form of AR, currently the most common, which uses the display of the smartphone as a "magic window" into the real world where we can see and interact with virtual objects overlaid onto the physical environment. Figure 17-1 shows examples of these different approaches.

Just like VR, AR might also sound to be a recent invention, but early prototypes can be traced back many decades. We already mentioned Sutherland's head-mounted display from the 1960s, but as soon as 1901, writer Frank Baum, who is best known for the children's book *The Wonderful Wizard of Oz*, described the idea of electronic spectacles that could overlay data onto real life. Of course, the technology did not exist at the time to make it happen; it wasn't until 1980 that inventor Steve Mann created the first wearable computer, called EyeTap, which was capable of overlaying text and graphics onto a real-life scene. Several researchers carried out pioneering work during the 1980s and 1990s, including Ron Feigenblatt, who proposed what we now know as the "magic window" form of AR in 1986; Jannick Rolland, who engineered key optical systems for AR displays; and Gudrun Klinker, who combined AR with mobile computing and sensing to enable real-word applications. Despite all this early work and the use of AR in research and industry since the 1980s, it's only been in the past decade, with the widespread availability of smartphones, that AR has become accessible to consumers.

© Andrés Colubri 2023
A. Colubri, *Processing for Android*, https://doi.org/10.1007/978-1-4842-9585-4_17

Figure 17-1. *From left to right: AR Sandbox by UC Davis W.M. Keck Center for Active Visualization in the Earth Sciences (projection-based AR), AR app using a QR code for object placement in real space (marker-based AR), and NormanAR, an app to display animations in AR, by James Paterson, Irene Alvarado, and Jonas Jongejan ("magic window" AR)*

Once mobile devices became powerful enough for real-time AR, software development kits like Vuforia and ARToolKit were introduced to allow developers to take advantage of these capabilities. Nowadays, both Apple and Google have built sophisticated AR frameworks directly into iOS and Android, so we don't even need extra software kits to develop AR apps for consumer-level devices. However, these built-in frameworks are often hard to learn, so this is where the AR library in Processing becomes handy (at least for Android)!

AR on Android

Google's framework to create augmented reality (AR) apps for Android, called ARCore (`https://developers.google.com/ar`). Phone-based AR experiences typically involve drawing digital 3D content overlaid onto the physical world, as seen from the perspective of the phone's camera, in such a way that the digital contents convincingly appear to be part of the real-world environment. This includes the contents updating their appearance as we change the orientation and position of the phone. Doing this requires applying complex algorithms in real time to recognize objects in the physical environment, such as walls, pieces of furniture, and even people, and determining the pose (position and orientation) of the phone relative to the world over time. Fortunately for us, ARCore handles all of these calculations automatically, and it provides an API (`https://developers.google.com/ar/reference`) to access the real-world features and attach digital contents to them from our code. While it is possible to access ARCore directly from Processing, the Android mode includes an AR library that makes it easier to use ARCore in our Processing sketches and apply Processing's drawing API to create AR content.

AR on smartphones has grown thanks to frameworks such as ARCore on Android and ARKit on iOS (`https://developer.apple.com/augmented-reality/`) and to the fast pace of technical improvement of mobile devices. The integration of real-world environments with digital contents is opening many new possibilities for phone-mediated experiences in the physical world. The AR experiments from Google (`https://experiments.withgoogle.com/collection/ar`) and the awesome ARKit list of AR apps for iOS (`https://github.com/olucurious/Awesome-ARKit`) are good resources to find projects making creative use of AR.

Requirements

Android devices need to run Android 7 to enable AR apps, and to ensure a good AR experience, Google further certifies devices to be officially supported by ARCore. The official list of supported devices is available at https://developers.google.com/ar/devices. The devices in that list should work with Processing as well to create AR projects.

Getting Started

Before getting into the code of our AR sketch, we need to remember to select the AR option in the Android menu to make sure that our sketch is built as an AR app, as shown in Figure 17-2.

Figure 17-2. *AR option in the Android mode menu*

While in VR you can pretty much turn any 3D Processing sketch into VR simply by importing the VR library and using the VR renderer, using AR requires a few additional steps. First of all, we need to add an ARTracker object to our sketch and call its start() function in the sketch's setup() function to get AR tracking going. This object internally interfaces with ARCore and handles the AR session in Processing.

The other two classes in the AR library are ARTrackable and ARAnchor. ARTrackable represents a surface that can be tracked in real-world space (such as a table or a wall), and ARAnchor is a point in space that remains fixed relative to a given trackable surface. We will delve into these concepts as we go through the next sections in the chapter. For the time being, a basic skeleton for an AR sketch in Processing would look like the code in Listing 17-1, where we just launch AR tracking and print to the console the trackable objects detected in each frame.

Listing 17-1. Basic AR sketch

```
import processing.ar.*;

ARTracker tracker;

void setup() {
  fullScreen(AR);
  tracker = new ARTracker(this);
  tracker.start();
  noStroke();
}

void draw() {
  for (int i = 0; i < tracker.count(); i++) {
    ARTrackable t = tracker.get(i);
    println("Trackable", i, t);
  }
}
```

As can be seen in the code, we can query the number of trackables using the count() function in the ARTracker object and then retrieve each trackable separately with get(), using the index of the trackable as the argument for the call.

Drawing Trackables

Trackable objects in Processing are limited to plane surfaces, even though the underlying trackable in ARCore (https://developers.google.com/ar/reference/java/com/google/ar/core/Trackable) can represent other kind of features in physical space, such as cloud points. Each trackable object contains basic information about the physical entity it represents, including size and status (whether it is being tracked, paused, or stopped). To draw a trackable plane, first, we need to apply the transformation that turns Processing's world coordinates into the trackable system; in this way, it is easy to represent points relative to the trackable plane that spans X and Z axes irrespective of its orientation with respect to Processing's coordinate system. We can retrieve the size of the trackable along each axis with the lengthX() and lengthZ() functions and call the transform() function before making any drawing, as shown in Listing 17-2.

Listing 17-2. Drawing trackable objects detected by the camera

```
import processing.ar.*;

ARTracker tracker;

void setup() {
  fullScreen(AR);
  tracker = new ARTracker(this);
  tracker.start();
  noStroke();
}

void draw() {
  lights();
```

```
  for (int i = 0; i < tracker.count(); i++) {
    ARTrackable t = tracker.get(i);
    pushMatrix();
    t.transform();
    float lx = t.lengthX();
    float lz = t.lengthZ();
    if (t.isFloorPlane() && lx < 1 && lz < 1) {
      fill(255, 100);
      beginShape(QUADS);
      vertex(-lx/2, 0, -lz/2);
      vertex(-lx/2, 0, +lz/2);
      vertex(+lx/2, 0, +lz/2);
      vertex(+lx/2, 0, -lz/2);
      endShape();
    }
    popMatrix();
  }
}
```

In the preceding code, we also check if the trackable is a horizontal surface (i.e., a floor) of less than 1 meter along each X and Z before drawing it (lengthX/Y() return dimensions in meters), because otherwise Processing will likely draw many quads for walls and large trackables. We can determine if a trackable is a horizonal plane by calling isFloorPlane(), as we did here. A similar function, isWallPlane(), allows us to know if the trackable is a vertical plane (i.e., a wall).

■ **Note** ARCore needs to find salient features or "key points" (such as edges or textures) in the physical space to detect trackable planes. Our AR sketches will not be able to properly detect and track flat surfaces without any features. Read more about this and other fundamental concepts of AR in the developer site from Google: https://developers.google.com/ar/develop/fundamentals.

Our preceding sketch should draw all the trackable planes being detected by the phone as we move around, as shown in Figure 17-3.

Figure 17-3. *Drawing planes for each trackable*

It is easy to test if a trackable is being selected by the user using the touchscreen; all we need to do is to call the isSelected(x, y) with the (x, y) coordinates of the touch point, adding this to our previous sketch results in in Listing 17-3 that demonstrates trackable selection, shown in action in Figure 17-4.

Listing 17-3. Selecting a trackable through touch interaction

```
import processing.ar.*;

ARTracker tracker;

void setup() {
  fullScreen(AR);
  tracker = new ARTracker(this);
  tracker.start();
  noStroke();
}

void draw() {
  lights();
  for (int i = 0; i < tracker.count(); i++) {
    ARTrackable t = tracker.get(i);
    pushMatrix();
    t.transform();
    float lx = t.lengthX();
    float lz = t.lengthZ();
    if (t.isFloorPlane() && lx < 1 && lz < 1) {
      if (mousePressed && t.isSelected(mouseX, mouseY)) {
        fill(255, 0, 0, 100);
      } else {
        fill(255, 100);
      }
      beginShape(QUADS);
      vertex(-lx/2, 0, -lz/2);
      vertex(-lx/2, 0, +lz/2);
      vertex(+lx/2, 0, +lz/2);
      vertex(+lx/2, 0, -lz/2);
      endShape();
    }
    popMatrix();
  }
}
```

Figure 17-4. *Output of the code in Listing 17-3, with one trackable selected by touch*

Using Anchors

Once we have trackable surfaces in our AR scene, we can attach anchors to them. Anchors in ARCore (https://developers.google.com/ar/develop/anchors) are essentially positions in space that are fixed relative to the trackable they are attached to. They allow us to make virtual objects appear to stay in place in the scene. Anchor objects in Processing are created with the relative coordinates they will have in relation to their parent trackable. Extending our previous example, we could add new anchors exactly when a trackable is detected for the first time. That event can be handled by adding the trackableEvent() function to our code, which will receive the trackable being detected as an argument. We need to keep track of all the anchors in our scene manually, for example, by storing them in a list and removing them when they are no longer being tracked. The code in Listing 17-4 does all of that.

Listing 17-4. Adding anchors to newly detected trackable objects

```
import processing.ar.*;

ARTracker tracker;
ArrayList<ARAnchor> trackAnchors = new ArrayList<ARAnchor>();

void setup() {
  fullScreen(AR);
  tracker = new ARTracker(this);
  tracker.start();
  noStroke();
}

void draw() {
  lights();
  drawAnchors();
  drawTrackables();
}
```

```
void trackableEvent(ARTrackable t) {
if (trackAnchors.size() < 10 && validTrackable(t)) {
  trackAnchors.add(new ARAnchor(t, 0, 0, 0));
  }
}

void drawAnchors() {
  for (ARAnchor anchor : trackAnchors) {
    if (anchor.isTracking()) drawSphere(anchor, 0.05);
    if (anchor.isStopped()) anchor.dispose();
  }
  tracker.clearAnchors(trackAnchors);
}

void drawTrackables() {
  for (int i = 0; i < tracker.count(); i++) {
    ARTrackable t = tracker.get(i);
    if (!validTrackable(t)) continue;
    pushMatrix();
    t.transform();
    float lx = t.lengthX();
    float lz = t.lengthZ();
    if (mousePressed && t.isSelected(mouseX, mouseY)) {
      fill(255, 0, 0, 100);
    } else {
      fill(255, 100);
    }
    drawPlane(lx, lz);
    popMatrix();
  }
}

void drawSphere(ARAnchor anchor, float r) {
  anchor.attach();
  fill(#CF79F5);
  sphere(r);
  anchor.detach();
}

void drawPlane(float lx, float lz) {
  beginShape(QUADS);
  vertex(-lx/2, 0, -lz/2);
  vertex(-lx/2, 0, +lz/2);
  vertex(+lx/2, 0, +lz/2);
  vertex(+lx/2, 0, -lz/2);
  endShape();
}

boolean validTrackable(ARTrackable t) {
  return t.isFloorPlane() && t.lengthX() < 1 && t.lengthZ() < 1;
}
```

In this code, we simplified the check for valid trackables by putting all the conditions (being a floor plane and larger than 1 meter along each direction) inside the validTrackable() function, and then calling this function when handling a new trackable event, and drawing all detected trackables.

Notice that the radius of the sphere is very small (0.05); this is because, as we mentioned before, ARCore's translation units are meters, so everything in our AR sketch should be scaled to sizes that are consistent with the real-world dimensions, as expressed in the metric system. It is also important that we dispose an anchor once it is no longer tracked with the line if (anchor.isStopped()) anchor.dispose(), to make sure we don't waste resources with anchors that are no longer active (anchors that are simply paused should not be disposed as they can be tracked again later, but those stopped are not going to be restarted). We should also remove the disposed anchors from our array list; we can do that in our sketch, or use the utility function clearAnchors provided in the ARTracker class. Figure 17-5 shows the result of our latest code.

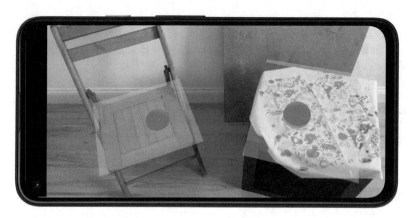

Figure 17-5. *Drawing 3D shapes attached to anchors*

Hitting Trackables

A typical interaction in AR is to move around an object along a trackable plane, for example, to find its best placement interactively. The AR library in Processing offers functionality that makes implementing such interaction very easy. The ARTracker class includes a get() function that takes an (x, y) touch position and returns the trackable hit by that touch point. We can then create a new anchor for that hit trackable, and the anchor will be placed exactly at the position on the trackable that's at the intersection of the trackable's plane with the touch pointer. As the pointer moves around, we need to keep disposing the anchor at the previous position and creating another one at the new position. Listing 17-5 demonstrates the technique.

Listing 17-5. Placing a 3D model in the scene attached to a trackable

```
import processing.ar.*;

ARTracker tracker;
ArrayList<ARAnchor> trackAnchors = new ArrayList<ARAnchor>();
ARAnchor touchAnchor;
PShape obj;

void setup() {
  fullScreen(AR);
  obj = loadShape("model.obj");
  tracker = new ARTracker(this);
```

```
  tracker.start();
  noStroke();
}

void draw() {
  lights();
  drawObject(touchAnchor);
  drawAnchors();
  drawTrackables();
}

void mousePressed() {
  if (touchAnchor != null) touchAnchor.dispose();
  ARTrackable hit = tracker.get(mouseX, mouseY);
  if (hit != null && validTrackable(hit)) touchAnchor = new ARAnchor(hit);
  else touchAnchor = null;
}

void trackableEvent(ARTrackable t) {
if (trackAnchors.size() < 10 && validTrackable(t)) {
  trackAnchors.add(new ARAnchor(t, 0, 0, 0));
  }
}

void drawAnchors() {
  for (ARAnchor anchor : trackAnchors) {
    if (anchor.isTracking()) drawSphere(anchor, 0.05);
    if (anchor.isStopped()) anchor.dispose();
  }
  tracker.clearAnchors(trackAnchors);
}

void drawTrackables() {
  for (int i = 0; i < tracker.count(); i++) {
    ARTrackable t = tracker.get(i);
    if (!validTrackable(t)) continue;
    pushMatrix();
    t.transform();
    float lx = t.lengthX();
    float lz = t.lengthZ();
    if (mousePressed && t.isSelected(mouseX, mouseY)) {
      fill(255, 0, 0, 100);
    } else {
      fill(255, 100);
    }
    drawPlane(lx, lz);
    popMatrix();
  }
}
```

```
void drawSphere(ARAnchor anchor, float r) {
  anchor.attach();
  fill(#CF79F5);
  sphere(r);
  anchor.detach();
}

void drawPlane(float lx, float lz) {
  beginShape(QUADS);
  vertex(-lx/2, 0, -lz/2);
  vertex(-lx/2, 0, +lz/2);
  vertex(+lx/2, 0, +lz/2);
  vertex(+lx/2, 0, -lz/2);
  endShape();
}

void drawObject(ARAnchor anchor) {
  if (anchor != null) {
    anchor.attach();
    shape(obj);
    anchor.detach();
  }
}

boolean validTrackable(ARTrackable t) {
  return t.isFloorPlane() && t.lengthX() < 1 t.lengthZ() < 1;
}
```

In this code, we are using an OBJ model loaded from the sketch's data folder to draw at the placement of the hit anchor. If all is correct in the code, the output would look like Figure 17-6. As before, we need to make sure that the dimensions of the virtual object are consistent with coordinates expressed in meters, so it has the correct size in comparison with the surrounding real objects.

Figure 17-6. *Placing an OBJ model in the scene*

■ **Note** Always remember to call dispose() on the anchor objects that are no longer needed; otherwise, they will continue to use device's resources.

Adding a User Interface

So far, all our AR examples did not include any interface elements, such as buttons, which has not been a problem, given their very simple interactions. As we start developing more complex AR apps, we may need to add a user interface, so the users of our apps are able to do things like changing settings, selecting virtual objects to show in the augmented space, etc.

Applying a 2D overlay layer containing the interface elements such as buttons and checkboxes is one way to implement a simple interface in our AR app. In order to draw this overlay, we only need to call the eye() function, which we already used with the VR library, after drawing all our 3D content and then draw the 2D UI, as shown in Listing 17-6.

Listing 17-6. Using a simple UI to select a 3D model to place in the scene

```
import processing.ar.*;

ARTracker tracker;
ARAnchor touchAnchor;
PShape plant, rocket, selObject;
PImage plantImg, rocketImg;

void setup() {
  fullScreen(AR);
  loadObjects();
  tracker = new ARTracker(this);
  tracker.start();
  noStroke();
}

void draw() {
  lights();
  drawObject(touchAnchor);
  drawTrackables();
  drawUI();
}

void mousePressed() {
  if (mouseY < 200) {
    if (mouseX < 200) {
      selObject = plant;
    } else if (mouseX < 300) {
      selObject = rocket;
    }
  } else {
    if (touchAnchor != null) touchAnchor.dispose();
    ARTrackable hit = tracker.get(mouseX, mouseY);
    if (hit != null && validTrackable(hit)) touchAnchor = new ARAnchor(hit);
```

```
    else touchAnchor = null;
  }
}

void drawTrackables() {
  for (int i = 0; i < tracker.count(); i++) {
    ARTrackable t = tracker.get(i);
    if (!validTrackable(t)) continue;
    pushMatrix();
    t.transform();
    float lx = t.lengthX();
    float lz = t.lengthZ();
    drawPlane(lx, lz);
    popMatrix();
  }
}

void drawPlane(float lx, float lz) {
  fill(255, 100);
  noStroke();
  beginShape(QUADS);
  vertex(-lx/2, 0, -lz/2);
  vertex(-lx/2, 0, +lz/2);
  vertex(+lx/2, 0, +lz/2);
  vertex(+lx/2, 0, -lz/2);
  endShape();
}

float angle;
void drawObject(ARAnchor anchor) {
  if (anchor != null) {
    anchor.attach();
    rotateY(angle);
    shape(selObject);
    anchor.detach();
  }
  angle += 0.01;
}

void drawUI() {
  eye();
  image(plantImg, 0, 0, 200, 200);
  image(rocketImg, 200, 0, 200, 200);
  noFill();
  stroke(255, 0, 0);
  strokeWeight(10);
  float x = 0;
  if (selObject == rocket) x += 200;
  rect(x, 0, 200, 200);
}
```

```
boolean validTrackable(ARTrackable t) {
  return t.isFloorPlane() && t.lengthX() < 1 && t.lengthZ() < 1;
}

void loadObjects() {
  plant = loadShape("plant.obj");

  rocket = loadShape("rocket.obj");
  float dim = max(rocket.getWidth(), rocket.getHeight(), rocket.getDepth());
  float factor = 0.3 / dim;
  rocket.scale(factor);

  plantImg = loadImage("plant-preview.png");
  rocketImg = loadImage("rocket-preview.png");

  selObject = rocket;
}
```

The eye() function in AR returns Processing's camera to 2D projection so we can draw flat user interface elements such as buttons, or any other 2D shapes and images with the Processing API. This is done in the drawUI() function, where we draw the images previewing the virtual objects and use them as selectable buttons to switch between the plant and the rocket models. Figure 17-7 shows the output of this code, with the rocket as the selected object and placed on top of a detected trackable plane.

Figure 17-7. *Selecting a virtual object with a basic overlay 2D UI*

Using Custom Shaders in AR

In Chapter 15, we learned how to write custom GLSL shaders to render the graphics in our Processing sketches under different lighting and texturing conditions, as well as to apply pixel filter effects. We can use shaders in AR sketches too, but we need to add some additional shader code to ensure that the brightness of the virtual objects is consistent with the lighting in the physical space.

We can reuse one of our shader examples from Chapter 15, such as the emboss filter from Listing 15-13. In the new AR version, we place a textured sphere at the anchor where the touch point hits a trackable plane, to be rendered with the emboss fragment shader. As before, we load our shader in setup() and then enable it with shader() in draw(). The entire code is shown in Listing 17-7, including the fragment shader.

Listing 17-7. Applying an emboss shader to a texture in AR

```
import processing.ar.*;

PImage earth;
PShape globe;
float angle;
PShader embossShader;

ARTracker tracker;
ARAnchor anchor;

void setup() {
  fullScreen(AR);

  embossShader = loadShader("embossfrag.glsl");
  earth = loadImage("earthmap1k.jpg");
  globe = createShape(SPHERE, 0.2);
  globe.setTexture(earth);
  globe.setStroke(false);

  tracker = new ARTracker(this);
  tracker.start();
}

void draw() {
  lights();

  if (mousePressed) {
    if (anchor != null) anchor.dispose();
    ARTrackable hit = tracker.get(mouseX, mouseY);
    if (hit != null && validTrackable(hit)) anchor = new ARAnchor(hit);
    else anchor = null;
  }

  if (anchor != null) {
    anchor.attach();
    shader(embossShader);
    rotateY(angle);
    shape(globe);
```

```
    resetShader();
    anchor.detach();
  }

  angle += 0.03;
}
boolean validTrackable(ARTrackable t) {
  return t.isFloorPlane() && t.lengthX() < 1 && t.lengthZ() < 1;
}
```

embossfrag.glsl

```glsl
#ifdef GL_ES
precision mediump float;
precision mediump int;
#endif

uniform sampler2D texture;
uniform vec2 texOffset;
uniform vec4 colorCorrection;

varying vec4 vertColor;
varying vec4 vertTexCoord;

const vec4 lumcoeff = vec4(0.299, 0.587, 0.114, 0);

const float kGamma = 0.4545454;
const float kMiddleGrayGamma = 0.466;

void main() {
  vec3 colorShift = colorCorrection.rgb;
  float averagePixelIntensity = colorCorrection.a;

  vec2 tc0 = vertTexCoord.st + vec2(-texOffset.s, -texOffset.t);
  vec2 tc1 = vertTexCoord.st + vec2(          0.0, -texOffset.t);
  vec2 tc2 = vertTexCoord.st + vec2(-texOffset.s,           0.0);
  vec2 tc3 = vertTexCoord.st + vec2(+texOffset.s,           0.0);
  vec2 tc4 = vertTexCoord.st + vec2(          0.0, +texOffset.t);
  vec2 tc5 = vertTexCoord.st + vec2(+texOffset.s, +texOffset.t);

  vec4 col0 = texture2D(texture, tc0);
  vec4 col1 = texture2D(texture, tc1);
  vec4 col2 = texture2D(texture, tc2);
  vec4 col3 = texture2D(texture, tc3);
  vec4 col4 = texture2D(texture, tc4);
  vec4 col5 = texture2D(texture, tc5);

  vec4 sum = vec4(0.5) + (col0 + col1 + col2) - (col3 + col4 + col5);
  float lum = dot(sum, lumcoeff);
```

```
  vec4 color = vertColor;
  color.rgb = pow(color.rgb, vec3(kGamma));
  color.rgb *= colorShift * (averagePixelIntensity / kMiddleGrayGamma);
  gl_FragColor = vec4(lum, lum, lum, 1.0) * color;
}
```

In the fragment shader, the calculations for the emboss filter are the same as before, but we now have the line color.rgb *= colorShift * (averagePixelIntensity / kMiddleGrayGamma), which adjusts the brightness of the rendered object. The colorShift variable is a vec3 value that represents the amount of brightness to be added or subtracted from the pixels. The averagePixelIntensity variable is a float value that represents the average brightness of the scene. Both are automatically calculated by the AR renderer and passed from the renderer to the shader in the colorCorrection uniform. The sRGB gamma parameters are used to apply the gamma correction for more pleasing visual results (more about gamma correction in this page: https://learnopengl.com/Advanced-Lighting/Gamma-Correction).

Overall, these changes in the shader code should enhance the visual appearance of AR scenes on different devices or under different lighting conditions. We can see the output of this code for the same space and virtual object placement, but with low and high lights, in Figure 17-8.

Figure 17-8. *Same 3D model placed in a real environment with low light (left) vs. high light*

■ **Note** For more advanced manipulations of the AR scene, we can get the underlying AR surface object using "ARSurface surface = (ARSurface) getSurface();" anywhere in the sketch. The surface object contains the AR camera and frame, from which we can get the current pose with surface.getPose() and lighting estimation with frame.getLightEstimate().

Drawing in AR

In this section, we will apply a few techniques we learned in this chapter as well as in previous chapters to make 2D line drawings with the touchscreen and then place these drawings in the AR scene. We will start with a sketch where we draw the lines into an offscreen PGraphics object, which was introduced in Chapter 9. The idea is to add lines to the PGraphics object once we are in the 2D view mode right after the eye() call. This is done in Listing 17-8.

Listing 17-8. Touch-based drawing layer in AR sketch

```
import processing.ar.*;

ARTracker tracker;
PGraphics canvas;

boolean drawingMode = false;
float uiHeight = 150 * displayDensity;

void setup() {
  fullScreen(AR);

  canvas = createGraphics(width, height, P2D);
  initDrawing();

  tracker = new ARTracker(this);
  tracker.start();

  textFont(createFont("Arial", uiHeight/2));
  textAlign(CENTER, CENTER);
}

void draw() {
  if (!drawingMode) {
    lights();
    drawFloors();
  }

  eye();
  updateDrawing();
  drawUI();
}

void drawFloors() {
  for (int i = 0; i < tracker.count(); i++) {
    ARTrackable trackable = tracker.get(i);
    if (!validTrackable(trackable)) continue;
    pushMatrix();
    trackable.transform();
    fill(200, 20, 20, 80);
    noStroke();
    beginShape();
    float[] points = trackable.getPolygon();
    for (int n = 0; n < points.length / 2; n++) {
```

```
      float x = points[2 * n];
      float z = points[2 * n + 1];
      vertex(x, 0, z);
    }
    endShape();
    popMatrix();
  }
}

void initDrawing() {
  canvas.beginDraw();
  canvas.background(255, 0);
  canvas.endDraw();
}

void updateDrawing() {
  if (drawingMode) {
    canvas.beginDraw();
    canvas.stroke(0);
    canvas.strokeWeight(2 * displayDensity);
    if (mousePressed) canvas.line(pmouseX, pmouseY, mouseX, mouseY);
    canvas.endDraw();
    image(canvas, 0, 0, width, height);
  }
}

void drawUI() {
  fill(0);
  rect(0, 0, width, uiHeight);
  fill(255);
  if (drawingMode) {
    text("PLACE DRAWING", 0, 0, width, uiHeight);
  } else {
    text("NEW DRAWING", 0, 0, width, uiHeight);
  }
}

void mousePressed() {
  if (mouseY < uiHeight) {
    drawingMode = !drawingMode;
    if (drawingMode) initDrawing();
  }
}

boolean validTrackable(ARTrackable t) {
  return t.isTracking() && t.isFloorPlane() && t.lengthX() < 1 && t.lengthZ() < 1;
}
```

The rest of this code should be familiar from what we already saw in this chapter. We draw floor plane trackables and use a simple UI to switch between the drawing mode, where the touchscreen input is used to draw the lines, and the placement mode, which at this point does not do anything yet. In Listing 17-9, we complete the logic of the example by generating a new anchor every time Processing detects a touch event (only when we are in placement mode) and then placing a quad textured with the PGraphics holding the drawing, at the anchor's position (remember that a PGraphics can be used just as a PImage).

Listing 17-9. Placing the user's drawing in the AR scene

```
import processing.ar.*;

ARTracker tracker;
ARAnchor anchor;
...
void draw() {
  if (!drawingMode) {
    lights();
    drawFloors();
    if (mousePressed) updateAnchor();
    if (anchor != null) placeDrawing();
  }

  eye();
  updateDrawing();
  drawUI();
}
...
void updateAnchor() {
  if (anchor != null) anchor.dispose();
  ARTrackable hit = tracker.get(mouseX, mouseY);
  if (hit != null && validTrackable(hit)) {
    anchor = new ARAnchor(hit);
  } else {
    anchor = null;
  }
}
...
void placeDrawing() {
  anchor.attach();
  noStroke();
  beginShape(QUAD);
  float r = float(canvas.width) / canvas.height;
  texture(canvas);
  vertex(0, 0, 0, canvas.height);
  vertex(0, 1, 0, 0);
  vertex(r, 1, canvas.width, 0);
  vertex(r, 0, canvas.width, canvas.height);
  endShape();
  anchor.detach();
}
...
```

This previous listing only contains the new code with respect to Listing 17-8; the rest remains unchanged. There are a few aspects to note in the preceding code: first, the dimension of the quad in the AR scene is adjusted to preserve the aspect ratio of the PGraphics image, which is r = float(canvas.width) /

canvas.height; in this way, our drawing is not distorted when placed in the real world. Second, we invert the texturing coordinates, so the bottom of the PGraphics corresponds to the top of the quad, and vice versa. This is because of the top-to-bottom orientation of the y axis when drawing with Processing (this applies both to onscreen and offscreen rendering).

Even though this code does all we set to do at the beginning of this section, allowing us to make a line drawing and place it anywhere in the AR scene, we could still apply some improvements to it. For example, we might reuse the vine drawing code from Chapter 2, where application of some basic shapes resulted in a somewhat abstract yet recognizable vegetation-like patterns. Incorporating this code is easy; we only need to place the calls that generated the vine shapes in the canvas object so they are drawn into the offscreen PGraphics. The new changes are shown in Listing 17-10.

Listing 17-10. Using a PGraphics surface to draw the vines offscreen

```
...
void updateDrawing() {
  if (drawingMode) {
    canvas.beginDraw();
    canvas.stroke(121, 81, 49, 150);
    canvas.strokeWeight(2 * displayDensity);
    if (mousePressed) {
      canvas.line(pmouseX, pmouseY, mouseX, mouseY);
      canvas.ellipse(mouseX, mouseY, 13 * displayDensity, 13 * displayDensity);
      if (30 * displayDensity < dist(pmouseX, pmouseY, mouseX, mouseY)) {
        drawLeaves();
      }
    }
    canvas.endDraw();
    image(canvas, 0, 0, width, height);
  }
}

void drawLeaves() {
  int numLeaves = int(random(2, 5));
  for (int i = 0; i < numLeaves; i++) {
    float leafAngle = random(0, TWO_PI);
    float leafLength = random(20, 100) * displayDensity;
    canvas.pushMatrix();
      canvas.translate(mouseX, mouseY);
      canvas.rotate(leafAngle);
      canvas.line(0, 0, leafLength, 0);
      canvas.translate(leafLength, 0);
      canvas.pushStyle();
        canvas.noStroke();
        canvas.fill(random(170, 180), random(200, 230), random(80, 90), 190);
        float r = random(20, 50) * displayDensity;
        canvas.beginShape();
        int numSides = int(random(4, 8));
        for (float angle = 0; angle <= TWO_PI; angle += TWO_PI/numSides) {
          float x = r * cos(angle);
          float y = r * sin(angle);
          canvas.vertex(x, y);
        }
```

```
        canvas.endShape();
      canvas.popStyle();
    canvas.popMatrix();
  }
}
...
```

With this last addition, our sketch is complete, and we can use it to draw vines and place them on any of the floor planes detected by Processing in the AR scene! A typical output is shown in Figure 17-9. We could continue to refine this sketch in many ways, for example, by trying to make line drawings in 3D. Right now, our offscreen canvas uses the P2D renderer, but it could be 3D as well, and in that case, we could draw 3D contents in this separate canvas to later place them on the real world (using the same drawing/placing switching). However, making a 3D drawing through a touchscreen interface may be tricky, so it is left as an exercise for the reader. Sketches from OpenProcessing like `https://openprocessing.org/sketch/95793` or `https://openprocessing.org/sketch/1362912` could help!

Figure 17-9. *Output of the AR drawing sketch in the drawing mode (left) and placing mode (right)*

Summary

This chapter provided a glimpse of the basics of AR in Android, showing us how Processing can be used to experiment with 2D and 3D shapes and quickly prototype ideas for interactions and experiences in AR. All of this is possible because the same drawing and input handling functions that we learned in the past chapters can be used in the AR library with only minimal changes. This allows us to bring non-AR projects into AR with ease, and for more advanced applications, we could still take advantage of the full-fledged ARCore API from within Processing.

CHAPTER 18

■ ■ ■

Creating XR Experiences

In this final chapter, we will go step by step through in the development of a full-featured VR drawing app with Processing for Android, as an example of using Processing to create interactive experiences in "Extended Reality." We will apply all the techniques we have learned so far, including gaze-controlled movement and user interface in immersive environments.

Challenges with XR Apps

In the previous chapters, we learned the basics of the 3D API in Processing and the libraries available in the Android mode to code interactive graphics in VR and AR. The term "Extended Reality" (XR) is often used to encompass technologies such as virtual and augmented reality, as well as a "mixed reality" (MR), which all blend real and virtual environments to some degree to create immersive and interactive experiences. In the last two chapters, we delved into VR and AR while leaving out MR. If we think of VR as complete immersion in a digital environment and, at the other end of a spectrum, of AR as a more limited immersion, with digital objects only overlaid on top of the physical environment, then we could consider MR as occupying the spectrum between these two ends. In this sense, MR would combine elements of both, allowing physical and digital entities to interact while the user maintains a sense of presence in the real world. Examples of MR applications or devices are Microsoft's HoloLens, Magic Leap 2, and the upcoming Vision Pro headset from Apple. There is even a standard called OpenXR that aims at providing high-performance access to VR and AR platforms and devices. (`www.khronos.org/openxr/`). In the end, there are no precise boundaries between these technologies; this is why XR is used as a general term to describe this spectrum.

Because VR and AR are clearly distinct in the Android platform, with Processing for Android, we are currently able to generate either a pure VR or AR experience, but not an intermediate "mixed" experience (such as a virtual environment with a camera view into the physical space). With this observation in mind, we need to go with one or the other for now; maybe upcoming Android devices would allow such blended experiences, and Google may combine its separate AR and VR frameworks into a unified XR programming interface. Such API could result in an XR library for Processing in the future!

Here, we will focus on designing and implementing an interactive experience in VR from the ground up as a particular example of the challenges in XR; an interactive experience in AR would also present us with unique challenges, some of which might be like those we encounter in VR but others specific to AR. In contrast with "traditional" computer graphics, where we can rely on representations (e.g., perspective vs. isometric views) and interaction conventions (e.g., mouse or touch-based gestures) that many users are familiar with, VR and AR are comparatively far less common, so users may find them confusing by lack of an accepted representation or interaction mechanisms.

We could say that a central goal, as far as VR is concerned, is to suspend disbelief and immerse the user in the virtual space, at least for a short while, even if the graphics are not photo-realistic or the interaction is limited. VR creates the unusual experience of being inside the synthetic 3D space but without a body. Recent input hardware demoed in tech and gaming shows (e.g., bicycle stands for biking in VR, air pressure to

© Andrés Colubri 2023
A. Colubri, *Processing for Android*, https://doi.org/10.1007/978-1-4842-9585-4_18

create the illusion of touch, even low electric discharges) illustrates ideas people have come up with to try to make VR experiences more physical.

We should also pay attention to the specific characteristics of the Google Carboard platform. Since we are generating the graphics with a smartphone, they are more limited than those from VR headsets driven by more powerful computers. First, it is important to make sure that phones can handle the complexity of our scene to keep a smooth frame rate. Otherwise, choppy animation can cause dizziness and nausea to the users. Second, Cardboard headsets have limited interaction input, typically only a single button. Also, since we need to use both hands to hold them (see Figure 18-1), we cannot rely on external input devices. The interaction in our VR app should take all these aspects of the experience into account.

Figure 18-1. *Students using Google Cardboard during class activities (photo by K.W. Barret, Google Expeditions)*

Drawing in VR

Making 3D objects in VR can be a fun activity, where we can sculpt figures unbounded by a flat screen or laws of physics, while being in the same space with our creations. Google's VR drawing app Tilt Brush (Figure 18-2) is a great example of how immersive and engaging drawing in VR could be. Inspired by Tilt Brush, we could try to implement our own drawing VR app for Cardboard! Tilt Brush took advantage of the high-resolution and spatial controllers of VR headsets such as the HTC Vive and Oculus Rift. As we discussed before, we will have to deal with the more limited graphics and interaction capabilities of the Cardboard headsets. Since we only have one button to make single presses, we are essentially constrained to use gaze as our pencil. For this purpose, some of the techniques in Chapter 16 to select 3D elements in VR space using the line of sight would become handy for this project.

Figure 18-2. *Google Tilt Brush VR drawing app*

■ **Note** Google ended the development of the virtual reality painting app Tilt Brush in 2021 but released most of the source code of the app, which can be found in this GitHub repository: `https://github.com/googlevr/tilt-brush`.

Initial Sketches

Sculping is indeed a good analogy for drawing in VR. Following this analogy, we could have a "podium" on top of which we do our VR drawing/sculpting, with some UI controls to rotate it when we need to change the angle we are working on. We should remember that Cardboard does not track changes in position, only head rotations, which are not enough to make a 3D drawing from all possible angles. Figure 18-3 shows a possible pen-and-paper concept sketch of a VR app addressing these limitations.

The point where our line of sight reaches the volume above the podium could be the tip of our pencil. The key functionality would be to connect this pencil to the movements of our head, without interfering with the UI. We could use button presses as the mechanism to enable/disable drawing, so when we are not pressing the button, we are free to move our head around and to interact with the UI. So the app could work as follows: while we are in the drawing mode, we stay at a static position from where we draw above of the podium. We could add an additional element of immersion by letting the user move freely around after the drawing is completed and, by doing so, be able to look at it from unusual angles. Back in Chapter 16, we learned how to implement free movement in VR, and we could use that technique in this project as well.

Figure 18-3. *Pen-and-paper concept sketch for our VR drawing app*

A Simple VR UI

Let's start by creating an initial version of our app only incorporating the podium and some initial UI elements, but with no drawing yet. As a temporary placeholder for Listing 18-1, we display a dummy shape to test rotation with the UI.

Listing 18-1. Starting point of our VR drawing app

```
import processing.vr.*;

PShape base;

void setup() {
  fullScreen(STEREO);
  createBase(300, 70, 20);
}

void draw() {
background(0);
  translate(width/2, height/2);
  directionalLight(200, 200, 200, 0, +1, -1);
  drawBase();
  drawBox();
}

void drawBase() {
  pushMatrix();
  translate(0, +300, 0);
```

```
    shape(base);
    popMatrix();
}

void drawBox() {
  pushMatrix();
  translate(0, +100, 0);
  noStroke();
  box(200);
  popMatrix();
}

void createBase(float r, float h, int ndiv) {
  base = createShape(GROUP);
  PShape side = createShape();
  side.beginShape(QUAD_STRIP);
  side.noStroke();
  side.fill(#59C5F5);
  for (int i = 0; i <= ndiv; i++) {
    float a = map(i, 0, ndiv, 0, TWO_PI);
    float x = r * cos(a);
    float z = r * sin(a);
    side.vertex(x, +h/2, z);
    side.vertex(x, -h/2, z);
  }
  side.endShape();
  PShape top = createShape();
  top.beginShape(TRIANGLE_FAN);
  top.noStroke();
  top.fill(#59C5F5);
  top.vertex(0, 0, 0);
  for (int i = 0; i <= ndiv; i++) {
    float a = map(i, 0, ndiv, 0, TWO_PI);
    float x = r * cos(a);
    float z = r * sin(a);
    top.vertex(x, -h/2, z);
  }
  top.endShape();
  base.addChild(side);
  base.addChild(top);
}
```

The podium or base is just a capped cylinder stored in a PShape, but it requires some extra code to construct the sides and the top cap according to the parameters in the createBase() function (radius, height, and number of divisions), since we need two different pieces: the sides of the cylinder and the ellipse to use as a cap. As we saw previously, we can store different kinds of Processing shapes inside a group, and the resulting PShape group is all we need to draw this base shape. Figure 18-4 shows this first version of the app.

Figure 18-4. *First step in our VR drawing app: a base shape and a dummy object*

As a first iteration for the UI, we will add three buttons: two to rotate the base and box along the y axis and another button to reset the rotation. Listing 18-2 implements this initial UI (the createBase(), drawBase(), and drawBox() functions are omitted since they are identical to the previous code).

Listing 18-2. Adding a simple UI

```
import processing.vr.*;

PShape base;
float angle;
Button leftButton, rightButton, resetButton;

void setup() {
  fullScreen(STEREO);
  textureMode(NORMAL);
  createBase(300, 70, 20);
  createButtons(300, 100, 380, 130);
}

void calculate () {
  if (mousePressed) {
    if (leftButton.selected) angle -= 0.01;
    if (rightButton.selected) angle += 0.01;
    if (resetButton.selected) angle = 0;
  }
}

void draw() {
  background(0);
  translate(width/2, height/2);
  directionalLight(200, 200, 200, 0, +1, -1);
  drawBase();
  drawBox();
  drawUI();
}
```

```
...
void createButtons(float dx, float hlr, float ht, float s) {
  PImage left = loadImage("left-icon.png");
  leftButton = new Button(-dx, hlr, 0, s, left);
  PImage right = loadImage("right-icon.png");
  rightButton = new Button(+dx, hlr, 0, s, right);
  PImage cross = loadImage("cross-icon.png");
  resetButton = new Button(0, +1.0 * ht, +1.1 * dx, s, cross);
}

void drawUI() {
  leftButton.display();
  rightButton.display();
  resetButton.display();
  drawAim();
}

void drawAim() {
  eye();
  pushStyle();
  stroke(220, 180);
  strokeWeight(20);
  point(0, 0, 100);
  popStyle();
}

boolean centerSelected(float d) {
  float sx = screenX(0, 0, 0);
  float sy = screenY(0, 0, 0);
  return abs(sx - 0.5 * width) < d && abs(sy - 0.5 * height) < d;
}

class Button {
  float x, y, z, s;
  boolean selected;
  PImage img;

  Button(float x, float y, float z, float s, PImage img) {
    this.x = x;
    this.y = y;
    this.z = z;
    this.s = s;
    this.img = img;
  }

  void display() {
    float l = 0.5 * s;
    pushStyle();
    pushMatrix();
    translate(x, y, z);
    selected = centerSelected(l);
```

```
    beginShape(QUAD);
    if (selected) {
      stroke(220, 180);
      strokeWeight(5);
    } else {
      noStroke();
    }
    tint(#59C5F5);
    texture(img);
    vertex(-1, +1, 0, 1);
    vertex(-1, -1, 0, 0);
    vertex(+1, -1, 1, 0);
    vertex(+1, +1, 1, 1);
    endShape();
    popMatrix();
    popStyle();
  }
}
```

The Button class encapsulating the selection functionality is the central element of this code. Its constructor takes five parameters: the (x, y, z) coordinates of the center of the button, the size, and an image to use as the button texture. In the implementation of the display() method, we determine if the button is selected by using the screen coordinates technique from Chapter 16: if (screen, screenY) is close enough to the screen center, then it is considered to be selected, in which case the button has a stroke outline. The UI events are triggered in the calculate() method, to avoid applying them twice, when the "mouse" pressed (corresponding to the physical trigger available in the VR headset) event is detected.

The placement of the buttons is determined in the createButtons() function, with the left and right rotation buttons placed to the sides of the base and the reset button slightly underneath. We also draw a stroke point to use as an aim to help with selection.

Let's review the display() function in the Button class, where, in addition to draw the button, we also test if it is selected. This may look like the wrong place to put that logic, since a display function should take care only of drawing tasks. As it turns out, the screenX() and screenY() calls require that the 3D transformations affecting the button are current; otherwise, they will return incorrect results. Since the transformations are applied when drawing the geometry, this is the reason to perform the interaction detection in that stage as well. The result of this sketch should look like the one shown in Figure 18-5.

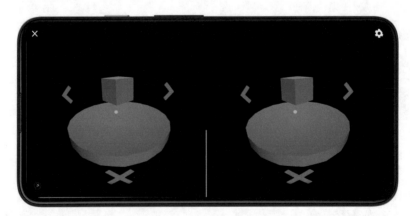

Figure 18-5. *Adding buttons to the UI*

Drawing in 3D

When we implemented the drawing app in Chapter 2, we only had to worry about making strokes in 2D. This was easy thanks to the pmouseX/Y and mouseX/Y variables in Processing, which allowed us to make a line between the last and the current mouse position. In three dimensions, the idea is the same: a stroke is a sequence of lines between successive positions of our pointer, no longer constrained to be contained on the plane. But if we don't have an actual 3D pointer in VR space, we need to figure out directionality in 3D space from gaze information alone.

We know that the direction of our gaze is contained in the forward vector, which is automatically updated to reflect any head movement. If at each frame, we project the forward vector a fixed amount toward the center of the scene, then we would have a sliding point that could generate the strokes in our drawing. In fact, this is not too different from what we did for 2D drawings, where the strokes were defined by the sequence of (mouseX, mouseY) positions. We can also compute the difference between the current and previous forward vectors, analogous to the vector (mouseX - pmouseX, mouseY - pmouseY) in 2D, to determine if we need to add new points to the drawing. Figure 18-6 shows the relationship between the difference vector and the corresponding displacement in the drawing.

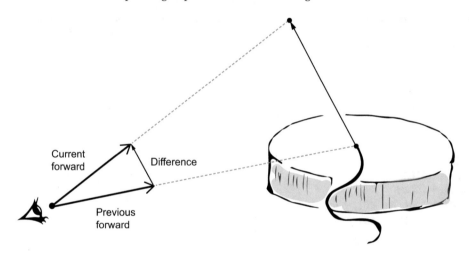

Figure 18-6. *Calculating displacement using previous and current forward vectors*

An important difference between 3D and 2D is that in 2D we don't need to keep track of all the past positions, only the last one. The reason is because if we don't clear the screen with background() at the beginning of draw(), we can simply add the last line on top of the ones that are already drawn in previous frames. But in 3D, we need to refresh the screen in every frame, since the position of the camera is not static and so the scene needs to be updated continuously. This means that all past lines, since the first position recorded in our drawing, must be redrawn in each frame. To do so, we need to keep track of all positions in an array.

However, if we want to break the stroke when the user stops pressing the trigger in the headset, then storing all positions along our drawing in a single array is not enough. We also need to save where those breaks occur. One possibility is to store each continuous stroke in a separate array and have an array of arrays containing all past strokes.

With all these considerations in mind, we can go ahead and start working on the drawing functionality. Since the sketch is becoming more complex, it is a good idea to split it into separate tabs with related code in each one. For example, we could have the tab structure shown in Figure 18-7.

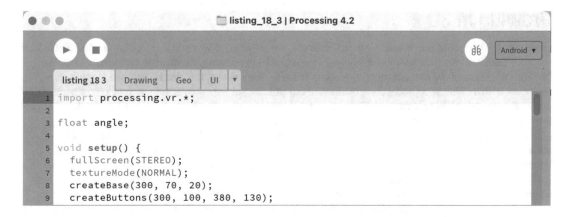

Figure 18-7. *Tabs to organize our increasingly complex VR drawing sketch*

Let's look at each tab separately. The main tab shown in Listing 18-3a contains the standard Processing's setup(), calculate(), draw(), and mouseReleased() functions. The rest of the functions we call from the main tab are implemented in the other tabs.

Listing 18-3a. Sketch's main tab

```
import processing.vr.*;

float angle;

void setup() {
  fullScreen(STEREO);
  textureMode(NORMAL);
  createBase(300, 70, 20);
  createButtons(300, 100, 380, 130);
}

void calculate() {
  if (mousePressed) {
    if (leftButton.selected) angle -= 0.01;
    if (rightButton.selected) angle += 0.01;
  }
  if (mousePressed && !selectingUI()) {
    updateStrokes();
  }
}

void draw() {
  background(0);
  translate(width/2, height/2);
  directionalLight(200, 200, 200, 0, +1, -1);
  drawBase();
  drawStrokes();
  drawUI();
}
```

```
void mouseReleased() {
  if (resetButton.selected) {
    clearDrawing();
    angle = 0;
  } else {
    startNewStroke();
  }
}
```

One observation about mouse event handlers is the following. The updates of the rotation angle remain in calculate(), because this allows to rotate the scene continuously by increasing/decreasing the angle in 0.01 steps, as long as we keep pressing the trigger button on the headset. In contrast, the mousePressed()/ mouseReleased() handlers get called only when starting and ending a mouse press event, so they are not useful to fire events during a long-press. On the other hand, clearing the drawing should be triggered only once after the button is released, and not many times while pressing it, so that's why clearDrawing() is placed inside mouseReleased(). So, we need to consider carefully which event handler is most appropriate for our code depending on the intended interaction.

■ **Note**   Tabs in a Processing sketch are entirely optional and do not affect how the sketch is run. We can leave all our code in a single tab, but using multiple tabs allows us to organize the code and make it more readable.

Moving on to the Drawing tab in Listing 18-3b, we can inspect the code that adds new positions to the current stroke in upateStrokes() and draws current and previous strokes by connecting all consecutive positions with lines in drawStrokes().

Listing 18-3b. Sketch's drawing tab

```
ArrayList<PVector> currentStroke = new ArrayList<PVector>();
ArrayList[] previousStrokes = new ArrayList[0];

PMatrix3D eyeMat = new PMatrix3D();
PMatrix3D objMat = new PMatrix3D();
PVector pos = new PVector();
PVector pforward = new PVector();
PVector cforward = new PVector();

void updateStrokes() {
  translate(width/2, height/2);
  rotateY(angle);
  getEyeMatrix(eyeMat);
  float cameraX = eyeMat.m03;
  float cameraY = eyeMat.m13;
  float cameraZ = eyeMat.m23;
  float forwardX = eyeMat.m02;
  float forwardY = eyeMat.m12;
  float forwardZ = eyeMat.m22;
  float depth = dist(cameraX, cameraY, cameraZ, width/2, height/2, 0);
  cforward.x = forwardX;
```

```
  cforward.y = forwardY;
  cforward.z = forwardZ;
  if (currentStroke.size() == 0 || 0 < cforward.dist(pforward)) {
    getObjectMatrix(objMat);
    float x = cameraX + depth * forwardX;
    float y = cameraY + depth * forwardY;
    float z = cameraZ + depth * forwardZ;
    pos.set(x, y, z);
    PVector tpos = new PVector();
    objMat.mult(pos, tpos);
    currentStroke.add(tpos);
  }
  pforward.x = forwardX;
  pforward.y = forwardY;
  pforward.z = forwardZ;
}

void drawStrokes() {
  pushMatrix();
  rotateY(angle);
  strokeWeight(5);
  stroke(255);
  drawStroke(currentStroke);
  for (ArrayList p: previousStrokes) drawStroke(p);
  popMatrix();
}

void drawStroke(ArrayList<PVector> positions) {
  for (int i = 0; i < positions.size() - 1; i++) {
    PVector p = positions.get(i);
    PVector p1 = positions.get(i + 1);
    line(p.x, p.y, p.z, p1.x, p1.y, p1.z);
  }
}

void startNewStroke() {
  previousStrokes = (ArrayList[]) append(previousStrokes, currentStroke);
  currentStroke = new ArrayList<PVector>();
}

void clearDrawing() {
  previousStrokes = new ArrayList[0];
  currentStroke.clear();
}
```

We have several variables in this tab, starting with array list of PVector objects holding the positions in the current stroke and an array of array lists, where each list is a completed stroke. Once a mouse released event is detected (in the mouseReleased() function defined in the main tab), the startNewStroke() function is called to append the current stroke to the array of previous strokes and initialize an empty array list for the next stroke. The rest of the variables are used to compute the new positions in the current stroke. The code is based on our previous discussion about extending the forward vector by a predefined amount depth (Figure 18-6). This puts the "pencil's tip" right above the drawing podium since depth is the distance between the camera and the scene center. We should not overlook the use of the object matrix, objMat, in updateStrokes(). It is necessary to ensure that the strokes are drawn correctly even if there are transformations applied to the scene (like a translation and a rotation around Y in this case). Notice how we apply these transformations at the beginning of updateStrokes(). Even though updateStrokes() is called from calculate(), which does not do any drawing, we still need to apply the same transformations we later use in draw() to make sure that the matrix we retrieve with getObjectMatrix() will apply all the transformations on the stroke vertices.

In the UI tab in Listing 18-3c, we have all the definition of our Button class and all the button objects we are using so far in our interface.

Listing 18-3c. Sketch's UI tab

```
Button leftButton, rightButton, resetButton;

void createButtons(float dx, float hlr, float ht, float s) {
  PImage left = loadImage("left-icon.png");
  leftButton = new Button(-dx, hlr, 0, s, left);
  PImage right = loadImage("right-icon.png");
  rightButton = new Button(+dx, hlr, 0, s, right);
  PImage cross = loadImage("cross-icon.png");
  resetButton = new Button(0, +1.0 * ht, +1.1 * dx, s, cross);
}

void drawUI() {
  leftButton.display();
  rightButton.display();
  resetButton.display();
  drawAim();
}

void drawAim() {
  eye();
  pushStyle();
  stroke(220, 180);
  strokeWeight(20);
  point(0, 0, 100);
  popStyle();
}

boolean selectingUI() {
  return leftButton.selected || rightButton.selected ||
         resetButton.selected;
}

boolean centerSelected(float d) {
  float sx = screenX(0, 0, 0);
  float sy = screenY(0, 0, 0);
  return abs(sx - 0.5 * width) < d && abs(sy - 0.5 * height) < d;
}
```

```
class Button {
  float x, y, z, s;
  boolean selected;
  PImage img;

  Button(float x, float y, float z, float s, PImage img) {
    this.x = x;
    this.y = y;
    this.z = z;
    this.s = s;
    this.img = img;
  }

  void display() {
    float l = 0.5 * s;
    pushStyle();
    pushMatrix();
    translate(x, y, z);
    selected = centerSelected(l);
    beginShape(QUAD);
    if (selected) {
      stroke(220, 180);
      strokeWeight(5);
    } else {
      noStroke();
    }
    tint(#59C5F5);
    texture(img);
    vertex(-l, +l, 0, 1);
    vertex(-l, -l, 0, 0);
    vertex(+l, -l, 1, 0);
    vertex(+l, +l, 1, 1);
    endShape();
    popMatrix();
    popStyle();
  }
}
```

The Geo tab, shown in Listing 18-3d only contains just for now the code that creates and draws the base, which is the same from before.

Listing 18-3d. Sketch's Geo tab

```
PShape base;

void drawBase() {
  pushMatrix();
  translate(0, +300, 0);
  rotateY(angle);
  shape(base);
  popMatrix();
}
```

```
void createBase(float r, float h, int ndiv) {
  base = createShape(GROUP);
  PShape side = createShape();
  side.beginShape(QUAD_STRIP);
  side.noStroke();
  side.fill(#59C5F5);
  for (int i = 0; i <= ndiv; i++) {
    float a = map(i, 0, ndiv, 0, TWO_PI);
    float x = r * cos(a);
    float z = r * sin(a);
    side.vertex(x, +h/2, z);
    side.vertex(x, -h/2, z);
  }
  side.endShape();
  PShape top = createShape();
  top.beginShape(TRIANGLE_FAN);
  top.noStroke();
  top.fill(#59C5F5);
  top.vertex(0, 0, 0);
  for (int i = 0; i <= ndiv; i++) {
    float a = map(i, 0, ndiv, 0, TWO_PI);
    float x = r * cos(a);
    float z = r * sin(a);
    top.vertex(x, -h/2, z);
  }
  top.endShape();
  base.addChild(side);
  base.addChild(top);
}
```

After all this hard work, we should have a working drawing app for VR! We can try it out in a Cardboard headset, and if everything goes well, we should be able to use it to create line drawing like the one shown in Figure 18-8.

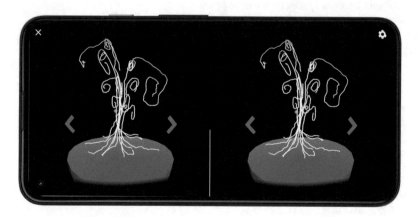

Figure 18-8. *Our VR drawing app in action*

365

Flying Around

With the VR drawing app in its current form, we can direct strokes with our gaze and rotate the drawing around the horizontal direction to add new strokes from different angles. Even though this is already quite neat, we could still improve the app in many ways.

A limitation in our current version of the app is that our position remains fixed in front of the drawing podium. Although we can change our viewpoint by moving our head and rotating the drawing around the horizontal axis, we would not be able to get any closer to it. We learned in Chapter 16 how to implement free range movement in VR, so we could make use of that code to implement this functionality in our app. Since we want to create a fly-by through the drawing, we could add a pair of animated wings in front of the view! These wings, fixed with respect to the users' position, would provide a visual reference to help them not feeling disoriented when "flying" around.

We will go over all the changes we should introduce to the tabs of the last version of the sketch. Let's start with the main tab in Listing 18-4a.

Listing 18-4a. Main tab with the modifications needed by the fly mode

```
import processing.vr.*;

float angle;
boolean flyMode = false;
PVector flyStep = new PVector();

void setup() {
  fullScreen(STEREO);
  textureMode(NORMAL);
  createBase(300, 70, 20);
  createButtons(300, 100, 380, 130);
}

void calculate() {
  if (mousePressed) {
    if (leftButton.selected) angle -= 0.01;
    if (rightButton.selected) angle += 0.01;
    if (flyMode) {
      getEyeMatrix(eyeMat);
      flyStep.add(2 * eyeMat.m02, 2 * eyeMat.m12, 2 * eyeMat.m22);
    }
  }
  if (mousePressed && !selectingUI() && !flyMode) {
    updateStrokes();
  }
}

void draw() {
  background(0);
  translate(width/2, height/2);
  ambientLight(40, 40, 40);
  directionalLight(200, 200, 200, 0, +1, -1);
  translate(-flyStep.x, -flyStep.y, -flyStep.z);
  drawBase();
```

```
  drawStrokes();
  if (flyMode) drawWings();
  drawUI();
}

void mouseReleased() {
  if (resetButton.selected) {
    clearDrawing();
    angle = 0;
  } else if (flyToggle.selected) {
    flyToggle.toggle();
    if (flyToggle.state == 0) {
      flyMode = false;
      flyStep.set(0, 0, 0);
    } else {
      flyMode = true;
    }
  } else {
    startNewStroke();
  }
}
```

We introduced a few new variables in this listing: a flyMode boolean variable to keep track of whether we are in fly mode or not and the displacement vector flyStep that we update by advancing along the forward vector when the headset button is pressed. Also, we added an ambient light, so the wings are visible even when they don't receive any directional light.

We also had to add some extra interaction handling in mouseReleased(). The problem is that now we need another UI element to switch between the normal draw mode and the fly mode. We do this by implementing a specialized toggle button with two alternative images indicating which mode we can switch to. The placement of this toggle button is not obvious: it could just be in front of our view as we start the app, but then it would be not visible if we are in fly mode, and we end up lost somewhere in VR. It would be better if this button is always visible when we do some specific gesture, for example, looking up. We can achieve this if the toggle button is not affected by the fly movement and always placed exactly above the camera position; the code in Listing 18-4b does that.

Listing 18-4b. UI tab with fly mode modifications

```
Button leftButton, rightButton, resetButton;
Toggle flyToggle;

void createButtons(float dx, float hlr, float ht, float s) {
  ...
  PImage fly = loadImage("fly-icon.png");
  PImage home = loadImage("home-icon.png");
  flyToggle = new Toggle(-ht, s, fly, home);
}

void drawUI() {
  leftButton.display();
  rightButton.display();
  resetButton.display();
  noLights();
```

```
  flyToggle.display();
  if (!flyMode) drawAim();
}
...
boolean selectingUI() {
  return leftButton.selected || rightButton.selected ||
         resetButton.selected || flyToggle.selected;
}
...
class Toggle {
  float h, s;
  boolean selected;
  int state;
  PImage[] imgs;
  color[] colors;

  Toggle(float h, float s, PImage img0, PImage img1) {
    this.h = h;
    this.s = s;
    imgs = new PImage[2];
    imgs[0] = img0;
    imgs[1] = img1;
    colors = new color[2];
    colors[0] = #F2674E;
    colors[1] = #59C5F5;
  }

  void display() {
    float l = 0.5 * s;
    pushStyle();
    pushMatrix();
    getEyeMatrix(eyeMat);
    translate(eyeMat.m03 + flyStep.x - width/2,
              eyeMat.m13 + h + flyStep.y - height/2,
              eyeMat.m23 + flyStep.z);
    selected = centerSelected(l);
    beginShape(QUAD);
    if (selected) {
      stroke(220, 180);
      strokeWeight(5);
    } else {
      noStroke();
    }
    tint(colors[state]);
    texture(imgs[state]);
    vertex(-1, 0, +1, 0, 0);
    vertex(+1, 0, +1, 1, 0);
    vertex(+1, 0, -1, 1, 1);
    vertex(-1, 0, -1, 0, 1);
    endShape();
    popMatrix();
```

```
    popStyle();
  }

  void toggle() {
    state = (state + 1) % 2;
  }
}
```

The Toggle class is like Button, but it is textured with two images, one for each toggle state. We place the toggle button so it always appear to be "floating" above the user by translating it to (eyeMat.m03 + flyStep.x - width/2, eyeMat.m13 + h + flyStep.y - height/2, eyeMat.m23 + flyStep.z), which cancels the translation to the screen center and the fly movement we apply in draw(), so it is placed at exactly (eyeMat.m03, eyeMat.m13 + h, eyeMat.m23), the camera coordinates plus a displacement of h along the vertical.

Finally, Listing 18-4c shows the code for the animated wings we draw while in fly mode. The geometry is very simple: two larger, rotating quads for the wings and a smaller rectangle between them to create a body.

Listing 18-4c. Drawing tab with fly mode modifications

```
...
void drawWings() {
  pushMatrix();
  eye();

  translate(0, +50, 100);
  noStroke();
  fill(#F2674E);

  beginShape(QUAD);
  vertex(-5, 0, -50);
  vertex(+5, 0, -50);
  vertex(+5, 0, +50);
  vertex(-5, 0, +50);
  endShape();

  pushMatrix();
  translate(-5, 0, 0);
  rotateZ(map(cos(millis()/1000.0), -1, +1, -QUARTER_PI, +QUARTER_PI));
  beginShape(QUAD);
  vertex(-100, 0, -50);
  vertex(   0, 0, -50);
  vertex(   0, 0, +50);
  vertex(-100, 0, +50);
  endShape();
  popMatrix();

  pushMatrix();
  translate(+5, 0, 0);
  rotateZ(map(cos(millis()/1000.0), -1, +1, +QUARTER_PI, -QUARTER_PI));
  beginShape(QUAD);
  vertex(+100, 0, -50);
  vertex(   0, 0, -50);
  vertex(   0, 0, +50);
```

```
    vertex(+100, 0, +50);
    endShape();
    popMatrix();

    popMatrix();
}
```

With these additions, we can switch into fly mode to fly through our drawing and switch back to the default draw mode to continue the drawing or start a new one, a sequence of steps we can appreciate in Figure 18-9.

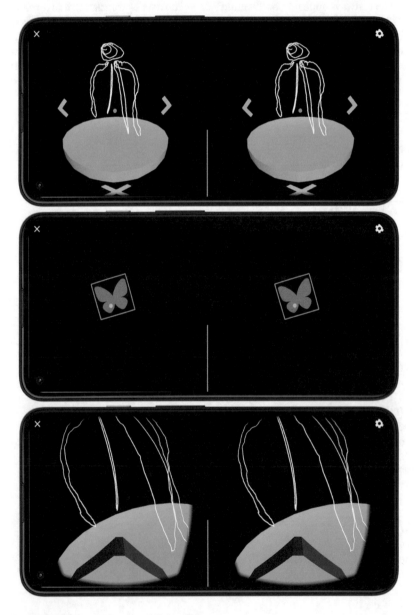

Figure 18-9. *Transition between draw and fly modes*

Final Tweaks and Packaging

We have arrived at a fully functional drawing app for VR, inspired by the legendary Tilt Brush! During this process, we encountered challenges that are unique to VR development: constructing an engaging and immersive 3D environment, adding UI elements that can be accessed using gaze alone, and moving freely in VR. Our app incorporates some techniques to solve these challenges, which we could explore even further in future VR projects. But for the time being, we only need to do a few final tweaks to get the drawing app ready for release on the Play Store.

Intro Text

When users open our VR drawing app for the first time, they may not be sure what to do first, so a good idea would be to introduce the basic mechanics of the experience. We should keep this introduction as brief as possible since users may not go further if bothered by too many instructions. We should also keep in mind that a successful VR experience should be as self-explanatory as possible.

We should draw the intro text page in eye coordinates, so it is facing the user irrespective of the head position and disappears as soon as the user presses the headset button to continue. Listing 18-5 shows the additions to the code to implement a simple intro, and the result is shown in Figure 18-10.

Listing 18-5. Implementation of the intro screen

```
import processing.vr.*;

float angle;
boolean flyMode = false;
PVector flyStep = new PVector();
boolean showingIntro = true;

void setup() {
  fullScreen(STEREO);
  textureMode(NORMAL);
  textFont(createFont("SansSerif", 30));
  textAlign(CENTER, CENTER);
  ...
}
...
void mouseReleased() {
  if (showingIntro) {
    showingIntro = false;
  } else if (resetButton.selected) {
    ...
  }
}
...
void drawUI() {
  leftButton.display();
  rightButton.display();
  resetButton.display();
  noLights();
  flyToggle.display();
  if (showingIntro) drawIntro();
  else if (!flyMode) drawAim();
```

```
}

void drawIntro() {
  noLights();
  eye();
  fill(220);
  text("Welcome to VR Draw!\nLook around while clicking to draw.\n" +
       "Click on the side buttons\nto rotate the podium,\n" +
       "and on the X slightly below\nto reset.\n\n" +
       "Search for the wings to fly", 0, 0, 300);
}
...
```

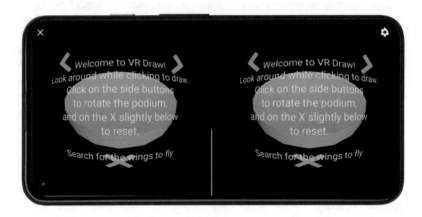

Figure 18-10. *Intro screen with some instructions on how to use the app*

The logic for the intro screen: we use the showingIntro variable to indicate whether we should be drawing the intro and set it to true by default. As soon as the user releases the first button press, the intro will go away.

Icons and Package Export

The final steps in the creation of the app are designing its icons; setting the final package name, labels, and versions in the manifest file; and then exporting the signed package ready to upload to the Play Store, all of which we covered in Chapter 3.

As for the icons, we need a full set including 192×192 (xxxhdpi), 144×144 (xxhdpi), 96×96 (xhdpi), 72×72 (hdpi), 48×48 (mdpi), and 32×32 (ldpi) versions, such as the one shown in Figure 18-11.

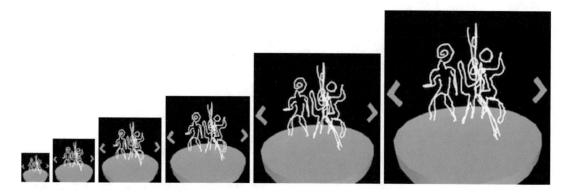

Figure 18-11. *App icons in all required resolutions*

As we have discussed already, the manifest file for the exported package should include a unique full package name, the version code and name, and the Android label that is used in the UI to identify the app.

Summary

We just completed our last full code project! This VR drawing app was probably the most complex from all the projects in the book, but it should have helped us to realize the challenges involved in creating VR experiences for users to interact in a virtual space. By addressing the challenges involved in this app, we had a hands-on opportunity to apply Processing's 3D API to implement immersive graphics and interactions in XR. Hopefully, all that we have learned so far gives us a useful toolkit to create new and original Android apps, not only for XR but also for watches, phones, and tablets, using Processing.

PART VII

Appendixes

CHAPTER 19

■ ■ ■

Appendix A: Gradle and Android Studio Integration

In this appendix, we will learn to export Processing sketches as Gradle projects that we can then compile from the command line or import into Android Studio.

Google Tools for Android Development

Android Studio is the official Integrated Development Environment (IDE) for Android. It is available for free from Google (https://developer.android.com/studio). Android Studio offers a full-featured interface to write and debug Android apps, which includes not only an editor for source code (Figure A-1) but also a visual UI designer.

Figure A-1. *Android Studio interface for code editing (top) and visual app design (bottom)*

A. Colubri, *Processing for Android*, https://doi.org/10.1007/978-1-4842-9585-4_19

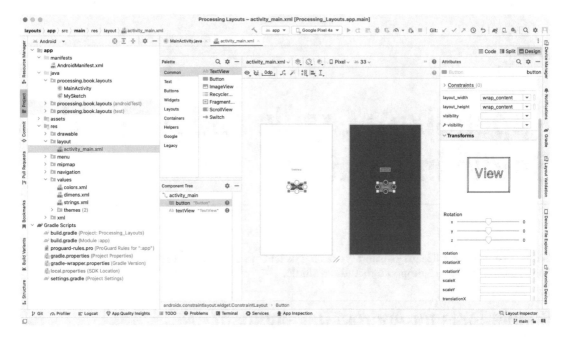

Figure A-1. (*continued*)

Android Studio uses a software called Gradle (`https://gradle.org/`) to build its projects. Gradle is a "build automation system" where we can specify all the information needed to compile the source code, resolve dependencies, and package the final app, in a set of build files written in a Groovy-based language, specifically customized for software-building tasks. This provides great flexibility to handle the complexity of Android projects, which often involve several files, among source code, libraries, and resources. Processing uses Gradle to build the sketches into apps but keeps this complexity hidden from the user.

Although Processing for Android aims at a different group of users (artists, designers, students) and uses (sketching, prototyping, teaching) than more advanced IDEs do, integration with Android Studio can be very convenient in many cases. For example, we may want to incorporate some interactive graphics we created with Processing into a larger Android app. Also, being able to access the underlying Gradle build files for our sketch allows us to tweak things in ways that are not possible from the PDE.

There are two main ways to combine Processing for Android with Gradle and Android Studio:

1. Exporting a Processing sketch as a Gradle project from the PDE. This project can be compiled from the command line using the Gradle Wrapper tool (`https://docs.gradle.org/current/userguide/gradle_wrapper.html`), which is included with the exported project or imported into Android Studio.

2. Importing the processing-core package into an Android Studio project and using it to access all the core Processing's API for drawing and interaction.

We will learn how use each one of these integration approaches in the next sections.

Exporting a Sketch As a Gradle Project

The Android mode has an option in the File menu called "Export Android Project" (Figure A-2). After we select this option, the mode will create a complete Gradle project, including assets and resources, from our sketch, and ready to compile from the command line. The project is placed in the "android" folder inside the sketch folder.

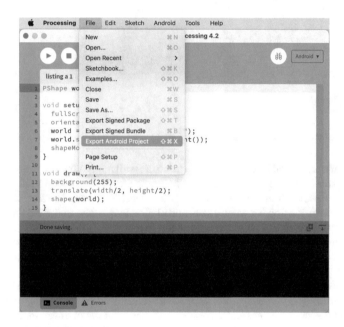

Figure A-2. *Export Android Project in the PDE*

Listing A-1 shows a simple sketch to test the export functionality in the Android mode.

Listing A-1. Sketch to export as Android project

```
PShape world;

void setup() {
  fullScreen(P2D);
  orientation(LANDSCAPE);
  world = loadShape("World-map.svg");
  world.scale(height/world.getHeight());
  shapeMode(CENTER);
}

void draw() {
  background(255);
  translate(width/2, height/2);
  shape(world);
}
```

After exporting it, the resulting Gradle project should have the folder structure shown in Figure A-3. The original sketch includes an SVG file in its data folder, which will be placed inside src/main/assets in the exported project.

Figure A-3. *File structure of an exported Android project*

Gradle projects are organized in a hierarchical structure, with a main build.gradle file in the top level folder containing the master options and another build.gradle file inside the app subfolder with the specific options to build the project, such as the dependencies and target SDK level. The Java source code generated from the sketch's code is inside app/src/main/java, and all files in the data folder are copied to assets. The processing core library is placed as a jar file inside the libs folder.

Once we generated this exported project, we can compile it using the gradlew command-line program included in the android folder. In order to do so, we need to open a terminal, change to the project folder, and run the command "./gradlew build".

The results of a successful build are the debug and release (unsigned) packages, which we will find in app/build/outputs/apk as app-debug.apk and app-release-unsigned.apk. The package name will be the one we set in the manifest file, or the Processing default if we did not edit the manifest that Processing generates automatically for us. This manifest file will be also copied into the exported project, so we can further customize it.

Importing into Android Studio

Once we have exported our Processing sketch as Gradle project, we can easily import it into Android Studio, since an Android Studio project is essentially a Gradle project with some additional files.

From inside the Android Studio, we have the import project under the File menu, inside "New ➤ Import Project…", and we can also select "Import Project (Eclipse ADT, Gradle, etc.)" from the Welcome screen, as seen in Figure A-4.

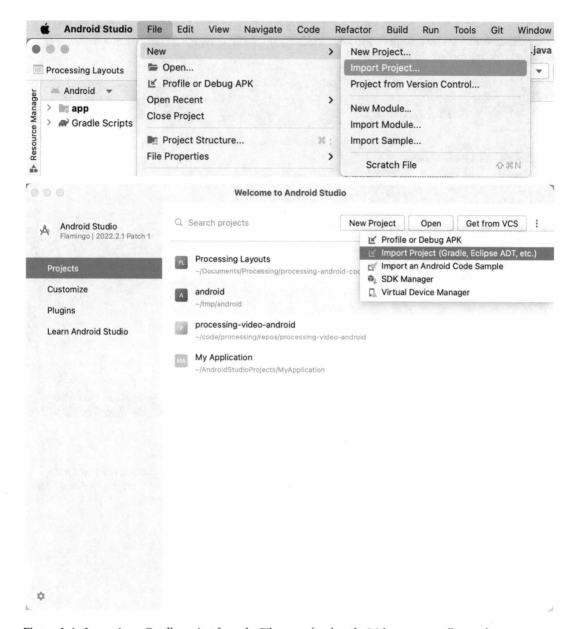

Figure A-4. *Importing a Gradle project from the File menu (top) or the Welcome screen (bottom)*

The import functionality will prompt us to browse for the folder containing the Gradle project using the system's file browser. The exported Gradle project from Processing is linked to the SDK we use in Processing's Android mode. If it is different from Android Studio's SDK, then we will be prompted to choose to use one or the other in the imported Android Studio project. In general, it is recommended to use Processing's SDK, because it will be certain that it will work with the project, but a newer SDK in Android Studio should be compatible as well.

After importing the project, we can use all the functionality in Android Studio to edit and debug the code (Figure A-5). We also have access to any function from the Processing's API since the core library is included as a dependency in the project.

***Figure A-5.** Processing sketch imported into Android Studio*

The code from our original Processing sketch is converted into two separate classes: the first for the main activity and the second containing the sketch itself, which is a subclass of PApplet, the core class that holds most of the functions and variables in the Processing API, shown in Listing A-2.

***Listing A-2.** Exported sketch code in Android Studio*

```
package processing.test.listing_a_1;

import processing.core.*;

public class listing_a_1 extends PApplet {
  PShape world;
  public void setup() {
    orientation(LANDSCAPE);
    world = loadShape("World-map.svg");
    world.scale(height/world.getHeight());
    shapeMode(CENTER);
  }
  public void draw() {
    background(255);
    translate(width/2, height/2);
```

```
    shape(world);
}
public void settings() {  fullScreen(P2D); }
}
```

Notice an important change with respect to our original sketch code: fullScreen() is now inside a new function called settings(), needed to properly initialize our sketch when running it outside the PDE and which always gets called before setup(). If we were using size() instead, it will also go inside settings().

Listing A-3 shows the main activity where the Processing sketch object is initialized and attached to a containing fragment inside the activity. This code is automatically generated by Processing when we export the Android project.

Listing A-3. Main activity for an exported Processing sketch

```
package processing.test.listing_a_1;

import android.os.Bundle;
import android.content.Intent;
import android.view.ViewGroup;
import android.widget.FrameLayout;
import androidx.appcompat.app.AppCompatActivity;

import processing.android.PFragment;
import processing.android.CompatUtils;
import processing.core.PApplet;

public class MainActivity extends AppCompatActivity {
  private PApplet sketch;

  @Override
  protected void onCreate(Bundle savedInstanceState) {
    super.onCreate(savedInstanceState);
    FrameLayout frame = new FrameLayout(this);
    frame.setId(CompatUtils.getUniqueViewId());
    setContentView(frame, new
        ViewGroup.LayoutParams(ViewGroup.LayoutParams.MATCH_PARENT,
                                        ViewGroup.LayoutParams.MATCH_PARENT));

    sketch = new listing_a_1();

    PFragment fragment = new PFragment(sketch);
    fragment.setView(frame, this);
  }

  @Override
  public void onRequestPermissionsResult(int requestCode, String permissions[], int[]
    grantResults) {
    if (sketch != null) {
      sketch.onRequestPermissionsResult(requestCode, permissions, grantResults);
    }
  }
}
```

```
@Override
public void onNewIntent(Intent intent) {
  if (sketch != null) {
    sketch.onNewIntent(intent);
  }
}

@Override
public void onActivityResult(int requestCode, int resultCode, Intent data) {
  if (sketch != null) {
    sketch.onActivityResult(requestCode, resultCode, data);
  }
}

@Override
public void onBackPressed() {
  if (sketch != null) {
    sketch.onBackPressed();
  }
}
}
```

It is important to keep the onRequestPermissionsResult() event handler so that our sketch can respond to the result of a dangerous permission request, as well as onNewIntent(), needed to handle any new intent sent to the activity (https://developer.android.com/reference/android/app/Activity. html#onNewIntent(android.content.Intent)). We should also keep the onBackPressed() method, which is needed to handle back presses received by the sketch.

Let's take a closer look at the relevant code to create our sketch object and add it to an existing view in Listing A-4, which we used in the onCreate() method in the previous listing.

Listing A-4. Adding a sketch object to a fragment view

```
sketch = new MySketch();
PFragment fragment = new PFragment(sketch);
fragment.setView(frame, this);
```

Here, MySketch is the class encapsulating our Processing code, like listing_a_1 before. PFragment is a system class from the Processing core library that handles integration with Android fragments. All we need to do after creating it is to set the view with the containing layout (in this case, a FrameLayout) and the main activity as arguments. These steps can be used in more complex projects with multiple views. However, in such cases, we would need to add a reference to the actual view object we want to use, which we will discuss in more detail next.

Adding a Processing Sketch to a Layout

Advanced users might want to work with Android Studio directly, using Processing as a library in their projects. To do so, we need to consider two important aspects:

1.   How to include the Processing core library as a dependency in the project

2.   Attaching a Processing sketch to a layout in the UI of the project

The Processing core library for the Android mode provided as a package that can be imported as a dependency in Gradle projects. In the settings.gradle of the project, we need to add `https://raw.github.com/processing/processing-android/repository/` as a maven repository, under the dependencyResolutionManagement block (Figure A-6). Once we have done this, we can add the processing-core dependency in the app's gradle.build file:

```
dependencies {
    ...
    implementation 'org.processing.android:processing-core:4.5'
    testImplementation 'junit:junit:4.13.2'
    androidTestImplementation 'androidx.test.ext:junit:1.1.5'
    androidTestImplementation 'androidx.test.espresso:espresso-core:3.5.1'
}
```

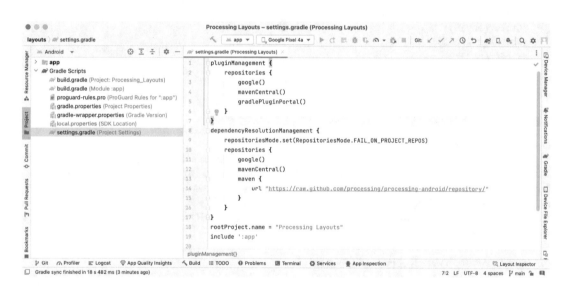

Figure A-6. *Adding processing-android maven repository to a Gradle project*

Once we have added processing-core as a dependency, we can write the class containing the sketch, an example of which is presented in Listing A-5.

Listing A-5. Writing Processing code in Android Studio

```
package processing.book.layouts;

import processing.core.PShape;
import processing.core.PImage;
import processing.core.PApplet;

public class MySketch extends PApplet {
  float angle = 0;
  PShape cube;
```

```
public void settings() {
  fullScreen(P3D);
}

public void setup() {
  fullScreen(P3D);
  PImage tex = loadImage("mosaic.jpg");
  cube = createShape(BOX, 400);
  cube.setTexture(tex);
}

public void draw() {
  background(0x81B771);
  lights();
  translate(width/2, height/2);
  rotateY(angle);
  rotateX(angle*2);
  shape(cube);
  angle += 0.01;
  }
}
```

As we saw earlier, the screen size must be initialized in settings() instead of setup() when working outside of the PDE.

Now, we will integrate the sketch into an existing layout. UI elements in Android are declared in layouts (https://developer.android.com/develop/ui/views/layout/declaring-layout), which in turn are described by XML files that are "inflated" as objects during runtime. If we create an "Empty Activity" project in Android Studio, we will end up with a layout for the main activity. If we want to add the sketch to the main activity, then we would need to retrieve the reference to activity and its ID from the resources object, like it is done in Listing A-6.

Listing A-6. Adding a sketch object to a fragment view

```
sketch = new MySketch();
PFragment fragment = new PFragment(sketch);
fragment.setLayout(R.layout.activity_main, R.id.activity_main, this);
```

In case the activity does not have an ID, we can add it by editing the corresponding XML file and adding an android:id attribute, as seen in Figure A-7.

Figure A-7. *Setting a name for the content layout to add to our sketch*

With all of this in place, we can implement the onCreate() method in the main activity to look something like the one shown in Listing A-7, where we set the layout of the fragment holding the sketch.

Listing A-7. Creating the activity that contains the Processing fragment

```
@Override
protected void onCreate(Bundle savedInstanceState) {
    super.onCreate(savedInstanceState);
    setContentView(R.layout.activity_main);

    sketch = new MySketch();
    PFragment fragment = new PFragment(sketch);
    fragment.setLayout(R.layout.activity_main, R.id.activity_main, this);
}
```

If we use the requestPermission() function in our sketch to request critical permissions, then we would also need to add the onRequestPermissionsResult() handler in Listing A-8. We did not need to do this when exporting the sketch as an Android project from the PDE, since in that case Processing adds this handler automatically.

Listing A-8. Creating the activity that contains the Processing fragment

```
@Override
public void onRequestPermissionsResult(int requestCode,
                                       String permissions[],
                                       int[] grantResults) {
  if (sketch != null) {
    sketch.onRequestPermissionsResult(requestCode, permissions,
                                      grantResults);
  }
}
```

We can now run our project and should see a screen similar to that in Figure A-8, where we have the Processing output inside the layout containing the sketch fragment.

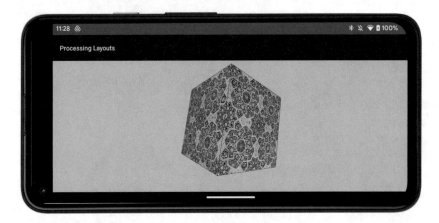

Figure A-8. *Running app with the Processing fragment embedded inside a content layout*

■ ■ ■

CHAPTER 20

Appendix B: Processing Libraries for Android

Processing can be extended with libraries written by members of the community to add new functionality. This chapter goes over some of the libraries available for the Android mode and ends with a guide on how we can create our own libraries.

Extending Processing with Libraries

Two features in Processing have contributed to its adoption as a teaching and prototyping tool. First, a minimal core API that is easy to learn and second, a library architecture that extends the Processing core with new functionality and hardware support. Some libraries offering important features (such as video or networking) are developed by the Processing Foundation, but many more are created by members of the Processing community and are called contributed libraries.

There are contributed libraries for a wide range of applications: 3D, computer vision, user interface, data handling, audio, machine learning, etc. A few of these libraries are specific to Android; others are only for PC or Mac platforms, but many can be used across the Java and Android modes.

Installing Libraries with the Contribution Manager

Installing a library is very simple to do through the Contribution Manager (CM) shown in Figure B-1, although they can be installed manually as well. We can search for a library using a keyword, by category, or simply by scrolling the list.

© Andrés Colubri 2023
A. Colubri, *Processing for Android*, https://doi.org/10.1007/978-1-4842-9585-4_20

Figure B-1. *Contribution Manager showing the Libraries tab*

All we need to do to install a library through the CM is to click on the install button. After we have installed it, we will receive notifications if there are updates available. The CM will allow us to install those updates, or to remove the library entirely once we no longer need it.

Contributed libraries typically include examples demonstrating their functionality. These examples can be found by opening the "Examples" option in the "File" menu and browsing to the "Contributed Libraries" category in the listing window (Figure B-2).

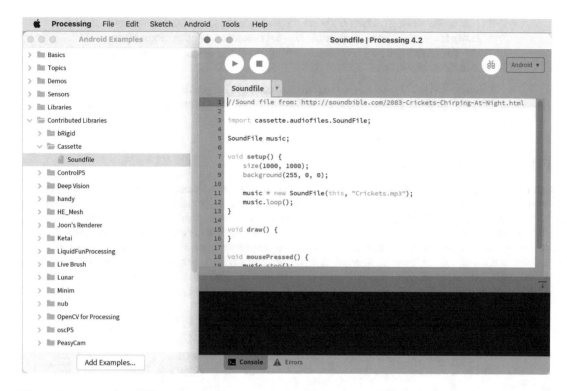

Figure B-2. *Contributed libraries examples*

In the following, there is an overview of several Processing libraries that are specific to the Android mode, or explicitly support it, in addition to the Ketai library for mobile sensing (`http://ketai.org/`), which we already covered extensively in Chapters 7 and 8. However, this does not mean that these are the only libraries that could be used on Android, since many libraries that were written originally for the Java mode are also compatible with the Android mode:

- oscP5 (`www.sojamo.de/libraries/oscp5/`): We can use oscP5 to send data between local and remote apps using the Open Sound Control (OSC) network protocol. This protocol was designed for communication among various multimedia devices, including computers, sound synthesizers, and light controllers.

- AndroidCapture for Processing (`https://github.com/onlylemi/processing-android-capture`): This library allows to transfer Android camera and sensor data from the Android device to a Processing sketch running on the computer.

- ControlP5 (`www.sojamo.de/libraries/controlP5/`): This is a GUI library to build custom user interfaces for desktop and Android mode. It has been around for a long time, so there are many examples of it in use, and it has a very characteristic look and feel. It is important to keep in mind that when used on Android, ControlP5 does not rely on the native Android UI widgets nor the standard UI creation techniques.

- Android SelectFile (`https://github.com/pif/android-select-file`): This library is Android-only, and it provides dialogs for selecting input and output files and folders, since the core Processing API does not offer that functionality on Android (it does on PC/Mac).

- TFLite for Processing (`https://github.com/codeanticode/processing-android-tflite`): It's another Android-only library that provides simplified access to the TensorFlow Lite library for Machine Learning on mobile devices (`https://www.tensorflow.org/lite`).

- Cassette (`https://github.com/shlomihod/cassette`): It provides sound basic playback functionality using the underlying Android APIs; therefore, it will not work on other platforms.

Installing Libraries Manually

Sometimes, a library is not available through the CM. In those cases, we can install the library manually by downloading the zip package containing the library files and then copying them to the sketchbook folder.

For example, the video library for Android is hosted in the following public GitHub repository: `https://github.com/codeanticode/processing-android-video`. This repository contains the source code of the library but also includes releases section from where pre-made packages can be obtained. We need to download the zip file for the version we want to install, typically the most recent. Once the zip file is downloaded, we can decompress it and then copy to the libraries folder inside the Processing sketchbook (Figure B-3). By default, the sketchbook can be found inside the documents folder.

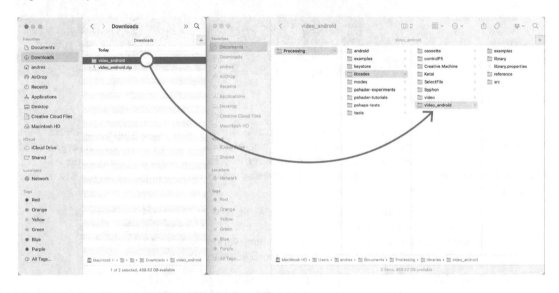

Figure B-3. *Installing a contributed library manually*

This library allows to play movie files and capture live video from the phone's camera. Listing B-1 shows how to load an mp4 file to show on full screen mode. The output of this code is shown in Figure B-4.

Listing B-1. Playing a movie file using the contributed video library for Anroid

```
import processing.video.android.*;

Movie movie;

void setup() {
  fullScreen(P2D);
```

```
  orientation(LANDSCAPE);
  movie = new Movie(this, "transit.mp4");
  movie.loop();
  movie.play();
}

void draw() {
  float w = height  * float(movie.width) / movie.height;
  image(movie, (width - w) /2, 0, w, height);
}

void movieEvent(Movie m) {
  m.read();
}
```

Figure B-4. *Example from Video for Android library playing a video file*

Writing New Libraries

We often find ourselves using a piece of code in our sketches over and over again. It would be easier to include the code in future projects if we were able to package it as a library. Also, if this code implements some general functionality that other people may find useful, we could also consider sharing it with the rest of the Processing community. As we saw in the previous section, there is very little restriction on what a library can do, and even though writing a Processing library involves some more technical steps, it is not that hard to write and distribute a library.

A first step in the creation of a new library is to modularize the functionality we want to make into the library, in a separate class that takes the sketch object as a parameter. Processing puts all our sketch code inside a class called PApplet, and this class also holds most of the Processing API we have seen throughout the book. For example, let's imagine we wrote several functions to draw regular polyhedrons, as outlined in Listing B-2.

Listing B-2. A polyhedron-rendering sketch

```
void setup() {
  fullScreen(P3D);
}

void draw() {
  background(255);
  drawTetrahedron();
  drawOctahedron();
  drawDodecahedron();
  drawIcosahedron();
}

void drawTetrahedron() {
  beginShape();
  ...
  endShape();
}

void drawDodecahedron() {
  beginShape();
  ...
  endShape();
}
...
```

If we move the drawing code inside a new class, we could do something like what is shown in Listing B-3.

Listing B-3. Encapsulating library functionality inside a class

```
Polyhedron poly;

void setup() {
  fullScreen(P3D);
  poly = new Polyhedron(this);
}

void draw() {
  background(255);
  poly.drawTetrahedron();
  poly.drawOctahedron();
  poly.drawDodecahedron();
  poly.drawIcosahedron();
}

class Polyhedron {
  PApplet parent;

  Polyhedron(PApplet parent) {
    this.parent = parent;
```

```
  }

  void drawTetrahedron() {
    parent.beginShape();
    ...
    parent.endShape();
  }

  void drawDodecahedron() {
    parent.beginShape();
    ...
    parent.endShape();
  }
}
```

Note how we create an instance of the Polyhedron class with the "this" keyword, which is a reference to the current sketch. This reference is stored in the parent field in the Polyhedron class, which we can use to perform any Processing call.

Once we have organized the code in this way, although it does not bring much immediate benefit to the sketch, it is easy to take the class encapsulating the special functionality into a separate library. After doing this, we would only need to import the library, and the Polyhedron class will be available to use, as shown in Listing B-4.

Listing B-4. Importing the polyhedron library

```
import polyhedron.*;

Polyhedron poly;

void setup() {
  fullScreen(P3D);
  poly = new Polyhedron(this);
}

void draw() {
  background(255);
  poly.drawTetrahedron();
  poly.drawOctahedron();
  poly.drawDodecahedron();
  poly.drawIcosahedron();
}
```

We no longer need to include the code of the Polyhedron class in our sketch, since it is now provided by the library. The advantage of this is that we can reuse our original code in as many sketches as we want just by importing the library. If we make improvements to the library or fix errors in it, all the sketches using the library will reflect the changes in the library.

The Processing Foundation provides a Processing Android library template with all the required files to create a Gradle project to build contributed libraries and where we can incorporate our custom code. The library template is available at https://github.com/processing/processing-android-library-template and includes a detailed step-by-step guide on how to import the template into the IntelliJ IDE and use it as the basis for a new library project.

Index

© Andrés Colubri 2023
A. Colubri, *Processing for Android*, https://doi.org/10.1007/978-1-4842-9585-4

397

Printed in the United States
by Baker & Taylor Publisher Services